PITTSBURGH THEOLOGICAL MONOGRAPH SERIES

Dikran Y. Hadidian

General Editor

29a

The Emergence of Contemporary Judaism

Volume One: The Foundations of Judaism
from Biblical Origins to the Sixth Century A.D.
Part Two: Rabbinic Judaism

OTHER BOOKS IN THIS SERIES . . .

THE EMERGENCE OF CONTEMPORARY JUDAISM

by
Phillip Sigal

Volume One

THE FOUNDATIONS OF JUDAISM
from Biblical Origins to the Sixth Century A.D.

Part Two: Rabbinic Judaism

The Pickwick Press
Pittsburgh, Pennsylvania

1980

Library of Congress Cataloging in Publication Data

Sigal, Phillip.
  The foundations of Judaism from Biblical
origins to the sixth century A.D.

    (His The emergence of contemporary Judaism ;
v. 1) (Pittsburgh theological monograph series ;
29-29a)
    Includes bibliographies and indexes.
    CONTENTS: pt. 1. From the origins to the
separation of Christianity.--pt. 2. Rabbinic Judaism.
    1. Judaism--History--To 70 A. D. 2. Judaism--
History--Talmudic period, 10-425. I. Title.
II. Series: Sigal, Phillip. Emergence of
contemporary Judaism ; v. 1. III. Series: Pittsburgh
theological monograph series ; 29-29a.

Library of Congress Cataloging in Publication Data

BM165.S53   296'.09'01   79-20355
ISBN 0-915138-30-1 (v. 1)
ISBN 0-915138-46-8 (v. 2)

Copyright© 1980 by
THE PICKWICK PRESS
5001 Baum Boulevard
Pittsburgh, PA 15213

To my life's partner

Lillian Fisher Sigal

This book is dedicated with profound
love and gratitude.

*"Many women have wrought capably
but you excel them."*

(Proverbs 31:29)

.

PREFACE TO VOLUME ONE, PART TWO

Upon completion of the manuscript for Volume One of this projected four-volume work on Judaism, it was decided that it be separated into two parts for publication. Volume Two already having been published, it was necessary to call these books Volume One, Part One and Volume One, Part Two. It appeared most logical to make the division at the end of Chapter Seven, for it is there that the Biblical religion reaches a watershed and has its continuity along two separate tracks. From that point on, with the expansion of gentile Christianity, the Judaic daughter-religion no longer belongs to a survey of Judaism. And Judaism itself now becomes transmogrified into a new evolving faith based upon progressive revelation and ethical monotheism, taught and developed by spiritual leaders called rabbis. Rabbinic Judaism seemed to stand logically as a separate entity beginning a new era and ushering in that form of Judaism which is still operative in the contemporary world.

During the course of researching and writing Volume One I did not generally find that I had cause to alter views expressed earlier in Volume Two. But I did find the need to clarify one view. In Vol. II, p. 288, I stated that there is no hint of divine femininity in Judaism prior to the kabalistic era. This should be understood to indicate that there was little or no femininity in deity in the standard Establishment Judaism since rabbinic times. The feminine principle discussed in Volume One shows how complex a matter it is and how the feminine principle had been shunted to the background by rabbinic Judaism until it came out again in Kabalism.

It seems appropriate at this time to reiterate my gratitude to all those whom I named in the Preface to Part One. But I also feel impelled to add to that my prayer that the memory of my sainted grandparents, Menahem and Sima Sigal and Yehoshua Alter and Sheva Weingarten, will be perpetuated in these volumes on Judaism which was their legacy to me. Most especially I express gratification for the earliest training in classical Hebrew sitting on the knees of my maternal grandfather, scholar and pious humanist, Yehoshua Alter, I picking at his beard and fondling his pocket-watch while he drank his numerous glasses of tea.

Phillip Sigal

CONTENTS OF VOLUME ONE (PART TWO)

CHAPTER 1

Proto-Rabbinic Judaism Matures

I. THE PHARISEE QUESTION[1]

A. *Background Comments*

In the course of the previous chapter I have identified the Pharisees as *perushim,* a complex of pietists and separatists who made up a segment of Judaism and included such known entities as Essenes and Qumranites as well as other unknown groups that proliferated at the time. Such pietists and ascetics who were also separatists existed long before as we can see from the Rekhabites.[2] During the post-exilic period these pietistic groups took heart from the Ezraic-Nehemian retrenchment and we hear nothing further about them or of their views. The hellenization process that set in with the third century B.C., however, brought them forward into opposition to Hellenism. They were behind the Hasmonean rebellion, but became disenchanted after 164 B.C. In contemporary writings these disenchanted pietists are referred to as *ḥasidim,* but soon thereafter the literature contains other terms such as *Essaioi* (Philo, Josephus), *pharisaioi* (New Testament, Josephus) and *perushim* (rabbinic literature).

The scope of this volume does not permit a comprehensive demonstration of the thesis that the term Pharisees has reference to an amorphous complex of pietists. A separate monograph is assuredly desirable for this purpose. All references to *perushim* in rabbinic literature and to *pharisaioi* in the New Testament and Josephus, the only three places where these terms are found, require a careful reexamination. At the same time it is fair to inform the reader that my view runs counter to the consensus that the term translated as "Pharisees" from the Greek *pharisaioi* and the Hebrew *perushim* refers to the predecessors of the rabbis, that the rabbis are Pharisees and that Pharisaism is the rabbinic Judaism which gained hegemony after 70 A.D. My thesis is here adumbrated publicly for the first time.

The post-70 rabbis saw themselves as the successors to a

chain of proto-rabbis or *ḥakhamim* (sages) beginning with the
third century B.C., and even with biblical Ezra of 450 B.C.
These proto-rabbis may at times have possessed certain characteristics for which one might use the adjective *perushite*,
pietistic. But they did not consider themselves members of
such a movement, nor would they accept for themselves the
substantive classification of *perushim*. In the spirit of one
of their first-century B.C. colleagues, Hillel, the proto-
rabbis were opposed to separatism. Hillel taught *al tifrosh
min hazibur* "do not separate yourself from the community."[3]
In order to attract the fragmented community to their authority after 70, the rabbis adopted some of the pietistic halakhah
into their system. But first they put it through their own
filter. This partly explains the two-fold phenomenon: on
the one hand there are wide discrepancies in halakhic opinions
in rabbinic literature, and on the other, there are strong
affinities between the pietism of the *ḥasidim* and *perushim*
of 170 B.C.-70 A.D. and rabbinic Judaism. In a sense proto-
rabbinism superimposed itself upon "pharisaism" after 70 A.D.
and this may explain why Josephus, in distant Rome, sees
Pharisaism as the major movement in Judaism.

Scholars of late first-century Judaism and the origins of
what is called "rabbinic Judaism" see rabbinic Judaism as
emerging from an academy of learning at Yavneh (Jamnia) near
the Mediterranean coast, and ultimately impressing itself as
"normative" for all of Palestinian and diaspora Judaism.
Modern scholarship also argues that the antecedent to rabbinic
Judaism is that which is called "Pharisaism" and that to all
intents and purposes there is an equivalency between Pharisaism and rabbinic Judaism.[4] But I consider Pharisaism to be
one only of many elements incorporated into rabbinic Judaism.
The rabbis sought to ameliorate the extremes of *perushim*. Proponents of rabbinic Judaism rejected the idea of extending
pietistic norms preferred by *perushim* into mandatory standards
of religious conduct obligatory upon all members of the community.[5] Furthermore, rabbinic Judaism rejected the idea of
separatism.

B. *The Pharisees in the New Testament*

The earliest literature that uses the Greek term *pharisaioi*,
a transliteration of the Hebrew *perushim* is the New Testament.
This term has reference to *ḥasidim*, who were rigorous in observance and separatistic. The opponents of these pietists
referred to them in a perjorative manner as *perushim*, pietistic separatists, in order to convey the notion that the true
Elect Community is still that which is under the priestly

leadership in Jerusalem. Among those who supported the priestly Establishment were Sadducees, a term of doubtful origin and obscure meaning. The proto-rabbis did not constitute a movement of their own, nor did they join in the pietistic separatism. They were individuals. Sometimes they were priests, and sometimes they were pietists. They bided their time, and after 70 A.D. were the best candidates available to assume spiritual leadership in Jerusalem.

But around the year 30 when Jesus preached they were not a major force in Judaism and were not among his *perushite* antagonists. It is clear that in the New Testament the *pharisaioi* are vehement antagonists of Jesus on grounds that proto-rabbis would not have supported. The *pharisaioi* are very meticulous about ritualistic observances in such matters as purities, dietary practices, the Sabbath and tithing. These *pharisaioi* are frequently in controversy with Jesus. In some instances the Pharisees are depicted as enemies of Jesus. In rare instances Jesus and the Pharisees appear to be in agreement, as in the case of the belief in resurrection.[6] But in matters of halakhah they are at odds. Either the Pharisees are depicted as being overly fastidious or as being hypocritical. The observances, the character and the integrity of the Pharisees are all brought into question in the New Testament (Mt. 23).

New Testament Pharisee halakhah is best represented by the Book of Jubilees and the Dead Sea Scrolls as has been shown in Pt. I, Chap. 7. That the Pharisees were especially pietistic is clear from the major role played by ritual purity, the washing of hands and immersion of utensils and other bodily ablutions, dietary practices and tithing, observances that were not universal among ordinary Jews. Adherence to such practices made a person a "Pharisee." But being a Pharisee was not equivalent to being a proto-rabbinic scholar, although a proto-rabbinic scholar such as Gamaliel I might be a Pharisee (Acts 5:34-39). Paul, a self-identified Pharisee, stresses this over-fastidiousness of ritualistic observance on the part of *perushim*.[7]

In the Synoptic Gospels the Pharisees are often mentioned in conjunction with the "scribes," recorded in the Greek as *pharisaioi kai grammateis*. The "scribes" or *sofrim* in Hebrew, should not be understood as forming another "party" in Judaism. Every faction had its own scribes, and therefore the term should be understood as denoting a functionary. Sometimes the scribes are *perushim*, sometimes they are of the priestly circles.[8] By the time of the New Testament, the *sofrim* were no longer always scholars or high court functionaries. They were not the proto-rabbis. They were either teachers of elementary school children or secretarial functionaries and copyists, or

both. But their status had dropped.[9] Neither the scribes nor
the Pharisees are the rabbis who emerge to leadership after
the war of 66-73.

There are superficial similarities between the Pharisees
and the founders of rabbinic Judaism. The Pharisees are said
to be followers of the *paradoseōs ton presbyteron,* "the traditions of the elders," as were the proto-rabbis. They were
"traditionalists" who developed a long history of supplemental
interpretation of the written scripture and accepted this
sacred tradition on a par with the Pentateuch. But there the
similarity ends. The proto-rabbis operated with a program of
leniency and pragmatism while the Pharisees were strict adherents of a restrictive, pietistic interpretation of scripture and meticulous adherents of a complex of pietistic,
ascetic-oriented practices which they inherited from their
elders and perpetuated in their fellowships, communities and
settlements such as Qumran.[10] Various beliefs attributed to
the Pharisees are also attributable to the people at Qumran
and prove nothing about the identity of Pharisees. Among
these beliefs are the doctrine of resurrection and a belief
in demons.[11] The Dead Sea Scrolls indicate a belief in a
Davidic Messiah, a doctrine also believed by Matthean Pharisees.[12] But on the other hand where some scholars see the
Pharisees as being believers in the love command at Mt. 22:
34-40 it should be noted, as I have indicated earlier, that
Pharisees did not govern themselves by this. It is not the
Pharisees but a *nomikos,* an expert in the halakhah, a proto-
rabbi, who is involved in that conversation with Jesus.[13]

It is argued that in the Gospel According to John the
Pharisees constitute a scholar class and are also authority-
figures, and therefore by implication are the predecessors
of the rabbis. But here again it must be understood that the
author of the gospel refers to the antagonists of Jesus in
the time of Jesus and bases himself upon the tradition that
the antagonists of Jesus were *perushim.* The author of John,
like the author of Matthew is willing to make it appear that
contemporary rabbis are the kind of people who opposed Jesus
two generations earlier. He desires that his contemporaries
identify the opponents of Jesus with the Yavnean rabbis who
were expelling Christians from the synagogues.[14] It is very
much as moderns will tar socially-conscious left-of-center antagonists with the brush of "communism," or misapply the
term "atheist" to agnostics or to those who believe in a
deistic naturalism. But the antagonists of Jesus were not
the predecessors of the rabbis, the proto-rabbis. They were
perushim with whom the rabbis had much in common, but from
whom the rabbis differentiated themselves. That the Gospel

According to John is written from this standpoint is borne
out by the fact that the Sadducees play no role in it. As in
Josephus' *Against Apion*, written during the last decade of
the century, where there is apparently a doctrinal consensus
on a basic question like resurrection, the Sadducees are not
present.[15]

The material in Luke-Acts at times reflects a friendlier
relationship. Evidently some *perushim* are affirmative toward
Jesus and some later become Christians. Some Pharisees warn
Jesus that Herod's men are out to get him (Lk. 13:31). Some
Pharisees attempt to help Paul before the Sanhedrin (Acts
23:6-9).

In sum, the term Pharisee comes up many times in the New
Testament, but there is no reference at all to first-century
proto-rabbis. The only person called "rabbi" in the New
Testament is Jesus.[16] When an actual proto-rabbi is referred
to in the New Testament, as in the case of Gamaliel I, he is
called a *nomodidaskalos*, a teacher of the *nomos* (halakhah);
while unnamed proto-rabbis are referred to with the term *nomikos*, "an expert in the halakhah."[17] It is true that on one
occasion Jesus is reported to have denounced Pharisees for
wishing to be called "rabbi" and admonishes his disciples
not to use the title.[18] But this does not change the fact
that in all the encounters in which Pharisees controverted
Jesus no proto-rabbi is named, and the title rabbi is not
used in reference to them along with "priest" and "scribe."
On the other hand there is a distinction between the expert
or teacher of halakhah (the *nomikos* and the *nomodidaskalos*)
and the Pharisees. When the two are together, the Pharisee
may oppose Jesus while the *nomodidaskalos* does not, or else
both terms are used to describe a friend.[19]

C. *The Pharisees in Josephus*

Josephus refers to the Pharisees as a *haeresis*. This
term is generally translated as "school of thought" or "sect."
There are difficulties with the nuances of the term "sect" in
current English usage, and it is best to understand Josephus'
Greek term *haeresis* as "a school of thought," a "movement,"
or even a "denomination" within a broader religious spectrum.
That Josephus so intended the term is supported by his use of
various forms of *philosophia* ("philosophy") as a synonym of
haeresis.[20] Josephus' discussion of Pharisees indicates
that they were a large movement among the definable articulate
movements. But the four *haereseis* do not include the broad
mass of people, the *ammei haarez*. That he lists a movement of

pharisaioi separate from the Essenes does not mean they were not similar in terms of being pietistic and separatist. He does not name other groups within Judaism which we know to have existed and is therefore not providing an accurate, comprehensive or technical picture of the broad spectrum of religious life in first-century Judah and Jerusalem. The so-called "fourth philosophy" spoken of by Josephus is a very militantly nationalist one. He informs us that the members of this group are in basic agreement with the Pharisees but insist that God alone is ruler of the Jewish people. This may easily be interpreted to signify that these militants engaged in a pietistic religious tendency, were strongly separatistic as regards the Jerusalem leadership, and favored the Qumran idea of a sacred war of the "sons of light" against "the sons of darkness."[21]

There is no contradition between the anti-Establishment and anti-Roman bias of the "fourth philosophy" and its agreement in religious matters with the Pharisees. There is also no contradiction between the opposition of some Pharisees to war with Rome and the Qumran philosophy that forecast a sacred war. At many junctures of history different segments of one movement or of separate but similar movements have taken varying positions on social issues and matters of war and peace. Nothing in Josephus' several discussions requires that we interpret the term *pharisaioi* as designating proto-rabbinic halakhic scholars or as the spiritual leaders or their disciples who emerged as the rabbis at Yavneh after 70 A.D. In fact, probably when Josephus really wants to refer to proto-rabbis as he does in reference to some Zealots, he calls them *sophistoi*. The proto-rabbis who were not Zealots had already before 66 become wary of remaining in Jerusalem and many of them had departed from the thriving schools in Jerusalem that went by the names of Hillel and Shammai to pursue their studies and research at Yavneh.[22]

One important question about the identity of proto-rabbis with Pharisees arises in Josephus' treatment of the Pharisees. He identifies a person commonly considered a proto-rabbi, Simon b. Gamaliel, and he refers to him as a Pharisee.[23] It is not necessary to regard this Simon b. Gamaliel as a proto-rabbi in the real sense of that word. This Simon is the son of an illustrious proto-rabbi, but was himself a political leader and Pharisee who was in favor of the war and opposed to Josephus' tactics of appeasement. Only one halakhah of his is known, but this is more related to economic and political policy in Jerusalem, to bring the price of pigeons down and curb inflation, than it is to normative halakhah (M. Ker. 7:1). But even if one will consider him a proto-rabbi there is no contradiction in the same person being both a political leader and a religious expert just as his father Gamaliel I is identified as a Pharisee as well as a *nomodidaskalos* in Acts. Otherwise, no other known proto-rabbis are named by Josephus and no clear identity of Pharisees and proto-rabbis can be inferred from Josephus' account.

Josephus' description of Pharisees as experts in the laws and as assiduous in their observance can fit Essenes and Qumranites as well. Not only that, but proto-rabbis are individuals and the *pharisaioi* constitute a *haeresis*, a movement. Nowhere does Josephus refer to the title rabbi although all of his works are written after the rise of rabbinism. It is apparent that Josephus, in far-off Rome, engaged in his writing labors, is not aware of the new direction of leadership. As a young man he adhered to the *pharisaioi* himself.[24] It is, therefore, little surprise that in his later writings he seeks to make them appear in the light of a reasonable philosophical society in order to help them gain ascendancy in the new Roman Order for Palestine. He does not mention the journey of some rabbis to Rome.[25] This can only underscore the fact that when the war ended in 73 A.D. after Masada fell, and after Josephus took up residence in Rome, the rabbis were not yet a major factor in the leadership. They emerged some years later when the work of Yoḥanan ben Zakkai at Yavneh began to be felt, and especially after he was deposed and Gamaliel II gained Roman recognition. Josephus did not carry the history of Judea past 73, and offered no detailed description of their religious life.

Unlike what Hadrian did in 135, Vespasian did not prohibit Jewish access to the Temple area in Jerusalem. Despite reported visits to the area by rabbis there is no discussion of rebuilding the Temple at that time in the rabbinic literature.[26] It appears that there is a hope for the ultimate restoration of the Temple. This is certainly implied in the Passover Seder ritual of R. Akiba.[27] But no action was taken. Nevertheless the militant national spirit continued and the pious hope for the restoration of the Temple is an expression of that spirit. It is apparent that Gamaliel II hoped to regain the power of his father Simon b. Gamaliel and evidently maneuvered to receive the position of Nasi, or "President" of the ruling council.[28]

We hear nothing of all of this from Josephus, nothing of Yoḥanan ben Zakkai, and nothing of Gamaliel II. Undoubtedly this is due to his completing his work with the devastation of Jerusalem. Be that as it may, we have no clear indication in Josephus that the scholarly group of proto-rabbis who emerged at Yavneh as a new semi-sacerdotal class of "rabbis," to become the spiritual leaders in Judaism are the former Pharisees.

D. *Pharisees in Tannaitic Literature*[29]

All of the tannaitic literature in the form in which we have it is later than the first century. But it embodies older traditions. These are, however, difficult to date, and frequently we can do little more than conjecture.

The term *perushim* which stands behind the term *pharisaioi* used by Josephus and the New Testament writers occurs many times in this literature. Not once, however, is it a term by which self-identity is indicated by the rabbis. *Perushim* are contrasted with *ammei haarez*, (literally, "people of the land"). They are contrasted with, or in controversy with *Zedukim* (Sadducees) and Boethusians. At times they are in controversy with certain individuals, such as Zadok of Galilee, and there are times when apparent *perushite* halakhah is given in the name of *hakhamim*, a term that is used of rabbis.[30] The complexity of the occurrence of the term leads to a variety of hypotheses. One recent one is that sometimes it is used to designate Pharisees, and sometimes it designates only pietistic people or separatists who, in effect, are anti-Pharisees.[31]

There is no doubt that the problem of who are the *perushim* in tannaitic literature is as complicated and difficult to solve as is the problem of who are the *pharisaioi* in the New Testament and Josephus. The *perushim* in Tannaitic literature, like the *pharisaioi*-Pharisees are either pietistic Jews, often ascetic, successors to the *hasidim* of the Hasmonean era and similar to Essenes and Qumranties, or they are separatists from the Jerusalem Establishment, or all three: pietistic, ascetic and separatist. While it is difficult to tell when *perushim* are pietists and not separatists, a careful reading of each passage will yield results in most cases.

The fact that *perushim* are in conflict with Sadducees does not necessarily imply that the *perushim* are proto-rabbis. The *hasidim,* Essenes and Qumranites are all *perushim* of one type or another and are in conflict with Sadducees. The *perushim* are also in conflict with Boethusians. It is difficult to ascertain precisely who the Boethusians are, but I see no reason to doubt the account that two men, Zadok and Boethus, dissented (*pirshoo*) from their teacher Antigonus' views, and formed two new segments of Jews.[32] The distinguishing feature of these *Zedukim* (Sadducees) and Baitusin (Boethusians) is that they rejected the concepts of an after life and resurrection.

They understood *perushim* to be pietistic and ascetic.

It is quite conceivable that this correctly places the
origin of the Sadducees in the early second century B.C. And
if this is indeed the case the Sadducee name is not directly
related to the Zadokite priesthood, but rather to the founder
of a school which grew into a small minority movement within
Judaism. Thus Zadokite priests could be Sadducees in theology
and halakhah. Our source, however, tells us that these two
men Zadok and Boethus looked askance upon the *perushim* which
signifies that the *perushim* were already going by that name,
and it therefore follows that this dissent by Sadducees and
Boethusians came into being after the dissent of the pietists
who are first called *ḥasidim* in the Books of the Maccabees.
In later times pietists were still called *ḥasidim*. The word
ḥasidim should be seen as not denoting a party but serving as
an adjectival noun, being descriptive of the religious patterns
of certain groups. The same is true of the term *perushim*.
It is a very broad all-inclusive term like the word "Evangeli-
cal" in modern times. When pietists dissent further from the
ranks of *perushim* they take on specific names such as *toḥle
shaḥar,* the Morning Bathers, or for that matter, the more
famous Essenes and Therapeutae.[33]

Perhaps it will be of some value here to examine several
sources where the terms we are discussing are used, in order
to see the difficulty we are up against. The first source is
that of the Babylonian Talmud (Yom. 19b). The Talmud records
an incident when a High Priest prepared the incense outside
the Holy of Holies. This was done in order to fulfill the
verse (Lev. 16:13), "In the cloud I shall appear on the
kaporet (at the place where expiation is executed)." The
verse was exegeted by Sadducees to mean that the priest must
not approach where God appears except behind a cloud of incense. When the High Priest emerged in great happiness over
his successful execution of the ritual his father admonished
him that he should not have acted as he did for "despite our
being Sadducees, we fear the *perushim*." It is apparent that
the *perushim* had another way of exegeting the verse but though
their exegesis is not given in this passage, the implication
is that they interpreted it to mean one must prepare the incense inside the Holy of Holies.[34]

The second source is the Tosefta (Yom. 1:8). There we
read of an incident where a Boethusian kindled the incense
outside of the Holy of Holies and then entered behind a cloud
which engulfed the entire room. Lev. 16:13 informs us that
the priest placed the incense upon the fire before the Lord
"and the cloud of incense covered the *kaporet* which covered

the tablets of testimony." The Boethusians exegeted this to mean that one must enter behind the cloud so that when one approaches the holy cabinet upon which was the *kaporet* where God appeared, there was already a cloud-cover upon it. *Ḥakhamim* differed with them, using the first part of the verse, "He shall place the incense upon the fire before the Lord," to argue that this signifies that the priest is to kindle the incense "before the Lord," after he enters the Holy of Holies. But the Boethusians reinforced their argument with Lev. 16:2 where God says "I will appear upon the *kaporet* in a cloud," taking it to mean that the cloud must be there before God is seen. The father of the priest was concerned that his son had followed the practice according to Boethusian exegesis ("Although we exegete, we do not practice so"), reminding him that priestly custom ordinarily complied with the *ḥakhamim*.

The third source is that of Sifra on Leviticus which is cited in the Palestinian Talmud (Yom. 39 a-b). Prior to this halakhic statement, however, the Talmud records an anecdote very similar to that of the Tosefta with Boethusians acting contrary to the practice of the *ḥakhamim*. Later on the Talmud refers to Sadducees who prepare the incense outside of the Holy of Holies because of Lev. 16:2. And *ḥakhamim* respond to them that Lev. 16:13, to place the incense upon the fire before the Lord, implies that the priest is to prepare incense inside the Holy of Holies. They exegete Lev. 16:2 to signify the use of an ingredient which provides fullness for the incense cloud because it should cover the entire *kaporet* (16:13).

When we read the biblical text (Lev. 16:12f.) very carefully we note that the priest is to take a pan of fiery coals from the altar and a fistful of incense and bring them "inside of the *parokhet*" (the veil). This expression may have a variety of meanings, but on the face of it the implication in this context is that he enters the room beyond the *parokhet* which is the Holy of Holies and there he places the incense upon the fire "before the Lord."[35] The Torah appears to be saying that the priest is to kindle the incense inside of the Holy of Holies, vindicating the exegesis of the *ḥakhamim*. Sadducees and Boethusians, otherwise strict constructionists as regards the Torah's text, appear to be stretching a point. Yet Lev. 16:2 leads them to this exegesis: that God is to be seen only from behind a thick cloud of incense. This implies that when one enters the Holy of Holies he should already have his view of the deity obstructed by the cloud of incense. We do not actually know how the Sadducee-Boethusian sages exegeted Lev. 16:12-13. There is ambiguity in the Torah, but we are not here concerned with this as a halakhic or exegetical problem. We are concerned only with the use of the terms

perushim, Boethusian, Sadducees, *ḥakhamim.* The three sources
have Boethusians and Sadducees in apparent agreement against
perushim and *ḥakhamim.* The crux now is: does this indicate
a parallelism for *perushim* and *ḥakhamim*? And if the *ḥakhamim*
are proto-rabbis, are the *perushim* proto-rabbis?

As we have seen, Boethus and Zadok, two disciples of
Antigonus of Sokho dissented from their master and established
two sectarian groups. It may be assumed that they had much in
common. Being without their literature we do not know what
they had in common and in what they differed from each other.
Apparently, since the same halakhah concerning the preparation
of the incense is given in the name of both they had cultic
practices in common. For the rabbis who edited these sources
the terms were interchangeable. But *perushim* and *ḥakhamim*
are not to be seen as equivalent. The term *perushim* is not
used in the accounts of the Palestinian Talmud and Tosefta.
And while the anecdotal account in the Babylonian Talmud
given above uses the term *perushim* the halakhic account uses
the term *ḥakhamim* (B. Yom. 53a). Furthermore, in the latter
statement the Sadducees are not "afraid" of the *ḥakhamim.*[36]
It is only in the possibly legendary context of the first
Babylonian source that a Sadducee priest says that Sadducees
are "afraid" of *perushim* and therefore should not follow
their own independent halakhah. Who are these *perushim* of
whom they are afraid? I am suggesting they are extremists who
sought to impose their views on the Temple priesthood, probably
including Zealots who threw fear into the priests. Some
perushim, instead, separated themselves from the Temple and
its cult. The *ḥakhamim* insisted upon their exegesis, but in
cases where they lost they threw no fear into the priests, and
they followed the Hillilite teaching not to separate from the
community. Of what were the Sadducee priests afraid? They
were afraid of the terrorist activities of the Zealots, and
of the power and appeal that the *perushim* and their pietism
had among the masses. This was especially so because the
priests suffered a high level of loss of credibility since
Hasmonean times.[37]

Evidently the rabbis who incorporated these passages into
their literature made no effort to clarify the arguments of
the *perushim* or of the *ḥakhamim* against the Sadducees. Scholars did make a halakhic statement they referred to the scholars as *ḥakhamim.* The only reference to *perushim* is in the
statement of the Sadducee father of the priest who explained
to his son that although they have their own exegesis they
do not follow its consequences because they are "afraid of
the *perushim.*" As a matter of fact, in the one source where
perushim are mentioned, the halakhah of the *ḥakhamim* is not

12

mentioned. We know nothing about what the *perushim* actually thought on this question except by implication that they did not approve of the Sadducee practice. It is even possible that this source in the Babylonian Talmud is an erroneous report, embodying obvious legendary material about how the priest was found struck down as he left the Holy of Holies. This would leave no room for his conversation with his father, a discrepancy which escaped the notice of the rabbis who compiled it.[38]

The reader may take this question of when to set afire the incense as a paradigm. Similar problems arise in other controversy literature involving Sadducees, Boethusians, *perushim* and *hakhamim*. In many passages *hakhamim* are juxtaposed to Sadducees or Boethusians. This does not make *perushim* of the *hakhamim*. It merely signifies that certain proto-rabbis took positions against disciples of Zadok and Boethus, preserving the traditions of Antigonos and Simon the Righteous, from whose schools of thought the two former had dissented. The schools that formed in oppostion to the schools of Zadok and Boethus ultimately became known as the Bet Hillel and Bet Shammai. From the later rabbinic perspective anonymous or unidentified *hakhamim* are opponents of Sadducee-Boethusian representatives, but are not *perushim*. They are the proto-rabbis in whose traditions rabbinic Judaism was nurtured.[39]

There are sources that have absolutely no value for a disposition of the problem. One of these is a well-known story in the Talmud. King Yannai (presumed to be the Hasmonean Alexander Jannaeus) gathered the *hakhamim (hakhme Yisrael)* for a party. A trouble-maker infused hostility in the occasion by telling the king the *perushim* are against him. Someone explained that the opposition was based upon the king's seeking the priestly role along with the crown. The *hakhme Yisrael* then separated themselves in anger. After some further agitation the king killed the sages (B. Kid. 66a). The story does not really have coherence and has many problems of historicity. But aside from literary and historical problems there is no evidence whatever that the *hakhme Yisrael* are identical with *perushim*. The *perushim*, not the *hakhamim* are accused before the king, and it is the *hakhamim* who are killed after the *perushim* take an oath of loyalty. Similarly when Yohanan b. Zakkai opposes Sadducees, this does not prove he is a "Pharisee." In key instances *perushim* are not even mentioned. These are instances when anonymous views are controverted by the Sadducees and it is not warranted to automatically declare the anonymous views as so-called Pharisaic.[40] In the same way it cannot be said the *ammei haarez* are synonymous with *perushim* and *hakhamim* simply because we have in-

stances where that term is used in opposition to Sadducees.
(T. Suk. 3:1; B. Suk. 43b). On the other hand there are instances where *perushim* clearly refers to people who abstain
from pleasureful activity or enjoyment, signifying pietists
(T. Sot. 15:11-12; B.B.B. 60b). The term denotes separatism
in an anecdote concerning a certain Judah ben Durtai and his
son who dissented from the *ḥakhamim* because of a difference
of opinion concerning whether the *ḥagigah* sacrifice may be
offered on the Sabbath (B. Pes. 70b). The term *perushim*
also designated such separatists as were placed in the same
category as *minim* (Christian Jews, Gnostics or "sectarians"
generally; T. Ber. 3:25).

The foregoing demonstrates that the term *perushim* is
used in tannaitic literature in several ways, and that it does
not in any of these contexts denote proto-rabbis. The rabbis
nowhere referred to themselves as *perushim,* and even where
perushim is juxtaposed to Sadducees it need not signify the
proto-rabbis. Not only *perushim*-pietists and separatists,
but also *ʿammei haarez* are juxtaposed to Sadducees, in addition
to *ḥakhamim.*[41] At one point, in a discussion of ritual purity,
we find Yosi b. Yoezer, one of the earliest of the proto-rabbis
carefully distinguished from *perushim,* and in other sources we
find *perushim* severely denounced by the rabbis.[42] There are
laudatory allusions to being *perushim* as God is *parush.* But
this exegesis of Lev. 11:44-45 and 19:2, "to be holy" as meaning that as God is considered a *parush* Israel is urged to emulate Him, signifies not that part of Israel is to be separated
from all Israel, but that Israel is to be separated from the
nations of the world and dedicated to God's will.[43] This
usage need have no significance whatever for our subject except to demonstrate the wide usage of the term and the im-
practicality of attempting to define it in the sense of a
"party" or a class of scholars.

Finally the terms *ḥaber, ḥaberim* ("fellows," "associates"),
are not synonymous with *perushim,* and do not signify rabbis.
The *ḥaburot* "fellowship societies" were organized specifically
for purposes of maintaining more rigorous standards of tithing and ritual purity, and in this sense their members were
pietistic. Some rabbis may have belonged to *ḥaburot.* But
being a *ḥaber* was not determinative of one's total life associations anymore than a modern person's life situation is
defined by a good co-op or one or two societies to which he
may belong. Furthermore, there were other *ḥaburot* in Jerusalem that were social welfare agencies concerned to help people
with a variety of life-cycle needs from circumcision to burial,
further complicating the effort to understand our terminology.
A *ḥaber* might also simply signify a disciple-colleague.[44]

One scholar has astutely and succinctly summarized the situation for us: ". . .we must be very cautious in drawing conclusions from similarities and differences between the regulations of the sects. The various sects with which Palestine of the first century swarmed might have had much in common although they differed from one another in basic and cardinal principles."[45] To use the term Pharisaism in English as if it represented a definable segment of Judaism and to see Pharisees as academic, judicial or sacerdotal functionaries (rabbis), is a highly unwarranted procedure in modern scholarship.

II. OBSERVATIONS CONCERNING THE SADDUCEES

The origin of the Sadducees or *Ẓadukim* is cloaked in obscurity. My inclination, in the absence of documentable evidence otherwise, is to give credence to the tradition that they were organized during the second century B.C. as a dissent from the emerging proto-rabbinic schools (Ab. de R. N. A, 5; B, 10). The original Sadducees were thus contemporaries of Yosi b. Yoezer. Perhaps the first Sadducean schools spawned a new moderate movement which moved away from some of the theological ideas of Sadduceeism in the Bet Shammai, while the disciples of Simon the Righteous and Antigonus spawned the Bet Hillel. But this is difficult to ascertain.[46]

It is wrong to think that Sadducees clung tenaciously to the text of the Pentateuch. They adopted evolving tradition. But they differed on how to interpret scripture. They were "strict constructionists," maintaining as R. Ishmael is quoted as holding over two centuries later, that the "Torah speaks in the language of humans," and therefore rejected radical new ideas or practices.[47] We cannot demonstrate how the Sadducees exegeted Torah and what post-Pentateuchal halakhah they practiced, for their literature was suppressed by rabbinic Judaism. The cases where Sadducee-Pharisee or Sadducee-*ḥakhamim* controversies are given may or may not accurately reflect Sadducee halakhah.[48] It is possible that their opinions have been distorted by their opponents and recorded in rabbinic literature in a manner that exalts rabbinic halakhah and not to preserve the historic accuracy of Sadducean halakhah. By the time of Yavneh, post-70, when the rabbis took control of Judaism, it was in their self-interest in the process of establishing their hegemony, to see the Sadducees as *minim*, and to make all other halakhah and beliefs appear to lack credibility.

An evident example of Sadducee practice of non-Pentateuchal halakhah is found in their acceptance of the ritual of beating the willow twigs on the last day of Sukot, although they objected to doing so when the festival fell on the Sabbath.[49] They too could see that the Torah allowed the priests authority to make rulings and innovate practices on the basis of Deut. 17:8-13. But they differed as to whether anyone who was not a priest of the Jerusalem Establishment had that authority. While the proto-rabbis claimed that authority for themselves, the Sadducees supported the Jerusalem priesthood as the exclusive authority. That the Sadducees had developed their own post-Pentateuchal halakhah is further evident from a collection of halakhah attributed to them. This is known as *sefer gezeratah* (Book of Decisions or Decrees). Sadducean oral interpretive Torah is also found in connection with additional matters of halakhah such as the cutting of the *ómer*, the first grain of the harvest, from which the date of Shabuot was calculated, and in matters of testimony. In the latter instance we have a case of Sadducean leniency over proto-rabbinic harshness.[50]

It is logical to assume that many of the practices, laws, and customs, that are a considerable portion of the halakhah, were maintained in common by all branches of Judaism. Different groups sometimes differed over details, as can be seen in a survey of the controversies. They sometimes differed over a major question such as what supersedes the Sabbath. But all branches practiced reinterpretation of Torah and expansion of the Pentateuchal civil and ritual guidelines. Members of different groups sometimes shared qualities of groups other than their own. Thus, Sadducees were also *ḥaberim,* members of fellowships who were pietistic about purity and tithes. People constituted themselves in separate movements because they differed on whose authority is legitimate, and on some theological doctrines such as the question of the resurrection of the dead which is not explicit in the Pentateuch. We cannot be certain as to precisely what the Sadducees believed about revelation and human authority, but can only assume that since they engaged in the process of halakhic development they had a view of progressive revelation as did the later rabbis. From Josephus we learn they rejected the resurrection of the dead, which we can also read in the New Testament. They undoubtedly accepted the limited references to the use of angels or divine messengers by God in the Bible, but rejected the expanded angelology and demonology that Palestinian Judaism acquired from Zoroastrianism.[51] It is quite conceivable that if we found Sadducee writings we would discover that the post-70 rabbis absorbed some of their halakhah just as we know that rabbinic literature contains elements that are also found in the Dead Sea Scrolls and in the New Testament.

Some proto-rabbis such as Simon the Righteous and Yosi b.
Yoezer, among others, down to Yoḥanan b. Zakkai, were priests
and enjoyed the priestly authority. But they also recognized
the right of non-priests to share in that authority on the
basis of the same passage in the Torah (Deut. 17:8-14).[52]
Thus after 70 when by act of God, the functioning priesthood
came to an end and the rabbis replaced them, the Sadducean
movement disintegrated. When it is considered how this, alongside the mass slaughter and massive deportation of Jews left
other organized groups such as Qumran and Essenes in a state
of disintegration, and how all the while they were confronted
with the growing Christian movement, it becomes apparent that
the only island of stability in traditional Judaism was Yavneh.
This historic reality is the explanation for the rise of rabbinic Judaism.

III. THE RISE OF RABBINIC JUDAISM

A. *From the Babylonian Exile to Yoḥanan ben Zakkai*

1. *587 B.C. To The Hasmonean Era.*

"Rabbinic Judaism" is a full-grown product depicted in the
Mishnah, Tosefta and the various tannaitic midrashim, and then
expanded into the talmudic literature.[53] The antecedents of
rabbinic Judaism go back to the earliest times and were taught
by the *kohen, nabi, ḥakham* and *sofer*. These functionaries
have been discussed in previous chapters. Each dispensed his
form of instruction, counsel and doctrine in his respective
school. During the last days of the First Commonwealth (pre-
exilic Judah) the *sofer* emerges out of the royal court context.
This functionary becomes a major post-exilic figure, but it is
the title *ḥakham* which becomes the lasting designation of
scholar and teacher. The *nabi* goes into decline and the *kohen*
loses credibility. The *sofer* however, should be understood
during his earlier period as more than a "scribe." He is a
scholastic, the learned scholar-researcher, as we can tell
from the description given Ezra the Sofer (Ezra 7:6, 10f.).[54]

Although priests still offer instruction, the last prophets
already give their own halakhic interpretations. It would appear that the great anonymous prophet, whom we call Deutero-
Isaiah, only cited extant halakhah but did not decide it, or
that Malakhi reflects an anti-divorce posture but does not

create new halakhah. It would be naive, however, to think
that these prophets of God who uttered the *dabar* of God did
not teach new halakhah to their immediate disciples and
wider circles, just as Jesus does in the New Testament. The
nebiim were regarded historically as transmitters of torah,
which includes the new oral interpretive torah or halakhah (M.
Ab 1:1).[55]

There is no certainty about who constituted the religious
leadership in Jerusalem and Judah from 587 B.C. to 458 B.C.,
or who served in this capacity in Egypt and Babylonia, the two
major diaspora centers. It appears that the sacrificial cult
continued in Jerusalem after the destruction of the Temple and
so presumably priests continued as religious authorities.
There also seems to have been a Temple in Babylonia and at
Elephantine in Egypt which again would require the service of
priests. The activity of Deutero-Isaiah, Ezekiel, Haggai,
Zekhariah and Malakhi indicates that the prophets also continued in their role as charismatic teachers.[56]

The permission granted by Cyrus for the exiles in Babylonia
to rebuild the Temple in Jerusalem and the execution of this
task under Zerubbabel and Joshua the High Priest did not immediately issue forth in a religious reformation, as we can
clearly see from Malakhi's stern denunciations.[57] With the work
of Ezra and Nehemiah to overcome the religious laxity the
sofer rises to temporary prominence in Judaic religious leadership. He soon comes to be identified with the *hakham*, the man
of wisdom. This is the title used by the Hasmonean spiritual
leaders and continues so down into rabbinic times. But it was
Nehemiah who was neither *kohen* nor *sofer*, but a secular governor, who apparently enforced the reformation of Ezra in matters related to the Temple, the Sabbath and mixed marriages.
This is significant because it bears out the historic fact
that only when governmental power was applied in the interests
of one faction of Judaism did a semblance of "orthodoxy" arise.
Otherwise there was manifest constant diversity. Nehemiah
used verbal excoriation and physical force to put an end to
mixed marriages. In the process he went beyond the limitations of the Torah, an act which sheds light on another aspect
of Judaism pertinent to the rabbinic period, that the norms of
the Torah can be superseded even without a new revelation.[58]

During the Ezraic-Nehemian era, a period of retrenchment,
religious conservatism was enforced by the state power exercised
by Nehemiah. It is difficult, however, to ascertain the lines
of spiritual development after Ezra and Nehemiah. Although
there continued to be prophets, we have no names of the apoca-
lyptists. Only when we encounter Ben Sira and Simon the Righ-

teous around 200 B.C. do we have the first names of proto-
rabbis.[59]

Our knowledge of religious life during Ptolemaic control
of Palestine (302-198 B.C.) is meager. Hellenism had been introduced and a process of acculturation began. At least three
points of view arose. There were those who insisted upon the
separatist-pietist arrangements covenanted by Ezra and Nehemiah. There were those who participated in moderate hellenization. And there were those who formed a more radical group
that ultimately went over to apostasy. But more important is
that this era is the time of the growth of the synagogue into
a major religious institution and the emergence of a non-
hereditary, sometimes charismatic spiritual leader, the proto-
rabbi. From Ben Sira's description of the ideal *sofer* ca. 200
B.C. we receive our first description of the emergent proto-
rabbi, a scholar and teacher who engages in prayer, and wel-
comes students without fees. He gives instruction, counsels,
pours forth wisdom, investigates obscure things, all without
benefit of the kind of direct revelation common in bygone
generations. He foreshadows the programmatic suggestions for
the rabbi of which we read in later literature. Furthermore,
as is clear from Ben Sira's great hymn to pre-existent wisdom,
which he identifies with the Torah, in the *sofer's* work all of
scripture and all of the interpretive torah receives the
authority and status of revelation. Rabbi Abudimi, a major
repository and transmitter of traditions between Palestine
and Babylonia reported on the tradition that prophecy exists
among the *ḥakhamim*. Thus, in effect, rabbinic theory assumed
for the rabbis the authority of both revelation and interpretation based upon their succession of both priest and prophet.[60]

Ben Sira and Simon the Righteous become the known links
between biblical Israel-Judah and rabbinic-talmudic Judaism.
Following them we know the "founders" of rabbinic Judaism by
name. But hovering in the background is another term which
has baffled historians and theologians, and which nevertheless
looms large in the rabbinic self-identification. This is the
term "Men of the Great Assembly."

2. *The Men of The Great Assembly*

We are informed that Simon the Righteous was of the last
remaining members of a "great assembly."[61] This term, *keneset
hagedolah,* "great assembly," is obscure. Later rabbinic Judaism attributes to it a wide variety of liturgical developments.
In effect, much of post-biblical Judaic ritual is attributed
to this "great assembly," an amorphous body that is alleged to

have existed from the time of Ezra to that of Simon the Righteous.[62]

The idea of a "great assembly" is not a figment of rabbinic imagination. We know of a series of major synods or assemblies. It is safe to say there was not a one-time synod that made so many innovations in Judaism. At different times such a body met in conclave to innovate needed practices or to affirm the religious developments of a recent period. (Neh. 5:7; 8:10). More than one is depicted in the time of Nehemiah. Such a *synagogē megalē* or "great assembly" occurred during the Hasmonean era, ca. 142 B.C. to establish the union of the priesthood and principate into one person (I Macc. 14:25-49). An *ekklēsia Israel* "assembly of Israel" declared the festival of Hanukah in 164 B.C. (I Macc. 4:59). But there is no evidence that such great assemblies were called to decide proto-rabbinic halakhah in the first century B.C. or first century A.D. A famous meeting of the year 65 A.D. was merely a small joint session of Hillelite and Shammaite scholars.[63] The schools were independent and scholars in each school deliberated halakhic questions arising from their study and life experiences. Each school had its followers and there developed no uniformity and no "orthodoxy." The proto-rabbinic period thus prefigures the whole future of Judaism in which local and contemporary authority plays a great role.

3. *The Proto-Rabbi*

Simon the Righteous is believed to be the first of the proto-rabbis known to us by name. Whether this is a historically authentic tradition is not relevant to rabbinic Judaism since no halakhah is given in his name. But the history of tradition is traced from him through others who are called *zugot* or "pairs," who are more familiar to us. The one exception to this is Simon's immediate disciple Antigonus of Sokho, of whom we know nothing.[64] The Mishnah seeks with this list to establish legitimate tradition from God through the prophetic line, including only the one priestly connection, Simon the Righteous, who is of special quality and is said to have been accompanied by the incarnate deity into the Holy of Holies (Lev. R. 21:12). The rabbinic implication is that the priesthood has legitimacy on rabbinic terms, and only if it is reinstated through the Zadokite line which ended with Simon the Righteous. As a matter of fact, by beginning the named proto-rabbis with Simon who emphasizes Torah and cult along with the ethical norms, the rabbis are tracing their ordination authority back to a priestly founder, thereby making the rabbis successors to both priests and prophets.

The chain of tradition which we are here discussing, as
listed in the first chapter of Mishnah Aḅot, from Moses to
Simon b. Gamaliel I brings us down to the great war of 66-73
and the emergence of rabbinic Judaism. The list is really a
theologico-halakhic affirmation that the entire interpretive
torah is legitimately set alongside the written Torah for
it is the product of continuous transmission from biblical
kohen, *nabi* and *ḥakham,* all of whom were represented among the
"men of the Great Assembly" among whom also sat Simon the
Righteous. This is what the rabbinic scholars of the first
and second centuries believed about the transmission of tradition and this became the premise of rabbinic Judaism.
Statements that constitute traditions of scholars known by
name began only with Yosi b. Yoezer and Yosi b. Yoḥanan, the
first of the "pairs."

The "pairs" of proto-rabbinic scholars are traditionally
referred to as *aḅot haOlam* "the fathers of the world," as are
also Ishmael and Akiba later, that is, the founding fathers
of rabbinic Judaism.[65] This list, including Gamaliel I, encompasses scholars who lived from before 170 B.C. to after
50 A.D., a span of almost two-hundred and fifty years.[66]
There are also other pre-70 scholars known to us by name, with
more or less halakhic teaching transmitted in their names.[67]
Among the pre-70 proto-rabbis we must include Yoḥanan b.
Zakkai, for although he is best known for his work at Yavneh
after 70, he was active since the second decade of the century
both in Galilee and Jerusalem.[68]

In these proto-rabbinic circles in which rabbinic Judaism
took root, the most productive groups were Bet Shammai and
Bet Hillel. The controversies between these schools produced
much anonymous halakhah. The schools were named for the two
famous scholars, Hillel and Shammai, of both of whom little
is actually known.[69] But it does appear quite likely that
these schools pre-dated both Hillel and Shammai, going back
to the period immediately after the Hasmonean restoration.
It is reasonable to assume that a religious renaissance would
give rise to divergent interpretation of scripture among
scholars, and that scholars and their disciples, forming
"schools," would seek to perpetuate their respective views.[70*]

These two famous schools ceased to function after 70 A.D.
We are informed that for three years the two schools debated
the question of whose authority should prevail and a *bat kol,*
a heavenly voice, called out that the halakhah shall be according to Bet Hillel.[71] According to our source this estab-

*See excursus at note 70.

lishment of Hillelism as the backbone of rabbinic Judaism, happened at Yavneh, but no further detail indicates when at Yavneh, or what were the circumstances. It appears that the points of view remained divergent for some time after 70 and that Yoḥanan b. Zakkai's assumption of authority became the occasion for a struggle for halakhic hegemony.[72] Yoḥanan b. Zakkai's school and relgious council, the *Bet Din* at Yavneh, superseded the two Jerusalem schools. Both Hillelite and Shammaite halakhah were probably accepted by Yohanan, for Yoḥanan is said to have received that tradition from both Hillel and Shammai (M. Ab. 2:9). There is some clue in the talmudic record that the halakhah was later more usually established according to Bet Hillel for several reasons. We are told they were prone to examine Bet Shammai's views and even to retract their own position in favor of Bet Shammai when the latter was proven correct. The tradition thus sought to explain Hillelite supremacy by presenting an image of more careful inquiry and humility in addition to leniency. It is also interesting that Bet Shammai placed no validity in a *Bat Kol* while Bet Hillel did (T. Naz. 1:1). The tradition that a *Bat Kol* confirmed the authority of Bet Hillel, therefore, is almost a taunt against Bet Shammai. Gamaliel II and R. Eliezer b. Hyrcanus, however, are outstanding men of the Yavneh generation who continued to follow the views of Bet Shammai. Once again, this underscores the ongoing diversity in Judaism contrary to all efforts to forge a uniform practice upheld by a central authority.[73]

When Jerusalem was destroyed in 70 A.D. the scholars at Yavneh turned to Yoḥanan b. Zakkai to pull things together. He literally remodeled the Covenant Community of Israel from a nation into an *ekklēsia*, a relgious assembly. It was taking a giant stride back in history to the days of the origin of Israel as an amphictyonic federation. Yoḥanan was an independent scholar, yet a disciple of both Hillel and Shammai. He was a contemporary of Jesus and familiar with the rising new branch of Judaism which insisted that the Messiah had come in the form of Jesus of Nazareth. He was an antinationalist who withdrew from the siege of Jerusalem to join the sages engaged in religious learning at Yavneh. When the smoke cleared, with the Gamaliel family in disrepute for being in rebellion in Jerusalem, this independent scholar and friend of Rome was in a position to lead the restoration of Judaism and Judaic communal life.

In some mysterious manner, however, for which we have no definite information as to how and why, Yoḥanan was removed from leadership and replaced by Gamaliel II. It is my view that he was removed because he had as much opposition in leading Jewish circles for his stance as had the Christians

who withdrew to Pella.[74] Secondly, his removal was probably
encouraged by those who thought him to be "soft" on Christianity. Thirdly, he was superseded because the Romans felt it
was time to return the helm to Gamaliel II and restore the
"pretender" to his "throne," no longer concerned that the
Gamaliel dynasty claimed to be descended from David. The appointment of Gamaliel II opened the way for the expulsion of
the Christians from the Synagogue, the alienation of Christianity and its separation from Judaism.[75]

The authority the Romans had given to Yohanan was now
transferred to Gamaliel. Yohanan b. Zakkai retired to Beror
Hayil and conducted a center of learning there, while Gamaliel
II became the formal Nasi and presided at Yavneh.[76] It is
probable that a coalition of Yohanan's opponents unseated him.
These would consist of his own former associates and disciples
who opposed his anti-war posture, the party of loyalists to
Gamaliel II, the priests who resented his anti-priestly stance
and persistent effort to "layicize" Judaism and grant equal
authority to centers other than Jerusalem, and finally any surviving Sadducees. This probably happened sometime early in
the reign of Domitian (81-96) and before his volatile behavior after 88. Priests and Gamalielites would each tend to
oppose Yohanan and logically form a coalition to seek an opportunity to unseat him.[77]

The major single contribution made by Yohanan ben Zakkai
which had vast permanent historical significance for Judaism
was his introduction of formal ordination of his disciples,
the laying on of hands to symbolize the transmission of
authority (P. San. 19a). This certified they may serve as
religious authorities whether they were priests or not, to
make halakhic decisions, and to govern the spiritual life of
the post-70 community. This was a direct challenge to the
priestly aristocracy. It created a wholly new formal and
authoritative democratic body, a meritocracy, through which
community leaders would no longer attain power and authority
by virtue of their priestly birth, but be appointed by virtue
of their attainment of a degree of competence in halakhah. A
second significant contribution is his replacement of Jerusalem as the center of authority by the academic center where
there presided an ordained scholar. The consequence of this
was a multiplicity of centers and of authority, thereby enabling Judaism to survive on a world-wide basis and to flourish intellectually. These changes signalled the true birth
of rabbinic Judaism. The members of this new scholarly
meritocracy envisioned by Yohanan bore the title "Rabbi."
Yohanan created a substitute for Jerusalem at Yavneh, and in
subsequent history, in every synagogue and center of higher

learning. He transmogrified a territorially-centered, central Temple-oriented theology dominated by a hereditary priesthood into a universal faith.[78]*

B. *The Achievements at Yavneh*

The Rabbis at Yavneh gathered the pre-rabbinic traditions and began the massive work of reconstituting shattered Jewish existence. They accepted the priesthood and the sacrificial system in theory, but rejected it as the pragmatic way for their time. They assumed for themselves the mantle of both priest and prophet. In their own persons they were perpetuating the biblical institutions. In the absence of the sacrificial cult Jews were to expiate their sins through deeds of love. In service to fellow-humans they were to offer up their surrogate persons to God, as once they offered the animal or vegetable surrogate. Yohanan b. Zakkai did nothing less than restate Judaic theology. With Hosea 6:6 as his motto "it is love I desire, not sacrifice," Yohanan made the sacrificial system appear superseded. This made the priests superfluous, and restored the pre-Solomonic legitimacy of multiple sanctuaries. Prayer worship was no longer merely a supplement to the true cult, or a concession to those in the diaspora and to those living in Palestine and unable or unwilling to appear at the Jerusalem Temple. It was now the God-ordained and God-willed form for His worship. This explains why a great deal of liturgical activity took place at Yavneh.[79]

It is impossible to unravel precisely the detailed contributions of Yohanan b. Zakkai as distinct from Gamaliel II at Yavneh. Yohanan undoubtedly set the mechanism of consolidation in motion, and through ordination and his restatement of Judaic theology he founded rabbinic Judaism. But it was Gamaliel II, who succeeded him sometime between 80-90 who introduced the policy of exclusion and brought about the permanent fissure in Judaism between rabbinic Judaism and Christianity. For example, while Yohanan sought to defuse priestly opposition and quarrelled with the Sadducees over a variety of halakhic questions, it was Gamaliel II who insisted upon belief in the doctrine of the resurrection of the dead as a pre-requisite for membership in theological Israel and consequent eligibility for salvation. In this way, although he benefited from Sadducees in his rise to power, Gamaliel II excluded Sadducees, Boethusians and others, by requiring specific theological affirmations, just as he excluded Christian Jews by instituting the *birkhat haminim.*[80]

*See expanded note 78.

Yohanan had not excluded priests. He only "retired" them. But in various ways he offered them ongoing honors and privileges. Some of these have continued to this day in that segment of Judaism which calls itself "orthodox." One of these is the priestly privilege called *dukhan,* to come before the congregation on holy days and intone the biblical priestly benediction, and to be called to the Torah first on Sabbaths and Festivals. He rejected the premise that the Temple, the priesthood and the cult were needed for Jewish salvation. But he did not abandon the institutions as such in theology, and made space for them in the liturgy of future expectation. The prayers included the hope for the restoration of the Temple and the sacrifices. But to emphasize the legitimacy of the synagogue and of such centers as Yavneh, Yohanan instituted *takanot* (enactments) that elevated Yavneh to the position of Jerusalem, and the rabbis to the position of the priests. Many rabbis, indeed, were non-functioning priests, descended from priestly families, and these helped in the transition. But other priests were bitter and undoubtedly played a role in procrastinating change.[81]

It is difficult to say how much halakhic material was arranged under the leadership of Yohanan ben Zakkai and to what extent the formation of the later Mishnah began to take place during his era. References to a Mishnah of R. Meir based upon the collection of material by R. Akiba is not very helpful, for this is post-Yohanan. There was an earlier "First Mishnah," but again it is difficult to tell whether this was part of Yohanan's work. Undoubtedly there was a body of mishnaic material that was even pre-70, such as Middot, Tamid and Yoma. Possibly Kinnim, said to have been arranged by R. Joshua b. Hananiah, was part of the work undertaken by Yohanan's disciples at Yavneh during his leadership.[82]

Regardless of how much arrangement of halakhic material took place at Yavneh, liturgical arrangement was prolific; and it was probably at Yavneh that the core of Judaic synagogue worship was structured. The central segment of worship is the *amidah*. Although most of its content is older, this was clearly arranged and instituted in a formal way at Yavneh. This, however, was probably the work of Gamaliel II, and not of Yohanan ben Zakkai. Similarly, other segments of the worship order, such as the paragraphs connected with the Shema which precedes the *amidah*, are probably pre-70, but were all arranged in the present form at Yavneh. This order as we have it presently affirms the basic theology of Judaism: creation, revelation, election, monotheism and redemption. The prayers include an invocation (*Borkhu*), a paragraph alluding to God as Creator, (*Yozer*) and Revealer, the source of

Torah as a sign of His love and Election of Israel (*Ahaḅah*),
the Shemȧ, and a paragraph affirming God as Redeemer, with
special references to the Exodus from Egypt (*Geulah*). The
same structure applies to both morning and evening worship as
we know it but for some generations the evening ritual was
not as widely observed as the morning order which was considered mandatory. It is, for example, clear that the prayer
after the Shemȧ, affirming God as Redeemer, is pre-70, and is
included in the priestly liturgy described in the Mishnah
(M. Tam. 5:1-2).[83]

Prayer or verbal worship accompanied by music is a very
old institution as can be seen in the existence of the Psalms.
The rabbinic revolution is constituted in declaring prayer to
be *aḅodah,* the equivalent of the sacrificial cult.[84] Rabbinic
halakhah introduced obligatory prayer. This meant primarily
that every individual was to participate in communal worship,
requiring a quorum (*minyan*) of ten. But failing that, the
individual remained obligated to daily private devotions to be
engaged in more or less at the hours when worship is conducted
in the synagogue, and with several exceptions known as "words
of sanctification," he was to use the same liturgy. But
while much of the liturgical halakhah as we have it is rabbinic
and post-70, there are many indications that the content of
the liturgy itself, and the antecedent halakhah is pre-rabbinic. Phrases and whole sentences, but more usually only words,
were here and there modified, and a liturgical "redactor"
combined various independent units into lengthier prayers such
as the *ȧmidah* or the paragraph accompanying the Shemȧ. Another "redactor" created the *shaḥarit.* But on the whole many
of the individual units of prayer still in use are pre-
rabbinic.[85] The Yavnean worship order is a direct outgrowth
of pre-70 Temple worship. Priests conducted a morning service (M. Tam. 5:1), and the *anshe maȧmadot*, representatives
of the people outside of Jerusalem who attended the sacrificial exercises in the Temple on a rotating system, engaged in
prayer while their fellow townspeople gathered in the synagogues
(M. Taan. 4:2-3; 2:2-5). Various discussions and halakhic
disputes in the rabbinic literature which reflect a pre-70
provenance also point to a variety of antecedents to the post-
70 worship order (M. Yom. 7:1).[86]

Another major achievement at Yavneh was the biblical canon,
to be discussed in Chapter Four. Although, like prayer, this
was basically a pre-70 collection, it took on its final form,
with the exception of perhaps a book or two, sometime during
the Yavneh period.

Yavneh was also the scene of exclusionary consolidation.

Just as the Ezraic-Nehemian retrenchment included the turning
in upon itself by the Jewish community so too the consolidation
at Yavneh involved a process of separation of the Jewish community. Ritualism became of greater importance because it
identified distinctiveness. Theologically one can see the
Destruction of 70 as the fulfillment of the worst admonitions
of the prophets of Israel. But at the same time the rabbis
were able to see their generation as the surviving remnant
which now had to undergo total repentance in order to bring
the messianic redemption. Rabbinism had now, from its own
perspective, to give battle with all those forces that might
diminish the piety and dedication that the rabbinic movement
thought necessary. Furthermore, where is was possible to take
over and incorporate those groups that proliferated prior to
70 the effort was made. In order to forge a halakhic consensus
and defuse the opposition of both Sadduceeism and Pharisaism,
(the various *perushite* groups), to reduce the tension among
Bet Shammai, Bet Hillel and independent scholars Yoḥanan ben
Zakkai and his successors incorporated Shammaite options,
preserved priestly prerogatives and took over much *perushite*
pietism. But Yoḥanan's successors saw gnosticism, apocalypticism and Christianity as superior dangers. They therefore
excluded their writings from the canon and took more serious
steps to exclude the followers of these religious tendencies
from the Jewish community. It is in relation to these and
other movements regarded by the rabbis as either extraneous,
heretical or aberrational that the catch-all term *minim*
(sectarians) has been applied.

Christian Jews were undoubtedly a major source of irrita-
tion to Gamaliel II. Dissenters generally were not tolerated
by him and he effectively used the ban to isolate them. He
in turn was temporarily deposed for his autocratic and au-
thoritarian ways. He practically persecuted the disciple of
Yoḥanan, R. Joshua, and excommunicated another, R. Eliezer b.
Hyrcanus. Other such instances, not recorded, may have
taken place. In this connection it has been pointed out incorrectly that Gamaliel was a Hillelite in controversy with
the priests and disciples of Yoḥanan. Rather, he was a
Shammaite, but the thrust of his controversy was with those
of Yoḥanan's disciples, who had never forgiven him for de-
posing Yoḥanan. Gamaliel, however, was consolidating the
newly acquired power of the Patriarchate and he took measures
against all possible dissent. His major measure was the isolation of Christian Judaism and the expulsion of Christianity
as such from Judaism, already referred to in Chapter Seven.
It is quite possible that this spiritual confrontation between
Yavneh and early Christianity is directly and indirectly reflected in the Gospel According to Matthew.[87]

Even if Matthew was written for a Syrian Church as some scholars argue, the long arm of Yavneh reached there. The famous rabbis such as Gamaliel II and Akiba travelled a great deal. They sent out apostles or *shelibim*, and they instituted halakhah specifically for Syria. The apostles or messengers of the rabbis went abroad to collect money, to deliver letters concerning religious life, to deliver money to ransom captives, and to visit synagogues.[88] At this time toward the end of the first century Yavnean Judaism separated the Christian branch from the trunk of Israel, and proto-rabbinic Judaism matured into what is commonly called "rabbinic Judaism." It is to the halakhah and theology of this new development that the next two chapters will be devoted.

NOTES

1. In addition to bibliographical items already cited in previous chapters, and the selection below, the "Bibliographical Reflections" in Jacob Neusner, *The Rabbinic Traditions About the Pharisees Before 70,* 3 vols. (Leiden: E. J. Brill, 1971) III, 320-368 should be read. Neusner's strictures on 19th and 20 century scholarship are sometimes aggressively negative, but his data and bibliographical summary are useful. Neusner's handling of the rabbinic literature should be read with caution. Solomon Zeitlin has questioned Neusner's competence with talmudic literature in "A Life of Yoḥanan Ben Zakkai," *JQR,* 62(1972), 145-155, and "Spurious Interpretations of Rabbinic Sources in the Studies of the Pharisees and Pharisaism," *JQR,* 65 (1974), 122-135. Neusner himself has honestly disclaimed being a talmudist, writing, "What I lack in the received virtuosities of Talmudic learning, however, I hope to make up in passionate interest," in *Invitation To The Talmud* (New York: 1973), p 26. See also Salo Baron, *A Social and Religious History of the Jews,* II, 35-46, 342-343, notes 43-44; Solomon Zeitlin, *The Rise and Fall of the Judaean State* I, 176-201. Martin Hengel, *Judaism and Hellenism,* II, 120, n. 480, cites O. Plöger's *Theocracy and Eschatology,* p. 8f., in support of his own views that many "pietistic and conventicle-like splinter groups" emerged from the hasidim and are unknown to us. He further suggests that men like John the Baptist may have emerged from them. Certainly Josephus' "guru" Bannus (Life, 2(11), seems to be an independent pietist. See also the recent work by Ellis Rivkin, *The Hidden Revolution* (Nashville, Tenn.: 1978). In order to highlight my different approach I have adopted Ellis' format of discussing *pharisaioi* in the N.T. and Josephus and *perushim* in rabbinic literature. All scholars identify the Pharisees with the rabbis. See n. 4. Thus G. Alon, "The Attitude of the Pharisees to the Roman Government and the House of Herod," *Scripta Hierosolymitana,* 7 (1961), 53-58, not only considers the rabbis to be the Pharisees but even calls the rabbis of Bar Kokhba's time by that term (p. 76).

2. For Rechabites, see Pt. I, Ch. 2. Additional Note 2.

3. M. Ab. 2:5. Herford, in his commentary on the text,

says this maxim is "fundamental to Pharisaism" as if Hillel is a Pharisee. The opposite is true. He is teaching that one should not be a *parush*, a Pharisee. At B.A.Z. 20b, Rashi makes an astute comment on *perishut*, (separatist pietism) when he remarks that such a-one even abstains from permitted things in order to impose greater stringencies upon himself.

4. See the "Bibliographical Reflections" cited at n. 1. All scholars such as Ginzberg, Finkelstein, Zeitlin, Neusner, Guttman, Herford, Moore, Rivkin, despite a variety of approaches and interpretation of particulars, consider the Pharisees as early, pre-70 rabbis, and identify rabbinic Judaism as Pharisaism. This is also true of historians such as Schürer and Baron, and New Testament scholars. That rabbinic or Pharisaic Judaism was "normative" was expressed by G. F. Moore, *Judaism* I, 3.

5. See B.B.K. 79b; B.B. 60b.; T. Sot. 15:5. The principle is not to enact a norm which the majority cannot abide by and for an individual authority not to impose his pietistic norms upon others. See Sigal, *New Dimensions,* Chap. 5.

6. See Jacob Neusner, *From Politics to Piety* (Englewood Cliffs, N.J.: 1973) pp 67-80 for a convenient summary of the N.T. passages; E. Rivkin, *The Hidden Revolution*, pp. 76-124. For agreement between Jesus and the Pharisees see Mt. 22:23-33; Mk. 12:18-27; Lk. 20:27-40; Acts 4:1-2.

7. Paul was a Pharisee before he became a Christian, Acts 23:6-9; 26:5; Phil. 3:2-7; see also Gal. 1:13-14 where he stresses his "former life" as one of zeal for traditions, although he does not refer to being a Pharisee specifically.

8. See further on this my *Halakhah of Jesus,* Chap. 2. The identity of Pharisees as *perushim* and their halakhah as Qumranic rather than rabbinic, is also there discussed, and is further amplified and illustrated throughout the work. David Flusser, *Jesus,* p 53 sees that Pharisees are not the later rabbis but sees the two groups "as forming a unity." I see this "unity" in terms of rabbinic Judaism having adopted some of the pietism after 70 A.D. Flusser, pp 53ff. distinguishes Pharisees from Essenes and Qumranites, but I think they are of "a unity" with those groups.

9. From the authority figure of Ezra the *sofer* to the idealized picture of Ben Sira 38, the *sofer* becomes a mere copyist at M. Git. 8:8, probably a town archivist at B.B.B. 21b; a learned person at B. Ber. 45b; but only a school teacher and not a proto-rabbi: B.B.B. 21a-b; T. Meg. 4:38; P.

Hag. 76c. He is referred to as a *lablar*, a *librarius*, as e.g. R. Meir was at B. Git. 67a. Josephus speaks of Temple scribes in the time of Ezra at *Ant*. XI. 5, 1 (128). These are the same functionaries as mentioned in the N.T. when "priests and scribes" occur together. The *sofer* is distinct from the *tanna* at B.A.Z. 9a-b, and in earlier usage the *tanna* is either the proto-rabbi or the reciter and repository of texts. In later talmudic usage the *tanna* is merely a repository and reciter of texts with no special intellectual or spiritual authority (B. Sot. 22a).

10. Rivkin, *op. cit.* pp 88f. uses this adherence to the traditions of the elders as an argument for the identity of Pharisees and the "scholar class" whose members become the rabbis.

11. Mt. 22:23-33; 9:32-34; 10-13; Lk. 5:29-32; 15:1-2; Mt. 21:9.

12. See Pt. I, Chap. 6; Mt. 22:42.

13. This is in contrast with Rivkin, p 97. Thus Mt. 22:34, that Pharisees approach Jesus, may be a detached reminiscence incorrectly attached to 35-40 and v. 35 "a *nomikos* who was one of them" was altered to make it consistent with v.34. It is of interest that suddenly *nomikos* is introduced to express a philosophic viewpoint absent at Qumran, and that at the end of the pericope there is no response whatever from the Pharisees. Possibly 22:34 belongs before 22:41.

14. Rivkin, *op. cit.* pp 98-104. Jn. 12:42f. clearly shows the people feared expulsion from the synagogue and therefore feared the "Pharisees," that is, the rabbis who, in their eyes, were behaving like the *perushim* of Jesus' time.

15. Rivkin sees this at p 103, note, but interprets it differently.

16. Mt. 26:49; Mk. 14:45; Mk. 10:51.

17. Acts 5:34; Mt. 22:35; Tit. 3:13; and elsewhere. Cf. Lk. 5:17.

18. Mt. 23:7-8. At its parallel, Lk. 20:45-47 the word "rabbi" is not used. This may point to the possibility that the Matthean source has a later interpolation of the word when Mt. was in controversy with the rabbis of Yavneh.

19. A lexicon or concordance may be consulted for all

instances of the use of the various terms. It will be found
that nowhere is it necessary to equate "Pharisee" with "proto-
rabbi." See Lk. 5:17; Acts 5:34; at Lk. 5:21 the scribes and
Pharisees suggest Jesus is guilty of blasphemy, but the *nomodidaskaloi* (v.17) are silent. It is not correct to equate
"scribes" and *nomodidaskaloi*, for every group had its scribes,
and the scribes here are Pharisaic scribes as elsewhere they
are temple scribes who accompany the priests.

20. See Rivkin's discussion of this, with which I concur,
in his *Hidden Revolution*, pp 316ff. His discussion of Josephus is at pp 31-75.

21. The references to Pharisees in Josephus are at: *Life*,
2 (10-12); 5 (21); 38 (191); 39 (197ff.); *War* I, 5.2 (110-114);
29.2 (571); II, 8.2 (119); 8.14 (162-166); 17.3 (411); *Ant.* XIII,
5.9 (171-173); 10.5 (288-295); 15.5 (399) - 16.2 (415); 16.5
(423); XV, 1.1 (3); 10.4 (370); XVII, 2.4 (41, 44); 3.1 (46);
XVIII, 1.1 (4); 1.2 (11); 1.3 (12-15);1.4 (16-17); 1.6 (23).

22. In the talmudic account of an encounter between Yohanan b. Zakkai and Vespasian at B. Git. 56a-b it is clear
that Yohanan wants an already-established center of learning
to be spared by the Romans. There are three other accounts of
this encounter at Ab. de R.N.A, 4: B, 6; Lam. R. to Lam. 1:31.
While the four accounts have significant differences they all
agree that Yohanan left Jerusalem and three of them agree that
he went to Yavneh. For a different view, that Yohanan was compelled to go there and that it was one of many "ghettos" or
"concentration camps" for Jews set up by the Romans see
Gedaliahu Alon, *Mehkarim Betoldot Yisrael* (Hebrew) 2 vols.
(Tel Aviv: 1957-1958) I, 219-238; see Neusner's discussion
of this, *A Life of Rabbi Yohanan Ben Zakkai*, pp 123ff. I concur with Neusner contra Alon, that Yohanan went to Yavneh voluntarily and there helped to inaugurate what later generations
have come to call "rabbinic Judaism." But did Yavneh have a
proto-rabbinic center before Yohanan came there? One source
clearly indicates it did (B. Git. 56b) the others (Ab. de R.
N.) are ambiguous. They read only ". . .I ask nothing of you
but Yavneh where I will go to teach my disciples. . ." and
". . .I ask of you Yavneh where I will teach Torah. . ." In
the light of B. Git. 56b I think these can be taken to imply
he asked to go to a place already known as a center where he
can resume the work he did in Jerusalem. See also Ab. de R.
N. B, 29 which clearly refers to a pre-70 period and to the
concentration of many sages at Yavneh. Josephus refers to
sophistai at *War* I, 33.2 (648ff.); *Ant.* XVII, 6.2-4, (149-167),
War II, 17.8 (433), 9 (445). Josephus' description of Zealotic
proto-rabbis helps explain the continuation of the nationalism

at Yavneh and its denouement in the Bar Kokhba rebellion. Cf. *Ant.* XVIII, 1.1 (4-10), 1.6 (23-24); *War* II, 8.1 (117), where it is clear that the *sophistēs* Judas is not a pharisee, which is the term used for his colleague Zadok.

23. *Life*, 38 (190)-39 (198).

24. *Life*, 2 (9-12).

25. The voyage of Gamaliel II, Joshua, Elazar b. Azariah and Akiba is recorded at Sifra 102b. where reference to them on a ship should be read in the light of Sif. Deut. 43. See also P. Suk. 52d and elsewhere. But not all references clearly place the four together and at Rome. At M. Er. 4:1 they are located at Brundisium, a port in Italy. See Louis Finkelstein, *Akiba, Scholar, Saint and Martyr*, pp 136f. See also Deut. R. 2:24. Here we have a rather disorganized account which reflects the fact that Romans in high position sometimes accepted Judaism thus bringing the ire of the Roman government upon Jews. The journey of the rabbis was presumably designed to seek amelioration of anti-Jewish policies. Cf. P. San. 25d.

26. See Smallwood, *The Jews Under Roman Rule*, pp 345ff.; B. Mak. 24b; at T. Ber. 7:2 Ben Zoma apparently visited the Temple site and at T. Ed. 3:3 R. Joshua apparently approves cultic offerings even in the absence of the structure; Ab. de R.N.A, 4, indicates Yoḥanan b. Zakkai travelled to and from Jerusalem after his move to Yavneh, and visited the Temple mount.

27. M. Pes. 10:6; Tam. 7:3; at B.R.H. 30a-b there is a discussion which theorizes about the rebuilding of the Temple, but the underlying implication is that this will be in an indefinite future. Cf. B. Bez. 5b; Suk. 41a; Shab 12b; T. Shab. 1:13.

28. M. Ed. 7:7; B. San. 11a. On the problems and understanding of the office of Nasi see Hugo Mantel, *Studies*, pp 1-53, especially 28-35; Sidney B. Hoenig, *The Great Sanhedrin*, (Philadelphia: 1953), Chapter V. Both of these scholars (Mantel, pp 32f.; Hoenig, pp 64f.) maintain that Yoḥanan ben Zakkai was not called *nasi*. The first to become post-70 *nasi* was to be Gamaliel II, and the title *nasi* thereafter denoted more than president of the *bet din* and head of the academy. The office of *nasi* became a quasi-political one, in effect taking into itself the old secular powers held by the Jerusalem priesthood under Roman power.

29. See Chapter Four for description of this literature.

30. M. Hag. 2:7; M. Yad. 4:6ff.; B. Yom 19b; P. Yom. 39a; T. Hag. 3:35; P. Hag. 79d; B. Nid. 33b; T. Yom. 1:8; T. Yad. 2:20. Sometimes "Boethusians" is used in a parallel pericope in place of Sadducees, indicating the persistent tradition that the two had much in common and originated under similar circumstances. See n. 32.

31. See Rivkin, *Hidden Revolution,* pp 125-179, especially pp 163-166.

32. Ab. de R.N. A, 5; B, 10.

33. T. Yad. 2:20 for *toḅle shaḥar,* and Chap. 6 above for Essenes and Therapeutae.

34. See also B. Yom. 53a; T. Yom. 1:8; Sifra 81b; P. Yom. 39a-b, and the discussion by Jacob Z. Lauterbach, *Rabbinic Essays* (Cincinnati: 1951), 51-83. Philo, *Spec. Laws* I, 13 (72) indicates the priest enters behind the cloud of incense in order not to see the *kaporet,* thus attesting to the Sadducee practice as the traditional one.

35. On the variety of meanings for the expression "inside of the *parokhet,*" and precisely which curtain is meant in different contexts see F. O. Fearghail, "Sir. 50, 5-21: Yom Kippur or the Daily Whole Offering?" *Biblica,* 59 (1978), 302-316.

36. B. Yom. 19b. See on this Jack Lightstone, "Sadducees Versus Pharisees," *Christianity, Judaism and Other Graeco-Roman Cults,* III, 211-213.

37. M. Ab. 2:5; Cf. T. Men. 13:21; B. Pes. 57a. where Abba Saul b. Batnit, 1st cent., denounces priestly families. Cf. *Ant.* XX, 8.8 (179-181).

38. Lauterbach argues that there is no reason to doubt the historicity of the legend at B. Yom. 19b. and points to its occurrence also at P. Yom. 39a. But the narrative at P. Yom. is quite different from that of B. Yom. Aside from other discrepancies the Palestinian Version does not include the statement, "we are afraid of the *perushim.*" The Palestinian version must be denied historicity, however, because it also has the discrepancy of the priest conversing with his father after emerging and of having been struck dead before emerging. The Palestinian version—and here I agree with the traditional commentators against Lauterbach, p 70, n. 18,—has the priest

being struck dead by angels in the Holy of Holies. Lev. 16:
17 says no *adam* shall be present in the Sanctuary when the
priest enters to do atonement, and R. Abbahu (P. Yom. 39a) says
this includes angels who have the appearance of *adam*, but refers only to when the priest acts correctly. But when he enters with the intention of acting incorrectly (in Sadducean
manner) the angels remain there and are capable of killing him,
which they did. Aside from the question of the identity of
the *perushim* in the Babylonian version I concur with Lauterbach's view of what underlying philosophic principles are reflected in this controversy over the smoke-cloud of incense.
The proto-rabbis and their successors, the rabbis, in the
quarrel with Christianity, sought to minimize the popular belief in the incarnation of the deity in the cloud of smoke, to
emphasize that one will not see the deity there. The Sadducee-
Boethusian groups retained the more primitive notions that are
implied in a strict construction of biblical texts and believed
it to be possible to see the deity in the Holy of Holies upon
the *kaporet*; they therefore, insisted upon entering behind a
thick-smoke-cloud. Furthermore, the smoke of the incense
would drive Satan away and prevent him from making accusations
against the priest and spoiling the atonement rite. See Lauterbach, p 74, n. 21.

39. E.g. B. Nid. 33b: the wife of a priest says that
wives of Sadducees are afraid of *perushim* and therefore they
show their menstrual blood to the *ḥakhamim*. For some strange
reason Rivkin, *op. cit.*, p 137 takes the terms here as synonyms. It is more likely that the wives of Sadducees, being
afraid of the pressures and perhaps of the curses of pietists
who will accuse them of impurity when they are pure, show
their blood to sages to be sure of themselves and receive expert advice. It does not mean the *ḥakhamim* are *perushim*. On
the basis of these views I am compelled to reject the conclusions drawn by Rivkin, pp 141f. He lists what he terms a
"legitimate line of reasoning" with sixteen points. His notion
that there are Pharisees (capital P) and pharisees (lower case
p) has merit. But while I once sought to draw that kind of
distinction I find it not as satisfying as a wholly new approach
to the subject. *Perushim* are pietists. They are pharisees
(lower case p) because they do not constitute a separate
party. *Perushim* are an incohate mass except when they are
Essenes, Therapeutae or the New Covenant (Qumran) movement.
Some proto-rabbis are also *perushim* of a sort. But the proto-
rabbis, the *ḥakhamim*, on the whole were opposed to *perushim*,
as exemplified in Hillel's dictum, "do not separate yourself
from the community" (M. Ab. 2:5). That *perushim* are sometimes
in support of the same halakhah as *ḥakhamim* only underscores
the broad affinities all the groups had. It would be gratu-

itous to think that even Sadducees and *perushim* never agreed.

40. B. Men. 65ab; Taan. 17b; B.B. 115b-116a.

41. Rivkin is thus partially correct, p 166, that there is no single meaning for *perushim*. It designates an incohate mass of pietists and separatists and its meaning can be determined only by the context. *Am haarez* is also juxtaposed to *parush* at T. Shab. 1:15.

42. Seven types of *perushim* are named. See Ab. de R.N. A, 37; P. Ber. 14b; M. Hag. 2:7; Sot. 3:4; B. Sot. 22b; P. Sot. 20c.

43. Sifra 57a, 86b; Mekh. to Ex. 19:6, ed. Laut. II, 206.

44. Rivkin, pp 173-176. See T. Meg. 4:15 for life cycle welfare *haburot*. Cf. M. Ab. 1:6.

45. Saul Lieberman, *Texts and Studies*, p 206. At p 200, Lieberman unnecessarily calls these societies "Pharisaic Haburah." See M. Dem. 2:3; passim; T. Dem. 2:2, 3, passim. They were "Pharisaic" only in the sense of being *perushite*, that is, pietistic.

46. Josephus, *Ant.* XIII, 5.9 (171, 173); 10.6 (293-298); XVIII, 1.2 (11); 4 (16-17); XX, 9.1 (199); *War* II, 8.2 (119); 8.14 (164-166); 9.4 (175). See Zeitlin, *Judaean State*, I, 176; Finkelstein, *The Pharisees*, I, 80f. II, 663, n. 20; Moore, *Judaism*, I, 68f.; Moore, p 70 (and see reference to Edward Meyer, n. 1), concedes that the tradition concerning Zadok and Boethus dissenting from Antigonus might have historical value.

47. Lauterbach, *op. cit.* p 31, n. 11.

48. A Rabbinic reference at B.B.B. 115b-116a indicates the Sadducees used the hermeneutical principle *kal vehomer*, deducing from the major to the minor and vice versa.

49. T. Suk. 3:1. The ceremony of beating the willow is not mentioned in the Pentateuch, and is termed a halakhah of Moses at Sinai. The occurrence of the plural "willows of the brook" at Lev. 23:40 is taken to signify two, one for the *lulub* and one for beating at the altar. And since it is a Sinaitic Mosaic tradition it supersedes the Sabbath. The Sadducees practiced the custom but rejected its superseding of the Sabbath. Cf. B. Suk. 43b.

50. Lauterbach, p 35, n. 15. The *Megilat Taanit*, a scroll of fasts, actually lists dates when fasting was not permitted. Modern scholarship places the origins of the scroll in the second century B.C. with additions being made over subsequent generations. The scroll did not retain authority. An English translation of it can be found in J. Newman, *Halachic Sources*, pp 76-82. On p 78 is found the reference to the Book or Decrees being abolished. The scroll had a commentary attached to it which is called "The Scholion" and dates to the end of the talmudic era, probably containing what was the oral tradition relating to the scroll. The Scholion informs us that this Book of Decrees was Sadducean halakhah. On the cutting of the *Omer* see M. Men. 10:3 where Boethusians insist the *Omer* may only be cut on a Sunday. For the question of false witnesses see M. Mak. 1:6 and B. Men. 65a.

51. Josephus, *War* II, 8.14 (175); *Ant.* XVIII, 1.4 (16); Mt. 22:23-33; Mk. 12:18-27; Lk. 20:27-40; Acts 23:6-9. A Sadducee as a *ḥaber* is found at B. Nid. 33b. See Appendix B.

52. The occurrence of the term *shofet* (a Judge) in addition to priest and levite at vs. 9, 12 can be taken to signify a non-priestly authority; Sif. Deut. 154.

53. For the terms used in this sentence see Glossary, and the fuller discussion of the literature in Pt. 2, Ch. 4.

54. For the *kohen* see Cody, *A History of the O.T. Priesthood;* for the *nabi* see J. Lindblom, *Prophecy in Ancient Israel;* for the *ḥakham* see O. S. Rankin, *Israel's Wisdom Literature.* The priest: II Ki. 12:13; the prophet: II Ki. 4:23; Ez. 8:1; 14:1; 20:1; the *ḥakham:* Prov. 22:17; Ben Sira 39:1-15. The *sofer* as a learned man at court is evident at e.g. II Ki. 22:8.

55. For the various references to prophets here see Hag. 2:10-14; Zekh. 7:1-14; 8:16-17; Is. 58:13-14; Mal. 2:14-16. At Jer. 18:18 the *dabar* of the prophet is parallel to the torah of the *kohen*. That *dabar* is revelatory is clear at Jer. 18:1, and frequently in prophetic writings. At M. Ab. 1:1 Moses receives torah (i.e. "instruction", not *the* Torah (i.e. the Pentateuch). See also Finkelstein, *New Light*, pp 3, 5, 13, 77, 132f.

56. See Pt.I, Ch. 3-5. Hugo Mantel, "The Dichotomy of Judaism During the Second Temple," *HUCA* 44 (1973), 56-87, argues that Babylonian religious authorities were also prophets, and that their writings have not been preserved. His only evidence, however, is Ezra 9:11.

57. See Ezra 1:1; 4:5-6; see denunciations at Ez. 11:18; 33:23f; Zekh. 10:2; 13:2f.; Mal. 1:6-2:9.

58. The use of the *sofer-ḥakham* is seen at II Ki. 19:2; 22:14; Neh. 8:1, 4, 9, 13; 12:26, 36; Ben Sira 38:24-39:11. Nehemiah's actions are at Neh. 13:4-14; 15-22; 23-27; limitations upon the prohibition of mixed marriage are at Ex. 34:16; Deut. 7:3-4.

59. Prophets are mentioned at Neh. 6:7, 10, 12, 14; see Chap. 5 above for Ben Sira. At Ben Sira 51:23 he conducts a *beth midrash,* which is best rendered as a "research institute," and at 51:29 he calls it a *yeshiḅah,* "a session," both terms known to us from rabbinic period. The Beth Midrash of Shemayah and Abtalion mentioned at B. Yom. 35b is of a period little over a century removed from Ben Sira. Ben Sira is cited extensively in rabbinic literature both as scripture and in the form of an earlier proto-rabbi: at times his words are introduced by the term *ketib,* "it is written," and at B. Pes. 113b the term used for rabbis, *tanu rabbanan,* "the rabbis taught" introduces his saying. Cf. B. San 100b; B.B. 98b; P. Hag. 77c. There are over twenty-five places where the citation in the literature is a quotation from B. Sira. He is also cited by another rabbi in the style of a rabbi: "R. Lazar said in the name of Ben Sira," P. Hag. 77c.

60. See Ben Sira 39:1-11 for the *sofer,* and Chap. 24 for Wisdom. The "program" for the rabbi is at M. Ab. 1:1 to be careful in judgement, to raise up many disciples, and to make a hedge for the Torah. The last item is often misinterpreted as being a signal to create restrictions. But see on this my *New Dimensions,* pp 47f., 66f., 215f, n. 1; 221, n. 21. On Torah and Wisdom see also Ben Sira 1:26; 19:20. On R. Abudimi see *JE* IV, 603, and B.B.B. 12a.

61. M. Ab. 1:2. The term Great Assembly is also mentioned at Mekh. I, 46; Sif. Deut. 16; P. Taan. 68a; Meg. 74a; and numerous times.

62. Attributed to the Great Assembly are such matters as the collection of sacred writings, B.B.B. 15a; B. Meg. 70d; liturgical matter: B. Ber. 33a; P. Meg. 17b; P. Ber. 4d; educational curriculum: P. Shek. 48c; the establishment of Purim: B. Meg. 2a. For a recent survey of the sources see Ira Schiffer, "The Men of the Great Assembly," *Persons and Institutions in Early Rabbinic Literature,* ed. William S. Green (Missoula, Mont.: 1977), 237-276. There is much literature on the question of who constituted the "Men of the Great Assembly" or what was the "Great Assembly." Schiffer reviews

a segment of the previous studies in his "Bibliographical
Study," pp 270-273. Significant essays are those of G. F.
Moore, "The Rise of Normative Judaism," *HTR*, 17 (1924), pp
307-373; L. Finkelstein, "The Maxim of the Anshe Keneset
Hagedolah," *Pharisaism*, 159-173. See also a survey of the
literature and views concerning The Great Assembly by Moore,
Judaism III, 7-11; Henry Englander, "The Men of the Great
Synagogue," *HUCA* Jubilee Volume (1925), 145-169. Englander
has an interesting, but unconvincing thesis that our Simon
the Righteous is Simon I, ca. 270 B.C. and that the "great
assembly" signifies the community as a whole. See also Vol.
VII of the Loeb Classical Library of Josephus, trans. Ralph
Marcus, Appendix B, "The Date of the High Priest Simon the
Just (The Righteous)," pp 732-736 where Marcus concludes that
Simon is Simon II.

63. A gathering mentioned at M. Shab. 1:4 which is given
as the locus of "eighteen decrees" cannot be included as a
"great assembly" notwithstanding Zeitlin, *The Rise and Fall*
II, 358f. Many rabbinical sources refer to those "eighteen"
with exasperating variants, contradictions and omissions. Cf.
T. Shab. 1:16; B. Shab. 13b; 17a-b; A. Z. 36a; P. Shab. 3c-d,
the latter probably being the clearest account. See also
Alexander Guttmann, *Rabbinic Judaism*, pp 102f. Asher Finkel,
The Pharisees and The Teacher of Nazareth (Leiden: 1964), p
17, has no warrant for his statement that the "vehicle of tradition" was a general assembly. The very fact that so many
differences of opinion existed at 65 A.D. indicates there was
no such regulator of religious affairs. Each school deliberated the issues independently, and each school had its own
following.

64. M. Ab. 1:3 It appears from the text of Abot that an
older list once ended here, for in 1:4 the two Yosis are
said to have received the traditions "from them," and the antecedent in 1:3 is only Antigonus. 1:1-1:3, therefore, may
have been an early list. Later, a new list beginning with the
Yosis at 1:4 with "from them" really referring to the men of
the great assembly of 1:1, was appended. Ab. de R. N. A, 4-5
has another list, and B, 5, 10, offers yet a third variation.
In my view, the different lists reflect different schools of
thought. See my *Halakhah of Jesus*, Chap. 3, and n. 35-36, for
further elaboration. There is much debate over whether Simon
the Righteous of M. Ab. 1:1 is Simon I who lived around 270
B.C. or Simon II who lived around 200 B.C. See for example,
George Foote Moore, "Simon the Righteous," *Jewish Studies in
Memory of Israel Abrahama* (New York: 1927). Since we know
names usually followed one another in rotation there is no
reason why there could not have been a Simon, Onias, Simon, Onias,

with a Simon at 270 B.C. and another at 200 B.C. whose father
was Onias, and whose son was also Onias. At B. Meg. 11a Simon
is connected with the Hasmoneans as a savior of Judaism, indicating Simon II. Neusner, *Rabbinic Traditions*, I, 57ff. is
overly skeptical, and appears to settle for only one "historical" Simon ca. 300 B.C., the Simon of the Mishnah being only
an idealized figure.

    65. M. Ed. 1:4; P. Hag. 77d; Shek. 47b.

    66. For dating the proto-rabbis see Travers Herford,
Pirke Aboth (New York: 1945) pp 25-38; see also Guttmann,
Rabbinic Judaism, pp 40-124 for a more thorough discussion of
the succession and halakhic difference. I do not agree with
Guttmann's approach on all counts, however, but the scope of
this volume does not permit a more comprehensive discussion.
For example, I do not regard rabbinic Judaism as commencing
with Hillel as Guttmann does, p 124. I regard Yohanan b.
Zakkai as the founder of rabbinic Judaism by virtue of his in-
stitution of ordination.

    67. For Yohanan the High Priest: M. Maas. Shen. 5:15;
Sot. 9:10; Par. 3:5; Yad. 4:6; T. Sot. 13:10; B. Sot. 47a-b
and a number of times in the Talmud. This Yohanan is enigmatic
and it is difficult to identify him. There is the Yohanan of
II Macc. 4:11, on whom see Tcherikower pp 88, 441. This
Yohanan received authority that improved the religious interests of the community. Perhaps for this reason he is much
lauded in tradition. Later literature saw a Yohanan as the
Hasmonean founder. See the Hanukah insertion in the *amidah*
of any traditional prayerbook. For Honi the Circle-maker:
M. Taan. 3:8; B. Ber. 19a; Taan. 23a; and elsewhere. Another
proto-rabbi is Menahem: M. Hag. 2:2; B. Hag. 16b. See
Neusner, *Rabbinic Traditions*, I, 389-419, for a fuller collection of names and references.

    68. See n. 22 above; Neusner, *A Life;* Gedalyahu Alon,
Jews, Judaism and the Classical World.

    69. See Herford, *Aboth*, p 32; Zeitlin, *The Rise and Fall*,
II, pp 104ff. The question of how much halakhah is attributed
to Hillel and to Shammai is an enigma. The problem is complicated by our inability to determine the authenticity of our
traditions to enable us to unravel what Hillel and Shammai
really taught, or what was the historic nature of the Bet Hillel
and Bet Shammai. See Guttmann's efforts in this direction,
Rabbinic Judaism, pp 59-124; and Neusner's more skeptical attitudes in his *Rabbinic Traditions* I, 212-340.

70. A parallel is provided by Zeitlin in his "Studies in Tannaitic Jurisprudence," *Journal of Jewish Lore and Philosophy*, p 300, n. 4. See also his "The Halaka," *Studies*, IV, p 32, but with some caution. The attribution Zeitlin makes there of "conservatism" to Shammai and Shammaites and "liberalism" to Hillel and Hillelites is an oversimplification. First, halakhah should be classified as "lenient" or "stringent" the accurate renderings for talmudic *kulah* and *humrah*. Secondly, even if Hillelites are usually lenient and Shammaites stringent, frequently they reverse their roles, as Guttmann has clearly shown, *ibid.* (n. 69), although he later makes light of it (p. 121). Thirdly, while he sees the origin of the schools with the two Yosis, I think this is too early. They should be dated to the time of stability and renaissance that set in with Simon the Ethnarch and John Hyrcanus. Thus at B. Tem. 15b, we read that all the *eshkolot* (from the Greek, *skholē*, a school) which arose in Israel from Moses until the death of Yosi b. Yoezer studied Torah like Moses, but not after that. Another saying is that no school from Moses to the death of Yosi could be reproached, but after that they could be reproached. These sources indicate change *after* the life and activity of Yosi b. Yoezer, which means sometime after 150 B.C. What these sources probably signify is that new schools arose, free from the old priestly teaching striking out more independently in the tradition of Yosi b. Yoezer who was an independent teacher dubbed as "a permitter." As disciples of his and their disciples in turn would seek to perpetuate this independent, basically lenient approach to halakhah, other schools would naturally form to represent a stricter approach, and perhaps to place a more narrow construction upon scripture. That Yosi was the inspiration for the later founding of new schools appears clear, and his epithet "the permitter" given him for his lenient decisions at M. Ed. 8:4; B. Pes. 16a; Ned. 19a; A.Z. 37b, shows that he was the inspiration behind the normal leniency of Bet Hillel. But neither of the two famous schools were utterly consistent. See also Lauterbach, "Midrash and Mishnah," *Rabbinic Essays*, pp 163-256. Lauterbach correctly traces the new form of mishnaic teaching to Yosi, the first teacher in whose name halakhah is given, p 185. The characteristic feature of mishnaic form is that it is a precise independent statement and not an exegesis of a scriptural verse. Yosi b. Yoezer is the first to whom such precise halakhic statements are ascribed. The significance of Yosi for the future of rabbinic Judaism is rooted in his introducing both a new form of teaching and an attitude (leniency) that broke with the Ezraic-Nehemian conservative retrenchment. The "reproach" referred to in the source that was possible after the death of Yosi undoubtedly means that the opposing schools confronted one another with reproach whereas

previously the priestly authority in Jerusalem spoke with one
voice. There was room for pietistic groups like Rekhabites
who might be more stringent than the "official" policy of
Jerusalem, but no place for a lenient opposition that would
set aside the halakhah of the priests. Now the followers of
the different schools would go their own way and enjoy equal
legitimacy. Undoubtedly this turn of events in Judaism was
the result of the usurpation of the priesthood by the hellenistic group ca. 175 B.C., and the ultimate failure of the religious rebellion when the Hasmoneans usurped the priesthood.
Dr. D. R. A. Hare called to my attention the comment by Jerome
to Is. 8:14, that the two houses of Israel which are in dis-
favor are Bet Hillel and Bet Shammai, and in a play on the
meaning of their Hebrew names, called them "profane" and "dis-
sipator" because of their *deuterōseis,* or "second torah."

71. The sources for this are at T. Ed. 2:3; B. Er. 13b;
P. Sot. 19a; Ber. 3b; Kid. 58d; Yeb. 3b. Cf. P. Suk. 53b.

72. Guttmann, *op. cit.* pp 107-113 reviews items of evidence to prove the schools ceased to exist before the end of
the first century, and probably close to 70.

73. The evidence for this is reviewed by Louis Finkelstein, *Akiba,* Appendix D, pp 304ff. Gamaliel I was also a
Shammaite in some of his views, e.g. at Ab. de R. N. A, 40
his view favoring study by sons of the rich coincides with
Bet Shammai *ibid.* 3, B, 4. It is either his halakhah or his
grandson's which agrees with Bet Shammai at M. Bez. 2:6-7.
Cf. M. Er. 6:2; Suk. 3:9; B. Ber. 43a; Yeb. 15a; T. Shab. 1:
22, not all of which are examined by Finkelstein since he con-
fined himself to Gamaliel II. But what we have here is the
anomaly of the supposed "House of Hillel," the grandson and
great-grandson of Hillel, both evincing Shammaitic tendencies.
This raises the serious questions of whether the Gamaliel
patriarchate dynasty was really descended from Hillel, and
for that matter, who Hillel really was.

74. S. G. F. Brandon, *Jesus and the Zealots,* pp 214f. rejects the tradition that Jerusalem Christians withdrew to Pella.
See also pp 208-212 and notes. He makes his main points on
this in *The Fall of Jerusalem and The Christian Church* (London:
1951). But see also a critique of his views by Barbara C.
Gray, "Movements of the Jerusalem Church During the First
Jewish War," *JEH,* 24 (1973), 1-7.

75. Gamaliel II could not immediately succeed his father
Simon b. Gamaliel I as head of the governing council in Jerusalem because the Romans were antagonistic to all Davidic de-

scendants, both Jewish and Christian after the fall of Jerusalem. We hear from Eusebius in the name of Hegesippus, *History,* III, 12, that Vespasian sought out all descendants of David to bring the royal line to an end. That the Gamalielites claimed maternal descent from David is clear at P. Kil. 32b; Taan 68a; B. Ket. 62b; San. 5a; Hor. 11b; these sources also indicate that the Babylonian Exilarch also claimed Davidic descent. See Geza Vermes, *Jesus,* p 157. A *beraita* at B. Taan. 29a informs us that Gamaliel II was the leader of the academy in Jerusalem in 70 and was warned that he was sought by the Romans, whereupon he escaped. By some time after 80 the Romans were apparently ready for political concessions to Jews and new arrangements for the governance of the province. See also David Goodblatt, "The Origins of the Recognition of the Palestinian Patriarchate," *Studies in the History of the People Israel and the Land of Israel* (Haifa: 1978), [Hebrew].

76. When Yohanan asked Vespasian for the "chain" of Gamaliel, B. Git. 56b, he was not asking, as some scholars think, (Neusner, *A Life,* p 121: Alon, *op. cit.* p 338) that Vespasian spare the Gamaliel family. He was asking for the symbol of authority. Yohanan retired: B. San. 32b; Sifre Deut. 144; T. Maas. 2:1

77. Alon, pp 323ff. provides names of some proto-rabbis who chose not to associate with Yohanan. Cf. Ab. de R. N. A, 14, B, 15; B. Hag. 14b, Shab. 147b. At M. Shek. 1:4; Ed. 8:3, we have glimpses of halakhic differences between Yohanan and the priests, the implication there being that he cannot govern them, those Sadducees who survived the war would oppose a man with whom they had past quarrels, as we see at M. Yad. 4:6; T. Yad. 2:9; M. Par. 3:5-8; B. Men. 65a where the synonymous Boethusians are named as Yohanan's opponents; B.B.B. 115b.

78. In the light of my own conclusions a few words are in order concerning Neusner, *Rabbinic Traditions* III, pp 239-319. There he offers his conclusions to his detailed form-critical research concerning Pharisees. It is evident that the task of redaction criticism remains, to put together again all the pieces atomized by Neusner. While his research is useful and his cataloguing of sources helpful, his conclusions are often open to question. The proto-rabbis as a class do not constitute a "Pharisaic party," which constituted "an important force in Hasmonean politics." Had they done so, we would have found them of some consequence in Hasmonean literature. His view at III, 306f. that the rabbinic tradition invented the relationship of Gamaliel to Hillel and the discipleship of Yohanan ben Zakkai is unwarranted. There is simply no reason to doubt that pre-70 oral and written traditions are embodied in our rabbinic literature. See Gerhardsson,

Memory and Manuscript on the transmission of oral torah, pp 71-189.

Jeremias is another scholar who amasses much data but whose conclusions have to be questioned. Thus in his *Jerusalem*, Appendix to "The Scribes" (pp 232-245), he concludes "that the leaders and influential members of Pharisaic communities were scribes." He offers a list of examples, beginning with Yosi b. Yoezer as the earliest example of a scribe who "belonged to a Pharisaic community or ruled their lives according to Pharisaic laws," p 254. He cites M. Hag. 2:7. But that pericope tells us nothing of the sort. It refers to Yosi as a priestly hasid (in the age of hasidic dissent from the Hasmoneans) whose tablecloth, despite his saintliness, would be considered as being able to convey uncleanness by contact. In other words, a *parush* would watch out even for Yosi. It does not say he is a scribe or a Pharisee as Jeremias thinks, but informs us that for Pharisees, that is, *perushim*-pietists, even a saintly person like Yosi is suspect. Thus again, Jeremias, p 266, indicates that the Psalms of Solomon reflect the bitterness between Pharisees and Sadducees. Yet the terms are never mentioned and there is no real certainty as to who precisely is contemplated in the various groups. The righteous elements who oppose the aristocratic "sinners" are called *hosioi*, "the holy ones," the same explanation as Philo offers for the name "Essenes." Thus we learn that the Psalms of Solomon are of the pietistic elements, the *perushim* in that broad sense, but not the "Pharisees" as defined by Jeremias, the predecessors of the rabbis. There is even some confusion in how Jeremias writes, p 266, that "the people unreservedly followed the Pharisees," and then he finds other people who are "the masses," the *ammei haarez*, who were also opposed by the Pharisees. Jeremias' other error casts light on all of the confusion in these pages in which his massive references do not rescue him. He calls Jesus' attack on the scribes and the Pharisees "an act of unparalleled risk," p 267, because they were so powerful, and were followed by the people (but not "the masses"?). He considers this an act which brought him to the cross despite his calling them to repentance "from the full power of his consciousness of sovereignty." If the call was from sovereignty, why did it bring him to the cross? But more to the point, as I have shown in Chap. 7, it was not anything Jesus said or did in theology or halakhah that brought him to the cross.

79. W. D. Davies, *The Setting*, pp 257f. sees this point correctly but does not indicate the rabbinic assumption of the dual role of preacher and Torah-authority. See Ab. de R. N. A, 4; B, 8. Yohanan includes thrice-daily prayer in

the examples of *gemilut ḥasadim*, the deeds of love, performed
by Daniel, which were the source of his salvation. See E.
Werner, *The Sacred Bridge*, pp 24ff. It is possible that some
sacrifcial activity continued at the site of the ruined altar
in Jerusalem, but if any, it was sparse and sporadic. See on
this K. W. Clark, "Worship in the Jerusalem Temple after 70
A.D." *NTS*, 6 (1959-60), 269-280.

80. M. San. 10:1 Akiba is adding a strict ruling to exclude those who would read intertestamental writings and
possibly the newly emerging and circulating Christian gospels.
That it was Gamaliel II, after 80, and not Yohanan pre-80 who
would be responsible for this exclusionary posture is evident
from Gamaliel's parallel move against Christians.

81. M. R. H. 4:1, 4; B. R. H. 29b; 21b; The *amidah* contains the prayers for restoration. Cf. B.B.B. 60b concerning
the importance of remembering Jerusalem. See Davies, *op. cit.*
p 260, n. 1. The continuance of the priestly benediction is
recorded at B. R. H. 31b. Apparently the priests wanted to
wear their sandals while officiating to indicate the synagogue
is of lesser sanctity than the Temple where they went barefoot,
but Yohanan compelled them to go barefoot to insist upon the
equal sanctity of the synagogue and to emphasize that the
rabbis will control the priests. Cf. for other *takanot* after
70a; P. Hal. 57c; M. Maas. Shen. 5:2. See also Davies, p.
263, n. 1.

82. References to early collections might be inferred at
M. San. 3:4; Ket. 5:3; Git. 5:6; Naz. 6:1; Ed. 7:2; the formula "They used to say. . .later they said. . ." at M. Ned. 9:6;
11:12; Git. 6:5; Nid. 10:6; Teb. Y. 4:5, may point to an
earlier form that was embodied in a previous collection. Cf.
also B. San. 86a; B. K. 82a; Meg. 31b.

83. B. Ber. 28b. Simon Ha Pakuli who systemized the
present Tefilah or *amidah* for Gamaliel II was utilizing older
prayers. On the *amidah* see the essays by Ismar Elbogen,
Kaufmann Kohler and Louis Finkelstein in *Contributions*, ed.
Jacob Petuchowski. I adopt the view of Finkelstein, p 92,
that the oldest portions of the *amidah* are pre-Maccabean and
that its systematization as we know it took place under
Gamaliel II at Yavneh. In general, credence must be given to
a persistent tradition that the basic rudiments of the liturgy
were quite old even in early rabbinic times: B. Meg. 18a;
Ber. 26b; 33a; Sif. Deut. 343; P. Ber. 11c. The major difference, however, between the *amidah* of Gamaliel II, and the
current one is that his included the anti-Christian clause in
the twelfth paragraph known as *birkhat haminim* (the berakhah

concerning sectarians) which is no longer present. See the
essays by Solomon Schechter and Jacob Mann in *Contributions,
op. cit.* pp 376, 416, and Finkelstein, p 164, all of which
have texts which contain the anti-Christian imprecation directed against *nozrim*. On the question of the origin and
development of the ancient liturgy in general, see Joseph
Heinemann, *Prayer in the Talmud* (Berlin and New York: 1977).
For the theology of this worship order see *Emergence* II, Chap.
3, and Chap. 10 below. See Louis Ginzberg, "Tamid the
Oldest Treatise of the Mishnah," *Journal of Jewish Lore and
Philosophy*, pp 277f. The question is raised at B. Ber. 27b
whether *arbit*, the evening worship is obligatory (*hobah*) or
optional (*reshut*), and although Gamaliel II attempted to declare it obligatory, two fourth-century Babylonian rabbis
still disputed the question.

84. Sif. Deut. 41.

85. M. Ber. 4:3, 7; M. Meg. 4:3; B. Meg. 23b, point to
this halakhah, among many other sources. Prayer was regarded
as more efficacious when conducted in the synagogue as communal devotion: B. Ber. 6a, 7a; P. Ber. 8d, and elsewhere.
See Heinemann, pp 218-275. See on the Synagogue, Pt.2, Ch. 4
below.

86. Heinemann, pp 22f. and Chap. 4. below.

87. Yohanan's disciples: M. Ab. 2:10; Gamaliel's
quarrels with these disciples and his deposition: P. Ber.
7c-d; Taan. 67d; B. Ber. 27b-28a; M. R. H. 2:8-9; P. M. K.
81c-d; B. B. M. 58b-59a; R. Elazar b. Azariah was elevated
to succeed Gamaliel temporarily: M. Zeb. 1:3; Yad. 3:5;
4:2. For misidentification of Gamaliel, see Robert Golden-
berg, "The Deposition of Rabban Gamaliel II," in *Persons and
Institutions*, p 38, citing Gedalyahu Alon. For a thorough
and useful discussion of the relationship to Mt. see W. D.
Davies, *The Setting*, pp 277-315. Douglas R. A. Hare of the
Pittsburgh Theological Seminary and I prepared a joint paper
for the Catholic Biblical Association's Matthew Task Force
which met at the annual conference of the society at Duquesne
University at August 1976. This is published here as Appendix D. Certainly Mt. 28:15 which tells of the Judaic taunt
that the body of Jesus was stolen from the tomb and that the
claim of resurrection is a deception, "until this day," implies
that the editor of Mt., living at some time away from the
events is living in an environment in which this is still being
charged. This environment could be post-70 Palestine, whether
in the Syro-Phoenician north, Galilee or Judea.

88.   See Davies, p. 295, n. 1; B. Z. Bokser, *Pharisaic Judaism in Transition* (New York: 1935), pp 23, 98ff.; P. Hor. 48a; M. Ḥal. 4:7-8; Shebi. 6:2; 5:6; Or. 3:9; A.Z. 1:8; B.K. 7:7; B. Pes. 8b.

CHAPTER 2

Rabbinic-Talmudic Judaism: The Sacred Rhythm

I. PARAMETERS

The scope of this volume does not permit more than a cursory survey of some aspects of the halakhah, highlights of the theology, and a brief discussion of the methodology of rabbinic Judaism. A series of separate monographs on the evolution of Mishnah, Tosefta, and the Talmuds, all with a careful eye on form, literary and redaction criticism is still required. To attempt the almost impossible process of dating the literature and ironing out the puzzle of correct attribution of sayings to the right scholars even then would be a quixotic endeavor. Consequently I am presenting a sketch of the end-product called rabbinic or talmudic Judaism. By this I refer to that Judaism which is the culmination of rabbinic exegesis, transmission, selection, interpretation and innovation during the first six centuries of the common era and which is embodied in the Midrashim and the two Talmuds. One should not think I am using the term "the rabbis" as if all thought alike, although occasionally there is halakhic and theological consensus reflected in the finished products of the sixth or seventh century.[1]

II. ON THE USE OF SCRIPTURE

A. *Targum*

Previous chapters discussed the developments that led from the Religion of Israel to Yavneh. We also noted that hermeneutical and exegetical principles were applied in successive periods to reinterpret scripture for contemporary needs. This process is called *midrash*. It is a process that is also used by Philo and the sages of Qumran. Midrash is a method by which the midrashist infers one or more meanings from a text that was not explicit in the text. But *targum*, or translation into Greek or Aramaic also often results in midrash.[2] The translation in such cases is no longer the

literal meaning of the Hebrew word, but the meaning read into
it or out of it by the translator. Targumists provided different meanings for words spelled with certain consonants because the consonants may be read with different vocalizations.
One example can be found at Gen. 22:14 where the Masoretic
text reads "And Abraham called the name of that place 'the
Lord will provide. . .'" The word for "name" spelled with
the consonants *shin-mem* can be read *shem*, "name," or *sham*
"there." It is taken in the second way and read "And Abraham
prayed *there*, in that place. . ." by Targum Onkelos. But it
is taken in the first way by one version of the Palestinian
Targum, thereby rendering the meaning of the verse as being

> "And Abraham called upon the *name* of the
> word of the Lord and said 'thou art the
> God who sees and is not seen'."[3]

Targumists use other methods of exegesis as well. There
are times when the targum might represent another text which
was ultimately set aside for our present Masoretic text. The
targum is primarily devised as a means to make scripture in-
telligible to the average person hearing scripture read in
the synagogue. It is also meant to remove theological problems
that a popular audience would be unable to comprehend. The
targum incorporates traditions that would otherwise be lost,
and often embodies traditions that help us to better understand the matrix of first and second century Judaism which
spawned both Christianity and rabbinic Judaism. We have already reviewed a significant example of this in a previous
chapter dealing with the *ākedah* of Isaac.

The point to be derived from this targumic application
of scripture is that the Judaic sages regarded every word in
scripture sacred and therefore as containing relevant and
significant meaning. The targumist would also use a verse in
one part of scripture through which to understand another
verse, that is, he would explain one verse by another. It
is therefore to be realized that targumic explanations which
seem fanciful are not the private imagination of the targumist
but the product of a careful and deliberate exegesis. Furthermore, the targumist also presents the sacred history sche-
matically seeing creation, the exodus, revelation and the
eschatological moment of redemption as interrelated.[4]

What has here been said about targum relevant to *ăgadic*
and theological material is also true of halakhah. Thus, the
Palestinian Targum, like the Greek translation, specifies that
the *ōmer* of first grain is to be presented before the Lord on
"the day after the first festival day of Pesah." This sup-

ports the rabbinic interpretation of the phrase "on the morrow of the Sabbath" and supports the rabbis' contention that the Festival of Weeks, Shabuot, is to fall on the fiftieth day from the first day of Passover.[5]

Furthermore, we have here an example of how the targumist used one verse in scripture to help understand another. The targumic interpretation of Lev. 23:11, 15 as the day following the first Passover festival day is based on Josh. 5:11 where the new grain of Canaan is eaten on the "morrow of the Pesah." The rabbinic halakhah of later times, therefore, that the *òmer* is to be presented on whatever day of the week is the day after the first of Passover, is found to be very early, present not only in the targumim, but also in the Greek Bible. This is an example of how we can determine early halakhic views from targumic literature. While it does not guarantee the rabbinic tradition is necessarily earlier than the view that insisted upon a precise rendering of Lev. 23:11, 15, as signifying a Sunday, it does show that rabbinic tradition had some very old antecedents.[6]

B. *Midrash*

The word *midrash* signifies both the process of research, inquiry and interpretation, and the results thereof embodied in literature. Through midrash the written Torah is adjusted to contemporary life. This is done in the fields of both *àgada*, theology or doctrine, and halakhah practice. The written Torah was carefully transmitted, despite the pious practice of private copyists rendering all or parts of it for their own use. The "official" scrolls used in the synagogue were the product of sofrim or of a *lablar*, text-reproducer specialists. There arose different schools of specialists and therefore there arose more than one *masorah* or textual tradition. This process of seeking to stabilize an official text was a very old one. We find Josephus referring to the books of the temple archives as his sources for the history of Israel. Nevertheless, in addition to the several versions that remained in the Temple library, private copies of scripture were made. Targums were composed, and midrash was developed in order to better understand the texts. These interpretations, including the translations which were in a real sense interpretations, were all transmitted orally.[7]

Out of targum and midrash applied to scripture, as well as innovative custom independent of scripture, grew the "oral torah." A preferable term for this body of teaching and practice would be the "interpretive torah," for some of it assuredly was written.[8] This evolving material, placed side by side with scripture was regarded as legitimate as the Torah and a proto-rabbi as early as Hillel refers to "the two Torot" (B. Shab. 31a). Thus while scripture was central, and regarded as containing God's revelation, the community had perforce to discover in it the way to preserve its traditions during an ongoing history.

Scripture was used extensively in liturgy. Not only were the Psalms used, but the prayers formulated by the liturgical developers were to a great extent paraphrases of scriptural verses. Furthermore, the midrashim are all exegetical works on scripture. Considering this extensive use of scripture for study and prayer, as a source of both liturgy and theology as well as the foundation for halakhic practice, it is no surprise that it was carefully nurtured and fastidiously transmitted. Similarly it is no surprise that the oral interpretations whether in targum or midrash, or the form in which the prayers were framed, were equally carefully nurtured and fastidiously transmitted, and regarded as Torah.

III. THE TRANSMISSION OF THE INTERPRETIVE TORAH[9]

At least three types of schools can be distinguished in our sources, the *bet sefer* and *bet midrash* or *bet talmud*. In the former was taught scripture; the latter served as a school of higher learning. Here was not only taught the halakhah, a condensed text, but its exposition, the talmud. The halakhah was the material which later became the fixed text that we know as Tosefta and Mishnah. The study technique was memorization and recitation. The overall oral interpretive material is frequently listed in rabbinic literature as *midrash, halakhot* and *àgadot*. The term "talmud" is basically synonymous with midrash. Both signify exegesis, exposition, analysis and other forms of inquiry and critique. Both midrash and talmud come to mean the result of the process embodied in evolving texts. Halakhot are the bare-bones fixed statement stripped of all expository material. The term *àgadot* is the plural of *àgada* and signifies all non-halakhic material: matters of belief, history, anthropology, liturgy, homiletics, biography, folk-lore, and so forth.[10]

According to rabbinic tradition many schools of the *bet sefer* type existed before the Christian era. It is stated hyperbolically that there were four hundred and eighty synagogues in Jerusalem before the destruction of the year 70, and that each synagogue had a *bet sefer* in which scripture was studied and a *bet talmud* in which mishnah was studied. The *tanna* (plural: *tannaim*) was the repository of the texts and recited them before the teachers and students. He was not necessarily a scholar. A photographic memory rather than acute intelligence was a pre-requisite. The quality of the *tannaim* varied, as may be expected. But a report from later times indicates the qualifications were demanding. The *tanna* was required to be able to recite all the extant texts of Mishnah, Sifra, Sifre and Tosefta, and a scripturalist was required to be able to recite Torah, Prophets and Writings.[11]

There are, however, many instances in the Talmud when a later rabbi calls upon a second version of a text in order to sustain his position on halakhah. This indicates that more than one text circulated and the texts probably varied in the different schools. Part of the objective of R. Judah the Nasi in publishing his Mishnah at the end of the second century was to stabilize the text. Nevertheless, he was not able to stabilize the halakhah as is evident from his incorporation of variant halakhic opinions into the body of his own work. The text was recited in the classroom of the *bet talmud* for purposes of analyzing and exploring the many-faceted ramifications. Here was exegeted new and innovated halakhah as well as *agada*. The *tanna* recited the text orally and the teacher and students discussed it orally. But this does not preclude the existence of written targumic, halakhic and agadic materials in the form of a teachers' aid, crib sheets archival deposits, and the like.[12] Teachers recited the oral texts four times, but probably when necessary even indefinitely, as is evident from R. Akiba. Pupils repeated after them until they were adept at reciting the texts. This method was followed by advance teachers expanding their knowledge as well as by novices. The method was one that was widespread in antiquity, known from schools of philosophy as well as from schools of law. Memorization of basic texts was the primary requisite and then the texts were orally expounded.[13] The texts or sayings of the teachers were reproduced rather accurately because they functioned with a rule that one must recite the precise words in the name of the person from whom he heard them.[14] For this reason, excessive skepticism on the part of form criticism which dates much of the tannaitic literature to a Yavnean and post-Yavnean period is unwarranted. Named authorities, as we have seen, begin with the early second century B.C., and although much material from pre-Yavnean days is anonymous, this emerged from Bet Hillel and Bet Shammai, which assures its pre-Christian provenance.

The oral interpretive torah is called God's "mystery" (*mysterion*). There can be no doubt that one tradition at least ascribes opposition to writing the *mysterion* to the desire to withhold it from the gentiles. This argument was that gentiles would appropriate the Mishnah as they had appropriated the Greek Bible and then called themselves "Israel." This is clearly a rebuke to the Christian claim to be Israel. And probably in reaction to the Christian Jewish community the rabbis favored and expanded the process of oral transmission so that only acceptable Jews admitted to the schools and higher academies would receive the interpretive torah, or God's *mysterion,* and thereby be considered Israel. Perhaps the reference to the orally transmitted interpretive torah as *mysterion* helps explain why written texts in the possession of academy students are called *megilot setarim* "scrolls of secrets" or "private scrolls."[15]

In any event the norm was oral transmission and this explains the brief, frequently laconic halakhic statements found in Mishnah and Tosefta that are bereft of all explanation and documentation. But the students who are the evolving scholars also remember the exposition which is *midrash* and *talmud.* This too continues to pass along in the schools. It is probably fair to describe this process as beginning with midrash on scripture which is then followed by the extraction of halakhah from the midrash. This halakhah is in turn expanded by talmud in the sessions of the schools. Ultimately it is extracted again either in the traditional form or in a modified one in Geonic literature. The rabbis were perfectly conscious of what they were doing but regarded their work as partaking of the nature of revelation. They believed that the holy spirit rested upon them and their work. At the same time, they believed that the entire substance of both the written torah and the oral interpretive torah was already revealed to Moses at Sinai. They were nevertheless aware of introducing *gezerot* and *takanot,* (prohibitory and positive enactments) into the halakhah derived from midrash and talmud. They were also aware of adopting *minhag* (custom) which was the historically-evolved practice of society with no reference to Sinai, scripture or midrash. They often finalized a halakhah simply because someone testified to seeing a rabbi do something in a certain manner.[16]

This oral interpretive torah continued to evolve, being expanded and adjusted from time to time. The hermeneutical rules (norms of interpretation) that were utilized were as old as scripture itself. Even Hillel, to whom they are ascribed, professed to have learned them from Shemayah and Abtalion of the first century B.C., two scholars who are called *darshanim* (expositors). That the hermeneutical system is part of a general cultural tradition in the Near East has been indicated in recent studies. But in addition to the technicalities of hermeneutics the rabbis employed other criteria in their de-

velopment of the halakhah. They were motivated by a large
number of principles that fall within five basic categories:
the humanitarian, aesthetic, historical, economic and intellectual. Furthermore, they sometimes expressed expectations
of special piety by urging people to voluntarily extend themselves *lifnim meshurat hadin,* acting beyond the requirements
of the halakhah. But more frequently the consensus maintained
the priority of leniency over stringency. It is to a brief
review of all of these elements that we now turn.[17]

IV. THE PROFILE OF CLASSICAL HALAKHAH[18]

A. *Prefatory Comments*

Observance of halakhah is the visible commitment one
makes to "theological Israel." People differ radically in
matters of doctrine, but what people treasure in their hearts
and minds is unknown to the outsider. Thus, in modern times
only a small percentage of those who identify as Jews affirm
a literal belief in the resurrection of the dead, despite its
being considered an absolute requirement for salvation in the
Mishnah. In this instance the ancient Sadducees have won
the day. But in the matter of observance of halakhah, if
one has ceased to abide by commemoration of the Sabbath and
the festivals, the observances of the life-cycle, at least
a minimal attendance at synagogue worship and the practice of
the ethical halakhah, there is hardly a basis upon which to
confirm his or her identity as being part of the faith-
community of Judaism. The practice of halakhah, whether
cultic, ritualistic or ethical, is the formal statement one
makes of one's faith. This commitment may vary in intensity
and in form from similar commitments made by others, but this
is in the very nature of the diversity of Judaic religious expression.

Halakhah was a major preoccupation of the ancient rabbis.
They emerged from the ruins of the war of 66-73 as heirs to
the leadership of a disparate and incohate community in
which "strict constructionists" of scripture, and a plethora
of pietistic and ascetic elements who added much detailed
ritual to the scant scriptural material vied with one another
for spiritual hegemony in Judaism. As noted previously the
rabbis sought to incorporate elements of all movements into
their new evolving consensus. Although organized Sadduceeism
and the Bet Shammai evaporated, representatives of their more
careful reading of scripture persevered even after the Hadrian-

ic period. Diversity remained a characteristic of Judaism, and was reflected in the different schools. For the most part the hermeneutics and the other criteria by which the earlier proto-rabbis and post-70 rabbis interpreted scripture and fashioned halakhah in a "loose constructionist" or "strict constructionist" manner contributed to radical departure from scripture in Judaic ritual. These developments had been going on since the time of Ezra. When we find them in their full-grown state in the second and third centuries, however, we discover a Judaism that is radically different from that of the Torah. But we must add this caveat: that we really do not know when the rituals of rabbinic Judaism were actually innovated. The antiquity ascribed to them by the tradition may be a valid conjecture. For example, the moment Moses taught "remember (or commemorate) the Sabbath day by sanctifying it," he might also have delivered himself of suggestions on how to do that. These recommendations may have been the rudimentary origins of such rituals as the proclamation of the sanctity of the Sabbath at its onset (*kiddush*) and the declaration of its termination (*habdalah*). This same suggestion obtains for much of rabbinic halakhah. But before we examine that we will turn to review the methodology of the rabbis as they interpreted scripture, adjusted it to contemporary needs and innovated or reconfirmed the inherited observances.

B. *The Motivating Factors Underlying the Halakhah*

In accordance with the usages of the Ezraic and post-Ezraic period the Torah halakhah was considered divinely revealed. But sofrim, ḥakhamim-proto-rabbis and rabbis not only legislated new halakhah, reinterpreted old halakhah and abrogated obsolete halakhah, but also defined the criteria upon which they based their activity. A survey of tannaitic and amoraic sources covering from 200 B.C.-600 A.D. enables us to infer the premises upon which they built. The criteria that motivated the sages in each generation and in varying geographic locales determined the specific halakhah by which Jews lived. One can portray a broad canvas of these criteria, ranging over such diverse considerations as doing honor to the deceased, the consideration of economic need, the desire to beautify religious practice, an intellectual commitment to leniency in halakhah, the urgings of piety, the compulsion of faith, theological commitment, the preservation of historic continuity, the adaptation of developing social custom and many more.[19]

The sages took under advisement over twenty such criteria, and were motivated by these ideas in their exegesis and abro-

gation of scripture and innovation of new practices. They used
scientific data in the halakhah of *kashrut* (B. Hul. 111b).
They upheld the validity of the law of the land in which Jews
reside in the principle of *dinà demalkhutà dinà*, a broad principle that the "sovereign law is law" which freed the Jew from
necessary resistance to government and consequent martyrdom.
They assumed full authority over marriage and divorce, and
ruled that because all marriages are made in accord with
and subject to their approval, they also possessed the power
to terminate a marriage even by retroactive annulment if some
aspect of it is found to have been inappropriate. Among their
criteria in liturgy was the emphasis upon *hidur mizvah*, beauti-
fying the act of pious devotion. They urged that social practice, domestic relations law and other areas of interpersonal
conduct be governed by two interrelated concepts: *mipnai tikun
haòlam* (the general social welfare) and *mipnài darkai shalom*
(domestic and civic tranquility). They eschewed excess piety
and restrictiveness by prohibiting the enactment of a *gezerah*
which could not be observed by the majority of the community.
A whole range of halakhah related to grief and bereavement
(*aḅelut*) was arranged out of consideration for *kevodan shel
aneeyim*, "deference to the poor."[20]

The rabbis and their predecessors saw halakhah as the
instrument through which human life was spiritualized and
beautified. It was not a yoke in the sense of a burden. Taking upon oneself the "yoke" of heaven or of the Torah or
mizvot, meant making a commitment to accepting guidance on the
path of life as a yoke guides a ploughing team of animals to
walk a straight line. Taking upon oneself the "yoke" of the
Kingdom of Heaven was to acknowledge God's sovereignty, a
commitment one fulfills by practicing loving deeds (Sif. Deut.
323).

The prophets of ancient Israel taught the objectives of
faith. The rabbis showed how to attain them. The halakhah of
the rabbis is the attempt to concretely express in real social
existence the ideals of the prophets. Halakhah is the instrument by which the Jew meets his needs in contemporary society.
Certain concepts are designated in the Torah *ledorot*, "for all
generations," such as the covenantal practices of circumcision
and the Sabbath, or the redemptive and eschatological cultic
celebration of Passover.[21] But on the whole the halakhah,
both Torahitic and rabbinic, is an ever-changing system of
practice subject to interpretation, adjustment, and even abro-
gation.

C. *Lifnim Meshurat Hadin: The Higher Standard*

Among these factors which governed the rabbinic outlook on halakhah was the concept of *lifnim meshurat hadin*. This phrase refers to a halakhic opinion which goes beyond the requirements of the norm, signifying that a person respond in a nobler way than mere compliance with the "letter of the law." The term *shurat hadin* denotes "strict law" as over against a flexibility that takes into account human welfare. Although this concept usually occurs in civil cases there are also examples of it in contexts of ritual. For example, the *shurat hadin* is that one is not to be believed when he testifies that he has committed a ritual sin. Although this is in itself contrary to the halakhah that one witness is adequate in ritual matters it is upheld on the grounds that a person cannot accuse himself. But an alternative view is that *shurat hadin* be set aside, and that an individual's testimony be accepted. This concept is also applied theologically. The first-century sage, Ishmael b. Elisha prays that God will show His mercy by entering into a *lifnim meshurat hadin* relationship with His people. Again, in reference to God's judgement, the phrase is used to express the hope that God will act *lifnim*.[22] The Talmud reflects one view that Jerusalem was destroyed as an act of God

> "only because they established their law according to the strict requirement of the Torah and did not practice *lifnim meshurat hadin*."

Here we have the principle interpreted as requiring the relaxation of stringency, the application of the quality of mercy. Another way of phrasing this approach to the halakhah is the term *midat ḥasidut,* which means that one must act with the quality of love, and signifies that a person should act beyond the halakhic expectation (B. Shab. 120a; Hul. 130b). To obey the law or to fulfill a ritual requirement precisely is insufficient. It is necessary to act out of consideration for the ultimate religious value, the love command. In this way, going "beyond" the halakhah is to remain "within" it (*lifnim*) on a higher plane.

D. *Leniency in The Halakhah*

Two technical terms used in rabbinic literature are *koolah* and *ḥumrah*; literally "the light" and "the weighty," but more properly "the lenient" or "permissive," and "the stringent." The sage who is *mekil* is selecting a permissive option; the one who is *maḥmir* is selecting a more rigorous or restrictive viewpoint. A natural conflict arose during the post-exilic period when *ḥakhamim* differed in their interpretations of the text of the Torah over which interpretive traditions would have an authority of equal validity with the written Torah. The solution seems to have come with Yosi b. Yoezer, a priest, who was highly instrumental in the subsequent ascendance of *koolah* over *ḥumrah*, of leniency over stringency, as well as in the rise to prominence of a willingness to chart new imaginative courses. Religious discipline in the community and the avoidance of severe schism was maintained by a tacit agreement for the legitimacy of halakhic options. The public was free to follow the loose construction of scripture, the lenient view, or to uphold a strict construction which resulted in a stringent view. Authority was shared by two or more schools of thought and by many proto-rabbis and post-70 rabbis. This approach continues to be the manner in which Judaic religious authority functions.

The older Ezraic-Nehemian conservatism continued to be reflected in the Book of Jubilees and the Zadokite Fragments. It served those who were in reaction to the incursions of hellenism. Proto-rabbinic scholars, however, at least since Yosi b. Yoezer (ca. 190 B.C.) moved in a more imaginative manner. Perhaps the earliest recorded example of this is the permission to bear arms on the Sabbath in self-defense, a decision which is contemporary with the last years of Yosi (I Macc. 2:40-42).

Major innovations became possible after Yosi introduced the era of halakhic individualism. In a significant move Yosi advocated three innovative permissive halakhot and was labelled "the permitter." He based his halakhah upon the hermeneutical rule of *kelal uperat, ein bekelal elah mah shebeperat,* "when scripture records a general term and a specific term, the general includes no more than is delineated by the particular" (Sif. 22b). The controversies of Bet Shammai and Bet Hillel were also resolved with the halakhah following the lenient option. Neither school should simplistically be labelled lenient (liberal) or stringent (conservative), for the tendency is to prefer the lenient halakhah without regard to whether it is Shammaite or Hillelite. This same approach of selecting the lenient option is found in the cases of a number of other scholars as well as in a variety of categories of halakhah.[23]

A few examples will suffice to illustrate. Normally the halakhah follows the third century Babylonian Amora, Abba Arikha (Raḅ), in matters of *isur vehetar* (matters of ritual whether prohibitory or permissive) and the halakhah follows

his contemporary, Samuel, in *dinei* (civil law). Nevertheless
when Samuel is more lenient in matters of ritual his halakhah
is preferred despite Rab's expertise.[24] Generally, R. Aḥa b.
Raba was stringent in his disputes with Rabina I who was lenient. The halakhah is said normally to follow Rabina except
in several cases where R. Aḥa was lenient and his halakhah is
preferred.[25] Similarly, the lenient halakhah of R. Yosi b.
Halafta is preferred over that of his colleage R. Yehudah b.
Ilai. Furthermore it is held that in a dispute over a matter
recorded in the Torah one follows the stringent view, but in
rabbinic halakhah one adopts the lenient opinion. Yet, clearly many "rabbinic" matters are really Torahitic in their
thrust. For example, rabbinic halakhah that affects the remarriage of a woman relates to the Torah's prohibitions of
adultery and bastardy should the rabbinic leniency be in error.
Nevertheless, the lenient halakhah is to be followed. In
effect then, even that which relates to the Torah receives
lenient advocacy. Similarly, if one examines the posture of
many significant scholars whose halakhah is generally preferred, such as Yoḥanan Kohen Gadol, R. Joshua b. Hananiah,
and others, one finds that their halakhah is the lenient
option. Another example of how the principle of leniency was
effected is in "the power of *hetar*," *koaḥ dehetera àdif*,
"The power of the permissive argument is preferable." The
rationale of the sages is psychological: one permits out of
certainty or conviction, but one prohibits out of doubt,
fear, anxiety or sheer cowardice to take a bold, challenging
and innovative step.[26] Finally, when R. Ishmael and R. Elazar
b. Azariah disputed a matter and the latter was *maḥmir*, stringent, while the former sought to ameliorate the halakhah, R.
Ishmael cited a rule that it is incumbent upon the stringent
one to prove his case (M. Yad. 4:3).

V. ASPECTS OF THE RABBINIC HALAKHAH

A. *Prefatory Comments*

Despite their activity in halakhah the rabbis espoused
the doctrine that Moses received the entire corpus of interpretive torah at Sinai. They often attributed traditions
whose source they had forgotten or which had been transmitted
anonymously to *halakhah leMoshe Mesinai*, oral halakhah transmitted by Moses at Sinai.[27] Here I will explore certain developments in limited segments of the halakhah that ultimately
became the historical Judaism that has survived to this day,
albeit frequently in radically modified form. Already in

the Torah with its governance of worship, dietary practices, sabbaths and festivals, purities, tithings and a complex ethical and moral code covering sexual and inter-personal relationships, we have the seeds of the rabbinic regimen that governed the life of the individual Jew from the time he arose in the morning throughout his day.[28] In order to sustain this corporate life of the covenant community rabbinic exegesis and interpretation increasingly regulated the religious life of the Jew at home, in society and in the synagogue, from birth to death, in matters economic as well as in ritual and ethics until it ultimately reached the intensive level described as "Judaism circa 1650" at the end of the second volume of this series.[29] The institution of the family was basic to all of this, and it is perhaps of value to turn to this first. In this as in other segments of the halakhah no effort is being made to present the halakhah in its precise chronological evolution, nor to draw distinctions between Judean and Galilean halakhah or between Babylonian and Palestinian halakhah. The scope of this volume does not permit this precision, nor will it permit me to explore all areas of the halakhah. In family halakhah, however, we see mirrored all of the facets of the halakhic system that are of interest to us: incorporation of the old, adaptation of the new, revision of the Torah's halakhah, expansion of particulars, an evolving sensitivity to human need while in the process of serving God's will, and a quest for forms that will give life to the essence of Judaism. Some of the flaws of rabbinic halakhah are also evident here.

B. *The Family*[30]

1. *Marriage*

The term for marriage in rabbinic literature is *kiddushin,* "sanctification," and implies that the nature of marriage is one of a sanctified relationship. It was God's will from the beginning that humans marry (Gen. 2:18, 24). Jewish scholars have been reluctant to apply the term "sacrament" to marriage, but the marital union was certainly regarded as sacred and as being in relationship with God. This is evident from the introduction of the *shevà berakhot,* the seven paragraphs of praise offered at the time of betrothal and marriage. The two ceremonies were later combined into one as Judaism still has them. Each berakhah contains the typical rabbinic formula of thanks and praise to God who creates humans and sanctions and blesses their union. These berakhot are known from the tannaitic period (200 B.C.-200 A.D.), but like all the berakhot and other prayers transmitted by the

known named scholars of the Talmud, these antedated the literature in which they are embodied. The originators of the berakhot are designated as a body of "elders and prophets" and
"the men of the Great Assembly." They are also called "the
early ḥakhamim" and "the early hasidim," pointing to the third
and second century B.C.[30]

The establishment of berakhot to adorn the marriage
event points to the metaphysical approach taken toward it.
Furthermore, rabbinic standards required a rigid sexual morality, underscoring their concept of the sanctified or sacramental
union. Just as *kadashim*, holy things related to the cult,
were not to be violated or profaned, so too must the marital
union be unviolable and unprofaned. Thus, in defining the
nature of the woman's status the rabbis termed her the equivalent of *hekdesh*, that which is sanctified to God. This is
expressed in another way: when husband and wife are worthy
the Shekhinah is with them. (B. Kid. 2b; Sot. 17a). Rabbinic
betrothal and marriage preserved older biblical and pre-
biblical aspects of a monetary arrangement and transfer of
property, but placed its emphasis upon the sacred and ethical.

Yet, the ancient practices of polygamy stood in the way
of a true sacramentalization of marriage in pre-medieval
Judaism and somewhat diluted it. Josephus not only cites the
biblical right for a man to marry several or many wives, but
says that is it "customary." Justin Martyr is therefore accurate when he criticizes this Judaic custom, even if it is
correct as some scholars claim, that it was rarely practiced.
Along with polygamy concubinage was an obstacle to true sacramental marriage. Concubinage was a very old pre-biblical
arrangement in which the man and woman entered into an agreement covering regular sexual relationship and entitling the
wife to her support, but with none of the legal rights of a
wife. She was neither married ceremonially nor required a
divorce when the husband chose to send her away. Although
this complex institution underwent radical transformation it
was still present among Jews, even in circumvention of the
prohibition of polygamy, as late as the sixteenth century.
Concubinage provided a legitimate form of easing sexual passion for the pious Jew and he could still look upon his marriage with his true wife as a sacred relationship. Acquisition
of Roman citizenship by all Jews in 212 contributed to the decline of the actual practice of polygamy since it was forbidden
to Roman citizens. On the other hand, because polygamy was a
regularized institution in the Parthian lands, the Babylonian
community tended to that direction. Talmudic evidence points
to both contrasting tendencies: the legitimacy of regularized
sexual relations with one who is not one's sacramental wife;

and the opposition to it.[32]

The shift in the rabbinic approach to the marriage ceremony indicates the growing effort to sacramentalize it. Biblically a man "takes" a woman and becomes her master, by sexual
intercourse, a gift of money or merely by handing her a document so stating (M. Kid. 1:1). But the rabbinic period transformed this informal male acquisition of the female into a
religious formaltiy by introducing the formula "You are hereby
consecrated (*mekoodeshet*, "sanctified") unto me. . ." recited
at the time of marriage. This formula in itself was a transformation of a pre-Yavheh clause in the *ketubah* which stated,
"You are my wife according to the law of Moses and the Judeans,"
with no mention of sanctification. Later the formula of con-
secration was added and the remainder of the formula became
"according to the precept of Moses and Israel." This accentu-
ated the theological identity of "Israel" as over the norms
that were practiced only in Judea in Roman times (P. Yeb. 14d).

The wife was subjected to a number of regulations that
underscored the inferior status of women but which were also
in accordance with the punishment of Eve for having succumbed
to the serpent. Eve was sentenced to be dominated by Adam
(Gen. 3:16). In rabbinic times the wife was obligated to observe the halakhah as required by the husband, to do all the
necessary household chores, to keep a low profile in public,
being forbidden, for example, to appear with her hair uncovered,
to work in the street, or engage in conversation. If the wife
violated these norms and her husband chose to divorce her he
could take advantage of her negligence by refusing to pay her
the marriage settlement recorded in the *ketubah*. In the
opinion of some scholars even the daughter of a wealthy
family who brings many maids into her marriage is to perform
all the household duties, and is to be required to do domestic
work of one form or another on the premise that idleness leads
to immorality and melancholy. There was no question, however,
of having a woman devote herself to scholarship, if she had
the leisure, despite the occasional exceptional references
we have to women like Beruriah who became learned. There was
even disagreement over whether a father could teach his
daughter Greek. But in any case this refers to the time
when a daughter was in her parental home. After marriage she
had no access to futher education. There are ambiguities in
reference to how a husband may treat a wife. Some locked
them in their homes, others gave them freedom.[33] But despite
the relatively low status of women in present-day terms,
much ágadic literature encourages love and tenderness on the
part of the husband toward his wife, and attributes to the
wife a central role in making possible a full and happy life
for a man. Early marriage was the norm except in certain

periods of economic stress. It was believed that marriages
were pre-arranged in heaven. Great emphasis was placed upon
a man's marriage with the daughter of a scholar or a woman's
with a scholar.[34]

2. *Mixed Marriage or Exogamy*

Marriage outside of Judaism with pagans was prohibited
despite the fact that the Torah had specified only certain
pagan nations and these were no longer clearly identifiable.[35]
But that mixed marriage was a reality is seen in the statement
of the Testament of Levi in which the son of Jacob is purported to prophesy that his descendents will marry gentiles
(14:6). Undoubtedly mixed marriages increased with the ever-
widening range of the hellenistic and Graeco-Roman diaspora.
As Jews found it difficult in some areas to find Jewish mates
they married gentiles. The Jews either disappeared into the
gentile communities or the gentiles were admitted to Judaism
and absorbed into the Jewish community. Although in theory
the proselytes were of equal status with any born Jew, in
matters pertaining to marriage a discriminatory provision persisted. Rabbinic Judaism had drawn up a table of ten grades
of persons according to descent and *gerim* or converts were
fifth on the list. They could marry into three grades above
them, but not into the priestly families, while they were
permitted to marry into some of the grades beneath them such
as *mamzerim* (bastards), or foundling children who were banned
to the average born Jew. This emphasis upon "family status"
or *yihus*, was exceptionally strong in Babylonian Judaism.[36]
This however, was not so much an emphasis upon "blood" as upon
socio-economic and intellectual background, for in the widespread mixed marriage in both Palestine and the diaspora much
non-Jewish blood entered into Judaism. The scholar, rather
than the royal or noble offspring, was regarded as a primary
choice for marriage. Not even the daughters of priests, the
supposedly highest noble order, were prior to daughters of
scholars. As one historian has put it,

> "Thus family purity tended to direct natural
> selection into intellectual channels. Here
> the survival of the fittest meant primarily
> that of the best educated."[37]

It is probably a truism that antagonism to mixed marriage and the fear of the consequences to Judaism led to an
array of separatist halakhah. Older prohibitions against the
use of heathen bread, wine, oil and cooked food, were revived
and invoked in rabbinic Judaism. Gentiles were declared

ritually impure so that any bodily contact caused ritual impurity.[38] They invoked the zeal of Phineas to declare as
Sinaitic the Zealots' first-century practice to execute anyone
caught in a sexual act with a gentile without a court trial.
They required chaperons when a Jew and a Gentile of the opposite sex were to be together, and extended the biblical
prohibition of mixed marriage with select nationalities to
all gentiles as did the circles who followed the Book of
Jubilees.[39] The rabbis thus incorporated many pietistic and
zealotic halakhot, and absorbed sectarian pietistic separatism
into rabbinic Judaism. This was done to insulate Jews socially
and prevent their mixing with gentiles in order to deter Jews
from mixed marriage. But this had no connection with racism,
ethnicity or nationality. It was a theological matter. A
marital union between a Jew and a gentile was declared retroactively null and void, there being no possibility of *kiddushin* between them since the gentile was not subject to "the
precept of Moses and Israel" (B. Kid. 66b, 68b). Ultimately
the rabbis retraced a few of their steps. Some of the prohibitions were lifted and some were modified. The pressure
of life was such that social mingling between Jews and gentiles could not be prohibited. But the invalidity of marriage with a gentile continued down into modern times when
this halakhah was finally disregarded. It should be borne in
mind that all of this applied only to marriages with gentiles
who did not adhere to Judaism. Marriages with gentiles who
became proselytes were the same as marriages with other born
Jews.[40]*

3. *The Levirate*[41]

Anthropologial studies of primitive marriage, family,
clan and tribal structures, indicate that a woman became the
property of the family. She was then subject to the head of
the family when her husband died, and the family head chose
for her another member of the family as a husband. Out of
this, it is supposed, grew the biblical levirate marriage
which I have discussed in Pt.I, Ch. 2. This is the rite of
yibum in which the brother-in-law (levir) of the widow
(*yebamah*) possesses the widow and provides seed for the deceased in order to perpetuate his memory.[42] The Bible also
provides for the rite of *halizah* in which the widow removes
from the levir a shoe, the symbol of possession, she spits
at him, and a court pronounces censure upon him for his being
a faithless brother (Deut. 25:7-9). *Halizah* later becomes a
paradigm of how the rabbis innovatively reinterpret written
torah in a way that reverses scripture. The rabbis advanced

*See excursus at n. 40.

halizah from a degrading rite of censure to the position of
preferred ritual contrary to the Torah where marriage of the
levir with the widow is the desideratum. After *halizah* the
widow is free to marry a person of her choice. The tension
and ambiguity between Torahitic and rabbinic halakhah endures
to this day, with some scholars preferring marriage, others
halizah.[43]

4. *Incest*

Most societies have some form of limitation of sexual
relations and marriage between kin. The Bible contains halakhic provisions that reflect a later time in the history of
Israel but also incorporates narrative traditions with contradictory halakhah pointing to the patriarchal period. For example, the paternal half-sister is allowed to Abraham but is
forbidden by Leviticus. The halakhah of incest applied to
both those who had maternal and paternal natural affinity and
to those who became legal kin through marriage such as a
mother-in-law (Deut. 28:23). The levitical roster prohibits
sexual relations between members of an external kinship, including parents and children, siblings, grandparents and
grandchildren, aunts and nephews, but not uncles and nieces.
So too the "in-law" categories are all prohibited: one's
sister-in-law, the wife of one's uncle, the wife of one's
nephew, and "step"-kin. Furthermore the rabbis ruled that the
corpus of halakhah related to incest applied from the time of
betrothal even if there was no marriage. On the other hand
incest halakhah was not applied to the kin of two people who
engage in improper sexual relations outside of marriage. For
example, a man's son by his legitimate marriage may marry the
daughter of his extra-marital sexual partner (M. Yeb.11:1). It
is also clear that incest halakhah applied to legal kin even
after the marriage is dissolved by divorce or death.[44]

An incestuous marriage is invalid and requires no divorce
for its termination except in several technical cases. Children born of such a union and products of certain other prohibited sexual unions such as adultery are considered *mamzerim*
(bastards), and are not eligible for marriage within the faith-
community. In addition to the biblical roster of incestuous
marriages which are invalid and whose offspring are *mamzerim*
rabbinic literature prohibited many new secondary categories
which are ascribed to the men of the Great Assembly. In effect
these new prohibitions are linear extensions. Some scholars
maintain only those that are specifically named in the Talmud
are prohibited but others argue that the linear extensions
should apply ad infinitum, although one is hard put to grasp

how one would have sex, for example with one's wife's father's mother's mother!

5. *Sundry Marriage Prohibitions*[46]

Among the many sundry marriage prohibitions in the Bible there are two of special interest because these categories are barred to all Jews. These are: a castrated male and a *mamzer*, both of whom are not to "enter the congregation of the Lord" (Deut. 23:2-3). The castrated male, the hermaphrodites (*tumtum*, one with undeveloped genitals, and *androgynus*, one with both male and female organs), the female *ailonit* who lacks generative organs and the sterile woman, are all barred from contracting normal valid marriages by rabbinic halakhah.[47]

The *mamzer* as we have seen above is the product of one form or another of prohibited marriage. It appears however, that Philo, LXX and the Palestinian Targum all defined *mamzer* as the product of a harlot. Some scholars, among them perhaps Hillel (though not the Bet Hillel), insisted that the status of *mamzer* is borne only by offspring of adultery. The Bet Hillel and Bet Shammai, however, are at one in including offspring of incestuous unions in the status of *mamzer*. Ultimately the halakhah was settled that a *mamzer* is the product of incest and adultery and this includes the foundling child who is presumed to be the product of harlotry and therefore possibly of an adulterous union. The *mamzer's* descendents forever are not to be eligible for marriage to a Jew. In modern times this is entirely ignored at least within the non-orthodox segments of contemporary Judaism[48]

The sages from the earliest post-biblical period to the end of the talmudic period, engaged in the interpretation of scripture and the creation of new categories and definitions as the requisites of history and social development required. Wars, migrations, transplantations of populations, servitude under occupying conquerors all resulted in grave disorientation of communal, clan and family stability. The proto-rabbinic and rabbinic effort was to preserve the family purity and exalt the ethical norms of the covenant people. The motive was to prevent the Jew from succumbing to the licentiousness and permissive sexuality of the hellenistic and Graeco-Roman societies. At times the ramifications of a complex halakhah might be harsh. A prohibitive posture designed to guard the morality of the Judaic community was not always fair to women. This posture also permeated the halakhah of divorce.

6. *Divorce*[49]

The Torah clearly allows divorce, although it legislates very little concerning procedures. Nevertheless, there is an anti-divorce sentiment in the Bible expressed by the prophet Malakhi. That there was a contrary trend of thought favoring easy divorce is expressed by Ben Sira who appears to favor a husband divorcing his wife on grounds that are not terribly demanding. Philo indicates that easy divorce was common procedure in Alexandria, although there is some ambiguity as to what Philo regarded as acceptable grounds. Both the Palestinian Targum and the targum of Onkelos interpret Deuteronomy 24:1 to have in mind *àberat pitgam*, any sinful matter, as the cause for divorce inherent in the words of the biblical text, "When a man takes a woman as wife but she finds no favor in his eyes because he detects an *èrvat daḫar*. . .and he writes her a bill of divorce. . ." The Hillelites interpret the term *èrvat daḫar* to mean for any reason whatever for which she finds no favor in his eyes, and Akiba goes as far as to allow a man to divorce his wife if he has a roving eye to prettier women. They are in stark contrast to Bet Shammai which requires that the wife be guilty of some sexual indecency, or a *daḫar* (a matter) which may be adjudged *èrvah*, sexual impropriety before the husband may divorce her. At Qumran divorce was prohibited entirely. Some rabbis express the anti-divorce sentiment in the tradition of Malakhi.

Rabbinic Judaism was heir to these varying views. While slowly giving way to Hillelite easy divorce as far as grounds for divorce are concerned, the procedural details in the rabbinic halakhah of tractate *Gittin* of the Talmud relating to writing the *get* (bill of divorce) and attesting to its writing and delivery crystallized in a way that resulted in a stringent divorce process. This was actually a "liberalization" of the halakhah. One must be aware that in the context of the social and economic subordination of women when Hillelite easy divorce became the functioning halakhah a husband could lightly dispose of his unwanted wife and subsequently she might remain destitute, or at very least at great social disadvantage. At first the only alleviation a woman possessed was the fact that at divorce her husband was obligated to pay the *ketubah* settlement. Under certain circumstances, such as in the event of a wife's insubordination, defiance of the husband's norms, or failure to perform her domestic obligations she might even be dismissed without the *ketubah*.[50] It was therefore helpful when the rabbis introduced protective delay tactics into the halakhah to retard the process of divorce in the case of impulsive husbands. The more liberal grounds for divorce were aggravated by the fact that the husband could divorce his wife without her consent (M. Yeb. 14:1).

There are instances where the wife may request a divorce and the rabbis will compel the husband to execute it. This is so when the husband is impotent, denies her conjugal rights, restricts her freedom of movement, has an unbearable sickness or works at an obnoxious occupation. This underscores the historic fact that the power to issue a divorce has remained in the hands of the husband even in a modern religious movement which by the end of the eighth decade of the twentieth century had provided for woman's equality in almost all other areas of Judaic life and rite.[51] Where a man's freedom to divorce is abrogated, when he falsely accuses his betrothed of infidelity and is compelled to marry her, the halakhah is not explicit that the wife may leave him. Philo, however, records the Alexandrian halakhah in that vein. The seducer-husband's right to divorce was restored if his wife later is discovered to violate sexual propriety or is religiously unsuited for him. Rabbinic halakhah of divorce here reversed the Torah by restoring his right. It interpreted the Torah's intention in compelling the seducer to marry the woman in order to protect her, but not to maintain an improper union. The rabbis went beyond the Torah in other instances. The husband's power to divorce is further circumscribed where the wife is insane or held as a prisoner. An interesting improvement in the rights of the wife was Gamaliel I's reversing the ancient right of the husband to treat his wife cavalierly. The husband had the right to annul a divorce without the wife being aware he has done so. That meant, for example, that if she were in a distant land and received the divorce after he annulled it and married another her second marriage is void and any child born of it in the interim is a *mamzer*. Gamaliel I broke this destructive hold of the husband upon his wife's life.[52]

Other restrictions of the husband's absolute power to divorce include when he is insane, intoxicated, or in a state of temporary mental incapacitation by fever. But the wife's consent was not required until the middle ages.[53] A continuing disability in the halakhah is failure of the rabbis to give the wife the power to divorce her husband. This disability is only partially relieved by the power granted to the wife to request a divorce at a rabbinical court. Originally the rabbis based this right upon a precedent set by the Torah where a woman was to go free if her husband denied her necessities and conjugal rights.[54] The rabbis saw in this a basis upon which to institute a denial of his right to consent. But they only gave the wife the right to sue in court and have the court compel the husband to execute the *get*.

One way for a wife to circumvent this restriction was to apply for a divorce in a gentile court which accepted the right of a woman to execute a writ of divorce. In modern times a civil divorce is accepted as adequate by the reform rabbinate, but not by others. Some ancient rabbis accepted a divorce executed in a gentile court but others did not, and the advocates of the latter stringent halakhah ultimately won their point which results in the need for two writs in all segments of Judaism other than the reform group.[55]

Another serious flaw in the traditional halakhah of divorce still practiced outside of the reform and conservative movements is the absence of provision for desertion. When a man has deserted his wife without writing a *get* and the rabbinical ecclesiastical court (Bet Din) is unable to locate him to compel him to issue a *get*, unless the rabbi accepts the civil law as adequate, the woman remains an *agunah*, chained to her husband, unable to remarry. Similarly, there is no provision for declaring him dead in order to classify her as a widow.[56]

7. *Parents and Children*

The attitude toward children is rigorous and humane. In a famous story concerning the death of the two sons of R. Meir, his wife consoled R. Meir with the idea that the children were valuable articles temporarily entrusted to them by God and now are returned to Him (Mid. Prov. 31:10). Sons were preferred to daughters and daughters had none of the rights of sons to inheritance and education. But children of either sex took precedence over the parents' obligations to their own parents under the fourth (fifth) commandment. Parents were to be impartial to their children except insofar as the subordinate status of daughters is concerned. They were not to treat them with physical violence, and never break a promise to them.[57]

Children under the age of twelve years and six months were to give their earnings to their parents. The daughter had the same obligations as a son toward her parents. But the father had no specific obligations to his daughter beyond her sustenance. The mother did not have specific obligations to her son, and if she were a widow, her sons or an uncle, and not she had the authority over her daughter's property, marriage and vows. The father's halakhic responsibilities toward her son included circumcising him, and in the event he is the first-born, redeeming him; teaching him Torah and an occupation, and getting him a wife. R. Akiba

adds to this the duty to teach his son to swim.[58] Honoring
parents stands analogously to honoring God. When a father is
in economic need the child is to succor him. Honor to parents
is to continue after death.[59]

Here again, as is manifest in marriage and divorce halakhah the rabbis mitigated Torahitic practice. The biblical
"rebellious son" was subject to parental charges and to
the death penalty if convicted by the court (Deut. 21:18-21).
This was so reinterpreted in rabbinic literature as to virtually be abolished (M. San. 8:1-5). A review of how the rabbis dealt with this harsh biblical regulation provides insight
into their creative exegesis and demonstrates how they applied
their hermeneutic to pragmatic halakhic revision (Sif. Deut.
218-220). The Torah's provision is very general. It does
not specify an age limitation or what is the definition of
rebellious, glutton and drunkard. The rabbis press each word
of the several verses to narrow the effects of the halakhah
substantially. They humanely reduce the period during which
the son is liable to the charges to a few months between
the emergence of signs of puberty and the growth of genital
hair. Furthermore, they limit "rebellion" exclusively to
the youngster's overindulgence in both meat and wine simul-
taneously, and only as part of a secular orgy. This they
deduce by means of the hermeneutical rule *gezerah shavah*
(analogy) from the use of both terms "glutton and drunkard"
elsewhere where they are explicated as meaning meat and wine
(Prov. 23:20). Since the Torah's wording provides for both
father and mother to seize him for charges, the rabbis rule
that if one parent demurs from charging the boy there is no
case. Furthermore, the parents must have first warned their
son before a court of three of the dire consequences of his
action. Only after that, if he persists is he flogged. And
only then does he become subject to the death penalty if he
is a repeated offender and is convicted before a court of
twenty-three judges. The ultimate reluctance to abolish the
halakhah altogether flaws the rabbis. But it is paradigmatic
of how they frequently used exegesis and hermeneutics in
order to refine the rough edges of the Torah and mitigate the
severity of the remnants of primitive custom.

Education of the male children stood very high on the
communal list of priorities. The *àgada* is replete with examples lauding the status and purpose of education. Efforts
toward universal education of children initiated by Simon b.
Shetah during the first century B.C., were expanded by Joshua
b. Gamla in the first century A.D. In some places each of
five children studied a book of the Pentateuch and each of
six studied an order of the Mishnah. Each student then
taught all the others his book, and in this way learning was

spread. Special concern was shown to educate the poor. Custom varied as to whether to begin education at five, or at six years of age. There are exaggerations in the Talmud such as the statement that there were four hundred synagogues in Bethar and each had four hundred teachers with four hundred pupils to each teacher. Nevertheless, the statement reflects the historical reality that synagogues were places of education and that many engaged in teaching and study. Universal education, such as it was, did not apply to girls.[60]

VI. THE STATUS OF WOMEN

Our discussion of the family and its relationship to the rights of women leads us directly to the question of the status of women. This has already been referred to in part in the material on marriage and divorce. Here we will look at several other items. The woman's subordinate position is demonstrated by her referring to her husband as *baʿal* and *ȧdon*, "master" and "lord," and being denied the right to inherit from her husband. She may inherit from her father, however, when there are no brothers. Biblical sources repeatedly admonish children to respect the mother and set the background for husbandly tenderness and respect. The position of the biblical woman was legally inferior to that of the women of Egypt and Babylon and of her Judaic sister in Elephantine. She could not serve as a witness except to testify to her husband's death and was not allowed to serve as a teacher. But deuteronomic halakhah, took pains to protect the impoverished widow along with orphans and aliens (Ex. 22: 21; Deut. 10:18, etc.). Again, unlike their counterparts in other Near Eastern countries women were not part of the temple staff in Israel.[61]

The widow and divorcee had the advantage over the minor girl or the married woman in that she had more independence. But the divorced woman still endured certain disabilities such as being prohibited from marrying her paramour or a priest. The rabbis encouraged men to support their former wives who were destitute.[62]

The first real revolution in the status of women in Judaism was the institution of the inalienable *ketubah*, the marriage certificate which put the husband's property in lien to his wife to pay a pre-arranged marriage settlement in the event that he divorces her or dies.[63] Equally with men women were subject to all the prohibitions of the Torah and to civil and criminal penalties. But neither the *ketubah* break-

through nor this negative equality alleviated their lack of
privilege or right in the sphere of religious life. Classed
with slaves and children they were exempt from certain standard rituals and therefore barred from public participation
in them. These include reciting the *shemà*, wearing *tefilin*,
dwelling in the booth at Sukot, carrying the *lulub* and *etrog*,
hearing the shofar at Rosh ha'shanah and the rites and obligations of the sacrificial cult except those that apply exclusively to women. Other rituals were designated as their obligations such as the lighting of the Sabbath lamp, reading
and hearing the Megilla of Esther at Purim, and the complex
of menstrual halakhah. Women were not required to observe
the biblical pilgrimages and later were not counted in the
prayer quorum, but while it was permitted to include them
among those who were called to the Torah, the custom apparently early arose not to do so. They were required to recite
the *àmidah* daily, to hang the *mezuzah* and to recite the
birkat hamazon, thanksgiving for food.[64]

There are no explanations for the discrepancies in these
ritual halakhot, as to why women were obligated to some and
not to others. Thus, for example, they are included in some
rituals related to a set time such as the *àmidah* or the reading of Esther. But they are exempt from some that are not a
set time for which they should be responsible, such as the
Sukot booth, which while it is required technically at a
"set time," that is, at Sukot, the mizvah of utilizing it
could be achieved at any time of day or night. The only possible explanation for inconsistencies is that our literature
reflects halakhah in flux with a growing tendency to include
women in ritual observance along with a continuing effort to
exclude them. There is no agreement in the lists in our
sources of the exempt mizvot which are subject to a set time.
One list enumerates only *sukah, lulub* and *tefilin*, but allows
a woman the mizvah of the garment fringes (*talit*), while another scholar opposes that. A second tannaitic exemption
list adds shofar and fringes to the previous list. Yet as
one rabbi notes, the study of Torah is not bound to a set
time and women are exempt while the eating of *mazah* is related
to a set time it being obligatory the first night of Passover,
and women are obligated. Examples of such discrepancies can
be increased by a very careful analysis of the halakhah. Despite the denial of their right to participate in the liturgical and synagogue ritual women frequented the synagogue daily.[65]*

This subordination of women was primarily the product of
the biblical story in which Eve leads Adam astray and part of

*See excursus at nn. 64-65.

her punishment is that the male will dominate the female (Gen. 3:16). The anti-feminist attitude is especially strong in Ben Sira, and continues among the early tannaim or proto-rabbis, right through the talmudic period into the middle ages. Women are regarded as the single greatest threat to a man's piety because of the danger of his falling prey to unchastity as a consequence of the woman's wiles and attractions.[66]

The ancient historian Josephus sums up the status of women at the end of the first century this way: "The woman, says the law, is in all things inferior to the man. Let her accordingly be submissive. . ." They were considered unable to make astute judgements and prone to gossip and sorcery. A modern historian has concluded that, "Probably there is an uneven balance of anti-feminist utterances in the talmudic literature. . ."[67] In sum it may be said that women had few civic and political rights and few religious privileges. But the tenor of the Judaic moral code demanded that they be respected, loved and treated with concern.

VII. ART AND THE HALAKHAH

The unearthing of the third century Syrian Dura Synagogue brought to view ancient Jewish art for the first time. The cycle of biblical images that appear on its walls give cause to revise old ideas concerning art in "normative Judaism" and to reflect on the antecedents of Christian art. One of the most significant historiographical and theological misinterpretations related to art has been the presupposition that the first (or second) commandment of the Decalogue prohibited art in the Religion of Israel and Judaism. No less a figure than the great art historian and critic Bernard Berenson assumed that "all pure Semitics (if such there be), have displayed little talent for the visual, and almost none for the formative arts. . ."[68]

A careful reading of the Hebrew text, of the commandment leads one to the recognition that it speaks of making images for the purpose of worship, not as art, and not as items for merchandizing. Opposition to images related to cultic exegesis impelled the Jews of Palestine to object to a statue of the Roman Emperor in Jerusalem. The Jews of Babylonia had no objection to the statue of a Zoroastrian king at Nehardea. The former was part of the state cult. The latter was not. Solomon had many sculpted items, including images of oxen, in his temple and was never accusedof violating the Decalogue.[68]

In the light of the anthropomorphism with which the
Bible is replete one would have expected God's encounter
with Israel to have been in some form which could be described
as is the figure described by Ezekiel on the throne-chariot
and by Isaiah in the sanctuary (Ez. 1; Is. 6). But the God
who appears consistently to Israel manifested himself as a
cloud or as fire as is evident in a great array of verses.
As a cloud He alights upon the expiatory seat of the cabinet
bearing the tablets of the Decalogue where He speaks to Moses
from between the cherubim (Ex. 13:21; 25:22). To bar images
of Yhwh was the only way to eliminate the possibility that
images of pagan deites would be called Yhwh and disruptive
syncretism would be institutionalized. One the other hand the
superior artistic skills attributed to Bezalel indicates art
was not absent in the Israelite tradition (Ex. 31:2ff). Even
if one rejects the historicity of Bezalel, the historicity of
Solomon and his magnificent temple attests to the use of
various art forms in the earliest Israelite period. This
bears out the fact that the Decalogue was aimed only at
prohibiting an image of Yhwh for worship.

During the first century militant Jews opposed even an
image of the Roman eagle in the vicinity of the Temple. But
this was in the nature of nationalist-political defiance
rather than religious zeal, and the Jerusalem priesthood ac-
knowledged that the culprits who tore it down are culpable.
Josephus excuses it on the grounds of religious requirements,
but that is his personal apologetic in his effort to reconcile Rome with the post-70 Jewish community.[70]

When we turn to the rabbinic literature we also find
that our presuppositions are not encouraged. The iconoclas-
tic rabbis were not as opposed to art as the Church Fathers.[71]
The latter were halakhically far more stringent during the
second and third centuries. This is evident, for example in
the writing of Tertullian who is analagous to a rabbi insofar
as he was not a bishop and could not advance his views with
episcopal authority. His scholarship was his "authority."
In the case of the Mishnah we find no real unanimity on the
definition of idolatrous images (M.A.Z. 3:5). But even more
interesting is how this mishnaic material on idolatry helps
us to perceive a permissive rabbinic view regarding creating,
using and enjoying art, even when images or articles are
representative aspects of idolatry. If images reminiscent of
idolatry are rabbinically permitted, *a fortiori* we can understand that the Decalogue does not prohibit engaging in art
as art. One view in the Mishnah states that if one finds an
object with a picture of "Drakon" he is to throw it into the
Salt Sea. "Drakon" is a representative of a serpent which

occurred frequently as a motif with paintings of gods to symbolize eternity, power and wisdom. The Tosefta parallel adds that if one finds an image of "the nursing mother and Serapis" he is also to throw it into the Salt Sea. The latter reference is speaking of Isis and Osiris, Egyptian deities that had been absorbed into the hellenistic pantheon and were common in Palestine (*ibid.*) R. Simon b. Gamaliel responds to this halachic statement by limiting the destruction of images to those found on valuable objects because they are likely meant as religious icons, but not when found on ordinary utensils more probably used in domestic life. This was the preferred halakhah as we can ascertain from the complex technical rules that obtained in rabbinic literature.[72]

The implication that flows from this brief review of one halakhah is that there was a segment of rabbinic opinion whose view was preferred in later literature that had no objection to art. This was contrary to the absolute interdiction of art by a Benedictine editor of Origen interpreting early Christianity. Thus too, Philo supports the contention that in traditional Judaism of that time, beauty in pictures and statues that adorned cities was appreciated, despite the contrary view of Philo that lauds Moses for banning art and sculpture. The explanation for the discrepancy is to be seen in Philo's interpretation of the Decalogue as prohibiting art related to religion but not art as art, a view that coincides with that of the second century R. Simon b. Gamaliel. Thus, artistic representations demonstrably not related to cultic use were permitted. One may fashion, purchase, possess and enjoy the objects, as is seen in ancient utensils permitted to Jews and on Jewish epitaphs in ancient cemetaries. The latter even included the popular ferry which took the dead to the other world. In fact, as we now know even *tyche* the goddess of fortune, was represented on utensils and permitted for use. R. Gamaliel is reported to have had a conversation with a Roman jurist Proculus who is surprised that Gamaliel bathes where there is a statue of Aphrodite in the light of the biblical ban on benefitting from pagan objects (Deut. 13:17-18). Gamaliel responds that the statue is art, and that the Torah requires that one destroy pagan gods, not pagan art images (Deut. 12:2f.).[73] All of this is in stark contrast to Tertullian's *De Idololatria* which prohibited a Christian from being an artist or enjoying any art form whatever, even a picture of a little child (Chap. 8).

VIII.   PROSELYTISM[74]

A.   *The Biblical "Ger."*

The biblical data inform us that in pre-proto-rabbinic times the *ger* is of a socio-economic stratum and not what we regard as a religious proselyte. He is something more than a *nakhri*, a gentile, for the *ger* enjoys a high degree of equality under biblical norms while the *nakhri* endures a high degree of discrimination. The *ger* is not a full member of Israel for to participate in the paschal sacrifice he must be circumcised, implying that normally he is not. Nevertheless it is clear from numerous references throughout the Pentateuch that he is integrated in most significant aspects of the religious life of the community. The *ger* is the forerunner of what was called the "God-reverer" in Graeco-Roman times. He became the ready audience for evangelization into Christianity. The biblical *ger* and talmudic *ger toshab* might have been originally a landless serf or urban laborer who took on part of his master's religion but he was later transmuted into the *ger zedek*, the religious proselyte, who became a full member of the faith out of conviction.[75]

From the beginning the *ger* was included in the love command, and this explains his basic equality before the civil and criminal law as well as his near-equal rights to participate in the community's ritual. We are not able to trace the precise process of the *ger's* evolution from a landless serf-resident-alien-semi-Jew to the classification of full-fledged, newly born Jew, the religious proselyte with whom we are familiar since rabbinic times. There is no indication of an initiatory rite in the biblical and intertestamental sources. But it appears to me that if he was required to undergo circumcision to participate in the soteriological and eschatological paschal sacrifice and become thereby a genuine physical member of Israel, it may be assumed that when a *ger* presented himself as a candidate for full religious absorption the initiatory rite was circumcision. In order, furthermore, to purify himself he would require an initiatory baptism. The circumcision signified that he entered into the covenant sacrament by offering of his flesh and blood a symbolic sacrifice as was required of any Israelite to enter the covenant of Yhwh. The purifying baptism was the normal expectation of any Israelite. One must surmise that any woman born into Israel became a part of the covenant by virtue of "belonging" to her father and then to her husband. Proselyte women undoubtedly underwent baptism as the rite of purification from menstrual impurity, and this served as their rite of admission into Judaism. Women were part of the covenant. The Torah pronounces the covenant as absorbing all of Israel: leaders, males, children, women and *gerim*, the high-born and the lowly (Deut. 29:9-14). This all-encompassing covenant was meant to include each succeeding generation into infinity.[76]

B. *The Rabbinic Ger*

The proto-rabbis of the intertestamental hellenistic era and the early post-70 rabbis actively engaged in proselytism (Mt. 23:15). In some instances like Onkelos and Aquila these converts became major figures of piety and learning (T. Hag. 3:3). The rabbis emphasized the status of the *ger* as "born again," as a full member of Israel. Consequently the category "semi-proselyte" was either advanced to full Judaism or absorbed into Christianity. There is little information in the apocryphal books, Philo or Josephus leaving us little to go on. It is apparent, however, that both a Jew who left his faith and one who converted from another faith and adopted Judaism were called *mumar*, "one who changes," and the Greek term *metabalein*, "to change," is used in the context of changing religions on several occasions. But ultimately *mumar* was reserved for a Jew who leaves the faith and *ger* for one who joins the faith. Philo, a diaspora contemporary of proto-rabbis refers to *gerim* as *proselytous* and considers them as having joined "the godly commonwealth," and as being full Jews. Philo was highly laudatory of proselytism and emphasized the equality of proselyte with the born Jew. He seems to have believed that proselytes do not require circumcision, just as Israel did not practice circumcision in Egypt. He speaks of the spiritual circumcision of sensual passions as all that counts in being true to God. It is possible, however, that Philo refers only to semi-proselytes when he appears to waive circumcision, in the light of the biblical requirement that a *ger* be circumcised to participate in the Passover. It is logical that *tebilah*, baptism of the female was a very early practice, ordained to overcome menstrual impurity and later also required of males before entering the people of God. At the end of the first century the rite of admission is disputed. This was probably stimulated by the ancillary question of whether a man requires immersion once he has been circumcised, but had nothing to do with the woman's requirement of immersion. The halakhah crystallized while the Temple still existed. It required circumcision, immersion and a sacrifice for a male, and immersion and sacrifice for the female. At Yavneh, the sacrifice having ceased, the question arose whether immersion is necessary in the light of the immersion purification rites

having been so intimately connected with the sacrificial cult
and the right to eat of holy things or enter the holy place.
Immersion was continued for all because of three reasons.
Being necessary for women owing to the menstrual cycle, it
was retained for men too. It may also have been inspired by
the impact of the symbolism of Christian baptism. And finally
it may have been retained because of the importance placed
upon the continued practice of purification immersions by the
pietists (*perushim*) who now accepted rabbinic halakhic guidance.[77]

As they disagreed on the rite of admission, proto-rabbis
disagreed on the desirability of admitting proselytes. Some
appeared to be content with semi-proselytes or as one scholar
refers to them, "spiritual proselytes." These proselytes are
the *theosebais, sebomenoi, phoboumenoi* and *iodaizontes* mentioned in Greek sources: "God-reverers" or "Judaic-like."
In some rabbinic sources they are called *yirei shamayim*
"those who revere heaven" (i.e. God). They were not all engaged in the same observances of Judaism and the proto-rabbis
apparently did not expect them to be. There were those who
accepted a commitment to all precepts except *kashrut*. R.
Meir, late first century was willing to accept any gentile as
a semi-*ger* who made a commitment before three colleagues not
to worship idols and others were willing to settle for the
Noahide laws. It seems that the common denominator of all
spiritual proselytes was that they accepted monotheism and
subjected themselves to the moral standards of Judaism. We
see here an analogy with what James and his Jerusalem Church
expected of the diaspora proselytes to Christianity. It may
in fact have been this vast diversity among spiritual proselytes that roused post-70 rabbis to seek consolidation and retrenchment through a re-examination of the whole question of
proselytism with a view toward stabilizing a uniform halakhah.[78]

Baptism was less urgent for some rabbis because theologically they saw circumcision as a vital element in the covenantal relationship with God while the rite of immersion was
merely purificatory. Furthermore, because Paul urged the "seal
of baptism" to replace "the seal of circumcision" with soteriological significance, some rabbis may have played down the
need for baptism. Eventually it was regularized and made
normative until modern times. On the other hand most rabbis
saw the blood of the passover and the blood of circumcision
in a dual salvational role. The participant in the paschal
event who thus partakes of redemption is to "show the seal" or
"he cannot enter." The midrashic presentation is very much
like a mystery. The seal of circumcision is his admission
card to the mystery. Only by participating in the mystery

does one attach oneself to the redeemed community and thereby
become redeemed. In this connection the midrash refers Ps.
50:5 "Gather My saints together unto Me, those that have entered My covenant by sacrifice," to the Israelites in Egypt
who underwent circumcision to join in the first paschal event,
implying directly that circumcision is a sacrifice. By
undergoing it one joins the company of God's saints.[79]

Once a gentile entered the faith the rabbinic halakhah
sought to protect his or her status and emphasized his or
her Judaic status by referring to a proselyte as a newborn
child. A proselyte was eligible for marriage to a Jew. He
or she enjoyed full equality in the halakhah and was entitled
to all the charitable and social benefits of a born Jew. The
question is taken up whether one who claims he is a *ger*
should be accepted without witnesses. While some rabbis
declined to do so in Palestine they approved it in the diaspora.[80] In a long litany the *ger* is in every way compared to
the Jew because scripture applies to both the same terms relating to God's love and concern, and to their status as his
servants and friends.[81]

IX. *ABELUT:* DEATH, GRIEF, BEREAVEMENT AND MOURNING[82]

Rabbinic Judaism worked on the material of scripture and
created a normative mourning ritual which is spiritually satisfying and psychologically gratifying to those who believe
and observe. This ritual has continued down into the modern
era, albeit with some additions and modifications designed
to simplify the rites, especially in the non-orthodox segments
of Judaism.

Theologically the first question to be posed is, why is
there death? A naturalistic response was never adequate, and
humankind yearned for immortal life. Two views predominate
in rabbinic thought. The first is that humans must die as a
consequence of Adam's sin recorded in the biblical story of
the Garden of Eden. The second is that death was predesigned
as an inherent feature of creation. The first explains the
presence of death in the world as a punitive act by God.
The second is essentially a naturalistic explanation. Both
proved inadequate. Consequently we find some rabbis leaning
to the view that death, like life is an inexplicable mystery.
Some see both life and death as forced upon the individual, a
phenomena which remains beyond human choice.

The human drive to deny the power of death led sages of

all religions in historical times to seek mitigations of its threat. The rabbis emphasized that death is not a "state" but a moment in time, a function, a process of transition from corporeal to incorporeal existence. That death was a form of "sleep" was an idea ready at hand in scripture. They articulated theological affirmations such as death frees the human from the obligations to mizvot, and that death is atonement for sins, two ideas that help us understand the "christianized" Judaic theology of Paul. They held out the hope that at death the righteous see God and attain the celestial radiance for which humans yearn. This mitigating view of death is perhaps neatly summed up in an epigram attributed to first-second century R. Meir who read the Hebrew *meòd* (very) of "And behold it was very good" (Gen. 1:31) as *mavet*, death, that "death is very good."[83]

Earlier Judaism has two competing views of death. One maintains there is total unconsciousness. The other argues for consciousness and fellowship with God. The intertestamental literature of the proto-rabbinic era transformed Sheol into an abode of souls awaiting resurrection. Treatment of the soul in heaven or hell becomes a prefiguring of treatment at the final judgement. This is the basic doctrine that entered rabbinic Judaism where one no longer finds the primeval denial of consciousness to the dead and where one reads of the souls awaiting judgement and resurrection. Hell-fire and eternal damnation are defended from scripture.[84]

The halakhah surrounding death and grief is conceptualized as serving two purposes. One is to affirm the value of the deceased as a human person. Put another way, respect for the dead is based upon the fact that the ultimate person is really the divine soul for which the body is only a temporary dwelling and respect for the deceased is really reverence for an aspect of divinity. The second purpose is to take the period of bereavement and mourning as a time to petition God's mercy. This concerns itself for the living. The halakhah aids in easing grief and making possible the sharing of the sorrow. In effect, in contemporary psychological terms the process of mourning delineated in the ritual halakhah becomes a true catharsis. Toward this end such practices as watching the body of the deceased and arranging for professional mourners and eulogists is deemed important. The same is true of *taharah*, the washing and perfuming of the body, a practice attested to in both the Old and New Testaments and in rabbinic literature. Demons are averse to water, scents and smoke of the burning spices that were applied. In this way it was believed, demons are kept from infesting the body. And out of respect for the equality of the dead and the economics of the living simple white shrouds were ordained as the garment for burial.[85]

The halakhah sets a four-stage mourning period. The first is the pre-burial period unknown in biblical halakhah and termed *áninut*. The mourner is exempt from religious observance except on the Sabbath. He or she refrains from festive foods such as meat and wine, and from over-indulgence. The second is called *shivah* for the seven-day period of its duration. It begins after the burial, and the mourner observes it either in the home of the deceased or in his own home. Generally all next of kin observe it together. In rabbinic times the biblical gashing of the flesh is transformed into rending a garment and is so regulated in terms of what to rend and how large a rent to make that it becomes merely symbolic of the rent in one's life. The rent is preceded by the ubiquitous rabbinic berakhah which in effect states one's acceptance of death as the righteous act of God who is faithful in judgement. Generally one is not to anoint oneself or use cosmetics, some engage in fasting, one allows the hair to grow and sits near the ground and one does not engage in one's occupation or in sexual relations.

The intense mourning period now ends. The third stage of mourning is called *sheloshim*, named for the period it lasts, thirty days from burial. During this period there is a modified *abelut;* the hair is still not cut and marriages and other festivities are postponed, as are business journeys. The fourth stage is engaged in when mourning for parents. The restrictions on festivities are extended for an entire year. The custom known in contemporary Judaism of reciting the "Mourner's kaddish" is a medieval development. Kaddish is an ancient eschatological prayer for the Kingdom of God and in the Sefardic version is expanded to explicitly call for salvation and the advent of the Messiah. It is in regular liturgical use only since late talmudic times and not yet listed as a prayer in mourning in the eleventh century. It is presumed to be a pre-70 prayer since there is no mention in it of the restoration of a destroyed Jerusalem.[86]

X. CONCLUSION

The foregoing is but a cursory glance at aspects of both rabbinic methodology and practice. The halakhah here outlined is largely selected from the orders of *Nashim* (Women, or Domestic Relations), *Nezikin* (Damages), and *Moed* (Festivals). All of the halakhot touched upon have parallels often cited from other orders of the Mishnah. Nevertheless much halakhah is here not touched upon because the scope of this volume does

not permit a more comprehensive survey of all areas of the
halakhah. As an alternative, the aspects chosen are in those
areas that are still widely observed in contemporary Judaic
life. For this reason I am not presenting the bulk of
halakhah of the order of Damages, the civil and criminal law
and the halakhah of jurisprudence, because this is inoperative.
This is also the case with the bulk of the halakhah of the
order of Purities of which only a small segment is still operative among a minority of traditionalist Jews. Similarly the
order of the Holy Things is not reviewed because of this order
only the dietary practices still play a significant role in
contemporary Judaism and these are surveyed briefly in the
second volume of this series, and will be again in Volume
Four.

On the basis of this criterion for selection I should
include a discussion of the aspects of the rabbinic halakhah
of the sabbath and festivals and the liturgy from the mishnaic orders of *Moed* and *Zeraim*. These will be included in
the following chapter under theology. In these areas the
halakhah is more intimately correlated with theology. Where
the practices related to Sabbath and festivals are not closely
connected to belief, they are seen as folk customs and aspects
of ethnic or communal identity. In that event many non-
theological books are available that describe the "customs
and ceremonies" of Judaism or the folk-lore behind them. In
the case of liturgy, much of the relevant material is surveyed in the theology of worship discussed in the next volume.
This is also true of such aspects of the life-cycle as relate
to the birth and the rites of passage of children, for to a
large extent these aspects of the halakhah crystallized
during the middle ages.

Furthermore, economy of space demands that this chapter
offer only paradigmatic selections and not become an attempt
to reproduce the Talmud in brief or serve as a latter-day
Mishneh Torah of Maimonides which has fully recorded almost
every detail of rabbinic halakhah. I have therefore offered
select examples of the rabbinic process. This included a
brief glance at how the rabbis exegeted scripture to create
halakhah, incorporated custom into halakhah, reversed
scriptural halakhah and innovated new halakhah.

NOTES

CHAPTER 2

1. Form critical efforts have been presented by Jacob Neusner in a number of volumes. See his *Rabbinic Traditions* (Chap. 8, n. 1); *Eliezer ben Hyrcanus, The Tradition and the Man,* 2 vols. (Leiden: 1973) *A History of the Mishnaic Law of Purities,* 22 vols. (Leiden: 1974-1977); *The Tosefta: Tohorot* (New York: 1977). Gary S. Porton, *The Traditions of Rabbi Ishmael,* 2 vols. (Leiden: 1976-1977).

2. See Lauterbach, "Midrash and Mishnah," in *Rabbinic Essays;* Gerhardsson, *Memory and Manuscript,* pp 33-70; Geza Vermes, *Scripture and Tradition in Judaism;* David Daube, "Rabbinic Methods of Interpretation," *HUCA,* 22 (1949); W. H. Brownlee, "Biblical Interpretation Among the Sectaries of the Dead Sea Scrolls," *BA,* 4 (1951), pp 54ff.; K. Stendahl, *The School of St. Matthew;* S. G. Sowers, *The Hermeneutics of Philo;* D. Patte, *Early Jewish Hermeneutic.* On the targumic use of scripture see Patte, Chap. IV, pp 49-86. On the various targums see Pt. 2, Ch. 4.

3. Gen. 22:14 is rendered by Onk. as "Abraham worshipped and prayed *there* in that place. . ." The Palestinian Targum renders it "Abraham worshipped and prayed in the name of the word of the Lord God." The passage is discussed by Patte, p. 56. It is also evident that the scriptural word *vayikra* "and he called," at Gen. 22:14, is being given a second meaning of "to pray," ("to call" in the name of the Lord, and the Hebrew *yireh,* "will provide" or "see to it," is reverting to its primary meaning "see."

4. Patte, pp 66f. The schematic is best exemplified in Targ. Neofiti I and Pseudo-Jonathan to Ex. 12:42 giving common identity to four nights in history: creation, the covenant or the *àkedah,* the exodus and the messianic redemption. See *ibid.* pp 70f. and the references to Roger LeDeaut and others.

5. Lev. 23:11, 15. Cf. also P. Targ. Neofiti I to Lev. 23:11, 15. See the discussion of *the calendar* in Pt. 1, Ch. 6; and Shabuot in Pt. 2, Ch. 3 below.

6. This view of Lev. 23 is also adopted in rabbinic literature at Sifra 100b; B. Men. 65a-b. That the rabbis interpreted "the Torah from the Torah" is clear at P. Meg. 72b where Noah is represented as deriving a dietary halakhah, that only "pure" animals are permitted for food, by interpreting Gen. 9:4 in the light of 8:20. The Greek to Lev. 23:11 reads "on the morrow of the first day" which implies the day after the first festival day. At v. 15 it reads "the morrow of the Sabbath" which implies a Sunday. But in the light of v. 11 the Sabbath here must be taken to mean the festival, as it is by the Targ. That Neofiti I contains pre-Christian halakhah is maintained by M. Ohana, "Agneau paschal et circonsision," *VT*, 23 (1973), pp 385ff. See also Jose Fauer, "The Targumim and Halakhah," *JQR*, 66 (1975), pp 19-26; Bernard J. Bamberger, "Halakhic Elements in the Neofiti Targum; A Preliminary Statement," *JQR*, 66 (1975), 27-38.

7. Gerhardsson, *Memory*, pp 43f., 49f. The term *lablar* is found in Latin as *libellarius*. R. Meir is a *lablar* at B. Sot. 20a; Git. 67a; Er. 13a; and a certain Naḥum is called a *lablar* at M. Peah 2.6, and see B. San. 11b and parallels for others. For Temple archives: *Ant.* III, 1.7 (38); IV, 8.44 (303); V. 1.17 (61); *Ag. Ap.* 1.8 (39-43). See also Lieberman, *Hellenism*, pp 21ff. where he points out that the proto-rabbis (*hakhamim*) tried to stabilize the temple scripture whenever there were discrepancies in the readings of several scrolls deposited there by selecting the reading from a majority of manuscripts. On the meaning of *lidrosh* at Ezra 7:10 as "to inquire" see LXX *zētēsai*. Lieberman, *op. cit.*, pp 48f., (notes 18-19 for numerous references) points out that the tannaitic midrashim "swarm" with interpretative translations. Lieberman, p 50 refers to the Septuagint as "the oldest of our preserved *Midrashim*" thus aligning himself with those who see *targum* as being *midrash* in many instances. He points to frequent agreement between tannaitic midrashic interpretation of words with that of the Septuagint.

8. Lieberman, *op. cit.*, p 84. J. H. Weiss, *Dor Dor VeDorshov*, 5 vols. (Vilna: 1911) III, 247, collects evidence for written halakhah. See also the evidence collected by H. Strack, *Introduction to Talmud and Midrash* (New York: 1959) pp 12ff.; 17; Julius Kaplan, *The Redaction of the Babylonian Talmud* (Jerusalem: 1973), pp 261-288. Kaplan believes that a certain amount of material was committed to writing and preserved in the academic archives and never circulated for public use (p 271).

9. The views expressed here follow closely the work of Gerhardsson, *Memory*, pp 71-189. My adoption of his basic positions on the question of the transmission of the oral

tradition does not preclude my disagreeing with him on such
details as his identification of "Pharisaism" with rabbinic
Judaism (p 25). The same stricture holds true for my use of
Patte.

10. The collective term *halakhah* is frequently used in
place of the plural *halakhot;* the former also denotes a single statement of halakhah. The term mishnah is also synonymous with the singular halakhah and with the collective
halakhah signifying an extended body of material. The term
beraita is used to signify a single halakhah as well as a
body of material, and frequently Tosefta refers to the extended corpus of *beraitot.*

11. P. Meg. 73d; Ket. 32c; B. Ket. 105a; Git. 58a; see
N. Morris, *The Jewish School* (London: 1937); Gerhardsson, p
59. See also N. Drazin, *History of Jewish Education From 515
B.C.E. to 220 C.E.* (Baltimore: 1940); E. Ebner, *Elementary
Education in Ancient Israel* (New York: 1956). The term
tanna also came to refer to all of the teachers listed in the
beraitot, Mishnah, Tosefta, and *midrash* halakhah. The body of
literature is called *tannaitic* from the Hebrew root *shanah,*
"to recite," Aramaic *tanà.* At. B. Sot. 22a, ". . .the *tanna*
recites and does not understand. . .," he is compared to a
magician who mumbles. See also B. Ber. 38b, 52b; Lieberman,
Hellenism, p 97; Gerhardsson, *op. cit.* pp 95f. For qualifications of the scripture and rabbinic text reciters see B.
Kid. 49a.

12. See n. 16. At B. Tem 14a-b we hear that the third
century scholars R. Yohanan and R. Simon ben Lakish used
texts (*sifra)* of *àgada*, despite the many references to a
prohibition against writing them, as at B. Git. 60a-b; at
B. Shab. 115a we hear of a targum of Job in writing; at B.
Ket. 49b, 69a, we hear that rabbis wrote halakhic correspon-
dence and thus were putting halakhic texts and opinions into
writing; cf. B. Shab. 6b; Ber. 27b; B. M. 116a; San. 57b; Hul.
60b; P. Ber. 9a, etc. B. San. 35a indicates court proceedings and the halakhic opinions of the judges on the case were
written. The prohibitions are recorded at B. Tem. 14b; Meg.
18b; Shab. 115b.

13. B. Er. 54b; Mekh. to Ex. 21:1 III, 1; B. Meg. 7b;
Ket. 22b; 50a; Ber. 28a; even advanced teachers were often
able only to recite the bare texts without having mastered
their exposition. See as an example, R. Joshua of the
Yohanan ben Zakkai circle, at M. Par. 1:1; Pes. 9:6; Yeb. 8:4,
as also R. Tarfon at T. Zeb. 1:8; B. Zeb. 13a; at Sifra 6a
R. Tarfon is in a dialogue with R. Akiba on a cultic question

and concedes that while he had heard the texts and himself recited them he was unable to apply them in the interpretive manner of R. Akiba. See Gerhardsson, pp 124ff.

14. M. Ed. 1:3; M. Ab. 6:6; B. Meg. 15a; Hul. 104b; Nid. 19b; Shab. 15a; Bekh. 5a; Ber. 47a; Er. 53a. See further Gerhardsson, pp 136-148 on the educational method utilizing conciseness and brevity. For methods to aid memory, the mnemonic techniques, see pp 148-156. The need to memorize such massive material resulted in a laconic style and contributed to the complexity of the talmudic literature. Alphabetical psalms, and similar acrostics used elsewhere, along with other methods of word association show that even in biblical times certain mnemonic techniques were understood as valuable for oral transmission and study of liturgical recital. See also Louis Finkelstein, "The Transmission of the Early Rabbinic Traditions," *HUCA*, 16 (1941), 115-135.

15. Tanhuma (Warsaw: 1910), "Vayera," 1.5 (p 25a); "Ki Tissa," 34 (p 127a). Cf. *Pesikta Rabbati*, trans. William G. Braude, I, 5:1 where this is expanded, and it is explicated that only he who possesses the *mysterion* is Israel. For private scrolls see B. Shab. 6b, 96b, and elsewhere. For various forms of written texts see B. Men. 70a; Shab. 156a; Gerhardsson, *op. cit.* pp 160ff.; Lieberman, *Hellenism*, pp 203f., and n. 12 above.

16. I do not fully follow Gerhardsson, p 176 who sees the later expository expansion as justifiably attributed to the originator of the halakhah. There are several stages: 1) scripture is interpreted by both targum and midrash. Targum also reflects the results of midrash. 2) a halakhah is formulated out of the midrashic discussions. 3) This halakhah is then further studied, over a period of generations, with new "midrash" or in this case what is called *talmud*. Some of the elements of *talmud* may of course be quite old. But they are basically seeking to penetrate the mind and reasoning of the formulator of the halakhah. Decisions reached by *talmud* are probably what are referred to as *gemarà*. See Chap. 4. In relation to *àgada* see Bernard J. Bamberger, "Revelations of Torah After Sinai," *HUCA*, 16 (1941), pp 97-113. That Moses received all of the details of both the written and interpretive torah is articulated many times: Sifra 105a, 112b; P. Meg.74d; Hag. 76d; and elsewhere. That the Holy Spirit functioned among the rabbis: B.B.B. 14a; P. Sot. 16d; Sheb. 38d; Lev. R. 9:9; B. Yom. 39b; T. Pes. 1:27. At B. Shab. 23a we find later talmudic rabbis explaining the validity of *gezerot* on the basis of Deut. 17:11; 32:7. The two verses are exegeted to affirm rabbinic authority to innovate. Z. H.

Chajes, *The Students Guide Through the Talmud,* trans. Jacob
Schacter (New York: 1960), has collected the *gezerot* and
takanot, pp 38-110; he discusses *minhag* (usage, custom) at pp
118-130. Examples of halakhah based on testimony of disciples
who saw their rabbis act in a certain manner are given by
Gerhardsson, pp 184f. See M. Suk. 2:5; 3:9; B. Ber. 24a,
38b, and elsewhere. Certain aspects of Chajes' discussion
must be read with caution because of his uncritical, orthodox
position.

17. The hermeneutical rules or *middot* were ascribed to
Hillel at T. San. 7:11 and with some variations at Sifra 3a;
Cf. Ab. de R.N. A 37. To R. Ishmael b. Elisha, 1st-2nd cent.
A.D., were ascribed thirteen hermeneutical rules at Sifra 1a-
b; but aside from the thirteenth and several variations,
Ishmael's are basically similar to Hillel's. To Ishmael is
also ascribed the principle that "the Torah speaks in the
language of humans," upon which was based his school's rejection of Akiba's atomizing hermeneutics, derived from the
early first-century scholar Nahum of Gimzo in which every
particle and letter becomes significant for interpretation and
expansion of meaning. See Sif. Num. 112. According to
Mekhilta of R. Simon ben Yohai to Ex. 21:1 R. Ishmael taught
that his thirteen rules were revealed to Moses at Sinai.
Cited by Strack, *Introduction,* p 288, n. 6. Thirty-two rules
of exegesis were also enumerated in the introduction to
Midrash Hagadol ascribed to R. Eliezer b. Yosi Hagelili. But
some of these rules, enumerated by Strack, pp 96-98, are
clearly used earlier by Nahum of Gimzo and Akiba at T. Sheb
1:7, and Eliezer b. Hyrcanus at B.B.K. 117b. Just as R.
Eliezer b. Yosi Hegelili receives credit for the thirty-two
rules although he was only a latter-day articulator of them
and not their originator, we may conjecture Hillel and R.
Ishmael received credit for rules they articulated and did not
originate. See David Daube, "Rabbinic Methods of Interpretation and Hellenistic Rhetoric," *HUCA,* 22 (1949), 239-264. Gen.
R. 92:7 already points to ten examples of *kal vehomer,* the inference from the lighter to the more stringent and vice versa,
in the Torah. See on this for more evidence, Louis Jacobs,
"The Qal Va-Homer Argument," *BSOAS,* 35, Pt. 2 (1972). More
uncatalogued rules were also used. See Strack, p 98 and
references, pp 296f.; notes 1-9. See also Raphael Lowe, "The
Plain Meaning of Scripture in Early Jewish Exegesis," *Papers
of the Institute of Jewish Studies,* ed. J. G. Weiss, (Jerusalem: 1964). On Hillel, P. Pes. 33a; B. Pes. 66a, 70a-b. See
Michael Fishbane, "The Qumran Pesher and Traits of Ancient
Hermeneutics," *Proceedings of the Sixth World Congress of Jewish Studies* (Jerusalem: 1977).

18. See Sigal, *New Dimensions*, Chapters 4-7, and Chap. 2 on the question of the tension between divine revelation and human authority.

19. In the decree of Artaxerxes purported to be reproduced at Ezra 7:11-26 we are told (v. 11) Ezra is "the scribe of the words of the miẓvot of the Lord, and of his statutes for Israel," an idea repeated in Aramaic at v. 12, and again at vv. 14, 21, 25, 26. The prevailing term is *dat*. This word can signify "law" in the context of a human agent ordering a *dat*, but it also signifies the more comprehensive term "religion" or the full range of God's will as at Dan. 6:6; 7:25, and here. So too it is used for a particular religious custom as at M. Ket. 7:6; T. Ket. 7:6f.; or for the full range of the faith, as at B. Suk. 56b where the reference is to one who apostatizes from one's *dat*, explicated at T. Suk. 4:28, P. Suk. 55d, as one's faith. Cf. B. Yeb. 70b, Pes. 96a. Twenty-two criteria for halakhic decision are enumerated Sigal, pp 218ff., n. 2.

20. The principle of d.d.d. is at B. Git. 10b; B.K. 113ab; Ned. 28a; B.B. 54b, 55a. The principle which expresses rabbinic authority over marriage and divorce is *kol mekadesh àl dàtah derabbanan mekadesh*, at B. Git. 33a, 73a; Yeb. 90b, 110a; B.B. 48b; Ket. 3a. The power to annul is termed *afkinhu rabbanan kiddushin minay*, "the rabbis withdrew the betrothal" declaring retroactively that there was no valid betrothal. On the importance of quality and beauty in worship, see B. Suk. 11b; 32a-b; Shab. 133b; Naz. 2b; B. K. 9a-b, Mekh. II, 25. For adaptation of pagan custom in ornamentation even in matters pertaining to the cult, see Lieberman, *Hellenism*, pp 128ff.; M. Yom. 3:9-10, B. Yom. 25b, 37a-b, for other examples of beautification in cultic-liturgical matters. M. Git. 4:2-9, 5:3, all relate to *tikun haolam*; M. Shebi. 4:3; Git. 5:8-9 to *darkai shalom*; see also the passages in the relevant tractates. The principle to consider the majority is formulated as *ain gozrin gezerah al haẓibur elah im ken rob haẓibur yakhol laamod bah*, with some variations in different texts. See T. Sot. 15:8; San. 2:13; B.A.Z. 36a; B.B. 60b; B.K. 79b; P. Shab. 3d. On mourning and the poor, B.M.K. 27a-b; that the lenient view should be adopted in matters pertaining to mourning is found at B.M.K. 18a, 19b, 20a, and elsewhere; cf. B. Er. 46a.

21. Gen. 17:7; Ex. 31:12-17; 12:14, 17. On the other hand the lengthy halakhic section called the "Book of the Covenant" at Ex. 21:1-23:19 has no such designation. It is a changeable body of practice subject to the vicissitudes of time and place.

22. M. Git. 4:4. T. Ter. 2:1-3; Pes. 3:7; B. Git. 2b, 3a; Hul. 10b; Ber. 7a; A.Z. 4b. In reference to the example concerning testimony of ritual sin, at B. San. 9b we are told a person is a relation to himself and therefore ineligible as a witness against himself. Cf. B. Ket. 18b, San. 9b, 25a; Yeb. 25b, for the principle that a person cannot testify against himself in self-accusation. See Saul J. Berman, "Lifnim Meshurat Hadin," *JJS*, 26 (1975), 86-104; 28 (1977), 181-193; Mekh. III, 182; P. Targ. Ex. 18:20, already draws the distinction between the act of justice (*shurat dinà*) and going beyond the norms of justice (*milgav leshurata lerashiàyim*) because one must show special compassion toward the guilty (B.B.K. 99b; B.M. 30b).

23. See Lauterbach, "Midrash and Mishnah," in *Rabbinic Essays*, pp 213-224. For Yosi's halakhah see M. Ed. 8:4. Cf. Sifra 22b. Sifra attributes the changes to *zekenim harishonim* "the early sages" which might be an allusion to Yosi, for at times a plural term conceals the identity of an individual in rabbinic literature. Lauterbach fails to note this possibility in his discussion of the question, *ibid*. Yosi was called *Sharya*, literally denoting "one who unbinds," virtually accusing him of destroying the scholastic discipline nurtured since Ezra. See a recent analysis of the Bet Hillel-Bet Shammai material by Alexander Guttmann, *Rabbinic Judaism*, pp 59-124. See especially M. Git. 4:5; Ed. 1:12f.; Nid. 1:1; Ed, 1:1. The lenient option is selected in cases of *abelut* (mourning), *èrubin* (creating continuity in space or time) and *àgunah* (a woman in limbo regarding her right of remarriage). See B.M.K. 18a, 19b; Bekh. 49a; Er. 46a; Yeb. 88a; Git. 3a, among many other parallels. The institution of *èrub* is too complex to detain us here. The reader is advised to begin with an article in *JE*.

24. B. Shab. 151b; Nid. 24b; Bekh. 49b; Hul. 11b; M. Taan. 2:8; B. Taan. 15b, 18a.

25. There were a number of rabbis called R. Aḥa. It is often difficult to be sure which R. Aḥa is meant. Scholars agree that the R. Aḥa in disputation with Rabina is R. Aḥa bar Raba bar Joseph, and that Rabina is Rabina I, both of whom flourished in the early fifth century. See Strack, *Introduction*, p 133. See B. Pes. 74b. Hul. 93b. There are, however, exceptions where apparently R. Aḥa and Rabina are in dispute and it is not clear whose opinion is lenient, but where the preferred halakhah is the stringent view. See B. Sot. 25a; A.Z. 26b, 33b, 75b. It is possible that the reports of these cases are in error, for it appears quite definite in Hul. and Pes. *ibid.* that whenever R. Aḥa and Rabina are in

dispute the halakhah follows the lenient view whether it is that of Rabina or R. Aḥa. This is explicitly corroborated by Rabbi Asher b. Yehiel at Hul. 7:11 and Alfasi to the text of Hul. 93b.

26. For Yosi b. Halafta: B.M.K. 17b-18a; Pes. 99b; R.H. 33a; Hag. 16b; Hul. 85a. Leniency also holds true regarding rabbinic sabbath halakhah which affects a primary Torahitic and covenantal institution. See T. Ed. 1:3; M. Er. 3:4; 5:5; P. Er. 21a; B. Er. 36a, 58b, 59a. For Yoḥanan Kohen Gadol see M. Maas Shen. 5:15; Sot. 9:10; P. Maas. Shen. 56d; T. Sot. 13:9-10; M.M.K. 1:10; B.M.K. 11a; Sot. 47a, 48a. For priority of the permissive: B. Ber. 60a; Bez. 2b; Er. 72b; Kid. 60b; and elsewhere. In general the rule prevails that *beshel sofrim holkhin aḥer hamekil*, "in soferic halakhah we follow the lenient view." In earlier sources it is found as *khol safek derabbanan lekoola*, "any question of doubt in a rabbinic mat- ter is decided leniently," at B. Bez. 3b; Shab. 34a; Er. 5b, 45b.

27. T. Peah. 3:2; Sifra 112b ". . .the Torah, its hala- khot, its details and its interpretations were given through Moses at Sinai." See B. Men. 29b. for the belief that Moses "ascended on high" to receive the Torah; B. Shab. 89a. For *halakhah leMoshe MeSinai* see P. Peah. 17a; Hag. 76d; many in- dividual halakhot are so ascribed, e.g. B. Men. 89a. See further Leo Landman, "Some Aspects of Traditions Received From Moses at Sinai," *JQR*, 67 (1977), 111-128.

28. The six orders of the halakhic collection called Mishnah incorporate the various areas of religious practice in the following way: 1) *Zeràim*, agricultural and liturgical halakhah; 2) *Moèd*, sabbath and festival halakhah; 3) *Nashim*, domestic relations and vows; 4) *Nezikin*, civil and criminal law, the system of jurisprudence, idolatry and some miscel- lany; 5) *Kadashim*, "holy things," or the halakhah pertaining to the cult and the system of tithing; 6) *Taharot*, purities, the halakhah pertaining to immersion in cases of impurity and to the *mikveh* or pool where immersion is conducted. Tosefta is a collection organized similarly and offers alter- native, supplementary and explanatory halakhah. The Talmud is the *midrash* or the combined commentary, analysis and critique of the two collections.

29. See S. Zeitlin, *Rise and Fall*, III, 261-327, 459-472; S. Baron, *Social and Religious History*, II, 215-321, 408-436.

30. See Roland de Vaux, *Ancient Israel*, I, 19-38; Louis Epstein, *Marriage Laws in the Bible and Talmud*, is a full pre-

92

sentation of all aspects of the question including polygamy, concubinage, the levirate marriage, intermarriage, incest, and miscellaneous aspects of the marriage system. For divorce see David Amram, *The Jewish Law of Divorce* (Philadelphia: 1896). See also E. Neufeld, *Ancient Hebrew Marriage Laws;* L. Epstein, *Sex Laws and Customs in Judaism* (New York: 1967); G. F. Moore, *Judaism*, II, 119-140; A. Cohen, *Everyman's Talmud* (London: 1932), 168-194.

31. The betrothal blessing is preceded by a blessing for wine, making for a total of two blessings. The six marriage blessings are also preceded by one for wine. They are certainly tannaitic and are referred to in the name of Rab who flourished as early as the late second century, B. Hul. 9a. (At B. Ket. 8a and elsewhere Rab is referred to as a *tanna*, that is, a scholar with the higher status of one listed in the Mishnah or Tosefta. See Chap. 4. The wedding berakhot are referred to in *beraitot* at B. Ket. 7b-8a, and as having been recited at the wedding of R. Judah ha'Nasi's son, mid-2nd Cent. B. Ber. 33a; Meg. 18a; Sif. Deut. 343.

32. Josephus, *Ant.* XVII 1.2 (14); *War* I, 24.2 (477); Justin, *D.* 134.1; 141:4. See Baron on monogamy, *History,* II, 223-229. As noted above the Qumran people and the Christian community opposed polygamy from the beginning. Ultimately under Christian influence in Europe, Judaism brought the practice to an end around the year 1000. See *Emergence* II, 108-112; 244-247; 457f. n. 42. Nevertheless the 3rd cent. Christian bishop of Rome, Callistus, legalized concubinage, and as late as the 16th century Martin Luther and Philip Melancthon, two leading reformers·, the latter a major Reformation scholar, approved concubinage for Philip of Hesse, a dedicated Protestant prince. See Baron p 244; Williston Walker, *A History of the Christian Church,* pp 338f. On concubinage see Epstein, *Marriage Laws,* pp 34-76. See also B. Yeb. 37b; 65ab; Epstein, pp 12-25; Neufeld, pp 118ff.

33. M. Ket. 5:5, 7:6; T. Sot. 5:9; 3:4; B. Sot. 20a; P. Peah, 15c; B. Git. 90a.

34. See C. G. Montefiore and H. Loewe, *A Rabbinic Anthology* (London: 1938), Chap. XXIII; Gen. R. 17:2; B. Yeb. 63a; San. 22a, 76b; B.M. 59a. On marriages with scholars M. Ab. 5:24; B. Kid 29b-30a; San. 76a; Sot. 2a; Pes. 49a.

35. This general prohibition against all gentiles on pain of death is first found at Jub. 30:7-10. The term "mixed marriage" applies only to a Jew who marries a gentile and should be understood as not applicable where a Jew

marries a proselyte to Judaism who leaves his or her previous faith. See Epstein, *op. cit.*, on the subject in general, pp 145-219.

36. M. Kid. 4:1; see the talmudic material on the chapter. Marriages permitted to a *mamzer* are: the proselyte and certain disadvantaged Jews. See M. Kid. 4:3; T. Kid. 5:1; B. Kid. 72b; P. Kid. 64c.

37. Baron, *History,* II, 235.

38. B.A.Z. 35b, 36b, 37b-38a, 57a; Nid. 34a.

39. Num. 25:7-8; B.A.Z. 36b; Kid. 68b.

40. Prohibition of gentile cooked food and bread; B.A.Z. 35b; 38a-b; oil, *ibid.* 57a, 58b, 59a; other limitations to impede contact are recorded at B.A.Z. 6b, 11b, 64b-65a. See further on this in *Emergence* II, for the medieval period when the Church also failed to break social contact between Christians and Jews despite repeatedly renewing prohibitive legislation and threatening the death penalty and excommunication. How the matter of mixed marriage developed in modern times will be taken up in *Emergence* Vol. IV. Meanwhile the reader may find it interesting to read Tama, *Transactions of the Parisian Sanhedrin,* trans. F. D. Kirwan (London: 1807) pp 154-156, for the first breakthrough in the modern period. The major change was the acceptance in 1806 of a civil marriage between a Jew and a gentile as valid, to accept the continued status of the Jewish partner as a Jew and to turn the back on any thought of penalizing those who enter into a mixed marriage. Nevertheless, the rabbis and laypeople at Paris continued to deny the possibility of *kiddushin* in an inter-marriage and the rabbis declined to officiate. On the other hand, in 1844 the Reform synod at Braunschweig (Brunswick), Germany, declared that mixed marriage between Jews and Christians or other monotheists is not forbidden if the children will be brought up in the Jewish faith. This is cited by David Philipson, *The Reform Movement in Judaism* (New York: 1907), p 212. But as late as 1871, as is clear from the Augsburg synod, cited by Philipson, p 446, this was not yet the general practice in Reform Judaism nor has it ever been such. The matter is in great flux in North America, however, as mixed marriages reach a very high percentage rate, some estimating between 25-40 percent of marriages entered into by Jews. Many reform rabbis officiate; few conservative rabbis do so; no orthodox rabbis officiate. Rabbis differ in how they regard the marriages, but generally the conservative and reform synagogue allow all his or her rights and pre-

rogatives to the Jewish spouse, and with consent of the parents will bring the child into the faith as a full-fledged Jew. My considered judgement is that under the socio-political and historical circumstances of our age, the "sacramental" nature of marriage can be entered into by a Jew and Christian who basically are both monotheists, do believe in the sacramental nature of marriage, plan to lead a Judaic life and raise their children as Jews. This degree of affirmation of Judaic faith should be sufficient for a rabbi to officiate at the marriage. Both the Jew and the Christian can say with intellectual integrity "You are consecrated unto me in accordance with the precepts of Judaism." "The law of Moses" may be retained in the formula if wished for they are still married in accordance with that law which prohibited only specific nations no longer identifiable.

41. See Epstein, *Marriage Laws*, Chapters 3, 5 and 6.

42. Gen. 38; Deut. 25:5-10; Ruth 3:9, 12-13; 4:1-17. There are sections of the Pentateuch where the institution of a levir marrying his widowed sister-in-law appears to be ignored: where a widow is to return to her father's house, Lev. 22:13; the estate passes to brothers or uncles, Num. 27:8-11; and there is opposition to a man taking his brother's wife, Lev. 20:21; 18:16. Epstein p 81, (and see n. 10) thinks that Lev. 18:16 is contra-levir. But these verses refer to improper sexual advances by the brother-in-law to his brother's "wife," not his widow. This becomes clear in P. Targ. to Lev. 18:16 where the targum interpolates one is not to dishonor his brother's wife "in the lifetime" of the brother, or after his death "if he have children," that is, when levirate marriage is not an excuse. In effect, therefore, Lev. 18:16 is not a contradiction to the levirate. The levirate provides exemption from the prohibition of incest at Lev. 18:16. Cf. B. Yeb. 55a; P. Yeb. 2b. Most of the entire large talmudic tractate of Yebamot is devoted to the complexities of the levirate and *ḥaliẓah* halakhah, and the ramifications of both, including the tragic situation of the *yebamah* who is in a state of *zikah*. This means she is "chained" to the levir, a unique form of *àgunah* (see glossary). She is not free to marry someone else when the levir neither espouses her nor undergoes the *ḥaliẓah* rite. See Epstein, pp 104-115.

43. M. Bekh. 1:7; B. Bekh. 13a; B. Ket. 64a; B. Yeb. 3a, 39b, 109a; P. Yeb. 12d-13a. In modern times opposition to *ḥaliẓah* arose as: a) an outmoded rite; b) as lacking intellectual integrity insofar as its ritual and symbolism are not a "preferable" means to liberate the "chained women"; c) that the concept is abhorrent to modern thought. I have written

a responsum for the Committee of Jewish Law and Standards of the Rabbinical Assembly which permits the local rabbi to waive *ḥaliẓah* and officiate at the remarriage of a widow who would normally require it. This has become a valid halakhic option.

44. Lev. 18:9. Lev. 18 in general is the comprehensive roster of the kinship degrees forbidden as incestual sexual relations and therefore for marriage. See Epstein, pp 220-274. For a complete chart of biblical incestuous relations see Epstein, pp 234f., for the earlier talmudic period, pp 258f. and for later additions, pp 259-262. Some attempted to apply incest halakhah even where marriage was not involved, e.g. at B. Yeb. 97a, where some maintained a person cannot marry his father's paramour, but despite Amos 2:7 this was not accepted as halakhah. Cf. M. San. 7:4.

45. Jub. 33:15; Philo, *Special Laws* III, 3; III, 5 (26); at Lev. 18:18 the sister of one's wife is permitted after the wife's death; inferred from this is that in all other cases the prohibitions continue after one's wife's death, at Derekh Ereẓ. 1; B. San. 76b; Yeb. 94b. For *mamzer* see B. Yeb. 94b; M. Yeb. 4:13. The term *mamzer* is not defined in the Bible and occurs only at Deut, 23:3 and Zekh. 9:6, the latter clearly being a reference to a foreign ethnic group. M. Yeb. 4:13 clearly reflects differences of opinion as to how to define *mamzer*, but all views agree that he is the product of one form or another of a prohibited union. Hence the out-of-wedlock offspring of two unmarried people who are not committing incest is not a *mamzer* in the halakhah although considered "illegitimate" in modern western law. Another exception is the product of the marriage of a *kohen* and a divorcee which is prohibited at Lev. 21:7; he cannot serve as a priest but he is not a *mamzer*. See also B. Yeb. 20a-21b; T. Yeb. 2:4; P. Yeb. 3d; Derekh Ereẓ 1. See Epstein, pp 259-261, B. Yeb. 22a.

46. Epstein, pp 275-332.

47. B. Yeb. 75b; 72a; Bekh. 42b; Yeb. 83a; M. Ket. 11:6; B. Ket. 77b; Philo, *Special Laws* III, 6 (36) condemns marriage to a sterile woman as lust; cf. T. Yeb. 8:4 which prohibits a man from marrying a sterile woman, in contradiction of M. Yeb. 6:6 which says that a barren woman divorced after ten years may marry another man who is also allowed to divorce her after ten years. The simplest explanation is that as in so many instances in all spheres of the halakhah there were different schools of thought and diversity in practice.

48. Philo, *Special Laws* I, 60 (326), LXX Deut. 23:2, P. Targ. Deut. 23:3; for Hillel, T. Ket. 4:9; B.B.M. 104a; at M.

Kid. 4:2 children who know their mothers and not their fathers and those who are foundlings and know neither are called *she-tuki* and *asufi* respectively, two categories that are differentiated from *mamzerim ibid.*, 4:1, while *shetuki* are included as *mamzerim* by Philo, *ibid.* For Bet Shammai and Bet Hillel, T. Yeb. 1:9f; Kid. 1:4; B. Yeb. 37b. The complexity of the halakhah is illustrated by the different approach of R. Akiba and the varying interpretations of his statement, for which see B. Yeb. 44a; T. Yeb. 11:5-8; B. Yeb. 92a, 49a; Ket. 29b; Kid. 68a. See Epstein, pp 281f. The complexity was sorted out by Maimonides, *Mishneh Torah* "Issurai Biah," 15:1, who concluded that only the offspring of incest and adultery is to be classified as *mamzer* and that has been the halakhah into modern times. That a *mamzer* is barred for "ten generations" (Deut. 23:3) means "forever" in rabbinic literature. See M. Yeb. 8:3. The prohibition of marriage with a *mamzer* has been declared inoperative by the Law Committee of the Rabbinical Assembly (Conservative).

49. Divorce is allowed at Deut. 24:1-4. This verse does not initiate the practice, but refers to it as if it is a well-known procedure. The right of the husband to divorce is denied him in two cases at Deut. 22:13-19, where he falsely charged his wife with infidelity and 28-29 where he seduced a woman and was compelled to marry her. This was obviously for their social and economic protection. For anti-divorce sentiment, Mal. 2:4-16; Ben Sira 25:26. Philo, *Special Laws* III, 5 (30); 14 (79, 80-82); M. Git. 9:10; Sif. Deut. 269; B. Git. 90a; P. Sot. 16b; M. Ket. 7:6. For Qumran: CDC 4:20-5:2; Rabin, *Zadokite Documents*, p 67, claims that CDC 13:17 permits divorce; however, he concedes that the Hebrew text is undecipherable. On the other hand, the Temple Scroll 57:17-19 clearly forbids a king to divorce his wife. At CDC 7:16f. "the king" is taken to be "the congregation" as Daube, *New Testament*, p 85 has pointed out in reference to Deut. 17:17, and it may be possible, therefore, to apply the law of the king at Temple Scroll 57:17-19 to all members of the community. B. Git. 90b records one rabbinic anti-divorce posture upon Mal. 2:14-16. For a complete picture of the halakhah of *gittin* see Amram, *The Jewish Law of Divorce*; Sigal, "The Future of Religious Divorce," in *New Dimensions*. On divorce procedure see Amram, pp 142-185 and his reference notes.

50. T. Ket. 12:1; B. Ket. 82b; Gen. R. 17:3; M. Ket. 5:1; 7:6; B. Ket. 72a-b; Git. 90a-b.

51. A wife may sue: M. Ned. 11:12; M. Ket. 5:5; 7:2-5; 7:9f. See Sigal, *op. cit.* It was possible that some women did issue divorces. Not only do we have the reference at Mk.

10:12 but a *get* issued by a woman to her husband was found at Wady Murabbaat, written in Mishnaic Hebrew and dated to the year 134. See Millar Burrows, *More Light*, p 33. Josephus says this is not according to Judean practice, *Ant.* XV. 7.10. (259). Perhaps some proto-rabbis accepted this procedure and it was later abolished.

52. Note 49 above. Philo, *Special Laws*, III, 14 (71, 84). In the case of the seducer of Deut. 22:28f. if his wife later turns out to be promiscuous or perhaps only flighty, according to M. Ket. 3:4-5 the husband is exempted from the Torah's prohibition and he may divorce. The term used at par. 5 is the Shammaite term of M. Git. 9:10, *debar èrvah*, some matter of questionable sexual propriety. See M. Yeb. 14:1; Ket. 4:9; for Gamaliel's halakhah, M. Git. 4:2; B. Git. 33a.

53. M. Yeb. 14:1; B. Git. 67b. Halakhic disabilities were unfortunately applied to a deaf-mute as we see at M. Git. 5:7; B. Git. 71a; M.B.K. 8:5; Yeb. 14:1.

54. Ex. 21:7-11 as interpreted at Mekh. III, 30; cf. M. Ar. 5:6. This ruling compelling a husband to issue a divorce under penalty of flogging created a basic ambiguity in rabbinic halakhah: on the one hand the theory was absolute husband-power, and his freedom to act (M. Yeb. 14:1); on the other hand the rabbis restricted that power when they saw fit and deprived him of that freedom (M. Git. 9:8).

55. M. Git. 1:5; B. Git. 10b; cf. P. Kid. 58c where it is alleged that gentile courts did not use a divorce instrument like a *get* as the ostensible reason for rabbinic rejection of gentile divorce decrees. This is not historically correct. See Boaz Cohen, *Jewish and Roman Law* I, 379, and *passim*, for a review of comparative practices and concepts. Actually the meaning of the statement is that the religious and moral conceptions of the Judaic halakhah (the "sacrament") are not present in gentile marriage and divorce which are only civil transactions, for "God's name is related to divorce only in Israel." See Cohen, pp 383f.

56. Amram, pp 172f. An annulment remedy is available under the jurisdiction of the Law Committee of the Rabbinic Assembly (Conservative).

57. B. Ket. 50a; Sot. 49a; Shab. 10b; Git. 6b; Suk. 46b.

58. M. Ket. 4:4; M. Kid. 1:7; T. Sot. 2:7; supporting daughters: M. Ket. 4:6; T. Ket. 4:8; B. Ket. 49ab; father's obligations to a son, T. Kid. 1:11; P. Kid. 61a; B. Kid. 29a-

30a. Examples of the mother's limitations, at M. Sot. 3:8.

59. Ex. 20:12; Deut. 5:16; Lev. 19:3; Philo, *The Deca-logue*, 22-23 (106-120); *Special Laws* III, 38-43 (224-241); 47 (261); P. Peah 15c; B. Kid. 30b; Mekh. II, 257ff. Sifra 87a; P. Peah 15c; B. Kid. 31b.

60. B. Shab. 119b; 127a; Gen. R. 49:4; 65:20; B.B.B. 21a; Shab. 119b; Kid. 30a; B.M. 85b; Ned. 81a; M. Ab. 5:24; the Bethar statement is at B. Git. 58a; cf. for other alleged statistics B. Ket. 105a. See above on the transmission of the Torah, and also at B.B. 21a on the limitation of elemen-tary classes to twenty-five, B. Pes. 3b for the requirement of conciseness by the teacher, and at B. Hag. 9b for the practice of repetition because "one who repeats his lesson one-hundred times is not like him who repeats it one-hundred and one times." They defined four types of students and ac-commodated their teaching to the four, M. Ab. 5:15, 18. On girls: M. Sot. 3:4; B. Kid. 30a; some thought girls should be educated but this view was not triumphant; Cf. P. Sot. 19a; B. Yom. 66b. Girls were not subject to the law of the re-bellious son (T. Sot. 2:8).

61. See Baron, *History* II, pp 235-241; Jeremias, *Jerusa-lem*, 359-376, and the literature he cites at p 359, n. 1; Sigal, *Emergence* II, Appendix A, and "Women in a Prayer Quorum." De Vaux, I, 39f.; husband as *baàl* Gen. 18:12; e-quality before children, Ex. 21:17, Lev. 20:9; 19:3; Prov. 19:26; etc.; husband's love and respect, Prov. 31:10-31. At Elephantine she paid property taxes showing she owned property she could obtain a divorce. In rabbinic halakhah she was not eligible to give testimony because of Gen. 18:15 which the rabbis took to indicate a woman is not reliable. Deut. 23:18-19 condemns the Canaanite practice of temple prostitution, but it appears this was a syncretistic element which intruded it-self in Israel according to II Ki. 23:7; I Ki. 14:24, and elsewhere. The woman singers at Ezra 2:65 are not listed with temple staff, nor were the dancers of Judg. 21:21. DeVaux, II, 383f. points out there is no feminine form for *kohen*. But note I Sam. 2:22 where the *Zoveot*, the women on the Temple staff may have been involved in cultic prostitution with the sons of Eli.

62. M. Kid. 1:1; M. Yeb. 2:8; M.B.M. 1:5; B.B.M. 8a; Lev. 21:7. On supporting divorced wives: Gen. R. 17:3. Amram, pp 101-131.

63. B. Shab. 14b; cf. Tobit 7:14; B. Ket. 82b; M. Git. 5:2.

64. M. Ber. 3:3; Kid. 1:7-8; T. Sot. 2:8; B. Ber. 20b; Kid. 33b-34a; M. Shab. 2:6; Gen. R. 17:8. The menstrual practices are referred to in various connections in many tractates of the Talmud, but the tractate Nidah of the sixth order of the Mishnah, Taharot is the primary source. The term *nidah*, from *nadad* in one of its primary significances means "to remove," and in Syriac usage, "to abominate." See Gesenius-Tregelles *Lexicon*, p 534, *nadad*, No. 4, and *nidah*. The biblical word refers mainly to impurity and specifically to menstrual impurity. See also Jastrow's *Dictionary*, II, 877f.; *nadah*; *piel:nidah*, to banish; and as a noun, "isolation," with special reference to menstruation. The biblical source for this aspect of purity halakhah is at Lev. 15:19-30; 12:1-8. It is clear from Lev. 15:1-17, 18, 31-33, that similar requirements for the male were of equal force for both the male and female. Yet, it is a measure of the woman's subordination that historically the onus was placed upon her observance of menstrual halakhah and no strong emphasis was placed upon the male's continued observance of these strictures after the destruction of the Temple in 70. Examples of special aspects of the cult that did not apply to women are at M. Kid. 1:8. On pilgrimage exemption, Ex. 34:23; on being called to the Torah: T. Meg. 4:11, B. Meg. 23a; the source is first century. The ultimate restriction upon women apparently stems from the first century refusal to allow her to read the Torah before the public as inappropriate, although she was allowed to be called as one of the seven honorees. See on these matters both Sigal, *Emergence* II, Appendix A, and "Women in a Prayer Quorum." In matters of civil and criminal prohibition and penalties for their violation, women enjoyed equality with men, with the exception that a woman would not be sold for theft. See M. Kid. 1:7; B. Kid. 35a; Pes. 43a; M. Sot. 3:8. Women participated in synagogue worship as is seen from *Ant.* 14:10-24 (260). This was based on Deut. 31:12; see B. Ḥag. 3a; P. Hag. 74d.

65. Cf. T. Kid. 1:10 and *beraita* at B. Kid. 33b-34a; B. Er. 27a; Pes. 43b; that women are not to study Torah: M. Sot. 3:4; B. Kid. 29b; women are exempt from the mizvah of reproduction although it is not bound to a set time, B. Yeb. 65b; that there were some who followed the lenient route in allowing female participation is seen at B.R.H. 33a where shofar is made optional for a woman though she is not obligated. This points up the true interpretation of *nashim peturot* used in the rabbinic literature: women are *exempt*, but not prohibited and hence these mizvot can become optional for them. Women are obligated to read the Megilah of Esther: M. Meg. 2:4; B. Meg. 4a, 19b; Ber. 15a; Ar. 2b-3a; this latter view is rejected at T. Meg. 2:7 and is a measure of the halakhic flux. Women's status is being almost fully equalized in the non-

orthodox denominations in Judaism. In the conservative movement, when they are not majority views, there are valid minority halakhic opinions, and therefore equally legitimate for
adoption by individuals or congregations, allowing for every
form of equality including testimony, signing religious documents, participation in all rituals of synagogue, including
the leading of worship, and at home. The only significant
lacunae at the time of this writing are the power to issue a
divorce and ordination. The latter depends upon whether the
faculty of The Jewish Theological Seminary admits women as
candidates for ordination. Women are ordained within the
Reform and Reconstructionist movements, and there too they
share equally with men in all ritual life. The movement
which styles itself "orthodox" has maintained the basic
halakhah of medieval period. Whence comes the custom of
segregating women in the synagogue is difficult to ascertain.
There are those who trace it to the Women's Court of the
Temple and to the fact that they sat on a raised gallery at
Sukot festivities, M. Suk. 5:2-4; cf. M. Mid. 2:5. Undoubtedly, however this was not designed to segregate them on a
regular basis, but rather to prevent pagan orgiastic exercises from arising, since the enthusiastic nature of those
festivities always threatened such excesses. Nevertheless,
archaeologists believe that their excavations of ancient
synagogues indicate that they had separate women's sections.
There is no hard evidence of this at Dura, however. At
Special Laws III, 31 (171) where Philo advocates seclusion
for the women he also mentions her attending worship. But
while he urges her to go through the streets when there are
few people there he does not indicate she was segregated in
the Synagogue, contrary to Baron, *History*, II, 241. See
also B.A.Z. 38a-b. It is interesting that medieval scholars
who enforced the prohibitions against women in ritual participation even read the talmudic text differently here. The
Talmud permits a gentile to participate in the cooking process
of the meal whose preparation was begun by a Jewish woman, for
instance, by stirring the contents of a pot, until "she returns from the bathhouse or the synagogue." R. Ḥananel (10th
cent.), Alfasi (R. Isaac of Fez 11th cent.), and R. Asher (13th
cent.), all read the text as "until she returns from the bathhouse or the market," eliminating the notion that women attended synagogue. But R. Yom Tov Lipman Heller noted in his
notes *Pilpuli Ḥariftah* n. 5, to R. Asher's commentary at Chap.
2, section 30, that R. Asher received his reading from Alfasi,
and that he has the text "or from the *synagogue*."

66. Generally the anti-feminism is related to sexism,
literally, in that the female is seen as a threat to the male's
piety because of her sexual attractions. Ben Sira 9:1-9; Mt.

5:28ff. with its warning by Jesus that one can commit adultery with the lustful eye is paralleled in rabbinic literature at Lev. R. 23:12; *PR* 24; Sif. Num. 115; P. Ber. 3c; B. Nid. 13b; but most especially in the words "anyone who looks intently upon a woman is as if he has come upon her," Kalah I. Many sayings can be found concerning lustful looks, potential for attraction to sexual sin, the danger of walking behind a woman or touching her hand while handing her money, and the like. See Moore, II, 267-275. On not conversing with women, M. Ab. 1:5; Cf. John 4:27. Much chagrin is often expressed over the berakhah which is part of the morning liturgy in which the worshipper thanks God "who has not made me female." While by modern standards this is a pejorative allusion to women, it must be seen in its setting as not necessarily so designed. It is provided for at T. Ber. 7:18 where the reason given is "because women are not obligated to perform the miẓvot," as also at P. Ber. 13b. Cf. B. Men. 43b. Abudraham, the medieval commentator on liturgy added (p 28) that one also thanks God he is not a woman because of her subjection to her husband who prevents her from fulfilling religious precepts even where she is able!

67. *Ag. Ap.* II, 24 (201); B.B.M. 59a; Baron, *History*, II, 239.

68. See M. Rostovtzeff, *Dura-Europos And Its Art* (Oxford: 1938); *The Dura-Europos Synagogue: A Re-Evaluation (1932-1972)*, ed. Joseph Gutmann (Missoula, Montana: 1973), and bibliography pp 157-159; *No Graven Images*, ed. Joseph Gutmann (New York: 1971) and bibliography, pp LVI-VXIII; Goodenough, *Jewish Symbols, passim.* Quotation cited by Gutmann, *No Graven Images*, p xiii.

69. *Ant.* XVIII. 8.2-9 (261-309) *War* II. 10.1-5 (184-198); Cf. B.A.Z. 43b; R.H. 24b; Meg. 29a. Gutmann, *op. cit.* p xxv. makes a telling point that when Philo writes in opposition to painting and sculpture because these crafts deceive the eyes he is really echoing Plato who was opposed to both amusement and imitative arts. His whole "Prolegomenon" is worth reading.

70. Josephus, *Ant.* XVII, 6.2-3 (151-163); *War* I, 33, 2-3 (649-653). See Gutmann, *No Graven Images*, pp 10ff.

71. This conclusion I reached in a still-unpublished paper which I have tentatively entitled "Aspects of Idolatry in Tannaitic and Patristic Literature." There I examine specifically M.A.Z. 3, and Tertullian's *De Idololatria.*

72. See the note to the A.Z. text by W. A. Elmslie, *The Mishnah on Idolatry 'Avodah Zarah'* (London: 1911); *Writings of Saint Justin Martyr*, trans. Thomas B. Falls; *The Fathers of the Church*, ed. Ludwig Schopp (New York: 1948), p 64; T.A.Z. 5 (6):1. The first halakhah requiring destruction of the images is an anonymous pericope (*stam mishnah*) and its teacher the *tanna kamma* or first teacher, both of which features generally assure that the halakhah is in accordance with that statement. This is, however, vitiated by a counter-vailing rule that when a disputing statement follows the *stam mishnah* the latter loses its precedence. See Moses Mielziner, *Introduction to the Talmud* (New York: 1968), p 191; Hermann L. Strack, *Introduction to the Talmud and Midrash*, p 21; B. San. 86a; Er. 96b; Git. 4a; Yeb. 42b; Shab. 81b, *passim*. In the face of the talmudic evidence to the contrary, Strack oversimplifies by calling the Mishnah "the authoritative norm." The Mishnah is only the repository of teaching. The norm was open for optimal selection. Frequently, in fact, as stated at B. Git. 75a, the preferred halakhah was in accordance with R. Simon b. Gamaliel II, 2nd cent., a Greek-educated rabbi with greater knowledge of the Graeco-Roman symbols and consequently the ability to distinguish between idolatrous ones and innocent art. See *JE* XI, 347f.

73. See *Tertullian*, trans. C. Dodgson, Library of the Fathers (London: 1842), p 110, Note B. See Erwin R. Goodenough, *By Light, Light*, p 257, n. 83. It should be added that even the anonymous *tanna* at M.A.Z. 3:1 who takes a stringent position only does so because he regards these images as potentially related to idolatry since they are of the sun, moon and Drakon, but he does not necessarily object to art. For the ferry: Saul Lieberman, *Hellenism*, pp 115, 120f., 127; *Texts and Studies*, p 252f.; B.A.Z. 43b; P.A.Z. 42d. For Tyche: Lieberman, *Greek*, p 171; *Hellenism*, p 134, n. 62; M.A.Z. 3:4 is explicit that a statue is proscribed only if it is to be used as an actual idol in the act of worship. Lieberman, *Hellenism*, 132, n. 40. For Gamaliel on Aphrodite: M.A.Z. 3:4; cf. 1:8 which permits fashioning ornaments even for idols as an occupation. See on economics as a motivating factor in halakhic leniency, Sigal, *New Dimensions*, Chap. VII and index "Economics."

74. Three useful books are: Bernard Bamberger, *Proselytism in the Talmudic Period* (New York: 1968) William G. Braude, *Jewish Proselyting in the First Five Centuries of the Common Era*, (Providence, R. I.: Brown University Dissertation, 1940); David M. Eichorn, *Conversion in Judaism* (New York: KTAV, 1966). See also above, Pt. 1, Chap. 2.

75. Only a few of the plethora of references are cited
here: Ex. 12:19, 48f.; Lev. 16:29; 18:26; 24:22; Num. 9:14;
Deut. 14:2; 26:11; 29:10; the *ger* is even involved in the
cult, Lev. 17:8; Num. 15:14ff.; but he must be circumcised to
participate in the paschal sacrifice, Ex. 12:48; the *toshab*,
however, is barred from it without qualification, indicating
that the *toshab* is not as acceptable as the ger. The LXX
uses either *proselytos* or *geiorais* for *ger*, and since *ger*
was not yet a full-fledged relgious convert, *proselytos* was
not yet the term for a full-fledged religious convert during
the 3rd cent. B.C. Yet Ez. 47:22 sees the *ger* along with
blood-progeny as being integrated into the tribes. Among the
Pentateuchal references cited, and many others, the Torah includes the *ger* in the observance of the Sabbath and the Day of
Atonement, leaven, certain norms of purity, sacrifices, festivals, etc. Solomon Zeitlin is way off the mark that those who
were not of ethnic Israel, descendents of Abraham, Isaac and
Jacob were not admitted to worship Yhwh. See his essay on
"Proselytism" in *Studies*, II, 407. He concedes this changed
in post-exilic times. But I think it was true always. Deut.
14:21 prohibits *nebelah* to Israelites but allows it to a *ger*,
while Lev. 17:15 implies an Israelite was permitted to eat it
as well but was then impure. At Lev. 17:13-14 blood is forbidden to the *ger*. See Finkelstein, *New Light*, p 10. That
the *ger* is a religious proselyte in rabbinic times is clear
from M.B.M. 4:10 where it is prohibited to remind the *ger* of
his ancestors' idolatry. Cf. P. Yeb. 8d.

76. The *ger* is under the love command: Lev. 19:33f; Deut.
10:19; Ex. 22:20; 23:9; equality: Ex. 12:49; 23:12; Num. 15:
16; on circumcision and covenant see above Pt.1, Ch. 2. Clearly
research is required on the question of a woman's entrance
into the covenant since her emancipation! It is my view
that this can be done through the medium of a more ritualistic
naming ceremony at the synagogue. The Christian has solved
this purpose since including women in baptism from the beginning.

77. On Onkelos and Aquila see Bamberger, pp 238f. Judith
14:10 attests to proselytism during the hellenistic era. From
the same period we have the biblical book of Esther which
tells us many converted for safety after Haman's fall. This
reflects admission of Persians in the eastern diaspora into
Judaism. The term *mumar* goes back to Jer. 2:11; B. Pes. 96a;
Suk. 56b; however, we must reckon with the fact that the
reading is not *mumar* at T. Suk. 4:28 and P. Suk. 55d but
rather, *nishtamdah*, "apostasized." At B. Pes. 96a the phrase
hamarat dat, "changing religion" is used to disqualify one
from participating in the paschal sacrifice. Cf. Zeitlin, p

410; *Ant*. XX. 7:1 (139); III Macc. 1:3; II Macc. 6:24. Philo
Spec. Laws I, 9 (51). At *QE* II, 2 Philo expresses the idea
that *prosēlytos* of Ex. 22:21 does not require circumcision.
For a brief survey of Philo on the proselyte question see
Wolfson, *Philo*, II, 352-374. Wolfson, pp 370ff. seems to interpret Philo as waiving circumcision only for the semi- or
spiritual proselyte. Zeitlin, p 411, denies there was any
rite. But Zeitlin contradicts himself by citing *Ant*. XX 2.4
(47-48) where Josephus indicates that circumcision was demanded of Izates, the converted prince of Adiabene after another
Jew had converted him without any rite.

78. Belkin, *Philo*, pp 45ff; B. Yeb. 46a-b; P. Kid. 64d.
Zeitlin, *op. cit.* p 413 argues for the introduction of proselyte baptism at famous pre-war conclave of 65 when gentiles
were declared subject to impurity in order to institute greater insulation of Jews, T. Zab. 2:1. Previously the rules of
impurity did not apply to gentiles, T. Neg. 7:10; Nid. 9:14;
Ahal. 1:4; Sifra 74d. The halakhic requirements of circumcision, immersion and sacrifice, M. Ker. 2:1, are based on
how Israel entered the covenant. Sif. Num. 108; B. Ker. 9a.
"Those who revere Heaven" are mentioned at Lev. R. 3:2, Gen.
R. 53:9. See Bamberger, pp 133-140. See Wolfson, pp 369-
374; Klausner, *From Jesus to Paul,* pp 29ff. Differences over
admitting proselytes: B. Yeb. 24b, 46b, 47a; Kid. 62b; Git.
88b. A.Z. 64b. On semi-proselytes see Saul Lieberman, *Greek
in Jewish Palestine* (New York: 1942), pp 77-90; especially,
P 81; P. Yeb. 8d; B.A.Z. 64b-65a; Ker. 9a; Gerim 3:1. P. Kid.
64d; B. Ber. 47b requiring circumcision and immersion.

79. Rom. 4:11; Ex. R. 19:5; the midrash uses the repetition of "live in your blood" at Ez. 16:6 to have the verse
refer to both bloods, that of circumcision and that of Passover, an interpretation already explicitly stated in the targums.

80. Ab. de R. N. 1; it is clear here that it was the
practice to marry proselytes, and the thrust of the lesson is
that the Jewish partner is to set a proper example of piety.
Equality: Sif. Num. 109, Sif. Deut. 281; B. Hag. 5a; M.A.Z.
1:4; B.A.Z. 13b; P.A.Z. 39c; his equality extended to his being included in the priestly atonement referred to at Ex. 28:
38.. Financial aid: Sifra 91a, 109b; Sif. Deut. 303, 110 indi
cates the *ger* is considered a full Jew for financial aid. On
witnesses to one's *gerut*: Sifra 91a; B. Yeb. 46b-47; P. Kid.
66b. The *ger* is newborn: B. Yeb. 97b-98a. Not to be re-
minded of idolatrous origins: Ger. 4:1; B.B.M. 58b, 59b;
Sifra 91a; T.B.M. 3:25; Mekh. III, 138. See also Sifra 58b;
B. Yeb. 72a-b; 46b-47b for proselyte admission rites. In

modern times an appropriate ritual is conducted with several prayers in Hebrew and English and formal documents are signed. In one the proselyte affirms his faith and in the other the presiding rabbi and two witnesses attest to the proselyte's having fulfilled the halakhic requirements. These now differ among reform, conservative and orthodox groups.

81. Braude, *op. cit.* p 22, referes to the passage at Mekh. III, 138-141 as a "litany." See further on the halakhah in reference to the proselyte, Bamberger, pp 31-123.

82. See Pt. 1, Chap. 2, III, H.

83. The rabbis take Gen. 2:17 *mot tamoot* "you will assuredly die" as more than merely a grammatical emphatic. They exegete this to signify that all humans after Adam will die, Gen. R. 16:6. At Gen. R. 30:8 there is exegesis of Gen. 3:22, "the human like one of us," where the Hebrew verb *hayah* ("has become") is deemed superfluous, and taken to signify what is signified by it elsewhere: that each person of whom it is said *hayah,* was at his end what he was at his beginning. If Adam dies it means he was pre-ordained since his pre-existence to die. He is celestial in his newly obtained knowledge, but he is different from the celestials in his destiny which is to die. This thought is expanded at Ex. R. 2:4 where Gen. 1: 2, "darkness *was* upon the abyss" is taken to mean death. Death was already present at the beginning, a built-in aspect of the cosmic reality. Life and death are compulsory, M. Ab. 4:22. Schauss, *Lifetime;* T. Gaster, *The Holy and Profane* (New York: 1955); Pt. 1, Ch. 5; A. P. Bender, "Beliefs, Rites and Customs of the Jews Connected With Death, Burial and Mourning," *JQR, Old Series* VI (1894-95), 317-47, 667-71; VII (1895-96) 101-118, 259-69. R. Meir: Gen. R. 9:5.

84. B. Ket. 103a; Ber. 18b; M. Ab. 4:16; death is sleep, Job 14:12; Dan. 12:2; freedom, B. Shab. 30b; atonement, Sif. Num. 112; M. San. 6:2; the righteous God, Num. R. 14:22 commenting on Ex. 33:20. See D. S. Russell, *The Method and Message of Jewish Apoclayptic,* p 356, with sources at Job 14:13-15; 19:25-27; Pss. 16, 49, 73, 78; Is. 24-27; Dan. 12:2; survival after death with consciousness is prolifically referred to in the intertestamental literature: Russell, pp 359, 362, 364f.; Jub. 7:29, 24:31; 23:31; I Enoch 91-104. Rabbinic view: B.R.H. 16b-17a; while Bet Hillel uses Ps. 116:6 to point to God's grace which saves from an inevitability of *gehinnom,* Zekh. 13:9 "a third will be brought through the fire. . .he'll call in my name and I will respond" is exegeted to establish the existence of temporary purgatory, and Is. 66:24 to validate permanent domicile in hell. The latter

fate is promised to *minim* (Christian Jews in the context), informers (a grave problem in Seleucid and Roman Palestine), and *apikorsim*. The last term is indefinable but refers loosely to those who reject the Torah, deny resurrection and lead the masses to sin.

85.   On respect for dead and last testaments, see B. Git. 13a; 28a; M. San. 6:2; B. Shab. 32a; San. 46b-47a; Sem. 9; M. Taan. 2:1; M. Ber. 3:1; M.K. 3:8f.   On *taharah* see Gaster, *op. cit.* pp. 164f., Sem. 8; II Chron. 16:14; Jn. 19:40.

86.   All four mourning stages are explicated at P.M.K. 83c.   *Aninut*, B. Ber. 17b ff.; B.M.K. 23b; Sem. 10; Deut. R. 9:1; B. Ber. 6a, 17b-18a; *shivah*, B.M.K. 15a-b; 23a; 27b; Ket. 6b; rending: Gen. 37:29, 34; Josh. 7:6; Job. 1:20; II Ki. 19:1; Is. 37:1; for all the practices listed, and more, see the talmudic references already cited; some biblical and intertestamental references are cited in Pt. 1, Ch. 2 and need not be repeated here.   Other select biblical references that reflect the practices of both pre-exilic and post-exilic Judaism are at II Sam. 3:31; 12:20; 13:19; 15:30; Ez. 26:16; 27:30.   Lam. 2:10; 5:15; Jer. 2:37; 6:26; 14:3-4; 16:6; Amos 8:10; Est. 6:12; Job 2:13; 30:31; Ecc. 3:4; *sheloshim:*   B.M.K. 22b-23a, 27b; a year: *ibid.*   Rabbinic sources at B.M.K. 20b indicate that the definition of "next of kin" for mourning is derived from the priest's next of kin at Lev. 21:1-3 with the addition of one's spouse.   Revisions of this halakhah of *abelut* have taken place in contemporary Judaism since the rise of Reform Judaism in the nineteenth century.   Some practices have been dropped, others modified, some simplified and others, such as the unveiling of a headstone, have been introduced.   See on this *Emergence,* Vol. IV.   The Kaddish is discussed in *Emergence,* II, and see also below, Chap. 3; its first mention as a regular part of daily liturgy is at Sof. 10:7.

CHAPTER 3

Rabbinic-Talmudic Judaism:
Theological Perspectives[1]

I. PARAMETERS

The purpose here is not to provide a systematic theology
of rabbinic Judaism. It is rather to briefly survey this
theology in its variegated rationalism, mysticism, messianic
utopianism and apocalypticism. And it will explicate the
rabbinic attitude toward sacred days and liturgy. As in the
case of my discussion of halakhah this chapter will not endeavor to separate early and late views. It is the finished
product which is presented as it is found in the compiled
rabbinic literature.

II. HISTORICAL SETTING[2]

Judaism emerged from the great war with Rome of 66-73 as
a "licit religion." Jews were free to practice their religion,
but they had to pay for this religious liberty. The Romans
appropriated the old half-shekel Temple tax and declared it
payable from all men and women from the age of three, both
in Palestine and in the Roman diaspora. This tax was directed
to the temple of Jupiter Capitolinus and became known as the
"fiscus Judaicus" because the tax was paid into a special
treasury of that name. Only those who paid it could practice
Judaism. Suetonius, speaking of the end of the first century,
indicated that those who were sympathetic to Judaism and
practiced it without becoming Jews to avoid paying the tax,
or Jews who tried to conceal their identity to escape the tax,
were prosecuted.[3]

The role the burden of this tax played in the Jewish revolt
of 115-117 near the end of Trajan's reign, is not clear. No
motive has been clarified with which to explain that revolt.
Certainly the constant payment of such a tax to a pagan temple
was a depressing reminder of the state in which Jerusalem found
itself and a provocative inspiration for messianism. Jews rebelled in North Africa (Cyrenaica and Egypt), on the island of
Cyprus, in Roman-Mesopotamia and briefly even in Palestine.

The Cyrenaican leader, Lucuas, is referred to as "king" by
Eusebius and there appears therefore, to have been a messianic
fervor involved. Lucuas does appear in Palestine at the head
of an abortive rebellion and is there executed. Aid was probably expected from Mesopotamia where Jews took advantage of
Trajan's preoccupation with Parthia by rebelling behind his
lines. Possibly the Jews thought they could upset Trajan's
victories in Parthia. It is also conceivable that the Adiabene Parthians with their interest in Judaism encouraged the
messianic rebellions as a way to overcome the threat of Trajan
consolidating his hold on the East.[4]

All these efforts failed. But this rebellion, in which
Jews are described "as if mad," underscores the continuing
messianic drive in Judaism which culminates in the Bar Kokhba
revolt less than two decades later. The Parthian connection
may indeed be important in the light of an obscure tradition
that circulated years later. It is cited with variants by
Simon b. Yohai in the second-century and R. Abba B. Kahana
in the fourth. R. Simon b. Yohai said, "If you see a Persian
horse tied among the graves of Palestine you can anticipate
the footsteps of the Messiah."[5]

Pro-nationalist militant forces were never entirely dormant.
And within a generation they followed Simon b. Cosiba to yet
another fruitless disaster.[6] The precise causes of the rebellion are not clear. But undoubtedly a major provocation
to the Jews was Hadrian's decision around 130 to rebuild
Jerusalem as Aelia Capitolina. Jews feared that a new pagan
capital on the site of Jerusalem spelled the ultimate end of
their dream for a restoration of the Jewish cult in a rebuilt
Temple. Such a fear could lead them to a last-ditch effort
to prevent the move by overthrowing the Romans.[7] Gamaliel II
had died. The more militant Galileans and Shammaites had
meanwhile gained supremacy within rabbinic Judaism.[8]

A matter of some debate in scholarly circles is the question
whether Hadrian introduced his measures to suppress Judaism before the revolt, thus provoking the revolt, or as punishment
for the revolt. The removal of Yohanan ben Zakkai from leadership in the eighties, and the diaspora outbreak in 115-117
certainly are two symptoms of a continuing nationalist mili-
tancy among Jews. This, like the combined civil war and revolt of 66-73 was an admixture of religious messianism and
secular nationalism. Rabbinic literature attributed anti-
religious attitudes to Bar Kokhba, accusing him of rejecting
God's help in battle, thus exhibiting a consciousness that
secular nationalism was an ingredient of the Bar Kokhba war
and retroactively disassociating the rabbis from him. It
also helps explain rabbinic opposition centered in such men

as R. Eliezer of Modim and R. Joshua b. Hananyah. The remark
of R. Pinḥas b. Yair who is reported to have said "since the
destruction of the Temple. . .advocates of arm and tongue
grew powerful. . ." may be a reference to the type of demagogu-
ery that urged the violence that culminated in the Bar Kokhba
rebellion.[9]

The foregoing remarks lead to my supposition that had the
Hadrianic persecutions preceded the revolt there would have
been greater rabbinic inclination to resist what was virtually
the suppression of Judaism. Hadrian was a cosmopolitan in
the style of Alexander the Great and Antiochus IV Epiphanes.
He provides a symbol of his emulation of Antiochus by his interest in a temple for Antiochus at Athens.[10] But Antiochus,
as we saw in Pt. 1, Ch. 5, introduced his suppressive legislation after rebellion stirred in Jerusalem and his chosen
High Priest was deposed. Hadrian's actions, therefore, may
also be presumed to have been introduced as punishment. The
revolt must have been provoked by Hadrian's decision to trans-
form Jerusalem into a pagan capital. This view has the ancient attestation of Dio Cassius. On the other hand Eusebius
sees this decision on the part of Hadrian as one made in the
post-revolt period.[11] The solution of this dilemma may be
to see Hadrian's decision in two phases. At first he decided
to rebuild Jerusalem in 130 as Aelia. This was sufficiently
provocative to Jews and brought on the revolt. But he did
not decide to place the Temple of Jupiter on the site of the
old Jewish Temple until after the war when he did so as
punishment for the revolt. And at the same time he began to
introduce his series of suppressive proscriptions against
Judaism.[12] This is to be seen as supported by references in
rabbinic literature to friendly communication with Hadrian
during his visit of 130.[13] It is all the more interesting
that these conversations are generally recorded as having
taken place with R. Joshua b. Ḥananiah, the perennial leader
of pacifistic forces, a survivor from the Romanophile circles
around Yoḥanan b. Zakkai.

The Bar Kokhba rebellion broke out in 132, and ended in
135 after less than three years. The name given to Simon b.
Cosiba in history, Bar Kokhba, "son of the star," is derived
from Akiba's hailing him as the "King Messiah" which was
taken as fulfillment of the words at Numbers 24:17, "a star
will step forth from Jacob." This verse was taken in an eschatological way in both targums and Qumran literature.[14]
From Justin we know that there were refugees who fled the war,
choosing not to participate (D. 1:3). From Bar Kokhba letters
we know that some Jews outside of Palestine refused to fight
and even profiteered from the rebels.[15]

Once again the Jews experienced calamity. The ancient historian Dio claims population loss was so astronomical that Judaea was depopulated. More important, Jerusalem was closed to Jews and Christian Jews, and temples to Jupiter and to Hadrian himself were erected on the site of the old Temple. The Christian community ceased being Jewish and Palestinian Christianity now became gentile like diaspora Christianity. To complete the job of de-Judaizing Palestine and preventing a resurgence of the Yhwh cult in a substitute Jerusalem, Hadrian also built a temple of Jupiter on Samaritan Mt. Gerizim. Furthermore, now was introduced the notorious Hadrianic persecution which is extensively embedded in rabbinic literature and which deeply influenced the course of rabbinic Judaism. The persecution consisted of torture and death meted out to anyone who violated the imperial proscription against circumcision, the observance of the Sabbath, ordination of rabbis and study of the Torah.[16] After the revolt R. Akiba underwent his dramatic personal martyrdom following his imprisonment at Caesarea.[17] The martyrdom of Akiba marks the last effort at Judean national independence until modern times. Akiba breathed his last professing the shemá, the oneness of God. This may be seen as symbolic of the transformation of the messianic-nationalist into the preacher of the Kingdom of God. Henceforth Judaism becomes what it started out to be, a medium of salvation-history, the expression of a religious association. The work of Yoḥanan ben Zakkai at Yavneh is now vindicated. Messianic faith remains a tenet of Judaism, but it recedes into the background, no longer a matter of immediate urgency and until modern times regarded as something not achievable through human action.

The center of a restored rabbinic Judaism moved to Usha in Galilee around 140, the climate for Judaism having improved almost immediately upon the death of Hadrian and the accession of Antoninus Pius as Roman Emperor in 138.[18] Academies were later established at Sepphoris and Tiberius. But meanwhile Usha became the center of leadership under R. Simon III, son of Gamaliel II. He received the post of Nasi, and it remained in his family by heredity until it was abolished by the Romans in the fifth century. The Nasiate, or as usually referred to, the Patriarchate, served in some respects as a central religious focus for all of world-wide Judaism. Even the Babylonian community at first accepted its authority in such basic aspects of religious life as calendar regulation. This was of especial significance since it enabled all Jews to observe their holy days at the same time and so contributed to similarity of worship, preventing radical geographic disintegration of Judaism into fragmentary bodies. Nevertheless, as is evident from analysis of the Palestinian and Babylonian Talmuds, there was wide divergence in many matters, precluding the rise

of a monolithic Judaism or a papal-like religious structure.
Furthermore, after the death of R. Judah I, editor of the Mishnah, rabbis other than the Nasi actually presided over the
academies, decided halakhah and served as spiritual leaders
even to the degree of appointing ecclesiastical judges who decided religious litigation. References to one or another
Nasi sometimes indicate the office had fallen to low estate
and was virtually dominated by rabbis. Even R. Judah himself,
known as "Rabbi" par excellence, did not have his way with the
halakhah in his own Mishnah.[19]

Jewish communities proliferated in Asia Minor, especially
at Sardis, at Smyrna, Ephesus, Magnesia and Philadelphia; and
at Antioch in Syria. As late as the end of the fourth century
Judaism was so attractive in Antioch that John Chrysostom delivered a series of sermons to obviate Jewish influence upon
Christianity. Sardis in Asia Minor yielded the largest synagogue ever discovered by archaeologists and the most Jewish
inscriptions found in the diaspora, outside of Rome. Dura-
Europos at the gate to Parthia was another major Jewish center
which yielded important archaeological finds for our understanding of the status of art in Judaism. Nisibis and Edessa
were significant centers in the east. Nisibis was probably
the first real center of rabbinic Judaism. To Nehardea
further south came R. Akiba to declare the calendar late in
the first century. From early beginnings in Nisibis under R.
Judah b. Bathyra before 70, the Parthian Jewish community
evolved into one of the major communities of Judaism's history.[20]

It has been shown that life was relatively normal for the
Jews in Palestine during the third and fourth centuries, and
that historians' assessments of major uprisings by Jews or
major persecutions by the Romans are unfounded. One scholar
has written,

> "Nothing can be found in the entire
> Rabbinic literature of the third and
> fourth centuries from which we might
> legitimately conclude that the Roman
> government deliberately persecuted the
> Jewish religion at that time. Conjec-
> tures by some Jewish scholars. . .are
> unfounded."

There was oppressive taxation and life was difficult. But
there was no specific impediment to Judaism, and the third
and fourth centuries is the period when the Palestinian
Talmud arose.[21]

The fourth century is the watershed in the relationship between Judaism and Christianity. The triumph of Christianity through the conversion of Emperor Constantine in 312 and the rise to power of Christian clergy spelled misfortune for Jews and Judaism. That which we know as the medieval subordination of Jews and Judaism based upon the views expressed in the Epistle of Barnabas, began to slowly pervade the relationship of the Christian Empire with Judaism from the time of Constantine forward, The Christian theological tradition emphasized the inferiority of Judaism considering it merely as a foreshadowing of Christianity. Basing himself upon an extreme interpretation of Paul's attitude toward the Torah, but using language distant in phrase and spirit from Paul, the fifth-century Alexandrian theologian, Cyril, referred to the Torah as "rubbish." As Judaism continued to flourish after the rise of Christianity its very life and expansion became a source of theological tension for Christianity. The solution of the pre-medieval Church was two-sided. It maintained that Jews are witnesses to Jesus through the Old Testament, but that in terms of the New Testament must survive only to be reconciled with the Church. Therefore, Jews must suffer appropriate punishment for their sins, most especially for the sin of the crucifixion of Jesus, but they must be allowed to continue to exist in order that they come to faith in Jesus. This attitude governed the next fourteen hundred years with little interruption, until the French Revolution.[22]

Church councils and imperial legislation both dealt with Jews. The councils reflect and seek to obviate extensive "Judaization" in Christianity which ran the gamut from intermarriage between Jews and Christians to Christians, including clergy, joining in synagogue worship and participation in festival celebrations. Imperial legislation reflects the ongoing effort to subordinate Judaism and Jews in political, social and economic matters, and abort any expansion through the acquisition of proselytes or slaves. Nevertheless, Jews were in a better condition than heretics. Jews were legal. Heretics were illegal and were dealt with violently.[23]

The rise of Christianity to supremacy must be seen as the cause for the decline of Palestinian Judaism relative to that of non-Christian Babylonia. Undoubtedly that had much to do with the publication of the calendar by Hillel II in 359. It should be noted that the Council of Nicaea in 325 ordered that Easter must be uniformly observed on the Sunday following the first full moon after the vernal equinox (March 21). The date was not to coincide with the Jewish Passover when many eastern churches observed it. The churches of Asia Minor were accustomed from earliest times to observe Easter on the

night of the fourteenth-fifteenth of Nisan regardless of the
day of the week, while Rome always observed the crucifixion
on Friday and the resurrection on Sunday. The *quartodecimans*,
those who continued to observe the Christian Passover on the
fourteenth of Nisan were condemned as heretics. The consequence of this decision at the Nicene Council was that
government authorities, bound by Emperor Constantine's Council
of Nicaea, opposed the messengers from Jerualsm who travelled
to the diaspora to announce the new moon of Nisan and the
date of Passover, especially since the observance of Easter
on the Jewish date continued in Syria, Cilicia and Mesopotamia.[25] We have a report in the Talmud of a coded message
to the Amora Raba (280-352). Messengers were sent by the Nasi
from Tiberius to announce the intercalation of the year, were
apprehended by the Roman authorities, but escaped (B. San.
10a). This undoubtedly reflects a time between 325 and 352
when Raba died, when on the strength of the Nicene decision to
prevent the observance of Easter on the date of Passover, the
imperial authorities prohibited the Nasi from publically an-
nouncing the Passover date. Since this prohibition was designed to assure the uniformity of the date of Easter observance among Christians, the rabbis concluded that a permanent
calendar must be published and the old system of annual proc-
lamations and special public announcements of intercalated
years, must be given up. Thus Hillel II published the permanent Jewish ritual calendar still in use today. Council decrees, and imperial legislation, all accelerated exhorbitant
taxation and economic oppression, and were sources of continuing deterioration in Judaic life. This explains the decline
of the schools in Palestine leading to the early and hasty
compilation of the Palestinian Talmud around 380-400 and to
the decline in the status of the patriarchate and its aboli-
tion in 429, four years after the death of the last Nasi,
Gamaliel VII.[26]

III. ASPECTS OF RABBINIC THEOLOGY

A. *Prefatory Comments*

The basic Judaic theology antedated the compilation of
both the Palestinian and Babylonian Talmuds. Nevertheless,
cultural conditions influence the thinking of scholars and
lead to theosophical and theological speculations that issue
forth in restatement or innovation of doctrine. For this
reason we find some theological difference between the two
Talmuds. The compilers of the Palestinian Talmud almost entirely exclude angelology and demonology, subjects which are
found extensively in the Babylonian Talmud. Perhaps the

Babylonians, under Zoroastrian influence, believed more
vigorously in these celestial beings and in their roles in
life and history, or they made more space for them in their
literature because of the popular culture. This is hard to
determine. It is equally difficult to ascertain whether
Palestinian rabbis gave no credence at all to these matters
and therefore omitted them from their literature. Obviously
this material did circulate in Palestine, not only in the
apocryphal works which were excluded from the canon, but in
the midrashic material which was later brought together in
various compilations. What has been said for angelology and
demonology may also be said for sorcery, magic, astrology, and
other elements commonly placed in the category of superstition.[27]

B. *A Survey of Aspects of Rabbinic Doctrines*

   1. *Cautions*

   It is reasonably safe to say that the rabbis of Palestine
and Babylonia taught the same basic theology. Both rooted
themselves in scripture and found support there for important
doctrines in Judaism. In the body of their teaching, however,
the astute student will find the rabbis sometimes differed
on particulars of theological interpretation. In such cases
frequently divergent opinions have remained legitimate versions of doctrine in Judaism. That part of ágadah which is
theology or doctrine, that is, the content of faith, therefore, is found to have a degree of diversity as has halakhah,
the content of practice.

   The theological literature from which we draw the content of faith or theology, the Talmuds and the midrashim, were
developed,[28] gathered and compiled over a period of many centuries. The rabbis of all these centuries formulated and
reformulated what we read there. In the process of restatement it is also possible for a teacher to reinterpret and
thereby change the content of the teaching. Polemics with
both gentile Christianity and Christian Judaism, with gnosticism, Hellenism, Zoroastrianism and its later Western form
of Mithraism, also affected proto-rabbinic and rabbinic
thought.

   There is in rabbinic theology a fluidity, as one
scholar has called it, that makes it impossible to accomodate
the mass of material to modern western systematic categories.[29]
It must be borne in mind that the rabbis expressed their theology in pithy apothegms and even in the course of halakhic

explanations. One must consider that in surveying rabbinic
theology one is really presenting a synthesis drawn from many
sources. As one writer has aptly phrased it,

> "The literature forms a large and chaotic
> museum containing many exhibits from which
> these pages will not attempt to wipe the
> dust of the ages."[30]

In the following account of rabbinic theology we can only
touch upon some significant aspects of several doctrines.

2. *The Doctrine of God*

Every theology, by virtue of its connection with the
Greek word *theos,* God, begins with a doctrine of God. Judaism begins with an implicit doctrine of the existence of God
in the very first line of its sacred literature, "In the
beginning, God (*elohim*) created. . ." (Gen. 1:1). A doctrine
of God as sole creator of all elements of the universe is
here presupposed. The very first paragraph of the Mishnah
presupposes the doctrine of God, and presents the companion
doctrine that human obedience to the sovereignty of His will
is the beginning of all faith by introducing the halakhah
concerning the reading of the shemá.[31] In this way the rabbis present the theological categories which are of the utmost
concern in all theology, the doctrine of God and the human relationship to Him. The human accepts upon himself the "yoke
of the kingdom of heaven," better phrased as the sovereignty
of God. In Judaism this God is defined as one and unique,
eternal, omnipotent, omniscient, omnipresent, both immanent
and transcendent, fully righteous, just and holy, abundant in
love and compassion. Sometimes attributes of God become contradictory, such as love and justice, but the resultant mystery aroused by inner theological contradiction is acceptable
to the believer. God's activity is found in creation, revelation and redemption, and his creative-redemptive characteristics are manifest in a continuing providence. All of these
characteristics are clear from scripture and are found abun-
dantly reiterated throughout rabbinic literature.[32] The rabbis connected sin with a loss of faith in God by maintaining
that "radical denial," that is, denial of the existence of
God, is closely related to the violation of the moral precepts
as well as the theological doctrines of retribution and the
divine love. The paradigm for this in targum is Cain.[33]

In the process of its struggle for survival after the
catastrophe of 70 A.D. rabbinic Judaism emphasized a purist

monotheism. Rabbinic theology attempted to exclude any dualism that could lead to a theory of *shtai reshuyot*, "two autho-
ities" or "powers" in the universe. The philosophical neces-
sity to provide for a mediator between a transcendent deity
and human beings, and to deny that a loving god can be the
source of evil and adversity influenced the introduction of
divine powers other than God in a mediational role. Philo attributes the dualism of separate sources of good and evil to
the Essenes, and despite scriptural evidence that the God of
Israel is the source of evil, the rabbis emended Is. 45:7,
changing God the maker of peace and creator of evil to "I make
peace and create all things," oblivious to the possibility
that this implies there is another source of evil.[34] The idea
of two authorities, one each respectively in control of the
beneficent and adverse aspects of life has its complete ear-
ler expression in Zoroastrian dualism. Its later expression
is found in gnosticism. The later all-pervasive philosophy
posited the idea that an evil god created the world and only
the elect who gain *gnosis* (knowledge) of the true transcendent
Unknown God and thereby can return to their celestial home,
are able to experience salvation.[35]

It is, however, extremely obscure as to whom the rabbis
address and polemicize against when they discuss dualism. The
objects of their opposition can be Philo's theosophy which
also admitted a dualistic principle, Christianity, gnosticism,
Judaic sectarianism or Persian Zoroastrianism. Later rabbis
might be employing against Christianity or gnosticism earlier
traditions used against Zoroastrianism. Sometimes they specifically name Zoroastrians when referring to *magi*. They might
refer to Hellenism, or they might simply be quarreling with
dualistic tendencies within rabbinic Judaism. One must be
aware that dualism existed side by side with monotheism and
that it was also part of Qumran theology and of rabbinic Judaism. A "two spirit" theology is apparent in the Testaments of
the Twelve Patriarchs and at Qumran, as well as in the rabbinic concept of the *yezer hara* and *yezer hatob*, the evil impulse
and the good impulse which struggle for control of the human
mind and conduct. The significant distinction between legitimate dualism and heretical dualism in rabbinic polemic against
a "two authorities" theology must be borne in mind. The rabbis opposed any concept that implied that another heavenly
being was an authority independent of God.[36]

And yet, even after that is said, one must be cautious in
how to interpret the heavenly being Metatron, and how to deal
with the concept of Shekhinah and Holy Spirit in rabbinic Judaism. For unlike gnosticism Christianity never affirmed two
deities; and conversely rabbinic Judaism never eliminated two

or more celestial manifestations on earth. But what the rabbis attempted to do was to identify each celestial figure that appears in or is exegeted from scripture, either as a subordinate being to God, or at times as in the case of the Shekhinah and Holy Spirit, as virtually God Himself. It is likely that most frequently the rabbis used these terms, as well as other terms used by targumists, such as *memrà* and *yekarà* to combat "two authorities" theology by referring them all to the Presence of God Himself. The rabbis were obviously confronted by the very suggestive passage at Daniel 7:9-14, which appears to describe two thrones and two divine beings, one with superior authority who invests this authority in another. They denied the implications of this by citing other scriptural verses that emphasize the "soleness" of God. Ultimately the midrash teaches that "the angel of Yhwh" always signifies the Shekhinah. For the rabbis the Shekhinah was usually God. But it is also possible at times that the Shekhinah is a detached entity, as is the Holy Spirit.[37]

According to Philo God used the *logos* to make the world, and this *logos* is the pattern from which all other beings were made. This is how Philo interprets Gen. 1:27, "God made the human after the image of God" (Gen. 9:6), that God made the human according to God's image, which is the *logos*.[38] Elsewhere he calls the *logos* the beginning (*arkhē*) as does Justin; and highly reminiscent of this is John 1:1 where the evangelist combines the *arkhē*, the beginning, with the *logos*, "In the beginning was the Word." Philo writes, "The *logos* is the image of God through whom the cosmos was framed," as John writes "Through him all things came into being." Both are obviously midrashizing Genesis 1 where all creation is the product of the word of God. But the affinity of their phraseology is of some importance. It points to the possible reason for rabbinic polemic against all such hellenistic categories of thought. They did not object that by God's word all things came into being. That was obviously scripture. They objected to how *logos* was hypostatized in hellenistic Judaism and then identified with Jesus in Christianity. This impelled them to abandon Philo and suppress him from their literature. But this polemic is post-70. It is not part of proto-rabbinic Judaism contemporary with the rise of Christianity, but of Yavnean rabbinism.[39]

According to the rabbis, God had no partner in creation. Although they argue this vigorously they only prove that Adam was not the partner and in no way refute the hellenistic idea of a pre-universe creation of the *logos* which becomes the partner, nor do they refute the function of *ḥokhmah* (wisdom) as partner in creation and even as the creator, known to us from biblical and intertestamental sources. One targumist translated *bereshit* at Gen. 1:1 as "by wisdom," interpreting *reshit* in the light of Prov. 8:22 where Wisdom personified says she was the beginning of God's creation. Later the midrash takes Wisdom to be synonymous with Torah, as it is by Ben Sira and elsewhere in intertestamental literature, and the midrash presents the Torah as saying that God used her to create the world.[40]

It was not possible for rabbis to eliminate entirely the elements that led from hellenistic theosophical speculations to gnostic and Christological ideas, any more than they could then or later eliminate anthropomorphism. Scripture presents God in human form and frequently interchanges Him with an angel. During the hellenistic period biblical Daniel and apocryphal apocalyptic writings present a human-like divine figure called "son of man." The hellenistic traditions coupled with the apocalyptic ideas spoke of "second god" who was a demiurge, partner of God in creation, and finally believe it to be incarnated in Jesus. This line of thought reaches its apogee in Johannine Christianity and it is quite likely that the rabbinic polemic which seems to appear in tannaitic literature toward the end of the first century is aimed at this, more so than at gnosticism. The terminology of the rabbis in which they argue against "two authorities" can apply equally to the Iranian and gnostic powers of good and evil and to the Christian equation of God the Father with Jesus the son. The rabbis countered the concept that God's names stood for his attributes of justice *midat hadin* and mercy, *midat haraḥamim* (Elohim and Yhwh respectively) to the notion that there were two authorities.[41]

Mention must be made here of Christian Jewish polemic against gnosticism as well. Peter is represented as arguing that the two *middot* of God, the attributes of goodness and justice belong to the same One God who is the only God. Peter is there in conflict with Simon Magus who represents all of gnosticism. Jesus is also represented as reciting the shema to Simon to confirm the existence of the Only God. Thus, it is argued that at least in its major form known to us Ebionism, the Christian Judaism of the Pseudo-Clementine literature was as anti-gnostic as rabbinic Judaism.[42]

One can find neither precision nor a monolithic approach in rabbinic literature. The Bat Kol, Holy Spirit, and Shekhinah all at times seem to be personified and enjoy an existence separate from God, but all also appear at other times to be a manifestation of God Himself, and coidentical with him.[43] To speak in dualistic terms in the sense of referring

to intermediaries between God and the world is a perfectly
normal Judaic way of discussing God and his activities, and
is evident all through the Old Testment. Thus, in reference
to who will be the celestial power that will help Moses to
lead Israel in the wilderness, God tells Moses it will be "my
malakh," and that "I will not go up in your midst." The
malakh (angel) of Yhwh is not coidentical with Him. But Moses
complains that God has not identified the *malakh* and God declares that it is *Panai*. This is an enigmatic verse. Onkelos
translates "Shekhinah" but the Palestinian Targum takes the
word to refer to God's anger, and translates the phrase "*Panai*
will go" to mean "the face of my displeasure will go away,"
and implies that after that Yhwh Himself will lead.

The targumists and the rabbis used the terminology of
dualism but they rejected any construction being placed upon
the texts that implied the existence of separate *independent*
celestial authorities. In this sense their monotheism remained purist. They used dualistic language, speaking of
separate personified entities to overcome the problem of God's
transcendence and to make more vivid his immanence. But they
did this within the parameters of Is. 43:10 "Before me no God
was formed, and after me there will not be," and 44:6, "I am
the first and the last; other than me there is no god."

Idolatry was present all around the rabbis. They mocked
the multiplicity of names of gods and the abundance of cults.
But their interest in idolatry was not so much to ridicule it
as to discuss the practices, rites and holy days in reference
to halakhic problems these presented to Jews in social and
economic matters. The rabbis were knowledgeable of pagan
mystery cults, but do not attack these as the church fathers
do because they have no relationship to Judaic rites while
they bear a degree of resemblance to the Christian faith in
a dying and rising saviour. Yet, from the rabbis' use of the
term *mysterion* to describe both circumcision and the Mishnah,
each as the *mysterion* of God, it is evident they were aware
of the religious significance attached to the word. In the
sacrificial rite of circumcision and in obedience to the interpretive torah they found that special element of mystery
in the relationship of God with the Jews.[44]

Nevertheless, along with this purist monotheism went many
appellations for God. We have already met with Holy Spirit,
Shekhinah and Bat Kol. There were a number of others ued as
metonymies such as "Heaven," and "Makom" (The One who chose
His place, or He who dwells in all Place, or Space).[45] These
contrast the transcendence and immanence of God which never
appeared contradictory to the rabbis. In all it has been

calculated that the rabbis used some seventy synonyms for God. This is an underestimation for others who find ninety.[46] But the important thing about these names is that each expresses a concept of God or describes an attribute of the deity, and in essence supersedes a pagan nature-deity. By understanding God and speaking of Him in these multifarious ways the rabbis established monotheism on a firm footing for Jews in the Western and Byzantine Roman Empires and contributed to the rise of Islam and its conquest of the Parthian-Babylonian east.[47]*

The rabbis sought to avoid the use of the actual proper name of God, Yhwh. This was probably due to various reasons. Perhaps there was a desire to prevent its use in magic, or to protect it from trivialization and desecration.[48] The result was the prolific use of the substitute synonyms for God and the institutionalization of the pronunciation *Adonai*, "Lord," instead of Yhwh. It is apparent that in rabbinic times there was lacking a clear explanation for reading Yhwh as Adonai and a definitive way to pronounce Yhwh. Thus, some rabbis speculate on whether the true proper name of God has four or twelve letters. They exegete Ex. 3:15 "this is my name forever" to refer to Yhwh, and "this is my commemoration for all generations" to refer to Adonai. A tradition is also cited that the Hebrew word *leòlam* (forever) in that verse is to be read *leàllam*, "to conceal," that the true Name Yhwh is to be concealed and when God's name is uttered it is to be uttered or commemorated with the reading Adonai (B. Kid. 71a).

The rabbinic view of the nearness of God is evident in their rejection of the need for angelic intercession. The worshipper or penitent, or person suffering adversity was told that he can cry out directly to God and need not plead with the celestial patrons of Israel, Michael and Gabriel, to intercede for him. God is said to bless bridegrooms, adorn brides, visit the sick and bury the dead, and humans are to emulate him.[49]

3. *The Doctrine of Redemption*

a. *Humans And Their Destiny--The Afterlife and Resurrection.*[50]

The doctrine of redemption refers to the individual's redemption from adversity and the ultimate oblivion of death,

* See Excursus at note 47.

and to the messianic expectation of the elect community, Israel. The sequence of the paragraphs of the amidah from the fourth prayer through the ninth, for knowledge, the inspiration to repent, forgiveness, redemption, healing, and prosperity, points to a segment of the amidah intimately related to the destiny of the individual. Some rabbis clearly interpreted the juxtaposition of the prayer for redemption with that of forgiveness to imply that those who originated the amidah designed the prayer for redemption as one for the individual (P. Ber. 4d).

Individual redemption or salvation does not require the observance of the mythical "six-hundred and thirteen commandments." No member of the Judaic faith was ever obligated to that number. The calculation merely attempts to summarize all the miẓvot that one can extract from the Torah, both the positive precepts and the prohibitions. But some of these apply to the priest, the levite, the master, the farmer, the employer, the child, the parent, the husband, the wife and so forth. There is no one individual of any status or occupation who is subjected to six hundred and thirteen. Salvation of the individual does not depend upon a statistical marathon. The great number of available miẓvot are opportunities, not absolute mandates, for salvation. The person who may be deprived of salvation is the one who fulfills no miẓvah at all. Even the fulfillment of one miẓvah in a consistent life-long pattern of excellence will win salvation for the individual (M. Kid. 1:10).[51] One rabbi even ventured a Paul-like suggestion that one's salvation may be achieved by faith alone, citing the same verse as Paul uses, "the righteous shall life by his faith." This comes from the fourth-century R. Nahman b. Isaac (B. Pes. 104a-b); but he was known as an accurate and expert transmitter of traditions, and implies that the Pauline tradition that faith is central in salvation was an alternative Judaic notion in the time of Paul. A corollary to this is that God grants grace and saves those who lack deeds. Even R. Matya b. Ḥeresh who stressed that deeds are required for salvation merely had in mind such salvific covenantal and sacramental acts as the paschal lamb and circumcision, not the piling up of a multiplicity of good deeds and the accumulation of merits.[52] Nevertheless rabbinic literature reflects a variety of efficacious merits. The merits of righteous ancestors (*zekhut aḅot* and *imahot*) assist descendants and the merits of children assist parents; the merits of the righteous (*zekhut ẓadikim*), assist society as a whole. Both merit and grace function side by side in Judaism, and play a role in the salvation of the soul as they do in the redemption of the people Israel.

It is an axiom in Judaism that the crown of God's creation is the human being. The Bible teaches that the human is created in the image of God and that the initial creation of but one human signifies that every human stands in equal status before God. Nobody, it is clear, can claim greater or purer ancestry when all look back to a common ancestor. Yet each human, though produced from the same mold as every other human, is unique.[53]

That the human is a body-soul composite, that the soul is from God, and is therefore divine, are early tannaitic beliefs. They are already current in Philo. Philo writes, ". . .the body was made through the Artificer taking clay and molding out of it a human form. . .that which He breathed in was nothing else than a Divine breath. . ."[54] That it should not be read off as a Philonic diaspora idea, but was current in Palestine also is evidenced by the fact that Josephus could expound upon it to his Palestinian audience.[55] But Philo and the rabbis differed on whether the human body was actually created by God. Philo takes God's consultation with others, "let *us* make the human" (Gen. 1:26) to signify that God used fellow-workers and that the latter are responsible for man's evil thoughts or deeds. Some of the rabbis, at least, stressed that God created the human directly.[56]

There is disagreement over whether there was also current a theory of the pre-existence of souls. One view is that this is a corollary of the immortality of souls. For that which is imperishable is also uncreated and is a segment of divinity itself. On the other hand there is a view that souls can become extinct, and a reference to souls yet to be created. One scholar has said, "Any attempt to systematize the Jewish notions of the hereafter imposes upon them an order and consistency which does not exist in them."[57] Thus one view is that at death the righteous souls are sent to be with God, and the wicked souls to a place of punishment. That there is a treasury or store-chamber for the souls of the righteous where they await resurrection, while those of the wicked are flung about carelessly and go zooming in the atmosphere, is inferred from the verse ". . .may the soul of my lord be bound up in the bundle of life, with the Lord your God, while He hurls the souls of your enemies as from the hollow of a sling" (I Sam. 25:29).[58] Frequently the place where the righteous souls stay is called *gan èden*, "the Garden of Eden," or Paradise. The latter is derived via the Greek *paradeisos* from the Persian *pairi-daeza*, "an enclosure" or park. The place where the souls of the wicked are punished is called *gehinnom*. Even a man of the status of Yohanan ben Zakkai was uncertain where his soul would go, whether to *gan èden* or *gehinnom*. The term *gehinnom* is derived from *ge hinnom*, the valley or glen that belonged to Hinnom. This was south of Jerusalem and there Molokh was worshipped and the wastes of the Temple cult were annihilated by fire.[59] Some maintain the stay in hell is for one year; others, that it lasts only seven weeks (M. Ed. 2:10). Some refer to this intermediate stage between life in this world and resurrection, the time of the soul's residence in heaven or hell, as "the World to Come" or *òlam habà*. Those who maintain that the souls of the righteous enter a storehouse for safekeeping until resurrection define *òlam habà* as the time after the advent of the Messiah. In this case the periods of this world and the hereafter are: this world of history (*òlam hazeh*), the days of the Messiah, the time of judgment after resurrection, the world to come (*òlam habah*), or *leàtid labò*, the coming future. At this time of *àtid*, the future, or in the world to come, the souls are reunited with resurrected bodies. But there is also a third usage of *òlam habà*, and this is to describe the messianic period itself, the paradisiacal existence in this world of history.[60]

The doctrine of resurrection is one of great import in the tannaitic period. No dogma is enunciated concerning the soul, how to define eschatological terms or of the messianic idea. But a dogma is declared of the concept of resurrection (M. San. 10:1; B. San. 90a), and it is even insisted that the doctrine is to be found in the Torah (B. Pes. 68a; San. 91b). Those who stress this doctrine exegete it emphatically from verses throughout scripture, and do not leave it to be derived only from the several texts where it is obvious. From the Danielic idea of a resurrection of the dead of Israel some of whom will enjoy eternal life and others damnation, is derived the later concept that both righteous and wicked will arise to judgment. Since it is believed that Elijah will herald the Messiah, Elijah is believed to be the mediating figure who revives the dead, or is at least present at the revivification of the dead. In this view the resurrection of the dead may precede the messianic advent. These are further symptoms of the absence of a consistent and systematic set of doctrines related to eschatology, and the presence of a wide variety of ancillary beliefs that accompanied the basic doctrine of resurrection.[61]*

Other ambiguities prevail. Some maintain that gentiles will not share in the World to Come, all of them being on a plane with wicked Jews who are deprived of salvation. Others hold the view that righteous gentiles will share in the World to Come along with righteous Jews. They also differ over

*See excursus at n. 61.

whether gentile children will attain the World to Come. One who denies them this privilege is the same R. Gamaliel of Yavneh who was instrumental in excluding Christianity from Judaism and in attempting to formulate an "orthodoxy" in rabbinic Judaism. These ambiguities are illustrated by the differences of opinion in an earlier period between Bet Shammai and Bet Hillel. The sages of both schools agree on the fate of the righteous and the wicked after final judgment, the one marked for bliss, the other for damnation. But they disagree over what will occur with the souls of those who are neither righteous nor wicked, an intermediate group. Shammaites maintain that they will enter hell and there endure some degree of purgation and then emerge. Hillelites argue that God will grant mercy to them and they will escape *gehenna*.[62]

In matters related to personal redemption just discussed as well as in matters related to collective redemption soon to be discussed, the rabbis build upon scripture, and also show affinities for the ideas of the apocryphal literature which we discussed earlier. Apocalyptic literature after Daniel was excluded from the rabbinical canon but remnants of it are found in ȧgadic sources and it is clear that the rabbis shared much of its mysticism and eschatology. The famous story of four who entered paradise is a rabbinic version of the apocalyptic pattern where revelation is made in a vision and is interpreted to the prophet by an angel, or the visionary tours the heavens and secret areas of the earth, having all he sees explained to him.[63] Although these books may be included in the books called *ḥizonim*, "outside books," which were placed on a prohibited index by some rabbis, much of their substance is found in rabbinic *ȧgadah* and in later midrashim.

Perhaps the most famous passage is that of the four who entered Paradise. Not only modern scholars differ on how this is to be taken. Rashi (R. Solomon b. Isaac, 11th cent.) and his grandsons who wrote the supplementary notes to the Talmud, Tosafot, reflect the same difference in the middle ages. Rashi writes that they went up into heaven; the tosafists write that it only appeared so to them; in other words, the latter maintain it was a dream-vision. Other medieval scholars enlisted on both sides of the argument. But it is clear from the talmudic tradition that this is similar to the apocalyptic ascents of a seer through the seven heavens, and the dangers attendant upon such an ascent.[64]

The Talmud relates that the well-known Akiba and his colleague Elisha ben Abuyah, who is famous as Aher, "the Other," that is, one who has become an adherent of another belief, along with two others, Ben Azai and Ben Zoma, entered Paradise. This clearly means they took a journey through the heavens. The passage is by no means clear after modern attempts to clarify it with the use of mystical texts. But it is clear that the *pardes* in the passage is a heavenly region. For we are told that Aḥér there saw Metatron and that the incident took place "on high." Further on we are informed that Akiba "went up unhurt and went down" despite the desire of the angels to hurt him. God, however, prevented the celestial forces from hurting Akiba because, He said, Akiba is worthy of availing himself of God's glory. Rashi so understood the passage, and indicates in early medieval pattern, that they entered heaven by making use of God's Name: "they ascended into the heavens by virtue of a Name." This incident is appropriately compared to Paul's ascent described in II Corinthians.[65] Undoubtedly the Talmud here preserves an old tradition of mystical ecstasy experienced by some of the rabbis. The four who entered Paradise did not enter together. They undoubtedly had individual experiences at different times. The results of their experiences as related by disciples are here given cryptically. Ben Azai could not withstand the experience and died. Ben Zoma went out of his mind. Elisha interpreted his experience in a way that took him out of rabbinic Judaism, as did Paul of Tarsus. Akiba, however, seems to have been capable of experiencing mystical ecstasy and successfully combining it with his rational halakhic activity.

But what must here be kept in mind once again, as I have frequently noted in other connections, is the authentic continuity of tradition. Apocalyptic with all of its esoteric material on the eschaton and the inexplicable celestial visions involving anthropomorphic experiences related to God, continued to play a role in talmudic and midrashic literature. This went on through the intervening centuries between the classical period of apocalyptic, the first century B.C. and the first century A.D., to the post-talmudic period and on into the early mystical literature of medieval times, ultimately flowering in the hekhalot literature and the Zohar.[66]

b. *The Messiah*[67]

A concept of the Messiah bringing about a great age of salvation would have no value to the dead. For this reason it is natural that Judaism developed an extensive theology of immortality and resurrection which held out the profound hope that each individual can share in ultimate salvation. Before this World to Come sprouts there is to be a messianic advent in which the Messiah sets the world aright in preparation for the great resurrection, final judgment and the eternal life of the righteous.

The technical Hebrew noun for the eschatological Messiah, does not appear in the Bible. The word *mashiah* is an adjective referring to an anointed king or priest until it is applied to the end-time redeemer at En. 48:10. What is comprehended by what we call "the messianic idea" before I Enoch is "the end of days" when redemption will take place. After that book, the hope that Israel will be redeemed is connected to the idea that the world will experience the *yemot hamashiah*, "the days of the Messiah." As in other aspects of Judaic theology, however, the messianic idea is weighted down with ambiguities. There is the concept of a utopia as presented in some prophetic passages promising universal abundance, peace, and harmony in nature. There is the concept of a convulsive "day of the Lord" which will be dark and destructive. There is the view that God Himself will be the redeemer, and the view that a great hero will arise. Even among those who hold he will be a Davidic king there are those who maintain he will not physically do violence but will subdue the world by "the breath of his lips." And finally there is also the Servant of the Lord concept, the servant who suffers as a vicarious atonement. This may or may not characterize the Messiah.[68]

It must be borne in mind that the rabbinic idea of the Messiah is drawn from the prophetic literature of the Bible and the apocalyptic writings. The rabbis undoubtedly reacted vigorously to the Christian claim that the Messiah has already come, and responded in some form to the *perushim* of Qumran. They rejected the Qumran Teacher of Righteousness but have some affinity with Qumran. Qumran's two-messiah idea appears in rabbinic use of the Elijah motif side by side with the Davidic Messiah. Furthermore, the Teacher of Righteousness as a messianic or eschatological figure is paralleled in the rabbinic Elijah lore. The lore sees Elijah as a great eschatological colleague and mentor of a number of rabbis.[69] But his role as ultimate authority in halakhah is reserved for the messianic age. At that time he will repeal old halakhah and proclaim new precepts.[70]

Elijah is part of the ambivalence in rabbinic ideas of the Messiah. The rabbis were undoubtedly reacting to Christian claims when they debated whether all or most Jews must fully repent before they will be redeemed. Whether they maintained that this repentance was mandatory or that the Messiah will be sent at a time determined by God without this repentance, they were of the opinion that Elijah will appear before and with the Messiah, to herald him and then to help effect the spiritual redemption of the people. He is believed in some esoteric midrashim to precede both the appearance of the Messiah and the self-revelation of God, and in other esoteric midrashim to be the revealer of the new complete Torah of which the Mosaic Torah will only constitute a very small portion.[71]

The messianic idea appropriated by the rabbis from scripture was that of a scion (*ẓemaḥ*, a branch or shoot) of the house of David who will be a wise and perfect king. On the other hand, in at least one source it appears there was a contrary tradition, that a Davidide will never again sit on the throne at Jerusalem (Jer. 22:30). Many eschatological passages do not mention a Davidic revival, and there is no evidence that Bar Kokhba was a Davidide. Thus we find that there were two facets to the messianic expectation: the political and the theocratic, the latter term being how one scholar has termed the messianic idea when it is distinct from the political.[72] This ambivalence is at the root of the attitude taken toward Jesus in the first century, and accounts for the ambiguities inherent in Zionism in the twentieth century. There are indeed many references to the end of days in apocalyptic literature, as in the biblical passages, with nobody that corresponds to a Messiah delivering Jews from subjection (En. 90:37ff.). On another level, however, the messianic figure is identified with the human-like figure which Daniel saw on the heavenly throne, and who is called in apocalyptic and New Testament literature, "the son of man." This figure is also related to the concept of a pre-existent Messiah who waits in heaven until the time for his appearance arrives. At Gen. R. 2:4 "the spirit of God" (Gen. 1:2) is taken to be the Messiah, thus supporting the notion of a divine and pre-existent Messiah.

The messianic age lasts until the final judgment. Even the Messiah is believed to be marked for death and after all the earth has been reduced to a pre-creation silence there will be a reawakening and a restoration. The last judgment will take place, The seat of God's personal reign will be a new heavenly Jerusalem come down to earth and there will be a real human existence in the physical world. The apocalyptic writers who described their visions of the eschaton were contemporaries of first-century proto-rabbis and it is not surprising that similar views are found in rabbinic ágadah and in the midrashim.[74] But in rabbinic literature there is neither a systematic presentation of the messianic idea nor an attempt to state a dogma concerning it.

The messianic expectation was largely the anticipation of the sovereignty of God in the world; *malkhut shamayim*, the kingship or "kingdom" of God foretold by the prophets. Zekhariah's vision of the day when the Lord will be king over all the earth and He will be one in the truest sense of the word because His Name will also only be One, became the closing line of the rabbinic liturgy.[75]

The conditions of life provoked the agonizing question of when this would happen. As a result there arose calculators. Some held the ages of the world are ideally three: two-thousand years of chaos, two-thousand under the Torah, two-thousand of the Messiah, but that sin has caused many years of the third age to be lost (B.A.Z. 9a). Others made a variety of calculations. Some rabbis were among calculators who depended upon different verses in Daniel and Habakkuk. But by the middle of the third century, the talmudic teachers, the amoraim, generally opposed messianic calculations. They saw it as a danger to faith for when the Messiah does not come at the computed time there are those who argue that a messiah will not come, that the doctrine is a delusion. Nevertheless calculators continued to function right through the middle ages. Along with calculations went signs, such as the forecast that the conditions of society would be unbearably bad on socio-economic, cultural and religious levels.

It is a late document that cites an early source on Elijah's role in bringing Israel to repentence, but the dramatic appearance of John the Baptist indicates that this belief concerning Elijah was current very early. Very early too it was believed that Elijah will restore the jar of manna preserved since Moses' time, along with other historical items. From somewhere Justin Martyr must have received his notion that Elijah will anoint the Messiah. Implicitly Elijah, who is borne by the spirit of God is also reminiscent of the spirit of God which hovers over the waters (Gen. 1:2) and is connected with messianic redemption. The midrash utilizes a *gezerah shavah* to indicate that the "spirit" in that verse is the Messiah, and the "waters" symbolizes the repentance of Israel. And as is well-known from Malakhi 3:23, Elijah is the agent of the eschatological repentance.[77]

Reference has been made earlier to the two-Messiah theory at Qumran. This has also found its way into rabbinic lore in different versions. According to one source Obadiah, verse 18, foretells that Esau (Rome) must be destroyed by Joseph, that is, a northern Messiah. A Messiah ben Joseph, therefore, precedes the Messiah ben David leading Israel in a fierce war in which cataclysmic events occur. The Messiah is slain in

Jerusalem and the Jews are at their nadir. At this time Elijah and Messiah ben David appear, and either Elijah or the Messiah revive Messiah ben Joseph who might resume the war, or God resumes the war himself. Elijah blows the ram's horn on the Mount of Olives. The primeval light of Genesis created on the first day before the luminaries which were not created until the fourth day, shines once more. The moon becomes as bright as the sun and the sick are healed. Elijah sounds the shofar a second time and the dead are resurrected. At a third sounding of the shofar the Shekhinah reveals itself to the world. In other midrashim the entire event is closed with the descent to earth of a heavenly Jerusalem with a new Temple. Elijah is said to be the agent of resurrection, having been granted this power when he resurrected the son of the Syro-Phoenician woman. Finally, Elijah supports the work of the Messiah. In some versions, he and the two Messiahs, along with the new high priest, the Kohen-Zedek (the priest of righteousness), which may be the priest-king Melchizedek (Gen. 14:18), rebuild the holy land. In some traditions Elijah is himself the high priest in the messianic era, identified with Phineas. Moses is told by God that because he has already sacrificed himself for Israel he will accompany Elijah in the era of redemption (Deut. R. 3:17).[78]

Malakhi's reference to Elijah's eschatological return is connected with "the great and terrible day of the Lord." This is related to the notion of a cataclysmic time when dreadful events will usher in the new era with great travail. This is referred to as "the pangs of the Messiah" in rabbinic literature, *ḥeblo shel mashiaḥ*. The word for "pangs" in Hebrew in this context is the same word as that used for the travail or pangs of childbirth.[79] This apocalyptic time of travail is followed by the advent of the Messiah and the golden age of his reign, or the appearance and reign of God himself without the human Messiah. This golden age will be characterized by utopian socio-economic and political conditions, marked by abundance of resources and universal peace. Another characteristic of the messianic age derived from numerous references in prophetic literature, is the restoration of displaced Jews to the holy land. This new redemption is to be so marvellous that it will eclipse the exodus from Egypt. Rabbis differed, however, over whether the northern ten tribes will join in this great messianic ingathering, or in any concept of "the World to Come."[80] Undoubtedly we see here a reflection of the historic hostility toward Samaritans. As for the other nations of the world, there is little clarity regarding their fate. The presence of Melchizedek, as noted earlier, indicates a view that gentiles will join in the redemption. But other biblical and apocalyptic references appear to speak of their subjugations, or conversions. The

latter is the implication of Zekh. 14:9, looking to the day
when all the world will worship the God of Israel. Clearly,
the anonymous preacher of Is. 66:21 believed that God will not
only include the gentiles in the new era but will choose
priests from among them. This heightens the presence of Melchizedek as one of the four eschatological figures.[81]

In this medley of concepts there was bound to be ambiguity. How long will the messianic era last before the resurrection, final judgment and the spiritual world to come are
inaugurated? Everyone agreed the messianic age will come to
an end, but there were many opinions as to its duration.
These ranged from forty years to three hundred and sixty-five
thousand years, each rabbi deriving his view by way of exegesis of scripture.[82] The doctrine of redemption thus incorporates at least three strands: the personal destiny of the
individual, the messianic promise and the cosmic end of days.

The rabbis did not shun the apocalyptic literature which
expresses the reaction to Hasmonean usurpation of both priesthood and kingship and the hellenization of the monarchy. This
in due course was followed by Roman and Herodian oppression
and further deterioration of the Jerusalem priesthood and the
quality of spirituality in Judaism. Consequently the apocalyptic writers seized upon the earlier prophetic "day of the
Lord" motifs to point toward the cosmic change which will be
wrought miraculously. They pictured great figures of the past
journeying in celestial realms within earshot of the Throne of
Glory on the great Chariot depicted by Ezekiel, receiving
revelations concerning this great cosmic day to come. They
portray details of the terror and of the messianic promises,
of the end of the world, of resurrection, of judgment and of
the new world in which humans will be like angels.[83]

The two Messiah idea referred to earlier in all probability originates with exegesis upon the suggestive phrases in the
oracle of Zekhariah where he asks the meaning of the two olive
trees in his vision (4:3), and the angel responds that they
are the two "sons of oil" (that is, the two anointed ones)
who stand with the Lord of all the world.[84] The one was to be
the anointed priest-Messiah and the other the anointed king-
Messiah, an Israelite of the house of David. The Psalms of
Solomon, however, point explicitly to the more pervasive idea
of a single Davidic Messiah. This clarity in liturgical material suggests that the idea had primary prevalence among the
people at the time of Jesus. Incidentally, too, it helps explain Jesus' rejection. In the end he was not perceived to
be the Davidic hero, and was therefore a source of deep frus-
tration. Only after his death did his followers begin to rethink alternative messianic ideas.[85]

Whether repentance of all Jews has to precede the redemption is a further source of ambiguity. This ambivalence
is indicated in the difference of opinion concerning the reading and interpretation of Is. 59:20. The masoretic text reads
"A redeemer will come to Zion and to those who turn (repent)
from transgression in Jacob." The Septuagint, however, renders the second part of this verse as "and he shall turn away
impiety from Jacob." Apparently from the earliest times it
was believed by some that the redeemer will effect the repentance, and two texts circulated. Either the Hebrew and
Greek texts reflect which view the editor espoused, whether
Jews will first repent or first the redeemer will come, or the
texts were later emended. But the ambiguity is embedded in
scripture, and carries over into the New Testament where Paul
cites this same verse in accordance with the Septuagint.[86]
While we do not know precisely how the proto-rabbis thought
about this, the disciples of Yoḥanan b. Zakkai reflect the
ambiguity. And in the light of the early textual variations
it is fair to say that this ambiguity existed early and lasted
through the rabbinic period (B. Yom. 86b).

Their differences also carried over into the question of
which month will be the time of redemption: Nisan, the month
when redemption is celebrated at Passover, or Tishri, the
month of equal eschatological import, when the creation,
God's kingship, and judgment are all commemorated at Rosh ha
Shanah. Similarly, there was no agreement on Bar Kokhba's
messianic claim for he effected none of the messianic signs.
Those, like Akiba, who supported Bar Kokhba simply saw the
Bar Kokhba revolt as a this-worldly messianic idea, all the
other eschatological elements then being relegated to the
post-messianic world to come. In reaction to the Bar Kokhba
debacle, however, most rabbis turned to an emphasis upon the
supernatural elements ascribed to the process of redemption.[87]

This dichotomy between the political and theocratic concepts endured into the twentieth century. When emigration of
Jews from various lands to Palestine began to sharply increase,
both Zionists and non-Zionists appealed to the respective
strands of the tradition that supported this position. Those
who opposed forcing God's hand through auto-emancipation ar-
argued that there is a "due time" when God will bring redemption. It is worthwhile here to cite in full the pertinent
midrash passage to S of S. R. 2:7 (3:5):

> "R. Yosi b. Ḥanina (third century) says,
> there are two adjurations here (in the
> adjuration of S of S 2:7), one directed
> to Israel, one to the nations of the
> world. He adjured Israel not to rebel

against subjugation by the nations,
and He adjured the nations not to make
too heavy the yoke upon Israel, for if
they make the yoke heavy upon Israel
they will provoke the end (*hakeẓ*) to
come before its time. . . R. Helbo said,
there are four adjurations here; He
adjured Israel not to rebel against the
kingdoms; that they should not press for
the end (*hakeẓ*); that they should not
reveal their mystery to the nations of
the world; that they should not go up as
a wall (en masse) from the dispersion. . ."

The midrash then adds variant lists of four occasions in history when Israel pressed the *keẓ* (the end) and suffered travail and defeat. Among these occasions the Bar Kokhba rebellion is listed in both variants.[88]

When are events of history to be judged eschatological?
Did the nations violate God's adjuration with the Holocaust?
And if so, is Israel's forcing of the *keẓ* legitimate? Or is
Israel's forcing of the *keẓ* merely compounding the violation
of God's dual adjuration? Another question may be: if
neither premise is correct, that is, neither the nations nor
Israel has violated the oath, are the events since 1948 then
to be seen as the vindication of the Akiba-Samuel position
concerning a this-worldly historical messianic event which
merely marks a political transition to the eschaton in which
Israel is no longer subjected to the rule of the nations of
the world? Either way these are theological themes which
call for full-scale investigation.

R. Yohanan, a third-century *ámora* spoke of the redemptive
process in erotic terms, comparing God's redeeming work for
Israel to the moment of sexual exaltation between a lion and
his mate. The rabbi says "woe to the nation that obstructs
at the time that the Holy One Blessed is He redeems His children." He asks: who would dare cast his garment between a
lion and his mate when "they copulate?" The context is a
homily on Num. 24:23 which is taken by the Talmud, targums
and the Greek translator in an eschatological way. Bilaam,
in one of his oracles asks "Who will live when God does
these things?" The Hebrew text is difficult, but its traditional interpretation was related to God's redemptive acts
and the warning to all not to obstruct or come between God and
His people.[89]

4. *Creation*[90]

The rabbis derived their concept of creation from Genesis and from sayings scattered through the writings of the preaching prophets. One of the questions addressed most vigorously by medieval philosophers is whether the world was created out of pre-existent, uncreated matter, or whether God created the world *ex nihilo*, out of no pre-existing matter. The general early rabbinic position was that God created the universe without pre-existent matter. This view is illustrated in the anecedote concerning a reply given by Gamaliel I or II to "a certain philosopher" who pointed out to him that God had good materials to use in His creation. To this R. Gamaliel is said to have responded that God created all of the materials to which he has reference: *tohu* and *bohu* (chaos), darkness and the watery abyss.[91]

The secrets of creation were much on the minds of the rabbis. But they were opposed to public teaching of this knowledge as they were also to that of the Throne-Chariot. The creation lore, *maàseh bereshit,* was not to be expounded to more than one competent disciple at a time. This had reference to investigating pre-creation, the nature of reality before what is described in the Torah came into being. The rabbis cite Ben Sira as their authority.[92]

The rabbis taught that God created the world alone as was noted in our discussion of "two authorities." The Babylonian rabbis were inclined to refute Iranian cosmology and therefore engaged in more detailed discussion in order to stress that God created both light and darkness, and that there was no separate Prince of Darkness who shared power with God.[93]

The rabbis taught that the Torah was the instrument of creation. This implies that the Torah was pre-existent.[94] We have already seen that Wisdom was personified and that the Torah was identified with Wisdom. This notion that God created the world with the Torah led to a basic optimism toward the world. Thus in a homily concerning why the first letter of the Torah in the opening account of creation is a *bet,* the second letter of the alphabet, rather than an *alef,* the first letter, the reply is an aphorism of optimism: "Because the *bet* is an expression of blessing. . .," *berakhah,* which begins with a *bet.* This is undoubtedly a position taken to refute gnostics who followed Simon Magus in claiming that creation was not the work of the good God, but of the demiurge, the subordinate of God who rebelled and declared himself supreme. Although they could point to Gen. 1:31, "And God saw that all

that He had made was very good," the rabbis had to use new
arguments in facing new challenges to the traditional theology.
They saw fit to quote Ben Sira in their effort to acclaim all
of creation as valuable and purposeful.[95]

Nevertheless, they could not escape scriptural difficulties. Gen. 1:26 "let us make the human in our image" implied
others were associated with God in the creation of Adam.
Rabbinic views ranged from the notion that God consulted the
angels, or the souls of the unborn righteous to the idea that
God utilized the plural of majesty. Proof that God created
the human alone, in any event, was offered from the next
verse (Gen. 1:27) "And God created the human. . ." With this
they also rejected the Philonic view referred to earlier that
God was assisted in the creation of humans in order that He
not be responsible for the evil part of human nature.[96]

Another difficulty confronted by the rabbis was the nature of the light created on the first day before the luminaries were created on the fourth day. Some taught that this
light is reserved for the righteous of the world to come.
But others taught, much in the same way as Philo, that the
first light was divine emanation from which the luminaries
and constellations all drew their light. A third way of understanding the light of the first day combines the two views to
see it as the light of divine emanation which was the garment
of God (Ps. 104:2) but is reserved for the world to come.[97]

5. *Revelation*[98]

Revelation is a central doctrine of rabbinic Judaism.
Although the Bible has no technical term for "revelation"
the entire Bible is replete with examples of God's communication with humans from Adam (the miẓvah of reproduction)
through Malakhi. The most common way of expressing this manifestation of divinity or theophany is with one form or another of God "speaking" or "saying," or the recipient of the
"word" announces *neum*, "the word of the Lord." The word of
the Lord is *noetic* insofar as it has real content which is to
be heard, understood and acted upon. It expresses the will of
God for humans to fulfill. The word of the Lord is also
dynamic insofar as it operated as a force which actualized the
will of God as in creation. "God said" is the typical expression in the Genesis account of creation.[99]

There is no other way for humans to describe a theophany
than in human terms. And this is the essence of the rabbinic
dictum that "the Torah speaks in the language of humans."[100]

We are unable to declare it to be either a physical or a
psychic process. Rather, it is a mystery because it is metaphysical, God not being corporeal. This mystery is underscored
by the repeated manifestation of God in cloud which is immaterial, yet a substance into which one cannot see. It is
ethereal, and in perpetual heavenly motion.[101]

But while revelation is a mystery, the record of it is
a human effort to set it down in writing and convey it to
others. The rabbis did not claim the revelation. They inherited the record. They believed that the mystery had indeed occurred and they believed the records to be true. But
at the same time they believed the records had to be understood and that the content of revelation as recorded had to
be lived out in a real world, their world in their time. The
recorded content had to be interpreted and this interpretation had to receive the needed authority that would allow the
Torah to be preserved as perpetual torah, ongoing instruction
to inform and enrich the spiritual life.[102]

The rabbis believed in *mattan torah*, that God "gave" the
Torah to Israel through Moses (Ex. 31:18), and in *kabalat
torah*, that Moses received the Torah. He immediately began
to teach it and it became the medium of tradition (Ex. 34:31-
32). Some rabbis sought to make belief in this doctrine a
pre-requisite for salvation:

> "These do not have a share in the world to
> come: the one who says that resurrection is
> not found in scripture; that the Torah is not
> from heaven. . ." (M. Aḥ. 1:1; San. 10:1).[103]

As it turned out, however, the rabbis were so prolific in
their interpretation that the interpretive torah became much
more abundant than revelation. But their theory allowed for
the interpretation to share in the authority of the revelation. Even more, the rabbinic interpretation, more so than
the words of the text, carry the authority for a halakhah or
a doctrine. As one observer has astutely remarked, "Here on
earth their opinion may overrule an opinion held in heaven."[104]

When the rabbis used the term *torah* they used it in a
comprehensive sense to signify the total body of religion that
is contained within the covenant between God and Israel. The
term Torah referred to non-Pentateuchal content as well as to
the interpretive commentary. The word *nomos* was used in this
same way by Jews in the hellenistic diaspora. Neither torah
nor *nomos* means "law" and it did not have the force of law in
antiquity. The judgment that post-exilic, proto-rabbinic or

rabbinic Judaism turned to a "legalistic" approach to religion is wholly unfounded.[105]

Torah (LXX *nomos*) means procedure or set of instructions at Ex. 12:49, as at Lev. 6:17; 7:1 and numerous other times. At Is. 2:3 torah (*nomos*) is parallel to *debar Yhwh*, "the word of the Lord," or divine revelation. At Zeph. 3:4 the priests do not do violence to "*the* Torah," but rather in a comprehensive way to divine teaching and the will of God. These examples can be multiplied many times over. Moreover *nomos* is used for Torah many times when torah cannot possibly refer to "law" such as at Prov. 3:1; 6:23 for parental instruction and Ps. 77:1 for history. Throughout scripture torah and *nomos* do not mean law, but rather refer to instruction and teaching, whether divine or otherwise. The term *nomos* represented the "constitution" of a Greek city-state, and for this reason, because it represented the total body of the revelation as the "constitution" of Jerusalem and Judah, the Greek translator chose the word *nomos*.

The rabbis distinguished between revelation and interpretation at times by using the term *torah shebeal peh*, the oral torah (literally, "the torah via the mouth"), that is, the torah that is not in written form. Their own torah, despite their consciousness of it being their own, had the authority of written and revealed scripture, and both Hillel and Shammai told a prospective proselyte that he was bound to accept both torahs (B. Shab. 31a; Aḇ de R.N. A, 15). This view prevailed centuries later when third-century rabbis asserted that the interpretive torah is the validating element of the Sinaitic covenant, that the importance of seemingly unnecessary verses in scripture derive from their use in interpretive torah, and that, in fact, the interpretive precepts are more precious than those of written scripture. Moreover, some rabbis held that many halakhot were revealed to Moses and they are all in the Mishnah. This all-embracing view of interpretive torah undoubtedly had an anti-Pauline edge on it, for the more the Christian argued against halakhah the more the rabbis elevated the halakhah. Furthermore, while the Church Fathers drew frequently upon the prophets, the rabbis argued that prophecy still functions in the words of the rabbis. Moreover, contrary to Paul's argument that Abraham's merit was his faith, they paralleled James' view that it was due to his deeds, and credited him with observing the entire torah (in their view: written and interpretive) even before it was revealed at Sinai. The rabbis inherited a tradition that Abraham's knowledge of monotheism came both by divine revelation and by his own efforts.[106]

6. *Providence and Free Will*

An apparent consensus in rabbinic teaching espouses
a doctrine of God's providence side by side with what appears
to some to be diametrically opposite, a belief in human free
will. This dual belief is possibly best expressed by R. Ḥanina who stated that "all is in the hands of heaven except
reverence for God." This leading halakhic authority and well-
known agadist of the second and third centuries was drawing
his doctrine from Deut. 10:12, but could have cited any number of other biblical verses. The very premise of God's
command to Israel is the freedom of choice to respond to it.
But Ḥanina was taking a position that the concept of free response pertains only to the moral sphere, whether the person
chooses to obey or disobey the will of God. All other things,
health, wealth, natural disasters, and the like, are "in the
hands of heaven." Providence determines human fate in socio-
physical terms.

Great mystery is inherent in this view, however, for
human choice can have socio-physical ramifications upon other
human beings, and upon oneself. Health is predetermined by
God according to this view. Yet it is the human being who
chooses to smoke or not to smoke, and this can be classed as
a moral choice since he is honor-bound to protect his own
life as well as not to harm others. Some rabbis, unable to
cope with the mystery of a coexistent providence and free
will, conceded the efficacy of astrological signs and planetary movements and asserted therefore, that the day of one's
birth is significant. Others, however, opposed any reliance
upon *mazalot*, the movement of planets and constellations.[107]

These differences of opinions were not crystallized into
dogma. The diversity of opinion was inherited from previous
centuries as is clear from Josephus' schematic description of
Sadducees, Pharisees and Essenes, all three of whom had a
different set of beliefs. According to Josephus, who phrased
it differently in his various writings, the "Pharisees" believed everything is the result of both fate and God, but the
human will also plays a role, and although moral behavior is
a matter of choice, fate or providence sometimes intervenes
and helps partially to determine it. This clearly falls short
of approximating the position of R. Ḥanina, who maintained
all moral action is human choice. Josephus described the
Essenes as believing that nothing is done by human free will
but that everything is in the hands of God, nothing occurring
except by decree of Providence. He asserted that the Sadducees insisted that all things are within human power. It is
clear that Qumran had an extreme doctrine of the power of

providence akin to what Josephus describes of the Essenes.[108]
Yet there was also a rabbinic view other than that of R.
Ḥanina that shared the Essene view. It would be incorrect to
overgeneralize about any of these groups. A case can be made
for rabbis sharing both the Pharisaic and Essene views. What
we have is a great medley of Judaic ideas concerning the
government of the natural order and how human needs are provided, as well as on the destiny of nations and the fate of
the individual.

Akiba did not argue that there is a paradox in that divine foreknowledge is contradicted by human free will as is
commonly thought, in his famous aphorism "All is *seen* (not
"fore-known") but the option (to act) is granted." He simply
meant that God knows human behavior as it is in progress and
humans are accountable for it. This is much the same as the
idea expressed by R. Judah ha Nasi in his sermon urging proper
conduct, that a person should be aware "there is an eye that
sees and an ear that hears and all your deeds are inscribed
in a book." On the other hand there were those who did argue
that the ways of both the righteous and the wicked are known
to God before they are created in the world. R. Yanai argued
that we have no control over the tranquility of the wicked or
the suffering of the righteous and he anticipated therefore
the view of R. Ḥanina. For what he is saying is not that
humans are totally devoid of free will but that the human
socio-physical lot is in control of providence. This view is
fully explicated in Tanḥuma to Exodus. From our sources consensus appears to prevail that there is human choice in moral
matters while human destiny is given over to providence. This
was really a traditional view, for centuries earlier Ben Sira
too expressed the idea that there is free will in moral choice,
as did the author of the Psalms of Solomon.[109] This ambiguity
concerning providence and free will carries over into halakhah.
It is wondered why a person must build a parapet to his roof
(Deut. 21:8) to prevent anyone from falling from it in view
of determinism which teaches that whoever falls from the roof
has already had his destiny to fall locked into the very laws
of nature since creation. Nevertheless the view is upheld
that despite determinism each human has the obligation to do
the right thing. Moreover, many rabbis pointed to prayer, repentance and good deeds as a way of over-coming adverse conditions of life. In effect this implies that human righteousness is able to frustrate divine determinism.[110]

The important thing here is that the rabbis did not attempt to suppress divergent thinking and to establish dogma.
Thus, they did not even agree on a nexus between sin and
death or sin and suffering. Some maintained the traditional
view expressed by the friends of Job, that suffering and death

is indicative of sin. Others denied this (B. Shab. 55a-b).
The ancient rabbis were troubled that the Torah's promise of
reward to the good and punishment to the wicked distorts human
perception. The reality we witness shows no causative nexus
between human behavior and the human predicament. Some rabbis
explicitly denied reward and punishment in this world and
taught a religion which demands of the human that he fulfill
God's will without reference to the circumstances and quality
of life and to the question of reward. This is a view expressed in later literature, but is also a view from the
earliest pre-Hasmonean proto-rabbinic era, given in the name
of Antigonus of Sokho. The question is neatly packaged in
the dichotomy between a second-century grandfather and his
grandson, Elisha b. Abuyah and R. Jacob. Elisha is said to
have become an unbeliever when he saw a person die after
fulfilling a miẓvah for which long life is promised in the
Torah (Deut. 22:6-7). His grandson exegeted the verse as
referring to the length of days in the afterlife and the
eternity of post resurrection existence. On this basis it
was possible to accept extreme views of providence in which
adversity cannot be avoided. Thus, when Moses is said to
have complained to God in heaven that Akiba should die a tor-
turous death at the hands of the Romans after a life dedicated
to Torah, God is said to have responded, "Quiet! Such is my
decree" (B. Men. 29b).[111]

God's decree is also seen by some as determined at the
hour of creation. In one exegesis of Gen. 1:1-5 the term
tohu vabohu (chaos) is taken to refer to the deeds of the
wicked, and God's command for light to appear to refer to the
deeds of the righteous. God's division of the light from the
darkness is interpreted as the separation of the righteous
from the wicked into two separate camps of humanity. But in
Qumranic terms the two groups, sons of light and sons of
darkness will meet on common ground on the day of judgment.
For, the homily continues: this is what is meant by evening
and morning constituting one day, that the deeds of the
wicked and the deeds of the righteous will both be judged on
the one day set by God for the judgment of all. We have here
a view that in the very origin of the cosmos were already incorporated the deeds of humans and conditions of life. This
also provides evidence of how pietistic views of the *perushim*
of Qumran, that there are predetermined components of the
human race, sons of light and sons of darkness, entered into
rabbinic literature (Gen. R. 2:5; 3:8).

While some rabbis excluded Israel from all planetary and
astral influence, basing themselves upon the verse ". . .be
not dismayed at the signs of heaven" (Jer. 10:2), others did

attribute some importance to these signs. Here, once more, we have no monolithic view and no dogma. Thus, it is explicated in some sources that even planetary movements, explicitly eclipses of the sun and the moon are the works of God. Yet some rabbis believed that human character is determined by the zodiac sign of his birth while others, conceding astral influence, maintained that observing mizvot can annul any adverse astral influence. Moreover, there is a clear effort to establish a consensus of scholars over a long period as denying any astral effect upon Israel. This was the great compromise the rabbis made with their cultural environment. They could not negate the science of their day so they accepted its significance but denied its efficacy in the case of God's Elect. This was done with such doctrines as providence and was also done with a wide variety of life-cycle rituals. In the case of the latter they retained ancient primitive rituals from a dim pagan past but ascribed to them new meaning in keeping with the concepts of Judaism.[112]

In sum, rabbinic literature provides us with a collage of opinions on providence and free will and does not leave us with any definitive point of view that can be considered a dogma. The consensus appears to be that in the face of utter uncertainty the human is obliged to carry forward the will of God and to have faith that ultimately good will prevail. The entire human race, at times, stands naked in the sight of God like Job, and can only say "my redeemer lives." But when all is said the assumption in Judaism remains that humans govern their own destiny as far as they can assess the daily consequences of their behavior, and that God hears prayer and acts on it, implying that no condition of life is unchangeable.

IV. THE THEOLOGY OF WORSHIP[113]

A. *Preliminary Observations*

Our survey of aspects of rabbinic theology has brought to the surface a rather lengthy roster of doctrines and principles. These include formulations concerning monotheism, creation, revelation, election, redemption, reward and punishment, hell and heaven, immortality of the soul, resurrection, providence, the messianic idea, free will, and many others that can be listed as subdivisions and ramification of these, such as vicarious atonement.[114] All of these and more are evident in the liturgy of synagogue and home. In the prayers delineated for Judaic worship since ancient times we find the

theology that spiritual leaders suggested to be the content
of Judaic faith. This theology consists of doctrines related
to both God and to history and they are celebrated in worship.
The great historic events, both the miracles that exalted
Israel such as the exodus from Egypt, and the sufferings that
overtook the people such as the destruction of Jerusalem, were
concretized in liturgical offerings and became part of regular
daily, Sabbath or sacred-day worship. The liturgy contains
praise, petition, and thanksgiving, mostly written and recited or chanted in first person plural.

It is significant that many different rituals arose in
Judaism and that great flexibility and diversity characterized Judaic worship throughout history. But the greatest portion of the core of every worship service was derived from
antiquity, some of it going back to pre-Hasmonean times.
What is today called the *Sidur* or *Maḥzor*, the "order" and
"cycle" of worship respectively has its origin in the ninth-
century Babylonian collection of daily berakhot made by
Gaon Natronai followed by the Sidur of Gaon Amram.[115] But
the basic elements of the order of worship sent by Amram to
Spain are traceable to the Talmud and to earlier sources, and
it is the work of Natronai and Amram which assured that historically the great variety of liturgical rites will be
based upon the Babylonian antecedent. Nevertheless, this does
not preclude the idea that many Babylonian texts originated
in Palestine. Some passages are believed to have been of
such great antiquity that the Talmud ascribes them to Moses
and expresses the belief that Moses received them in revelation from God. The basic prayers are either taken bodily
from the Book of Psalms or culled from various biblical
verses and therefore are in Hebrew. But from the beginning
many rabbis asserted the right to pray in any language.[116]

The institution of prayer is of highest antiquity. It is
evident throughout the Bible as a natural response of humans
to deity, or as a natural turning of the human heart to deity
for sustenance and healing. The notion of centralizing the
cult in Jerusalem never came to full fruition, and after the
destruction of Jerusalem in 587 B.C. the rural sanctuaries and
gathering places where people met with prophets on Sabbaths
and New Moons (II Ki. 4:23) surfaced as a viable new institution. It replaced the temple in the cities and towns of
Palestine and the diaspora and after 70 A.D. it became the
new worship center.[117]

The theology of worship may be said, therefore, to begin
with the premise that one can worship God anywhere. That God
is not territorially-oriented is a basic breakthrough of an-

cient Judaic theology. The priests were bound in self-
interest to pagan ideas of a central worship place conducted
by a sacerdotal class, but rabbinic Judaism built upon the
alternative worship experiences developed throughout pre-
rabbinic history which liberated God and worship from this con-
fining theology. These then are the first principles of a
rabbinic theology of worship: the content of public worship
derives from revelation, public worship (like private devotions) can take place anywhere, in every language, and may
consist of varying rites.[118]

That the synagogue form known from earliest rabbinic
Judaism is very old and pre-Hasmonean is clear from a reading
of the prayers recorded by Ben Sira. Although it is difficult
in this as in other matters to date rabbinic literature, it is
reasonable and logical to assume that the order of worship conducted in the temple at Jerusalem before 70 A.D. as described
in the Mishnah, if not pre-Hasmonean, is from the time when
the Hasmonean priest-kings reorganized the temple and state
during the second century B.C.

Form-critical textual and historical studies of the liturgical elements have been made to find the regular literary
patterns that recur in Judaic worship, and to determine the
probable date of origin of prayers. In this regard I proceed
on the premise that many of the regular prayers used in
synagogue literature had a history of oral transmission, and
that there existed variants of these prayers in different
centers of worship long before the rabbinic text as we have
it was crystallized. Rabbinic worship in my view, is in direct
continuity with proto-rabbinic, pre-Hasmonean and earlier
post-exilic worship. Thus the psalm of Ben Sira referred to
previously already contains most of the theological doctrines
that we will find in rabbinic worship. Ben Sira did not
originate the psalm, but rather interpolated a well-known
prayer of his time. Thus a perusal of Ben Sira's prayer at
Chapter Fifty will yield the following concepts: God is the
guardian of Israel, redemption, creation, the ingathering of
diaspora, the concern for Jerusalem and the Temple, the restoration of a Davidic scion, references to the God of Abraham
and Jacob and reiterated thankfulness. There appears to be no
reference to Isaac and there are lacking stanzas of personal
petition for knowledge, repentance, forgiveness, healing, help
and the prayer for peace. Nevertheless, elsewhere (35:12-20)
Ben Sira implies that individuals offered such petitions and
that God hears, and at 36:1-17 a number of other concepts are
incorporated in a prayer. Among these are God's overawing the
nations of the world so that all will see Him as the only God,
a theme which is included in High Holy Day worship. What we

see in Ben Sira, then, is an older version of a developing
liturgy, elements of which became permanent facets of rabbinic
liturgy.[120]

B. *The Content of the Liturgy*

    1. *The Berakhah*[121]

      The primary element of Judaic worship is the berakhah.
The usual translation of *barukh atah adonay,* "blessed art
thou," does not render the fullest theological significance of
the term *barookh,* which, as Abudraham has pointed out, signifies that God is the source of all blessing. A literal translation would then include the idea "You, O Lord, are the
source of blessing," and therefore by implication when reciting the entire berakhah one acknowledges God as the giver of,
or the one who blesses with the particular gift one enjoys.
A berakhah is a thanks-offering. But more, it is also a confession of faith in God as the source of all gifts. Sometimes the opening berakhah formula is followed by an additional formula, *elohenu melekh haolam.* This means "our God, king
of the universe," or perhaps "eternal sovereign." In either
case the source of blessing is identified with the additional
confession of faith in God as the power under whose sovereignty the worshipper places himself. This signifies that
the worshipper accepts the kingship of heaven, *malkhut
shamayim.* It is evident that this is precisely what the rabbis (B. Ber. 12a), had in mind when they said that a berakhah
is not appropriate unless it includes the Name and the Malkhut
(Yhwh and His Kingship). The formula *barukh atah adonay* is
biblical and exhibits continuity in liturgical forms. Berakhot are said before enjoying any gift of God, such as food or
clothing, or partaking of any material benefit. A berakhah is
also said before performing a ritual. Here the meaning is
clearly set out as affirming the worshipper's status within
the Elect community symbolized or expressed by his being called
upon to enter into the sanctity of this mizvah about to be performed. An example of this is the berakhah upon donning the
tefilin. This begins with the normal formula already translated above: *Barukh atah adonay elohenu melekh haolam*; and
then it continues (as translated): "who has sanctified us
with His mizvot by commanding us to don the phylacteries."
Thus the wearing of the phylacteries at worship is seen as a
sanctifying and sacramental act and is intimately bound up
with the affirmation of the *malkhut* of God enjoyed by the
Elect. It should be noted that other berakhot are said daily
that confirm this notion by thanking God explicitly for the

election of Israel and the revelation of Torah. Moreover, the recital of berakhot so many times a day--some sages required one-hundred! (B. Men. 43b), is designed to bring about that sense of holiness required of the "kingdom of priests" (Ex. 19:6).

2. *The Core Prayers*

The prayers that constitute the core of synagogue worship were inherited from the past but organized into a set pattern and formalized at Yavneh toward the end of the first century. It was here that the halakhah of prayer and the formal order of synagogue liturgy were determined. The order of worship remained substantially unchanged since that time except for haphazard additions of *piyyutim* throughout the centuries, and the accumulation of new elements such as the psalms and hymns added by medieval kabalists and readings and prayers included since the nineteenth century. As will be seen in a subsequent volume, contemporary synagogue practice allows for abridgment of the worship order by a process of selection. But the worship order has remained that of Yavneh.[122]

It has been noted correctly that the institution of thrice-daily worship by rabbinic authorities and the obligation to recite berakhot at so many junctures of the human day must have had the theological motive of awakening piety. The core prayers are also built around the concept of berakhah and themselves constitute elongated berakhot. Two berakhot before the shema and one after it in the morning worship and two before it and two after it in the evening attest to faith in the One God as creator of the universe who selected Israel as His people to whom He revealed His Torah for which purpose He redeemed them from Egypt (M. Ber. 1:4). At night a second berakhah is introduced especially oriented to petitioning God's guardianship during the crucial time of sleep when the human is as dead, and for awakening again in peace. The very heart of worship, the amidah, consists of a series of berakhot, and we find that the order to the amidah, of Rosh haShanah is still precisely as delineated by Akiba (M.R.H. 4:5). There we find the first three and last three berakhot as they are still, assuming the "priestly benediction" mentioned by Akiba includes the prayer for peace which closes the amidah.[123]

The opening of this order of worship begins since earliest times with an invocation, calling upon the congregation to give praise to the Lord who is worthy of praise. The preliminary berakhot which today consititute the first part of the order of worship (*birkhot hashaḥar*), and the hymnal passages (*pesuke dezimra*) which follow, are not found as part of public worship in talmudic times. The Sidur of Amram, however, does indicate that the opening public prayer was the paragraph that precedes *pesuke dezimra*, known as *barukh sheamar* "Praised is He who spoke and the world came into being." Thus acknowledgement of the creator was the first act of public worship by the ninth century. After the ámidah each worshipper said a private prayer which, as I have indicated in Part 1, Ch. 7, is undoubtedly the element of worship after which the Lord's Prayer is modelled. Other well-known elements of the worship order such as Hallel and the Torah reading along with the prophetic supplement called *haftarah* are also quite old, certainly pre-Christian. From earliest times there is evidence that different versions of the prayers circulated and ultimately two versions became standardized, for example, for the prayer before the shemá and after the shemá, one being used in the morning and one in the evening. Various other signs of flexibility are seen in the abridged prayer called *habinenu* which substitutes for the long ámidah, abbreviated versions of the Grace After Meals, and different arrangements and wording of the ámidah paragraphs.[124] One need but catalogue every prayer recited and list them either in the sequence of the worship order or in an alphabetical pattern, and one can arrive at the full complement of Judaic theology. Sometimes one short prayer offers several doctrines and brief formulae become mini-treatises.

In the sequence of the order of worship we encounter the following beliefs: a) God is the source of all blessing; b) God creates all things; c) God renews creation each day; d) a chorus of angels daily sing of His holiness, which serves as a model for His Elect on earth; e) God alone performs acts of salvation, miracles and healing; f) His love for Israel prompted His election of her and giving her the Torah, and the worshipper prays for the competence to understand it and the courage to observe it; g) monotheism; h) the duty to love God with all one's physical, rational and spiritual power; i) the obligation to transmit the word of God to future generations; j) the obligation to give witness to the faith with such symbols as *tefilin* and *mezuzot*, which in turn, like the Sabbath, serve as a sign of the bond between the Jew and God; k) the affirmation of a nexus between righteousness and reward and sin and punishment; l) the obligation to don fringes as reminders of the mizvot, now fulfilled in the prayer shawl worn at worship; m) the affirmation of faith in God's dependability for help and redemption; n) God is the redeemer.[125]

The above takes us through the berakhah paragraphs before and after the shemá and the shemá itself. We now come to the àmidah. The àmidah is the same each day but the content varies for each sacred day, Sabbath, and New Moon, except that the first three berakhot and the last three berakhot remain permanently the same. There are also some minor changes, for instance, to the weekday àmidah for New Moons, Ḥanukah, Purim and various fast days.

The first three berakhot of the àmidah constitute a mini-theology in themselves. The worshipper affirms the God of Abraham, Isaac and Jacob, thereby implicitly relating himself to covenant and election and to the doctrine of merits of the fathers. He describes God as one who recompenses with love, creator of all who remembers the pious deeds of the ancestors and brings a redeemer to the descendants. The worshipper recognizes this may be for God's own sake, or out of love, even if the community is not deserving. This first berakhah then concludes with mention of the belief that God is savior and shield, the shield of Abraham. The second berakhah relates to God the creator and savior whose unshared power is seen both in His control of nature and involvement in the life and history of human beings. No less than five times the worshipper affirms the doctrine of the resurrection of the dead in one short Hebrew paragraph. Some modern translations have tendentiously rendered the Hebrew words for "to restore life to the dead" or "to revivify the dead" as if they read "immortality." But the Hebrew clearly makes reference five times to faith in God's miraculous power as creator to re-create life not only by reviving vegetation annually, healing the sick, sustaining the fallen and liberating the bound, but above all by keeping faith with those who sleep in the dust, to revivify them and bring them to salvation. Here resurrection and salvation are parallel terms. The third berakhah affirms the holiness of God, a fitting climax to the previous two, and incorporates within itself in public worship elements from the mystical content of the experiences of Isaiah (6:3) and Ezekiel (3:12).

The daily àmidah then includes a variety of personal petitions, and the sacred day àmidot include paragraphs that relate to the occasion. In the last three berakhah paragraphs, always the same, the worshipper prays for the return of the Shekhinah to Zion, acknowledges God as God, offers thanksgiving to Him for His continuous goodness, expresses faith that the compassion of God is without end, and closes with a prayer for that peace which is really eschatological in the context of the return of the Shekhinah to Zion. This highlights the eschatological elements that abound especially in the daily àmidah. Not only is there the intensive emphasis upon resurrection and redemption at the beginning of the àmidah, but paragraphs ten through fourteen are messianic and eschatological in content, as are paragraphs seventeen and nineteen.

This same eschatological emphasis is found in the *birkhat hamazon*, the giving of thanks for food, or Grace After Meals, in the kaddish prayer and in the closing adoration of every order of worship, the alenu. Thus, in the Grace we find one paragraph thanking God for His sustenance; a second for the land, the exodus, the covenant, the Torah and once more for sustenance; a third which is messianic, asking compassion for Israel, Jerusalem, the temple at Zion and the Davidic monarchy; and a fourth which incorporates a large number of ideas and affirmations of faith in God's goodness and benevolence culminating once more in eschatological lines. These include a prayer for the advent of Elijah to announce "the good tidings of consoling salvation," with an added Sabbath prayer for that time which is a complete Sabbath, the Sabbath as paradigm of the world to come, and the climax prayer for the messianic era and the life of the world to come.[126] Similarly the kaddish in its entirety is a messianic prayer, an affirmation of God's holiness, and a prayer for the advent of the kingship of God the *malkhut shamayim*. It is clear from the above that the past redemption and the eschatological redemption to come, including this-worldly messianic elements and other-worldly resurrection, along with reiterated references to the covenant-election-revelation complex and to creation, occupy a very high proportion of the entire liturgy. This same conclusion would be reached by careful analysis of the additional prayers for the Sabbath, the High Holy Days and the pilgrim festivals, as well as other special days of the liturgical calendar. Each sacred day receives additional prayers with emphasis upon the theme of the day: human repentance and divine kingship and judgment at Rosh haShanah, atonement at Yom Kippur, and so forth.[127]*

In conclusion it is worth citing a midrashic passage that teaches a basic halakhah and theology of worship. The halakhah stresses that prayer should not be aloud (I Sam. 1: 13), that it should take place three times daily and not be telescoped into one event (Dan. 6:11), that it be at the times of day when the major shift takes place in the position of the sun, morning, early afternoon, and evening (Ps. 55:18), and that one precede petition (*tefilah*) with adoration (*rina*) as Solomon did in his paradigmatic prayer at the dedication of the first temple (I Ki. 8:28).[128]

* See excursus on *kiddush* and *kaddish* at n. 127.

It is a truism by now that the synagogue order of worship grew gradually out of biblical times into the rabbinic era. Different versions of each prayer circulated until the wording as we have it was standardized probably in the late talmudic period, and even then did not become monolithic. It is a fruitless task to attempt to restore an "original" text when oral transmission was employed over long spans of time and across vast geographic space from Egypt to the Persian Gulf.[12] There is also evidence that some prayers were simply expanded to accommodate new conditions or needs. Thus, the famous *birkhat haminim* which we discussed in Chapter Seven, (Part I) designed to expel Christians from synagogues, was not a wholly new berakhah paragraph added to the amidah, but was an expansion of the prayer against *perushim*.[130] This, incidentally is one more item of evidence that the proto-rabbis were not "Pharisees," but rather opponents of *perushim*. The process of attempted standardization of worship continued for centuries but was never fully accomplished. Variations in wording persisted, berakhot emerged with a variety of doxology patterns. But a relatively uniform order and wording of liturgy was finally arranged by the Babylonian Geonim. The diversity of Judaic theology and halakhah, however, is once again demonstrated in the historic reality that no simple prayer order gained absolute hegemony and down into modern times dozens of rites were accepted as legitimate, as they continue to be in the twentieth century.

V. THE THEOLOGY OF THE SACRED DAYS

A. *The Sacred Days*[131]

Rabbinic Judaism took over the Pentateuchal calendar of holy days in the form in which it found it. By then this meant a Pesah and Mazah festival combined in one (Passover), beginning on the fifteenth of the month Nisan; the Festival of Weeks, Shabuot (Pentecost), occurring on the fiftieth day from the bringing of the omer on the second day of Passover; the first day of the seventh month now referred to as Rosh ha'Shanah, a New Year festival; The Day of Atonement (Yom Kippur); and Sukot (Tabernacles), beginning on the fifteenth day of the seventh month and lasting for seven days, concluded by the Azeret or assembly of the eighth day. In addition to these rabbinic Judaism appropriated from the proto-rabbinic tradition the festive celebrations of Purim and Hanukah. The halakhic material of Tosefta and Mishnah was gathered in separate volumes for each festival, with the exception of Shabuot and Hanukah. But Shabuot was stabilized in the Mishnah while Hanukah was not.[132]

At the head of the roster of sacred days stands the weekly Sabbath, equalled in halakhic significance only by Yom Kippur. The other days which I indiscriminately refer to as festivals, holy days, or sacred days and which some books refer to as "feasts," are all of equal sanctity in the halakhah except for Yom Kippur, Hanukah and Purim. Yom Kippur is of a greater sanctity, on a par with the Sabbath. The latter two are of lesser sanctity, more or less on a par with *hol hamoèd*, the intermediate days of Passover between the first and the seventh day of the festival, and the six intermediate days between the first day of Sukot and the Eighth Assembly Day or Shemini Azeret. In the Hebrew one finds such terms as *moèd* ("appointed time" or "time of gathering"); *hag* (derived from the term for a sacred procession around the altar); azeret (assembly); *mikrà kodesh* (holy convocation).

Rabbinic Judaism added a sacred day to each one of the Pentateuch except Yom Kippur. This additional day is known as *Yom Tov Sheni Shel Galuyot* (the Sacred Diaspora Day) and was observed for the second day of Passover, an eighth day appended to the seventh day, a second day appended to Shabuot, a second day appended to Rosh haShanah, the second day of Sukot and a second day appended to the Eighth Day of Assembly after Sukot. This day was urged upon Jews residing outside of Palestine only, and became regularized through the Babylonian Talmud and its ultimate hegemony in European Judaism. These extra days were ultimately discontinued by Reform Judaism during the nineteenth century and made optional in Conservative Judaism around 1968.[133]

Pesah, Shabuot, and Sukot are known as the "pilgrimage festivals" because of the biblical requirement that pilgrimages to the sanctuary be made at those crucial junctures in the agricultural calendar. They were times of harvest and gifts of first products were to be presented to the priests. In time these nature-oriented sacred days were historicized and connected with redemption (Pesah and Sukot) and revelation (Shabuot).[134] Rosh haShanah and Yom Kippur were never commemorative of agricultural or historical times. Purim and Hanukah, whatever their earlier associations may have been, were history-oriented from the beginning of their inclusion in the roster of Judaic sacred days.

In addition to these sacred days the Judaic liturgical calendar includes a number of official fast days. Aside from Yom Kippur the significant ones are five in number. Four of

these are connected with the fall of Jerusalem in 587 B.C. and
one, observed on the day before Purim, is associated with the
peril presented by Haman and based upon Est. 4:16. The former
four consist of the following: a) the third day of Tishri,
marking the assassination of Gedalyah, governor of Jerusalem
after the destruction of 587 B.C. (II Ki. 25:22-26); b) the
tenth day of Tebet, marking the beginning of the seige of Jerusalem in 589 B.C. (II Ki. 25:1); c) the seventeenth of Tamuz,
marking the breach in the walls of Jerusalem in 587 B.C. (II
Ki. 25:3); d) the ninth of Ab. marking the sack of Jerusalem
and the burning of the temple (II Ki. 25:9). That these four
fasts were very old is evident at Zekh. 8:19. But c and d
are not observed on the days recorded in the Bible, because
when they were standardized by the rabbis after 70 A.D. the
rabbis chose the dates that were crucial in the Roman seige.
On the other hand anthropologists might attribute the choice
of the seventeenth of Tamuz to the fact that it was already a
long-time judaized pagan fast day in Babylonia where their
neighbors bewailed the god Tamuz who was believed to sink into
the netherworld on the eighteenth of that month. Similar explanations are provided for other days. Be that as it may,
the five fasts remained deeply rooted in Judaism in their
historicized form until modern times. Not even the reestablishment of Israel in 1948 has dislodged them entirely
from the liturgical calendar, although all five have undergone modification and are observed with varying degrees of
meticulousness in the different denominations.[135]

B. *Aspects of Theology*

The survey of the theology of worship above presents the
major theological principles that can be gleaned from the
Judaic liturgy. These same concepts, beliefs, and doctrines
are embodied in the symbolism and observances of the holy
days and the fast days. We will briefly review how this works
its way through the calendar occasions by beginning with the
first sacred day of the liturgical year, Rosh haShanah, although that is considered the first day of the seventh month.

1. *Rosh HaShanah*

The Bible refers to the month of the exodus as the first
month of Israel's calendar (Ex. 12:12). But eventually, in a
process too complicated to recall here the New Year was observed on the first day of the seventh month and is called a
"trumpeting of memorial" or of "remembrance." It introduced
the period leading to the Day of Atonement on the tenth of the

same month, and became known as Rosh haShanah, the new year.
It cannot be determined at how early a time in the proto-
rabbinic period this occurred. On the one hand it is a situation which is taken for granted in the earliest rabbinic
sources. But on the other hand, neither intertestamental literature nor Philo know of a "New Year" holy day. Philo refers
to it as "the opening of the sacred month" and "trumpet feast."
He thinks of the trumpets as alluding to the revelation at
Sinai and as a warning of the mighty consequences that flow
from revelation. This is only a mild allusion to the theme of
judgment which became central in the rabbinic Rosh haShanah.
But Philo still does not think of Rosh haShanah as the new
year for he refers to Shemini Azeret as the "closing," the
last sacred day of the year. This suggests that it was not yet
a universally observed day in its rabbinic form. But it was
probably emerging, for tannaitic literature reflecting the
views of the Hillelite and Shammaite schools which are undoubtedly antecedent to, and contemporary with Philo, contains
the complex of ideas which we associate with Rosh haShanah.[136]

The idea of "remembrance" in the reference to the day at
Lev. 23:24 was soon interpreted to mean human remembrance before God, and thus it became a day of judgment. The rabbinic
legacy also emphasized commemoration of the creation, and of
the kingship of God over the universe. But it highlights the
observances of a typological day of judgment. On this day,
it is believed, all humans are judged and their fate for the
coming year is decided. Repentance is still possible and
Rosh haShanah inaugurates the ten day period of repentance
when humans are still able to win reprieve from any adverse
judgment, so that when the decreee is to be sealed at the
close of Yom Kippur the person may yet win atonement and enjoy
the blessing of a good year. The motif of a book of life is
highlighted, with one view that there are three books, one
for the wicked, one for the righteous, and a third for the
intermediate.[137]

The ritual and the liturgy of Rosh haShanah embody the
great themes of Judaic theology.[138] Among the most suggestive
aspects of the liturgy is the selection of the binding of
Isaac (Gen. 22) as the Torah reading of the second day. In
this way creation and the resurrection motif of the targumic
version of the story are brought into juxtaposition. The
kingship theme is highlighted in the *shofar* ritual when a
ram's horn is sounded to the recital of verses that speak of
God's sovereignty, remembrances, and events of the past that
are connected with the sounding of a ram's horn including the
revelation at Sinai. And it is of utmost consequence to our
thesis that in all three sets of verses we find the same

themes reiterated. In the *malkhuyot* verses (kingship) God's sovereignty is exalted and climaxed by the eschatological hope of God's universal kingship (Zekh. 14:9). In the *zikhronot* verses (remembrances) we have the affirmation of creation. A major element of remembrance is the universe itself and all events and secret things which are revealed before God since the first day of creation for "this day is the beginning of your work." Thus the Rosh haShanah day has the cosmic importance of the day of creation itself. God's saving wonders at different junctures of history are recited and finally petition is made that God remember the àkedah and the exodus. Once more Isaac is juxtaposed with the exodus and allusion is made to the typology of Isaac as the sacrificial paschal lamb. The berakhah itself closes in an interesting fashion: God is petitioned to remember the àkedah and the covenant. This appears to juxtapose the covenant and Isaac, and allude to the sacrificial act of circumcision and the paschal lamb along with the expiation of Isaac. The *shoferot* verses (telling of the use of the ram's horn) emphasize the theophany at Sinai, and lead on to the ram's horn soundings that will herald the messianic redemption.[139]

In sum Rosh haShanah enshrines the three leading motifs of Judaic theology: a) creation, b) the complex of revelation-covenant-election and c) redemption. All three embody the sovereignty or kingship of God and therefore clearly speak in terms that point to the ultimate consummation of all of these motifs, the sovereignty of God, or what is often referred to as the Kingdom of Heaven. Rosh haShanah thus commemorates the cosmic birth and the cosmic consummation.

2. *Yom Kippur*[140]

Biblically this was the occasion of cultic expiation. The goat sent to Azalzel, the demon of the wilderness, was the vicarious atonement that bore the sins of the community. The priest offered another goat on the altar. Apparently we have here a relic of ancient obeisance to a demon-god side by side with the expiation made before Yhwh. In rabbinic times, however, the emphasis is upon penance, transformation of character and atonement as a consequence of human repentance. The fast is seen as an opportunity to place oneself in subordination to God by a form of penance: "You are to afflict yourselves." But the rabbinic view went beyond that. Rabbis saw both death and Yom Kippur as agencies of atonement. But *teshuvah,* repentance, had to take place before death and with the observance of Yom Kippur. The prevailing view insisted that penance must be accompanied by change of character and the reconciliation with God must be preceded by reconciliation with fellow humans (M. Yom. 8:8-9).[141]

Philo indicates that Yom Kippur was already understood in highly spiritual terms and reflects the fact that confession and entreaty for forgiveness played a major role in the liturgy as early as the first century B.C. in the diaspora. He writes of the Yom Kippur liturgy already occupying the entire day during which the worshipper asks for remission of both voluntary and involuntary sins, reminiscent of the *al het* prayer and other *selihot* (*Spec. Laws* II, 32 (193ff.)). There is a strong emphasis placed upon morality as a central motif in the morning *haftarah* from Is. 58. And in the afternoon the book of Jonah is recited as a second *haftarah* with its emphasis upon God's universal forgiveness. The symbolism of Jonah is further suggestive in that he descends into the watery depths and rises again. Sin and hell are overcome by God's compassion and the possibility of atonement, a possibility that awaits not only a repentant Jew, but even a penitent pagan sinner.

The cycle of Yom Kippur liturgy emphasizes confession, penitance, God's compassion, and atonement. The *Neilah* service which has come to mean metaphorically the closing of the gates of heaven, is a borrowing of the last of the day's worship at the temple when the gates were shut for the night. The agadic notion is that at this hour the book of life is sealed. The liturgy closes with the cry of Israel at Carmel after Elijah wrought his miracle against the prophets of Baal, "The Lord, He is God" (I Ki. 18:39). In this way allusion is made to Elijah, harbinger of redemption, and the shofar is sounded as it will be at the hour of the messianic advent. And so, at its ultimate moment Yom Kippur too takes on the significance of pointing to the eschatological hour of reconciliation with God and the advent of the spiritual Kingdom.

One further comment is of interest. In the course of the centuries additions were regularly made to the worship order in the form of *piyutim*. These were woven into the texture of the basic liturgy. And thus we find that in the second berakhah of the amidah which celebrates God's creative and regenerative power in nature, in society, and in the life, death, and resurrection of the individual, *Neilah* has an added line. This again bears out the notion often reiterated in this volume, of the high significance of Isaac's akedah. The *piyut* refers to Isaac and alludes to events recorded in scripture. The poet then turns in entreaty to God and cries out,

> "O Lord, Your name is interwoven with us,
> Bring nigh your salvation.
> Redeem us soon;
> Revive us with your dew
> *As you did for him* who mediated at evening.[142]

This indicates the tenacity of the daring concept of Isaac's
resurrection and of the ákedah having been more than a "binding." From the pre-Christian targums into medieval *piyut* the
idea fascinated the sages and synagogue poets. And thus the
closing moments of Yom Kippur reflect the all-pervasive
rabbinic theology which centers on redemption, individual and
communal, historical and metahistorical. And finally it
should be noted that in the closing line of the well-known
abinu malkenu prayer ("Our Father, our King") the worshipper
throws himself at the mercy of God's grace. He confesses
". . .be gracious unto us and answer us, for we possess no
deeds; deal with us in loving righteousness and save us."
In the great diatribe about faith and works, Yom Kippur
crystallizes the ancient theology that no works can stand
alone: in the moment of ultimate confrontation the human must
be the recipient of God's loving and undeserved grace.

3. *Sukot and Shemini Azeret*

Of all the sacred days only Shemini Azeret, the Eighth
Day of Assembly, has no apparent agricultural, historical or
theological significance. This apparent lack, however, is
made up with an early post-talmudic introduction of the
geshem prayer for rain embellished by a *piyut* that relates to
the doctrine of the merits of the fathers and particularly to
the ákedah. We read ". . .you convinced his parent to slaughter him and to spill his blood like water. . .For Isaac's sake,
be gracious with a flow of water. . ." In this way the observance of Azeret was accommodated to the water libation
ritual of the ancient temple that climaxed the festival of
Sukot.

Sukot was originally an agricultural festival, later
historicized, and the booths (sukot) that are the symbol of
the festival were said to commemorate the temporary structures
in which Israel dwelt in the wilderness. In this way it was
also theologized to recall God's deliverance of Israel from
Egypt. The *lulab* or palm branch joined by the willow, myrtle,
and citron, based on Lev. 23:40, probably originally associated with the harvest, were transformed by rabbinic ágadah into
symbols of the patriarchs, or different components of the community, and even of parts of the human anatomy. They were

carried in processions around the altar.[143]

Once again, however, we find that rabbinic liturgical arrangement has brought the eschatological motif to the forefront. The *haftarah* reading for the first day of Sukot is from Zekh. 14, an eschatological chapter in which the observance of Sukot is seen to become a universal one (vv.16-19). The punishment for those who will not join in the worship of God will be that no rain will fall for them. Rain is the symbol of regeneration and drought of death. Sukot with its water libation ceremony and its prayer for rain is thus made to allude to the eschatological rain and to the regeneration which is eternal life. In this way Sukot comes to balance Pesah, and the two, in the symmetry of each occurring on the fifteenth day of the "first" month of each half of the year, become twin festivals of redemption. This, furthermore, accommodates itself to the tradition that the future redemption will be in Tishri, and not in Nisan (B.R.H. 11b). The eschatological typology of Sukot is indicated by the rabbis' choice of Ez. 38:18-39:16 as the *haftarah* of the Sabbath that falls during Sukot, a selection which deals with the great apocalyptic struggle at the end of days, the war of Gog and Magog.

There can be no question of the rabbinic desire to bind Shemini Azeret into this same redemptive mood when they selected I Ki. 8:54-66 as the *haftarah* for the day. It provides hope and consolation that the dedication of the temple by Solomon is typological for the future temple that will arise when the great messianic day of Zekh. 14 and Ez. 38 will come about. And there too the dedication of the temple is bound up with the observances of Sukot, the *hag* (v. 65) just as the eschaton and Sukot are united at Zekh. 14.[144]

(Simhat Torah, the popular festival widely known and occurring as the second day of Shemini Azeret, or, where only one day is observed being meshed with Shemini Azeret, does not come under our purview here since it is of medieval origin. See Emergence II, index).

4. *Hanukah*

The festival of Hanukah is not mentioned in the Judaic Bible. It is based upon the reports in I and II Maccabees of the rededication of the temple by the Hasmoneans in 164 B.C. and the subsequent observance of an eight-day festival. This observance was then embodied in a halakhah by Judah the Maccabee, his brothers, and an assembly, for permanent annual observance of an eight-day festival (I Macc. 4:36-61; II Macc. 10:1-8). It is possible that the latter source gives a correct account, that the first Hanukah was a substitute Sukot that year, and consequently the festival of dedication was observed for eight days. On the other hand, tradition recorded that Moses, Hezekiah and Zerubbabel dedicated the altar in eight-day festivals.[145]

In any event, the festival of Hanukah was celebrated as a festival of rededication of the temple. It should not be seen as commemorating the victory of "Hebraism" over "Hellenism" as if there is an absolute antithesis between the two. As has been noted in Pt. 1, Ch. 5, hellenism was an influential ingredient of Judaism, and the Hasmoneans themselves were probably of hellenistic circles, even if not of the extreme variety. Theologically, Hanukah commemorates monotheism and its victory over pagan polytheism.

The divine fire alighting upon the altar which would signal the return of the Shekhinah to the temple did not occur and the Hasmoneans kindled the menorah themselves. This became the act of commemoration since it is also a cultic act which can be performed anywhere. For this reason the light-kindling custom of Hanukah need not be a borrowing from pagan solstice festivals. But again, if it is, we have another clear example of "judaizing" a pagan practice and bringing it within the parameters of Judaic theology. Thus, assuming the pagan light-kindling custom signified the regeneration of the sun at the annual solstice, the Hanukah light-kindling custom symbolized the regeneration of the monotheistic true religion in Jerusalem. The prayer recited at the occasion, *àl hanisim* ("for the miracles"), inserted into both the àmidah and Grace After Meals, is a very old one.[146] As is generally the function of Judaic liturgy, this prayer brings the "lights" festival within the orbit of Judaic theology. The prayer acknowledges the miraculous ways of God with his chosen people and the great redemption that took place in the days of Mattathias and his sons. It lauds God for the victory of the weak over the strong and few over the many, emphsizing that with God it is neither numbers nor power that prevail. So too the *haftarah* for Sabbath of Hanukah, consists of selections from Zekhariah, and contains the verse, ". . .not by might nor by power, but by my spirit, says the Lord" (4:6).

In sum the *àl hanissim* transforms the hellenistic Hasmonean military adventure into the redemption of the Jews from the grip of polytheism and the salvation of monotheism for its historic yet-uncompleted mission. And equally important, the prayer makes no mention of the events beyond the liberation of

the temple, thus signifying the theological significance of
Hanukah under the aspect of eternity as over against any tem-
poral national idea.

5. *Purim*[147]

Purim celebrates the saving of the Judaic community of
Persia, an event purportedly described in the biblical Book of
Esther. That it was a commonly observed festival during the
first century is clear from Josephus but its origin is obscure.
Scholars have debated whether the Book of Esther is historical
or merely a fictional work that explains Purim. Some believe
that Purim had its origin in the eastern diaspora, and represents the absorption into Judaism of a pagan festival with
mixed Persian-Babylonian themes. The style of observance preserves eastern New Year features such as amusements, banqueting, exchange of gifts, and the motif of casting *puru*, lots,
which fits the Babylonian idea that human destiny is determined at the New Year.[148] While scholars have been far from
developing a consensus on the origin of Purim, the current
weight of opinion is on the side of a historical core embellished by legendary and fictional elements.[149] Consequently
Purim is to be seen as a Judaic adaptation of a pagan festival
that had carnival aspects to it, and that the Book of Esther
is an effort to rationalize it. The story probably adopted a
basically historical record of a crisis in Persia but dis-
guised the names of the protagonists.

The argument is often offered that Purim or the Day of
Mordecai (II Macc. 15:36), could not have existed before the
time of Ben Sira since the latter does not mention Mordecai
among the historical heroes of Israel. But Ben Sira does
not mention Ezra either. Neither Philo nor Qumran mention the
day of Purim or the Book of Esther, but this may only be because the book was theologically repugnant, lacked mention of
divine intervention, and rationalized the sexual deviation
of a Jewish woman giving herself to a pagan king. Furthermore,
since Qumran observed only the Pentateuchal festivals, eschewing also Hanukah, it had no need of a book that told of
the ostensible events behind the occasion. As late as the
third century A.D. Babylonian rabbis disputed the sanctity of
the Book of Esther, but it is not clear whether they simul-
taneously objected to observing the festival of Purim (B. Meg.
7a; San. 100a). Some rabbis might have objected to Purim on
the grounds that Lev. 23:2 ". . .*these* are my festivals,"
refers emphatically to those listed at Lev. 23 and no others,
an emphasis repeated at Lev. 23:4, 37 and therefore refused
to prohibit work on Purim (P. Meg. 70b). On the other hand,

they could not object to Purim while celebrating Hanukah.
Moreover, the rabbis had a record of innovating halakhah.
They believed that all of their innovations were already known
and legitimized at Sinai, and specifically some held that the
scroll of Esther was recited to Moses at Sinai. Its Sinaitic
status was emphasized by giving it the same permanence as the
Pentateuch declaring its reading to be an eternal obligation
as is the Pentateuch's, in the face of the eventual messianic
annulment of Prophets and Hagiographa (P. Meg. 70d).

It may be considered surprising that the rabbis took so
emphatic a positive position toward salvaging a book and promoting the observance of a festival recorded in it when this
book does not contain any theological values normally associated with biblical Judaism. It is hardly convincing that the
book became popular during the Hasmonean era as an inspiration
to Jews to have faith in the final outcome. There is no martyrdom in Esther. The king is innocent of wrongdoing, hardly
the image Hasmoneans would want to project for the Selucid
monarch. The only point of contact between Esther and the
Hasmonean era is the hatred of, and vengeance against pagans,
and the mass conversions (Est. 8:17) parallel to the forced
conversion of pagans to Judaism by the Hasmoneans.[150] The
chauvinistic ethnicity in the book, and its consequences, the
extermination of men, women, and children (8:11) and the rage
of vengeance expressed at 9:5f., 13, 16 are hardly calculated
to enhance the religious life.[151]

We are therefore left with the question: how did Purim
originate, and what was the theological rationale for rabbinic
continuance of this observance? The rabbis sought to theologize Purim and give it religious and ethical meaning because
it was a popular festival. They created liturgy for it, a
Torah reading of the Book of Esther from a scroll, analogous
to the Pentateuch. They stressed the giving of gifts and
charity. They could not eliminate the bacchanalian aspect of
the ancient carnival festival so they permitted a lack of
sobriety on Purim, and to blur the theme of vengeance urged
people metaphorically to allow themselves to fall into such
abandon that they no longer knew the difference between Mordecai and Haman. They established the Torah reading from Ex.
17:8-16 on the continuous obligation to destroy Amalek, the
treacherous enemy of Israel, thereby elevating Purim to cosmic dimensions. It then becomes the typological event of all
efforts to destroy God's people, which are forever thwarted
by God who personally conducts the war against Amalek in every
generation. The reading of the *megilah,* the Esther scroll,
was declared to be as significant as the cult, and with a
touch of anachronism some rabbis argued that one must interrupt torah study just as priests and levites were to interrupt

the cult to hear the reading of the *megilah*.[152]

It appears quite likely that the following reconstruction is plausible. Jews of Susa adopted the pagan festivities at some unknown time between the Babylonian exile and the advent of Alexander the Great. These Jews constituted a major community in the diaspora as is seen from a gate of the Jerusalem temple which commemorated the Persian capital with a sculptured design of the royal palace. Susa's Jews exported their pre-Spring festival but neither Mordecai nor Esther had any religious standing anywhere, and so their order that all Jews of the Persian provinces celebrate their Persian festival (Est. 9:20-22) had to be voluntarily adopted (vv. 23, 27f.). At the height of Persian power the entire Near East was under the sway of the Persian monarchy and so the order of Mordecai is patently presented as one that encompasses Palestine, Egypt, and the Graeco-Roman diaspora as well. It is apparent, however, that there was resistance to it and that Esther is represented as sending a second order (9:29-32). It is also quite likely that a Jew of Susa wrote the book in the hope of universalizing the Susa festival.[153] The festival was probably only gradually incorporated into Judaic life and after 70 (there is no evidence for its observance in the Temple), the rabbis saw the need to theologize it, and create a halakhic superstructure to overcome its pagan and secular associations.

6. *Passover*[154]

It is possible that the oldest sources in the Bible indicate there were originally in Israel two separate festivals, the ḥag hapesaḥ (Pesah festival) and ḥag hamaẓot (Mazot festival).[155] At Deut. 16:1-8 it appears that the paschal lamb is no longer to be offered at one's home but only at the central sanctuary, and that the pilgrims also then celebrated the Mazot festival. Scholars incorrectly assume the people were to go home after offering the paschal lamb and observe the Mazot festival at home, thus seeing some discrepancy in how the logistics would all work out. But Deut. 16:7, that they were to go to their "tents" means precisely that: to their temporary dwellings at the region of the sanctuary. In any event, the two festivals (if they were two) were thus incorporated as one pilgrimage festival observed in Jerusalem in monarchical times (II Ki. 23:23; II Chron. 35:16-19). The process of this consummation which was certainly stabilized before the first century is a complex one and will not detain us here.

There is unanimity among all the documents referring to

the Pesah and Mazot celebrations that they commemorate the redemption of Israel from Egypt. There is no real agricultural
or mythic reminiscence left in the Pentateuch regardless of
how these festivals originated in pre-Israelite times. Passover in Judaism is inextricably bound up with the doctrines of
election, redemption and revelation. The redemption takes
place as fulfillment of the promise that was part of the
covenant-election, and with the purpose of consummating this
election with the revelation at Sinai (Ex. 3:12; 6:3-8).

There is a striking difference between the Paschal sacrifice and all other sacrifices in Judaism. In the case of all
other sacrifices either the whole sacrifice is burned on the
altar, or if some of the flesh is to be eaten, part of it is
given to the priest and part to the celebrants. But in the
case of the paschal sacrifice, it is entirely eaten by the
celebrants. This is probably due to the high antiquity of
the paschal offering which goes back to a time when the head
of a family, clan, or tribe was the officiating priest. This
antiquity of the ritual allows us to surmise that at one time,
although it was not wholly consumed on the altar, it was never-
the less expiatory. For this reason it was accompanied by the
detailed blood ceremonies at Ex. 12. In this case it was the
purgative and protective use of blood, the "life" of the
victim as substitute for the celebrant which saved the celebrant. At later times the *ōlah* or whole burnt-offering
served the expiatory purpose by its total annihilation. The
process by which this change took place, and when it was
finalized is no longer possible to determine. Originally,
then, the paschal offering was an expiatory communion meal.
By absorbing its flesh the celebrants became one with it in a
figurative or psychic communion. This notion is still preserved in both the Passover Seder when each celebrant is to
see himself as delivered from bondage, and in the Christian
eucharist.[156]*

This expiatory paschal communion meal included maẓah (unleavened cakes) and maror (bitter herbs) (Ex. 12:8f.). Whatever primitive religious custom these rituals are drawn from,
in historical times they are symbolically related to the experience of the bitterness of bondage and the subsequent redemption. Other rituals were added in the course of time, but
the narration of the historical and miraculous events and their
explanation functioning as a liturgical order to accompany the
ritual is already enjoined at Ex. 12:26f. (M. Pes. 10:5). The
reason given in historical times for the maẓah represents the

*See excursus   at n. 156.

rationale offered at Ex. 12:34, 39, that they baked unleavened bread because there was no time for the dough to rise since they had departed in haste. Yet this tells us little, for they had eaten mazah with the paschal lamb, and in any case had been enjoined to eat unleavened bread for seven days (Ex. 12:15, 18). The real question is why unleavened bread was attached to the paschal lamb in the first place. No doubt this was because leaven and fermentation were regarded as agents of degeneration and were symbolically inappropriate as part of an expiatory sacrifice and communion meal in which holy food is consumed. There was probably a universal view of leaven as an agent of corruption, and the rabbis later considered the role of the *yezer hara,* the evil inclination in humans, as leaven in the dough. If the paschal-mazah sacrificial meal was expiatory it is understandable that the bread to be eaten had to represent naturalness, and contain no elements of imperfection.[157]

Something of value can be learned from the traditions preserved by Philo who conveys to us alternative diaspora practices, norms that were observed because of the distance from the Temple in Jerusalem and a continuing desire to observe the paschal offering because of its expiatory mystique. Philo calls the Passover festival *diabatèria,* "the Crossing-festival" by which he means the crossing of Israel from Egypt to freedom.[158] He points out that the people as a whole are raised to the priesthood in celebrating the paschal offering. Philo also alludes to the Seder liturgy, that people gather "to fulfill with prayers and hymns" the festive custom. Philo makes no mention of the blood ceremonials and we need go no further than Deuteronomy (16:1-8) to read that in later times this blood ritual was no longer part of the celebration of the paschal offering. This was not only because if was held at the central sanctuary in Palestine, but even where it was still conducted in private homes as it was done in the diaspora according to Philo, the blood ceremonial was not observed. In this Philo is at one with contemporary proto-rabbis who referred to the "Pesah of Egypt" and the Pesah of the generations" (later times) as subject to two distinct sets of halakhic norms, and attest to the fact that the blood ceremonial is no longer observed. [159]

Deuteronomy might embody the first major evidence for the evolution of the pesah celebration. But surely the process from the "Pesah of Egypt" in Exodus to the rabbinic literature was a gradual one. Despite efforts by the authorities behind Deuteronomy to centralize the paschal observance in Jerusalem, Jews in diaspora lands observed it in their homes. This tradition reflected in Philo is found among the Elephantine Jews in a papyrus dated to 419–418 B.C. It is clear from the post-exilic sources that in Jerusalem the offering was performed by priests and levites and the people participated in the meal. The account of the paschal offering at Jubilees 49 prohibits its being eaten outside the sanctuary, and appears to sanction only one sanctuary. But this author also reflects the fact that an innovation had been made since Pentateuchal halakhah was recorded. He refers to wine being taken at the meal and retrojects the drinking of wine to the generation of the Exodus. It is probable that sometime between the effort to confine the sacrifice in Palestine to Jerusalem, and the Hasmonean era when Jubilees is compiled, red wine was introduced to the family ritual as a substitute for the blood ceremonial of which the individual family was now deprived. It is true that wine could have been introduced as part of family merriment, but the fact is that in the earliest times when the paschal offering was performed at home and each family head was the "priest" and it was a family celebration, wine was not included. The reason must be that they had the blood ceremonies, and when these came to an end the wine was substituted. In place of smearing the blood they drank the wine to parallel eating the sacrifice and thereby absorbing the expiatory power of the blood-substitute. Similarly, in later times when the paschal offering was no longer made after 70 A.D., the mazah was substituted. It was declared to represent the paschal lamb, and was named the *afikomen*.[160]

From the New Testament we see that the Palestinian paschal celebration was held in Jerusalem but not necessarily at the Temple. Various details in the gospels corroborate rabbinic literature and Philo's halakhic details in *Questions and Answers, Exodus*.[161] But there is no way to tell from the gospels whether the meal was a family meal or a fellowship meal of males. The Last Supper of Jesus and his disciples cannot be used as a normal example. But it is evident that women were in Jerusalem for the occasion, and if so it is reasonable to surmise that families gathered together. The Last Supper indicates that a first century Seder included reclining, a dish other than bread to open the meal, a dipping, bread passed around, wine taken. In Luke's account of wine before the bread we have the kiddush. The Seder is concluded with psalms. Neither Josephus nor the literature of Qumran teaches us anything new about the Passover festival.[162]

The Mishnah and Tosefta offer us the fullest picture of Passover observance in the last years of the Temple and in the early decades of rabbinic Judaism. Here we find the full-blown ritual which is the source and basis of the ritual of contemporary Judaism. The liturgy and rituals fully described

in tractate Pesahim become the foundation of the Passover
Hagadah, one of the most popular Judaic liturgical manuals.
The Hagadah itself is an excellent theological source-book
for Passover, for not only its rituals but its songs reflect
a theology deeply immersed in the eschatological hope. The
Hagadah, however, is a compilation of medieval times and not
germane to our discussion.

The rabbinic material that can be dated to the first
century or to the early second century recalls for us an
earlier halakhah and an older Pesah ritual. In the rabbinic
literature, whether applying to before or after 70 A.D., there
is an emphasis upon the use of wine. The rabbis introduced a
wide variety of practices designed to minimize the possibility
of leaven being present in one's home or in the community.
This may have been under pietistic influence of the Jubilees-
Qumran circles. All leaven was to be removed and burned on
the thirteenth and fourteenth of Nisan. But the proto-rabbis
were not separatists and for them Jerusalem had primacy. To
encourage people to come they allowed the sacrifice to be
eaten throughout Jerusalem and not only at the Temple. In
these and other ways we find how proto-rabbinic halakhah modified earlier halakhah. For example, contrary to the Torah,
the remains of the sacrifice did not have to be burned on the
first day (the fifteenth) but could be burned on the sixteenth,
and even later if the sixteenth was a Sabbath.[163]

The tenth chapter of Mishnah Pesahim is the most comprehensive source for the ritual and liturgy of Passover when the
Temple still functioned. This liturgy and ritual have been
incorporated into rabbinic Judaism. Four cups of wine are now
required for the Seder. This is the first halakhah mentioned
that is related to the ritual of the evening, and this indicates its importance. This importance can be understood only
if it is the consequence of something profounder than family
merriment, something more theological like the substitution of
the drinking of wine for the blood ceremonial. The explanation for four cups supports this view. Each cup is a reminder
of one of God's redemptive statements at Ex. 6:6-7. Each time
an individual formally drinks one of the cups he is identifying
with the salvation of Israel in Egypt. It is as if he is redeemed, as if he has experienced expiation. Each of the rituals of the Seder is now accompanied with a berakhah formula
referred to previously in the theology of worship. There now
takes place a dipping, perhaps a substitute for dipping of the
hyssop in blood. There is a dipping of lettuce or another
vegetable into salt water. This is called *karpas* from the
Greek word for fruit or vegetable. There is another dipping
of *maror* into *haroses*, a mixture of nuts, apples, wine and

cinnamon, or similar ingredients, which constitute a pulp that is reminiscent of the clay used by Israelites to fashion bricks during their sojourn in Egypt. There was a difference of opinion as to whether *haroset* is really a mizvah. In any event, it remained a permanent part of the Seder. Dipping the *maror* into the *haroset* identifies with the bondage expressed in the making of bricks, symbolizing the bitterness that arose out of the mortar. At this point the child is instructed to inquire of his parent why it is that this night Jews eat only mazah, and not *hamez*, why they indulge in *maror*, eat only roast meat and dip twice.[164]

The recital of the events follows. The core of the Hagadah remains to this day the passages recorded in the Mishnah and explicated in the Talmud, a midrash to Deut. 26:5-8 (B. Pes. 116a). An integral part of the Seder is the formula of Gamaliel I. He requires that each person enter into communion with the generation of the Exodus, for each person must regard himself as having been redeemed. Here we have the effort to continue the expiatory concept. Gamaliel requires that each person recite a formula which becomes reminiscent of the Pauline eucharistic formula, which indeed Paul may have imitated from Gamaliel's Passover formula. Gamaliel asks that each person recite: "This is the Pesah, in remembrance (or which is eaten because. . .) of Makom's (God's) protection of the houses of our ancestors in Egypt; this is the mazah in remembrance of our ancestors' having been redeemed from Egypt; this is the *maror* in remembrance of the Egyptians' having embittered the lives of our ancestors in Egypt." Each formula is accompanied by a taste of the item, and the theological explanation is communion. The Gamaliel formula and rite makes a true communion meal out of the Seder even after the sacrifice is no longer brought and eaten. Hallel is recited.

The liturgy of the Seder consists of midrashic passages. It is designed to stimulate long discussions and we find the prototype of this in an anecdote recited at the Seder in which a group of rabbis discussed the exodus all night.[165] During the course of the recital a midrash affirms faith in God's eschatological promise to Abraham during his mystical experience (Gen. 15), as an ever-recurring divine fulfillment. It is emphatically asserted in a midrash to Deut. 26:8 that God Himself is Israel's redeemer to counter arguments of early Christians and gnostics that God did not directly deal with Israel. Emphasis is placed upon God's personal intervention, "the Holy One, Blessed be He, Himself, in His own glory and in His own person. . .(For God says, 'I will go through the land of Egypt. . .') I and not an angel. . .I and not a seraph . . .I and not a messenger. . ."

A hymn is used at the Seder known as *Dayyenu*. This is very old, dated to the second century B.C. It is a litany of deep theological import referring to the exodus, God's judgment on Egypt, the miracle of the crossing of the water, the miracle of God's concern in the wilderness, the gift of the Sabbath, revelation at Mount Sinai, the gift of the land and the Temple for expiation of sins. All of these items in the roster relate to the redemption of the future. The eschaton is to be as the creation, a new creation, and so the divine events which were the glory of the beginning of Israel will be paralleled in the eschataological time. It is of interest however, that *Dayyenu* does not include the Davidic dynasty in the roster of God's gifts. This may point to the eschatological view that did not believe this to be mandatory in God's plan.[166] That creation remained a Passover theme is seen in rabbinic discussion previously alluded to that the world was created in Nisan. In the recital of Ps. 136, the rabbis provided specifically for lauding God as creator in conjunction with His role as redeemer.[167]

The theology of the rabbis expressed itself primarily in the Seder liturgy. But the concept of total withdrawal from the corrupting leavening agent expressed itself in a rather stringent halakhah. This halakhah requires that many foods be restricted lest a suspicion of fermentation taints them. All products that contain any amount of grain ingredient are therefore prohibited. The halakhic rubrics related to leaven are many, dealing with searching for it before the festival, removing it, even annihilating it, selling valuable leaven for post-Passover retrieval, and others. Dishes and utensils that cannot be *kashered*, that is, those of earthenware or wood, must be set aside and special Passover dishes and utensils provided. Glass, metal, and silverware can be *kashered*. The process of *kashering* involves immersing the object in water that has been brought to a boil. There are differences of opinion on this as there are on what types of objects may be *kashered*. There are also differences of opinion over what type of food products and which specific items need be eschewed on Passover or require special inspection and labelling. There are frequently injustices committed against the consumer and travesties perpetrated upon the integrity of Judaism. The rabbinic halakhah became more prolific and complex with passing centuries, but the seeds are found in the talmudic sources. To discourage laxity the rabbis declared that any *ḥameẓ* not removed before the Passover is permanently forbidden. It is technically required that the home be thoroughly divested of all leaven in every form. Since this is practically impossible the device of "selling the *ḥameẓ* was later devised, in which a fictional sale to a gentile takes place, the owner

"repurchasing" it after Passover. This in turn is preceded
by a search for leaven on the night of the thirteenth of Nisan
which then theoretically turns up any ḥameẓ that has not been
consumed or sold. A perusal of the tractate Pesahim yields
sufficient data on how complex has become the halakhah of Passover as regards the presence, possession, and use of leaven,
not only as concerns products that are in themselves leaven
but those that have but a fraction of leaven ingredients.
This halakhic rigor taught by the rabbis was an inevitable
outcome of a restrictive exegesis of the words of the Torah
and possibly an influence of *perushite* piety in which the
rabbis had to prove their religious mettle.[168]

Modern technology points to various areas of Passover
halakhah that require revision. Among them are those that
relate to questions of chemical transformation in foods, and
the question of whether leaven traces are absorbed into the
surface of modern glazed china, glass, plastic, pyrex and
even glazed ceramic utensils. Rabbinic methodology and the
manifest optionalism it stimulated in religious practice is
valuable in current restudy of Passover halakhah.[169]

7. *Shaḇuot*[170]

The Torah ordains that, "on the morrow of the Sabbath"
an *ȯmer*, a sheaf offering of the harvest is to be brought
and waved before the Lord (Lev. 23:9-14). This day of the
sheaf offering is manifestly a *moėd*, a festival of the Lord,
reckoned in the roster of festivals, but it it not declared
to be a sacred day. A *mikrȧ kodesh*, a holy assembly, is not
called for, and work is not forbidden. The Torah then continues (vv. 15-22) with a requirement that "from the morrow of
the Sabbath, from the day that you brought the *ȯmer* of waving,"
fifty days are to be counted. On the fiftieth day an offering of new grain is to be made along with specified animal
sacrifices. Now a *mikrȧ kodesh* is to be announced and work is
forbidden (v. 21). It is generally assumed that this festival
of the fiftieth day, Pentecost, is identified with that which
is called Shaḇuot (Ex. 34:22; Deut. 16:9-10), *Yom habikurim*
(the day of the first fruits) when an offering of new grain is
ordained (Num. 28:26), and *ḥag hakaẓir* (the harvest festival)
when the first grain is reaped (Ex. 23:16)

These biblical verses have caused no end of uncertainty
and religious disputation. They have even figured in sectarian
separation and schism. No date for the festival is given.
What is meant by "the morrow of the Sabbath," or which Sabbath,
is obscure. When to begin the count of fifty days is an enig-

ma. One could count from whatever day one begins to harvest
(Deut. 16:19) and complete chaos would ensue. Unlike the
other sacred days in the comprehensive levitical roster (Lev.
23), Shabuot does not have dedicated to itself a mishnaic
tractate. We are, therefore, not in possession of a significant amount of clarifying literature. The historic consequence has been that in antiquity so-called Sadducees differed
from those who are called Pharisees on the question of the
date of Shabuot, and in later history Karaites differed from
rabbanites. Moreover it is unclear as to when the revelation
at Sinai became the focus of the celebration at Shabuot.

We have seen that ancient agricultural festivals were
historicized in the Torah itself, for example when Sukot is
arbitrarily connected with the exodus at Lev. 23:39-43. The
process of historicizing was part of a process of theologiz-
ing. The Judaic thrust increasingly became the celebration
of the mighty acts of God centered in the three great miracles: creation, revelation, and redemption. The one leg of
this significant theological tripod that was not connected
with a sacred day and was therefore not commemorated appropriately was revelation. In time the Judaic sages saw an opportunity based on scripture itself to connect revelation with
Pentecost. But before the rabbis fully proclaimed Pentecost
to be "the time of the giving of the Torah" other sages
taught that this was a most significant day of days. Perhaps
as the fiftieth day of a counting-cycle they saw it in a
Pythagorean sense as the perfect day, and hence the day of
revelation. When this happened and in what circles it had
its origin is something we no longer can determine. It is
not clearly reflected in the pre-exilic literature, nor is
it evidenced in post-exilic canonical literature. But that
Pentecost was already a most significant occasion unrelated
to the harvest during the early hellenistic period is manifest
from its treatment in Jubilees. But here again there is confusion regarding the dating. 171[*] Unfortunately our present
texts permit neither a solution to the problem of dating Pentecost nor to the question of when it became the celebration
of revelation.

The proto-rabbis and the priestly Establishment in Jerusalem functioned with the same lunar calendar. But they differed over whether "the morrow of the Sabbath" at Lev. 23:11,
15 refers to Sunday or to the day after the first day of Passover. The Sadduccean priests argued that no matter when Passover occurred, the sheaf offering should be made on a Sunday,

---

[*]See excursus at note 171.

and Pentecost would always fall on a Sunday. The only calendrical difference, therefore, between the proto-rabbis and the priests was over the question of the *ómer* and consequently over the date of Pentecost. The solar calendar of Jubilees and Qumran led those who followed them to many other differences.[172]

The argument over dating Pentecost was supplemented by other halakhic differences related to the *ómer* upon which the dating of Pentecost depended. The proto-rabbis argued that the *ómer* had to be reaped at night after the first day of Passover even if Passover fell on Friday and the reaping took place at the onset of the Sabbath. They argued that the *ómer*, like other elements of the cult, supersedes the Sabbath. This proto-rabbinic halakhah was rejected by the Qumranites who permitted only the Sabbath offering to be brought on the Sabbath, but no other (CDC 10:17-18). It was also rejected by Boethusians and presumably by the Sadducean priests who normally permitted no cultic activity at night.[173]

The question remains as to when the doctrine of revelation was attached to Pentecost. There is no clear statement on this in our literature. But it is only natural to expect that some spiritual leaders, perhaps induced by a non-farming urban population, would find the agricultural motif of Shabuot inadequate. Just as historicization was applied to other elements of tradition they would search for a historicizing motif for Pentecost. That motif was already at hand in both the biblical tradition and in the circle of Jubilees. It was easy enough to see that Israel came to Sinai in the third month (Ex. 19:1) and that within a few days the revelation took place. It was a slight matter of careful exegesis to decide precisely on which date the revelation took place. By combining the *ómer* count of fifty days with a computation of the sequence of days at Ex. 19:1-15 some sages arrived at the conclusion that "the third day" (Ex. 19:16) when the theophany took place was the sixth day of Sivan.[174]

Jubilees (1:1) records a tradition of the revelation on Sivan 16 and therefore the *ómer* as offered after Passover, a tradition which can be as old as the third century B.C. Considering this, and also that the Book of Joshua records that the new grain (*ómer*) was eaten the day after Passover (5:10f.), we can discern a difference of opinion over dating Pentecost already prevailing from earliest times. Similarly, whether to celebrate Pentecost as a festival of revelation was undoubtedly a matter of serious debate into proto-rabbinic times in light of the fact that the motif is absent from the Bible. For strict constructionists like the priests this would suf-

fice to discourage an uncertain celebration. For loose constructionists like the proto-rabbis the tradition that the
revelation at Sinai took place in the third month would suffice to attach to the festival at hand, Pentecost, the theologically significant motif. That this motif would become
universal after the destruction of the Temple and the cessation of the colorful first-fruits ceremonial, would be inevitable.[175]

The rabbinic halakhah that applies to Pentecost is the
same as that which applies to all sacred days and is rooted
in biblical norms. These come under the general rubrics of
rejoicing on the festival (Deut. 16:11) and resting from one's
occupation (Lev. 23:21). Similarly, the Pentecost liturgy is
the basic festival liturgy with the same features as other
festivals: the Hallel, the same ámidah, but including particulars that relate to Shaḫuot such as the formula "the time of
the giving of our Torah" which is inserted in the ámidah. The
ten commandments are read as the Torah lection. The Book of
Ruth is read at Pentecost (Sof. 14:18), usually as a private
matter. The significance of reading Ruth is in her acceptance
of Judaism with her famous line, "Your God is my God. . ."
The book thus becomes a paradigm of Sinai repeated: receiving
the Torah. And for the same reason in the nineteenth and
twentieth centuries there developed an increasing tendency to
celebrate confirmation for boys and girls at Shaḫuot time.
This expresses the concept that they are confirmed in their
faith as Ruth was, and as Israel was at Sinai in the beginning.

8. *The Fasts*

There are a number of fast-days in Judaism. Some are
public fasts in time of drought and pestilence, and others
are private fasts for penitence, remembering a deceased next
of kin and other personal matters. There are, however, four
major public fasts that commemorate historical occasions, the
fast of Esther (B. Meg. 2a), and the great fast of Yom Kippur.[176]

With the exception of the ninth of Aḫ and Yom Kippur
which are twenty-four hour fasts, eating and drinking is proscribed only from sunrise to sunset. On fast-days a variety
of liturgical changes, omissions and additions are made in
the public worship order. Anthropologists have sought un-
successfully to explain the reason for fasting. There is,
however, one thing all fasting has in common. It is a form of
abstinence which is designed to help the one who fasts to
orient himself or herself spiritually and to focus on non-

materialistic hopes and aspirations. As penance fasting is psychologically purgative. Fasting is generally accompanied by abstinence from sexual relations and other material pleasures and therefore provides a spiritual catharsis. All of the fasts recall the sinfulness of Israel, God's anger and punishment and the human need for repentance and forgiveness. The Torah lection is the paradigmatic story of the Golden Calf, and the prophetic lection is Is. 55:6-56:8 reassuring the community of God's love. There are more stringent halakhot for Tisha B'ab which is treated as a day of mourning (B. Taan. 3a).

9. *Minor Festivals*

The Judaic festival roster provides several additional days which are not commemorated in any manner other than by minor liturgical revisions and some small-scale observances. These include what was once a major biblical festival Rosh Hodesh, the New Moon. They also include Lag Beomer, the thirty-third day of the fifty-day *omer* cycle between Passover and Shabuot and the fifteenth day of Shebat, the Palestinian New Year for trees. Lag Beomer serves to break the lenten-like period of the seven weeks from Pesah to Shabuot known as *sefirah,* when a variety of abstentions were engaged in such as refraining from cutting the hair, listening to music, or solemnizing marriages. But actually the Lag Beomer day is not known until the time of the geonim.[177]

10. *The Sabbath*[178]

The Sabbath was of supreme covenantal importance. At Ex. 31:13-17 we have the paradigmatic passage which describes the Sabbath as a perpetual *ot*, a sign that God has sanctified Israel. Each member of Israel is to sanctify the Sabbath at the pain of death and "being cut off" for its violation. Furthermore, the Sabbath is to be observed forever as a *berit olam*, an eternal covenant. The Sabbath, moreover, is the sign that God is the creator. These ideas are repeated in a variety of ways in many other passages in scripture. To these key theological concepts of sign, covenant (election), sanctification (of both Israel and the Sabbath), the perpetuity of the Sabbath and its function in Judaic religion and creation, there is added only one other at Deut. 5:15, the commemoration of redemption from Egypt. In this way the biblical Sabbath becomes a composite of all of the major theological concepts of Judaism. Its observance, in effect marks the affirmation of a creedal statement. This basic Sabbath theology is expressed in the kiddush which was discussed earlier. We can surmise that the death penalty for Sabbath violation came to an end by the first century when the Judaic court lost the right to impose the penalty, if it was really imposed for Sabbath violation until that time.

As noted in Pt.1, Ch.2, the Sabbath grew in importance with the spread of the diaspora and most especially after the Babylonian destruction of the Temple in 587 B.C. When observance of the cult was no longer possible it remained possible to cling to such symbols of the sanctified covenantal relationship as circumcision, the Sabbath, and holy days. Abstention from work and rituals of commemoration were possible everywhere, and without reference to the cult. In this sense the Sabbath was an excellent medium as a "sign" of the covenant in the diaspora. One scholar has duly noted that the Sabbath is in truth a sacrament, "a sacred sign by which a religious community is bound together. . ."179

Like the various historical or anthropological puzzles that confront us with the origin and evolution of the sacred days as they appear in the Bible, the Sabbath too has ambiguities. From the earliest times its violation is singled out by the biblical preachers as a "counter-sign" of Israel's infidelity (Jer. 17:19-27; Ez. 22:26). But it is by no means clear what is forbidden on the Sabbath, on the negative side, and what rites of commemoration are expected on the positive side.

The Old Testament is replete with Sabbath references. The leading prohibition often reiterated is to do no *melakhah*, but the term is never defined. The Sabbath is sacred as a source of both humanitarian (Ex. 23:12; Deut. 5:14) and cultic concern (Num. 28:9-10; I Chron. 23:30-31). The intertestamental writings and both Philo and Josephus attest to the great significance of the Sabbath.180 The Sabbath halakhah of the Pentateuch is enlarged by Jeremiah and Nehemiah and further expanded by the circles which produced Jubilees and the Zadokite Document. The constant evolution of prohibitions from the simple interdiction of agricultural labor and the kindling of fire in the Pentateuch to the complex Sabbath halakhah of later talmudic times is bound up with the centrality of the theology of the Sabbath. It was the way the ancient sages thought it best to secure the individual's consciousness of the covenantal holiness of the day.

It appears that the term *melakhah* may be connected to the term *malakh* which signifies a "calling" or an occupation.181 Certainly the sparse prohibitions found in the Pentateuch and

alluded to in Amos, Jeremiah and Nehemiah are all connected
with probable occupations in agriculture, trade and commerce,
and the transportation related to these occupations. Jubilees
and the Zadokite document take us beyond this criterion and
introduce a variety of new prohibitions which may not be
connected with one's occupation. What we notice is that from
the earliest times, while the proto-rabbis differ significant-
ly with the pietists they too begin to collect a large variety
of prohibitive halakhot which would lead to a quiescent
Sabbath. But unlike the pietistic circles the proto-rabbis
considered these not to be scriptural prohibitions, but
rather *shebut*, a form of cessation from tasks that is rabbinic
in status. It is clear that as the rabbis took control of
religious life after 70 they adopted, adapted and expanded the
pietistic Sabbath observances in order to create a wholly
quiescent day. This spiritualized approach to the Sabbath was
based upon Is. 58:13 and some read that as implying withdrawal
from every form of physical and mental exertion and mundane
thought and deed. Some of the halakhot incorporated into the
corpus were almost trivial, but they served the overarching
principle of changing the profane into the sacred and creating
a celestial moment in the midst of mundane time. This quiescent, spiritual moment in time became symbolic of the eschatological seventh millenium. The Sabbath was seen as a fore-
taste of the messianic age, and the latter was considered to
be the perfect Sabbath when the original perfect creation
will have been restored.[182]

Although rabbinic formulations of detailed proscriptions
of activity on the Sabbath were manifold, the principles of
the proto-rabbis which were the product of their tendency
toward leniency and their use of the love command as opposed
to the pietists in pre-rabbinic times, continued to function
after 70 and made the rabbinic Sabbath more humane. Thus
the principle of saving life took precedence over the Sabbath,
even when the danger to life was not direct but merely likely.
They kept in effect the whole range of circumstances which
supersede the Sabbath.[183] Thus, contrary to the *perushim* as
reflected in the New Testament and Dead Sea Scrolls, healing
was permitted, for example, in the case of a sore throat
being treated on the Sabbath (M. Yom. 8:6); and when considered meritorious, fasting was permitted (B. Shab. 11a; P.
Taan. 67a) despite the prohibition in Jubilees. In effect,
the rabbis multiplied prohibitions in ever-widening concentric
circles from their basic thirty-nine proscribed activities
(M. Shab. 7:2), ultimately arriving at a legendary total of
1521 derivative prohibitions (P. Shab. 9b-c). But simultane-
ously they sought for relief and opportunities to relax restrictiveness in the interest of humanitarian concerns. They

were doubtful that the heavy pressure of Sabbath prohibition
was indeed proper when they conceded that the Sabbath halakhah
was a mountain of interpretation resting on a hair of scripture (M. Hag. 1:8; T. Hag. 1:9). The probability is very
great that the rabbis inherited the pietistic Sabbath and
worked energetically at providing a way around the multitudin-
ous restrictions that flowed from it. The rabbi as scholar
and exegete may be seen as a halakhic engineer. The ancient
rabbis developed so many valuable principles for this purpose
that contemporary Judaism can still apply these for religious
advantage.[184] The governing principle related to the Sabbath
was for the rabbis no less than that attributed to Jesus (Mt.
12:8; Mk. 2:27; Lk. 6:5), that in effect the Sabbath is committed to the charge of human authority and that society is
not in abject subordination to the Sabbath (Mekh. III, 198).

The other aspect of Sabbath is its commemorative one.
The same verse at Is. 58:13 which led to the scrupulous re-
straint from activity that was related to economic gain or
one's occupation, inspired the rabbis to stress that it contained the idea that the Sabbath is to be called an *óneg*, a
delight (B. Shab. 118a-b). The conception of *óneg shabbat*,
enjoying the delights of good food, drink, clothing and
music, has remained a major Sabbath mode to the present time.
The rabbis added to the beauty of Sabbath celebration when
they converted the practical provision of lighting a lamp
before the Sabbath to provide light on the Sabbath into a
divine command and a sacred ritual, and adorned it with a
berakhah (M. Shab. 3; B. Shab. 25b). The kiddush proclaimed
its sanctity at the beginning of the day (M. Ber. 6:1) and the
festive Sabbath dinner is opened by an offering of thanks for
sustenance pronounced over two loaves as symbolic of the
double portion of manna enjoyed by the Israelites on Friday
to obviate the need to gather it on the Sabbath (B. Shab. 117b;
Ber. 39b). At the end of the Sabbath a *habdalah* (separation)
ritual is conducted in which the sacred is declared separated
from the profane.[185]

The sanctity of the Sabbath waives mourning during the
seven-day bereavement period following the death of a next-of-
kin, and although it is permitted to do so, it is deemed preferable not to feel the need to console the bereaved or visit
the sick on the Sabbath (B. Shab. 12a-b). Similarly, its
sanctity, and the preference for a quiescent day which deters
one from a variety of activities promoted a fuller ritual and
study regimen at the synagogue. This is something, as noted
earlier, that is already a historic custom in the time of
Philo. Considering these elements of positive joyous celebration and spirituality it is an error, as one scholar has appropriately noted, "to concentrate attention on the micrologic

casuistry of external restrictions or relaxations ignoring the real significance of the day for religion itself."[186]

In the light of this it must be asked how the editor of the Mishnah arrived at, or why he conceded to the restrictive posture of thirty-nine principal prohibitions. This same enigma bothered the later rabbis. The number thirty-nine is ascribed by R. Judah the Nasi to Moses, and this is probably derived from his older contemporary, R. Nathan, who based it upon a flimsy homily (Mekh. III, 206; B. Shab. 97b, 70a). More logical, however, was the ascription of the thirty-nine types of activity to the categories of activity involved in the building of the portable wilderness sanctuary (Mekh. III, 205). Nevertheless, the computation of thirty-nine remains an enigma and attempts by third and fourth century rabbis to explain it are unsatisfactory.[187] In sum, it appears that the rabbis inherited a mass of detailed opinions and restrictions related to what one may do, where one may go and generally how one is to conduct oneself on the Sabbath. Rabbis differed concerning this mass of material for centuries. Ultimately it was the geonim and medieval rabbis who tried to bring order out of the morass of halakhah, and although a monolithic Sabbath halakhah was nearly achieved by the sixteenth century, this was undercut by a new extensive diversity from the eighteenth century to the present.

175

NOTES

1. Samuel S. Cohon, *Jewish Theology* (Assen, The Nether-
lands: 1971), especially Chapters Three and Four; G. F.
Moore, *Judaism;* Solomon Schechter, *Some Aspects of Rabbinic
Theology* (New York: 1936); Ephraim Urbach, *The Sages, Their
Concepts and Beliefs* 2 vols. (Jerusalem: 1975). Urbach's
volume contains an extensive bibliography, II, 1051-1076.
See also Louis Ginzberg, *Legends of the Jews,* especially the
reference notes; Kaufman Kohler, *Jewish Theology Systematically
and Historically Considered* (New York: 1928); A. Marmorstein,
The Doctrine of Merits in Old Rabbinical Literature and *The
Old Rabbinic Doctrine of God,* Three Volumes in One, (rpt. New
York: 1968); Montefiore and Loewe, *A Rabbinic Anthology.*
Among Christian scholars one might consult R. Stewart, *Rabbinic
Theology* (Edinburgh and London: 1961).

2. Smallwood, *The Jews Under Roman Rule,* Chapters Thir-
teen-Twenty, pp..331-538; see also Michael Grant, *The Jews in
the Roman World,* pp. 231-260. In what follows in section II
I confine myself to Palestine. I will discuss Babylonia in
Chapter Four.

3. Smallwood, pp. 344f., 371-376; 376, n. 3. Apparently,
according to Suetonius, the Romans under Domitian examined
people for circumcision, to determine whether they were liable
for the tax. Some Jews practiced epispasm as in the days of
Antiochus IV, a surgical process which concealed circumcision.
Smallwood errs in speaking of race and nationality, and of
those who lived as Jews as "converts," although Suetonius
clearly says they were not. Those who "concealed their nationality" were probably either practicing Jews who attempted epispasm or Jews who wanted to cease being Jews by not living as
Jews. Any total proselyte would naturally have to pay the tax.
The question arises with Christians who were Jews. They were
circumcised and therefore liable. But pagan Christians undoubtedly escaped the tax, as did apostate Jewish families
with the first uncircumcised generation. The non-proselytes
who lived as Jews also became subject to charges of "atheism"
toward the end of Domitian's reign, as were Christians. For
only Jews were exempt from the imperial cult, and all others
who declined to participate in it were accused of "atheism"
and treason (*maiestas*). See Smallwood, pp. 379f.

4. Smallwood, Chapter 15, pp. 389-427; Baron, *History*, II, 94-98. See Eusebius, *History* IV, 2 (1-4). Baron, p. 370f., n. 10, cites the suggestion of F. M. Heichelheim from a book review in the *Journal of Egyptian Archaeology* XXII, 106, that Adiabene might have been involved.

5. S of S R. 8:9, 3; the tradition can look back upon Cyrus of Persia who restored the exilic community's right to Jerusalem, and forward to the Parthians who had already stood at the gates of Jerusalem at 40 B.C. and were regarded as likely saviors of the Jews from Roman domination.

6. The true name of Bar Kokhba is now settled as Simon b. Cosiba from a collection of Hebrew, Aramaic and Greek letters found at Murabba'at and Naḥal Hever issued by Bar Kokhba, in his name, or referring to him. See Smallwood, p. 439f.; n. 46, citing the documents published in *Discoveries in the Judaean Desert* II, nos. 24, 43-44; see also Yigal Yadin, "Expedition D" *Israel Exploration Journal,* 11 (1961), 36-52 where item 3 is The Greek Papyrus, and Yadin, p. 50, points out that it attests to "Kosiba" as the proper pronunciation of the patronymic. At P. Taan 68d the name is rendered as "Kozbah." In the absence of a Josephus the Bar Kokhba rebellion is not well chronicled. See Smallwood, pp. 428-466.

7. Louis Finkelstein, *Akiba*, p. 251 maintains that enactments suppressive to Judaism were made from 126 on, and were an important cause of the revolt. The name "Aelia" is that of Hadrian's family and Capitolina for the temple of Jupiter.

8. For Galilean and Shammaite supremacy, see Finkelstein, *ibid.*, pp. 238f., 258.

9. See P. Taan. 68d; B. Shab. 33b; Gen. R. 64:10; M. Sot. 9:15 for R. Pinḥas; Solomon Zeitlin, "The Assumption of Moses and the Revolt of Bar Kokhba," *Studies,* II, 181-225; p. 205 and n. 107. At B. San. 93b we have a report that the rabbis put Bar Kokhba to death as a false messiah.

10. Grant, *The Jews,* p. 245.

11. Dio and Eusebius are cited by Smallwood, p. 432. Dio wrote "In Jerusalem he founded a city to replace the one that had been destroyed and called it Aelia Capitolina, and he erected a temple to Jupiter on the site of the Temple of God. This caused a long and serious war. . ." Cf. Eusebius, *History* IV, 6 (4), where he says this took place as a punishment for the rebellion. Smallwood is probably correct, p. 434, in

arranging the compromise which I have adopted.

12. See also Baron, *History*, II, 374, n. 22 where he cites Saul Lieberman in support of the thesis that the anti-Judaism laws were introduced in reprisal for the revolt.

13. Gen. R. 10:3; 28:3; 78:1; Lev. R. 18:1; Ruth R. 3:2; Ecc. R. 9:4; 12:5; Lam. R. 3:23; 8; B. Hul. 59b-60a; Shab. 119a, 152a; the editorial "may his bones rot" after Hadrian's name in many sources does not alter the fact that the sayings represent a time when intellectual discourse was carried on between Hadrian and some rabbis, or that later rabbis had reasons to believe such a tradition. If that was true during his visit to Palestine in 130, it is unlikely that he had been attempting to suppress Judaism since 125 (see n. 7).

14. P. Taan. 68d: R. Simon b. Yohai reports that R. Akiba interpreted "a star will step forth from Jacob" with a play on the Hebrew word for "star" (Kokhab), saying Kozbah will step forth from Jacob. At Rev. 22:16 Jesus is the "morning star," and Cf. the allusion at II Peter 1:19; cf. also the exegesis at CDC 7:19, *IQM* 11:6-7. For rabbinic reference to the "kingdom" that was set up by Bar Kokhba and endured for two-and-a-half years see B. San. 93b, 97b; but in the Bar Kokhba letters referred to at n. 6 he is called Nasi, not *melekh* (king). See also Samson H. Levey, *The Messiah: An Aramaic Interpretation*, pp. 21-27.

15. D. 108:3; Smallwood, pp. 444, 453. For the letters, above, n. 6.

16. *Ibid.*, pp. 457, 459f., 462. See for Hadrianic prohibitions: B.B.B. 60b (study of Torah, circumcision, miẓvot); San. 14a (ordination); Ber. 61b (torah); Meilah 17a (Sabbath, circumcision, purities); Gerim 1:1 (circumcision, baptism, other miẓvot unspecified, and the need to practice Judaism in concealment); Ecc. R. 2:17 (Sabbath, circumcision); Lev. R. 32:1 (circumcision, Sabbath, maẓah, sukah, lulab, tefillin, the blue thread in the *talit*).

17. For a famous legend of the "Ten Martyrs" see B.A.Z. 17b-18a; Solomon Zeitlin, "The Legend of the Ten Martyrs and its Apocalyptic Origins" *JQR*, 36 (1945), reprinted in *Studies*, II, 165-180. For the story of Akiba's martyrdom see B. Ber. 61b; his trial before Tineius Rufus, the legate who ploughed under the site of the Temple after the revolt, P. Taan. 69b; Lam. R. 1:41; 3:44; his teaching in prison, B. Pes. 112a; Yeb. 105b, 108b; San. 12a; P. Yeb. 12d. Smallwood, p. 465, n. 147 also cites M. Git. 6:7, but that text does not explicate that the halakhah on divorce "brought from prison" is necessarily

a halakhah of Akiba. Other rabbis were also in prison at different times.

18. Mantel, *Sanhedrin*, 140-174.

19. Baron, *History*, II, 125, 197; Cf. B. Ket. 103b; M.K.
17a; 17b; P. San. 20c; A.Z. 39b. It is clear from all the
talmudic discussions that rabbis who were not patriarchs defined theological parameters and fashioned the halakhah which
remained the permanent repository of the ritual and ethics to
which each succeeding generation appeals.

20. Smallwood, Chap. 9. See further on Babylonian Judaism, Chap. 4 below. For R. Judah, B. Pes. 3b; Kid. 10b; Yeb.
102a; P. Yeb. 12c. For R. Akiba in Nehardea, M. Yeb. 16:7; B.
Yeb. 115a; at Ber. 63a we have a reference to Akiba as setting
the precedent for calendar regulation, but a more important
passage delineating a second century struggle between Palestine and Babylonia over halakhic authority. The importance of
Jewish communities in the second century in Syria and Asia
Minor is attested to in the Epistle of Polycarp and the Martyrdom of Polycarp, as well as in the concern over Jewish influence upon Christians evinced by the Epistles of Ignatius.
For these works see *Ancient Christian Writers*.

21. Saul Lieberman, "Palestine in the Third and Fourth
Centuries" *Texts and Studies*, pp. 112-177, rpt. from *JQR*, 36-
37 (1946); The quotation is from "Jewish Life in Eretz Yisrael
as Reflected in the Palestinian Talmud," *ibid.*, p. 181,
abridged from a longer statement in the *JQR* article, p. 125.
See also pp. 127ff., 143, 148; Lieberman's conclusion: "There
is no evidence either for the persecution of the Jewish religion. . .or for Jewish rebellions. . .The only exception is an
insignificant local insurrection of a part of the Sepphorian
Jews" (p. 153). For the Palestinian Talmud see Chap. 4.

22. Grant, *op. cit.*, pp. 282-290. See also James Parkes,
Conflict, pp. 133-370. Wilken, *Judaism and the Early Christian
Mind*, p. 228 cites Cyril's commentary to Is. 60:7. The subordination of Judaism to Christianity is based on a midrash
at Barn. 13:2-6, to Gen. 26:23, "the older shall serve the
younger." The older is seen to be Judaism, the younger,
Christianity. This midrash is transmitted through Justin, St.
Augustine, and others into the concrete positions of medieval
popes, e.g. Innocent III. See *Emergence*, II. Parkes, *op. cit.*
pp. 153f., 185-195.

23. *Ibid.*, pp. 174-184. See Appendix One, pp. 379-391
for both the imperial laws and council canons affecting the
Jews beginning with the first known council at Elvira, Spain

around 300 and running through the eighth century.

24. Baron, *History*, VIII, 368, n. 52, indicates the reason for Hillel's action is "shrouded in darkness."

25. Walker, *History of the Christian Church*, pp. 61f.; 108f.; Lieberman, *Texts*, pp. 115ff.

26. Lieberman, *op. cit.*, pp. 117f.; Grant, *The Jews*, pp. 286f. The Palestinian Talmud was compiled in two stages, the first at Caesarea around 350 and the second at Tiberius toward the end of the century. See Louis Ginzberg, "Introductory Essay: The Palestinian Talmud," *A Commentary on the Palestinian Talmud* (New York: 1971) I, xxxvii ff.

27. It seems to me that Louis Ginzberg, *ibid.* xxxiv f. is too certain that the largest part of the angelology and demonology of the Babylonian Talmud does not represent the theology of its compilers, and that this is also true of sorcery, etc.

28. See Chap. 4 for a survey of the literature.

29. Raphael Loewe, "Foreward" to Roy Stewart, *Rabbinic Theology*, p. vi.

30. Stewart, *ibid.*, p. 2.

31. M. Ber. 1:1 On God see also Pt. 1, Chap. 2, above.

32. Stewart, pp. 18-45; Urbach, *The Sages*, I, Chapters II-IX, Moore, *Judaism*, I, Part II, Chapters I-V.

33. The one who denies God's concern is said to hold *let din velet dayyan*, "there is neither judgment nor judge"; the "atheist" is called *kopher beikar*. See Gen. R. 26:6, Sifra 111b; T. Sheb. 3:6. See also P. Targ. to Gen. 4:8 where denial of divine justice is said to originate with Cain. He also denies an afterlife and reward and punishment before killing Abel.

34. Job 2:10; Is. 44:6; 45:7; 46:4; Deut. 32:39.

35. Philo, *Every Good Man* XII (84); cf. B. Ber. 11b for the rabbinic emendation as a "felicitous expression." It is used in this felicitous manner in the daily morning liturgy. See also Moore, *op. cit.* III, n. 110, pp. 115f.; Alan F. Segal, *Two Powers in Heaven*. The main caution I suggest in Segal's work is his conclusion that rabbinic arguments against the "two power theology indicate they developed an

"orthodoxy." Judaism implied its own mild form of dualism in such terms as the Shekhinah and Holy Spirit. This dualism was akin to the Christian idea of the major and subordinate manifestations of deity in "Father" and "Son."

36. Philo's dualism is evident in his use of the *logos*. Different types of dualism, however, have to be distinguished. Segal, pp. 7f., n. 8 concedes "two authorities" is a better term than "two powers" since what the rabbis really opposed was the concept that any heavenly being is able to exercise independent authority. We cannot delineate the heresy attacked by rabbis because we have no accurate understanding of the term *min*, usually translated as "sectarian." What it probably means is the same as *haeresis*, a point of view, and signifies "variegated species" or "types." See Segal, p. 5, n. 2. But not all dualism was "heretical" and worthy of attack. At Qumran, IQS 3:17, we find that the human is under the dominion of the spirits of truth and perversity, coming from light and darkness respectively, under the dominion of the prince of lights and the angel of darkness. The God of Israel and his angel help only the sons of light. See also Test. Jud. 20:1; Test. Asher 1:3ff. On the "two inclinations" in rabbinic Judaism see Urbach, *The Sages*, I, 471-483, and his references collected at II, 894-900. Some polemics were, of course, directed against Christianity, without reference to precise terminology or the specialized meaning of concepts. Thus R. Abbahu 3rd-4th century Caesarean scholar, attacks the christology at P. Taan. 65b, denying the godhood of any human, rejecting the "Son of Man" claims by anyone and denying that any human can "go up to heaven" in a live state. It is not clear what R. Abbahu would do about Enoch and Elijah whom the Bible has transported alive to heaven. That the dualism under attack in rabbinic literature is largely that of dual independent authority is seen at Sif. Deut. 329.

37. See Segal, *op. cit.*, Chapter Two: Mekh. II, 31f. to Ex. 15:3f and II, 231f. to Ex. 20:2; Ex. R. 32:9: "angel of Yhwh" in scripture is the Shekhinah. The Shekhinah appears detached from God at P. Targ. Ex. 25:8; 29:45, where God speaks of causing His Shekhinah to dwell in Israel; Sif. Num. 94, 106; Mid. Prov. 22:29. Urbach, *The Sages*, Chap. III, erroneously denies that Shekhinah is ever a separate entity in talmudic-midrashic literature. The concept of the Shekhinah as a feminine divine figure becomes prevalent only in mysticism. For the Holy Spirit as a separate entity see Lev. R. 6:1 where the Holy Spirit converses with God and is there to be seen as separate from them; at Ecc. R. 12:7, "the Spirit returns to God" is referred to the Holy Spirit at the destruction of Jerusalem; and at B. Pes. 117a it is ambiguous whether

Shekhinah and Holy Spirit are synonyms or euphemisms for God
or are emanations of the divine and to be understood as separate entities. On the other hand, at Mekh. II, 23f. Holy
Spirit and God are synonyms. Yet at Mekh. I, 105f. where
hen, "grace," is identified as the Holy Spirit and something
which God "pours out" on persons, it is a separate entity
from God. There are biblical roots for this at Is. 44:3
where God pours out His Spirit, and where the Spirit is parallel to "blessing." Thus to receive of the Spirit is to receive a beneficent divine activation of some form.

38. Segal, pp. 159-181; 205-233; Philo, *Q G* 2, 62.

39. *All. Int.* III, 31 (96); *On Confusion of Tongues,*
146; *Spec. Laws* I, 16 (81); Justin, D. 61; T. San. 8:7; for
Wisdom see Prov. 8:22-31, especially v. 30; Wis. 7:25ff.,
9:4, 9; for Paul's use of the same ideas see Col. 1:15-17.

40. Fragmentary P. Targ. to Gen. 1:1; Gen. R. 1:1; Wisdom
is Torah: Ben Sira 24:22; IV Macc. 1:17, and elsewhere.

41. For the two attributes related to God's names see
Ex. R. 3:6 which cites a dictum by a third century Palestinian
amora, R. Abba b. Memel: God tells Moses "When I judge mankind I am called elohim. . .when I have compassion on my world
I am called Yhwh." See also Sif. Deut. 27; Sifra 85b; Mekh.
II, 28. The last reference is interesting because it interprets the name *El* as representing the attributes of compassion,
citing Ps. 22:2 and Num. 12:13, the former in which El is
addressed in a prayer for compassion and the latter in which
El is evoked as healer. See Marmorstein, *Old Rabbinic Doctrine,* II, "Essays in Anthropomorphism," for a comprehensive
discussion of the question in both Palestinian àgadah and
Philo.

42. Schoeps, *Jewish Christianity,* pp. 121-130 Hom. 3:57;
4:13; 18:1-3; Recog. 3:38; Schoeps argues that Christian Judaism dealt with gnostic questions and used gnostic terms but
was not gnosticism (*ibid.* pp. 127ff.).

43. See n. 37; the references to Bat Kol are abundant,
conveniently collected in *JE* II, 588-592. The Torah acts as
intercessor at S of S R. 8:14, 1. See Targ. usages of "glory"
and *memrà* at Ex. 32:34; 33:2f.; 33:12, 14; Onk. and P. Targ.
to Ex. 33:14; P. Targ. 33:17-23. The same condition of an
intermediary, personified and both coidentical with and sepa-
from Yhwh is seen in the appearance of Yhwh to Abraham. Three
persons appear and one is identified as Yhwh (Gen. 18:1, 13-15,
17-22), two others as men (vv. 2, 16) and later as angels

(19:1), as men again (vv. 5-14) and angels (v. 15). The point is that Yhwh is one of three human-like figures, and two of these are angels who function on behalf of Him. Again, in the story of Jacob's wrestling with a celestial power at Gen. 32: 23-32, the entity is first a man (v. 25) but appears to be a demonic figure of the night who must flee before dawn (v. 27) and whom Jacob understands to be God Himself (v. 31). Again, at Ex. 3:2 a *malàkh* of Yhwh appears to Moses in the burning bush. But it is God who speaks from the midst of the bush (vv. 4ff.)

44. Saul Lieberman, *Hellenism*, pp. 115-127. For *mysterion* see Tan. Gen. Vayerà 5; PR 5; Gen. R. 50:9. See above Chap. 2. A major text emphasizing all aspects of rabbinic monotheism is at Sif. Deut. 329 to Deut. 32:39. It reads,

> "'See now, that it is I,' this is the answer to those who say there is no authority in heaven. As for the one who says there are two authorities in heaven, answer him by saying that it is already written 'and there is no god with me'. Or [if he argues] to the effect that he [the deity] has no power to cause death or restore life, to do evil or good, [respond] the teaching is 'see now that it is I, I who cause death and restore life.' And a further verse (Is. 44:6), 'thus saith the Lord, King and redeemer of Israel, the Lord of Hosts, I am first and last, and other than me there is no God.'"

45. Such halakhic statements as "death at the hands of Heaven," e.g. Sif. Deut. 96, or the phrase "reverence [or fear] of heaven" at Aḅ. 1:3, indicate the usage of this metonym.

46. See Marmorstein, *The Old Rabbinic Doctrine of God*, I, 54f.; II, 105f.

47. The most important names or titles of God are gathered by Marmorstein, I, pp. 56-147, with profuse references. An interesting àgadic epithet for God is *ish*, "man," and doubly interesting because this homily is said to have been preached in Tarsus, the home of Paul, by Nahum b. R. Simai who used Ex. 12:3 either in a Pesah sermon or a sermon on *Shabbat hagadol*, "the Great Sabbath," the Sabbath prior to Pesah. Nahum, (also known as Menahem, e.g. at B. Pes. 104a), is dated to the second-third century, and is likely engaging in anti-Christian polemic. He was known as a great pietist, considered "a wholly holy man" (P.A.Z. 42c). At P.R.K. 5:17 he is reported to have

preached in Tarsus that "they shall take unto them, each person (*ish*), a lamb," means that they should take unto them The Man (God), the Holy One, who is called "the Man of War" (Ex. 15:3). Nahum went on to explain how one takes God unto oneself: with the two lambs offered up daily in the Temple; for Ex. 12:3 mentions lamb twice, as does Ex. 29:39 which ordains the two daily lambs. The argument is hardly vigorous after 70 A.D. since Jews no longer offered up the two lambs in the Temple, but it is evidently designed to argue that there is not just one lamb (Jesus) who absorbs all sin, but that the Paschal lamb, prefiguring the lambs of the Temple, and their recall at Pesah time, is the mode of expiation. "To take God unto oneself" signified becoming one with God, enjoying expiation, an experience which becomes possible when one engages in the surrogate for the lamb offering, the Seder, and the daily doing of acts of benevolence as Yohanan ben Zakkai stressed (see Chap. 2 above). The term *makom* was used for God in the oldest literature. It is reported at M. Mid. 5:4 that it was part of a liturgical formula recited when a priest was found to be proper for the priestly service in the days of the Temple. This indicates it was in use during the first century. So too a passage of Mekh. II, 41f. to Ex. 15:6 uses *makom* throughout, except where it quotes scripture. "Heaven," having been attributed to Antigonus of Sokho of the second century B.C., is apparently of very early usage (M. Ab. 1:3).

48. Moore, *Judaism*, I, 425ff.

49. An angel intercedes at Zekh. 1:12; and at Job 33:23f; but rabbinic passages stress God's direct aid and accessibility; P. Ber. 13a.; Gen. R. 8:13; B. Sot. 14a. To emulate God: Mekh. II, 25; B. Sot. 14a.

50. Urbach, *The Sages*, I, 214-285, 420-523; Moore, *Judaism* I, Part III, 445-552; II, Part VII, 279-395; for a specialized treatment of the doctrine of merits and its relationship to human destiny see Marmorstein, *The Doctrine of Merits in Old Rabbinical Literature*.

51. Schechter, *Aspects*, pp. 164f. B. Mak. 24a; San. 81a. The 613 count is at B. Shab. 87a; Mak. 23b; cf. Hab. 2:4. Some rabbis used Ps. 15 as their paradigm, and stressed v. 5, "he who does these things will never slip." It should be noted that what is listed consists only of ethical and moral principles between the human and his fellow-human. The implication of this view is that the observance of cultic practices is not a *sine qua non* for salvation. The text at M. Kid. 1:10 should be translated "anyone who does not perform, (at least) one mizvah," and not "who neglects to perform a single mizvah,"

as if it means he must perform all miẓvot.

52. It is possible that alternate readings at M. Ab. 3:19
reflects a tradition that God does not judge humans according
to deeds, but rather exercises grace. The standard texts read
a paradox, "The world is judged by goodness, and everything is
according to the deed." Taylor, *Sayings of the Jewish Fathers,*
Appendix, p. 152, cites, a) "but not according to the deed";
b) "not according to the multiplicity of deeds." See also
Mekh. II, 69 where *ḥesed* is exercised by God in the absence
of human merit; Ex. R. 45:6. For R. Matya b. Heresh, Mekh.
I, 33f. See the extensive discussion by Marmorstein, *The
Doctrine of Merits,* and Schecter, *Aspects,* pp. 170-198.

53. Bar. 14:17; 21:24 for a Jewish view of man as goal of
creation; see also Gen. 2:7; M. San. 4:5; Sifra 89a; P. Ned.
41c. One view of man being created in God's image is that he
is to be righteous, as God is, Tan. Bereshit 7.

54. *On Creation* 46 (134-135); Gen R. 14:8. Man is both
celestial and terrestrial: Gen R. 8:11. For Philo, *ibid.* 47
(137) the body is the "sacred dwelling place or shrine" for
the soul "which man was to carry as a holy image, of all images the most God-like [the soul]." The translations here and
in the text are by G. H. Whitaker.

55. *War,* III, 8.5 (372): "All of us, it is true, have
mortal bodies, composed by perishable matter, but the soul
lives forever, immortal: it is a portion of the Deity housed
in our bodies." Trans. by H. St. J. Thackeray.

56. *On Creation* 24 (75); Gen. R. 8:5; according to this
source there was consensus that interpreted Gen. 1:31, that
God saw that His creation was *"very* good" ("very" is *meòd* in
Hebrew) as referring to Adam. The consonants of Adam (aleph,
dalet, mem) may be rearranged to form meòd (mem, aleph, dalet).

57. Tan. Pekude 3 maintains that on the basis of Deut.
29:14 all souls of all time were created during the first six
days of creation. Urbach, I, 234ff. claims that the rabbis
did not have this concept until the second half of the third
century. He rejects the notion that the rabbis believed in
the immortality of the soul. See T. San. 13:4, and B. Hag.
12b; Quotation is from Moore, II, 389.

58. B.R.H. 24b; Shab. 152b; Sif. Num. 40, 139; Aḅ de R.N.
A, 12. There is no way to date this usage of I Sam. 25:29
since it is recorded as "another interpretation" which can
signify either an old tradition whose source is no longer clear

or a later one. The notion of a storehouse of souls was carried through into medieval philosophy and was used by those who thought that there is no "life" after death until resurrection, the souls meanwhile being stored with God. See *Emergence* II, 147f. See also Josephus, *War*, III. 8.5 (374) for the idea that the souls of the righteous survive in heaven to await resurrection. See Lieberman, *Texts*, pp. 239-242.

59. On the term *pardes* see the Dictionaries; also the comment by Gordis, *Kohelet*, at 2:5. See B. Ber. 28b, and frequently, for terms *gan èden* and *gehinnom*. For the *gehinnom* or *gehenna* of punishment see B. Er. 19a; Yom. 72b; Suk. 32b; Sot. 4b; R.H. 17a; and elsewhere. For *gan èden* see B. Pes. 54a; Ned. 39b, and many other references. See Samual J. Fox, *Hell in Jewish Literature* (Illinois: 1972).

60. At Sif. Deut. 307 when the text speaks of punishing or rewarding in *òlam habà* it can refer to either the abode of the souls or to the eschatological post-messianic judgment and retribution. In the same passage, however, a certain philosopher refers to his dying and says "*tomorrow*, my portion will be with them (the martyrs) in *òlam habà*," an obvious reference to the abode of souls, where he will be "tomorrow." M. Ed. 2:10 limits hell to twelve months, except for such major sinners as apostates; T. San. 13:5. See Lieberman, pp. 236ff. Sif. Deut. 47; B. Zeb. 118b; T. Ar. 2:7; PR 21. B.B.B. 74b; 122a; Ket. 111b; Sif. Deut. 317, and elsewhere. Cf. Samuel, B. San. 99a; Ber. 34b; Shab. 63a, Pes. 68a, for his statement that this world and the days of the Messiah are the same except for Israel's political freedom. This implies that all the eschatological visions connected with *òlam habà* refer to the post-messianic, post-resurrection period. See also P. Peah 16b; San. 27c; M. Ab 3:15; T. San. 12:9.

61. The obvious texts are Is. 26:19; Dan. 12:2; Ez. 37; Hos. 6:2; I Sam. 2:6. See B. San. 90b-92; Yeb. 97a; Bekh. 31b. At B. Hag. 12b we see resurrection as something separate from life after death. Furthermore, where scripture tells of resurrection from the dead in such episodes as are connected with Elijah and Elisha at I Ki. 17:10-24; II Ki. 4:18-37, we have evidence that the notion that resurrection could happen was believed. At Lk. 7:11-15 Jesus is hailed as a great prophet because through him God has resurrected a woman's only son who had died. The phenomenon of resurrection itself did not surprise them. Again, in the story of the raising of Lazarus at Jn. 11 the phenomenon of resurrection does not dismay the priests; it is the effect Jesus' actions might have upon political stability that rouses them. That at the restoration of the dead to life the restored ones will be led to

the presence of Elijah is found at P. Shab. 3c in the famous
beraita of the second-century scholar, R. Pinḥas b. Yair. Cf.
P. Shek. 47c; B. Sot. 49b; S of S R. 1:1, 9. At M. Sot. 9:15,
however, which may well provide the original text of R. Pinḥas,
we read "the resurrection of the dead will come *through* Elijah." S of S R. also contains such an alternate reading.
That is, Elijah will be the agent who revives the dead at the
time he heralds the Messiah. At B. Pes. 68a we hear that at
the resurrection the dead will appear as they did in their
former life. Therefore, the living will recognize the dead
and believe that Elijah has performed the miracle. See Ginzberg, *Legends*, IV, 233f., and references at VI, 340f. where it
is the Messiah who resurrects the dead, whereupon the Jews believe Elijah is truly Elijah and the Messiah is truly the
Messiah. There was also current the notion that God will himself resurrect the dead, and another, that the righteous will
be able to resurrect the dead as did Elijah and Elisha (B. Pes.
68a). At B.A.Z. 20b the *beraita* of R. Pinḥas is given without
reference to Elijah, but while Alfasi cites it that way in his
abridgment, he corrects it with the Palestinian text. This is
also noted by the commentary of S of S R., *matnot kehunah* by
R. Issachar Ber (Baerman) Ashkenazi of the sixteenth century,
the first commentator of the midrash who used critical judgment on the text. There are other textual problems to be
noted here. Although annotations in the text of P. Shek. 47c
refer the reader to B. Sot. 49b, this *beraita* of R. Pinḥas is
found in a truncated form in our standard versions of the
Babylonian Talmud, and does not include his well-known stages
leading from fear of sin through purity, saintliness, and so
forth, to the holy spirit, resurrection and Elijah. The
beraita occurs in different versions. These are given at p.
42, n. 1 in Buchler's discussion of the passage in *Types of
Jewish Palestinian Piety*, pp. 42-67, but Buchler does not discuss the Elijah sentence. It should also be noted that the
clause in the *beraita*, "the holy spirit leads to resurrection
of the dead," may very well mean not only that one who is
blessed with the holy spirit will arise at the end of days,
but that one blessed with the holy spirit will have the power
to resurrect the dead, as noted above from B. Pes. 68a. This
is the way Moses Hayyim Luzzatto understood the *beraita* in
his *Mesillat Yesharim*, trans. Mordecai M. Kaplan (Philadelphia:
1948), p. 228, where he writes that the communion with God enjoyed by the righteous will lead to their being entrusted
with the key to the revivification of the dead as it was given
to Elijah and Elisha. See above, Pt. 1, Ch. 6, n. 72 for Elijah, and Pt. 1, Ch. 5, n. 116 for resurrection and immortality.

62. Gentiles will not share in the World to Come: B. Git.
45b; B.B. 10b. They will: T. San. 13:2; B. San. 105a.

Whether gentile children will be excluded: T. San. 13:1f.; B. San. 110b. The intermediate group: T. San. 13:3; B.R.H. 16b-17a.

63. Urbach, I, 651f. The four who enter paradise: B. Hag. 14b. The word "Paradise" in this passage may be taken to mean that people believed literally that the four entered Paradise, or that it signifies the realm of theosophy. L. Ginzberg, among others, held that the Talmud was reporting what it believed to be a literal apocalyptic-like journey through the heavens. See *JE* V, 138f., 683. See Pt. 1, Ch. 5, n. 113.

64. T. Hag. 2:3f.; B. Hag. 14b-15b; P. Hag. 77b; S of S R. 1:4, 1. See Gershom Scholem, *Major Trends in Jewish Mysticism* (New York: 1961), pp. 52f.; *Jewish Gnosticism, Merkabah Mysticism and Talmudic Tradition* (New York: 1960), pp. 14-19.

65. Scholem, *Jewish Gnosticism*, pp. 16f.; II Cor. 12:2-4.

66. See Scholem, *Major Trends*, pp. 40-79.

67. Urbach, I, 649-692; Moore, II, 323-376; Pt. 1, Ch. 2; Klausner, *Messianic Idea*, pp. 391-517.

68. Is. 43:11-12; Num. 24:17; Is. 11:1-10; 52:13-53:12. Moses is said to be the Ebed Yhwh, the Servant of the Lord, of Is. 53 at B. Sot. 14a. A suffering Messiah is spoken of at Ruth R. 5:6; cf. Klausner, p. 405f.

69. Ab. de R.N. B. 13; PRE 1; B. San. 97b, 109a, 113a-b; Ned. 50a; Ber. 3a; Yeb. 63a; Lev. R. 9:9; Deut. R. 5:15; B.B.M. 59a-b, 85b; Yom. 19b; Shab. 33b; Taan. 22a; B. Ber. 58a; B. Hag. 15b; Meg. 15b; Git. 6b; and numerous others.

70. B. Shab. 104a; Yeb. 102a. The Talmud indicates that solutions to certain enigmatic questions will have to await Elijah's eschatological coming by using the term *teku,* an acronym for *tishbi yetarez kushyot veabayot,* "The Tishbite [Elijah is said to be of Tishbi] will respond to questions and problems." See M.B.M. 3:4-5. For early references to Elijah's origins see *Vita Prophetarum, The Lives of the Prophets,* trans. C. C. Torrey (Philadelphia: 1946), pp. 32, 47. That Elijah was a Tishbite we read at I Ki. 17:1. *The Lives* is dated to the first century (*ibid.* p. 1). For the Elijah lore in general see a useful recent work, Aharon Wiener, *The Prophet-Elijah in the Development of Judaism* (London: 1978), and for the period here under discussion, pp. 43-77. Much of the Elijah lore is derived from midrashim called Seder Eliyahu

Rabbah and Seder Eliyahu Zutta, which are said to have been compiled during the second century (*ibid.* p. 57). A new edition of *The Lives*, trans. and ed. Douglas R. A. Hare and to be published by Doubleday is forthcoming.

71. P. Taan. 63d; B. San. 97b-98a. See the medieval Bible exegete, R. David Kimhi (*Radak*) at Mic. 2:13 which reads "The breaker will go up before them; they will break through departing through the gate; their king will pass before them with the Lord at their head." Radak cites a midrash which takes "the breaker" to be Elijah, and "their king" to be the Messiah. The new Torah which Elijah will offer is based upon Is. 2:2-4, and may have some connection with a special meaning for *pleroō* at Mt. 5:20 where Jesus says he has come to "fill out" the Torah, or perhaps "expand it" to its messianic proportions. Medieval kabalah engaged in much speculation about the content of both the pre-existent Torah and the Torah in the messianic age when humans will once again be as they were before Adam's sin. See on this Gershom Scholem, *On the Kabbalah and its Symbolism* (Frankfurt am Main: 1965), pp. 66-86. Essentially the kabalists worked out an explanation of relativism in the human understanding of the perpetually perfect Torah. That is, in different ages the Torah is understood in a manner appropriate to the age, and in the messianic age it will be grasped in its utter spiritual fullness when the spiritual transformation of humans will no longer require the severe demarcation of sacred and profane or prohibited and permitted. As Scholem phrases it, p. 73, ". . .the Torah remains an essentially unchanging and absolute entity. But at the same time, seen in historical perspective, it takes on specific meaning only in relation to the changing state of people in the universe, so that the meaning itself is subject to change." See also the comment to Is. 51:4 "A Torah will proceed from me," at Lev. R. 13:3. See the discussion by W. D. Davies, *The Setting*, pp. 156-190.

72. Moore, II, 327.

73. En. 46:2; 48:2; Dan. 7:13f. See further, Moore, II, 335ff. For the pre-existent Messiah; B. Pes. 54a; Ned. 39b; P. Targ. Zekh. 4:7; Ps. 72:1, 17; Sib. Or. 5:414ff. Cf. Urbach, I, 684, and notes.

74. See Moore, *ibid.*, pp. 338-345 and the numerous references he gathers; pp. 346-357 for rabbinic sources.

75. Zekh. 14:9; the verse closes the *álenu*, the prayer called "Adoration." See Hertz prayerbook, pp. 208ff., or the end of any morning, afternoon or evening worship in any standard prayerbook.

76. Moore, pp. 35ff.; Sigal, *Emergence* II, 303f. At B. San. 97a rabbis draw upon a variety of scriptural verses.

77. Moore, pp. 359f.; PRE 43; Moses instructs Aaron to preserve a jar of manna at Ex. 16:33f.; at Mekh. II, 124f. the manna is listed as one of the ten things (or according to some, twelve) God created just before the first Sabbath. Among these is also the cave in which Moses and Elijah received revelation at Sinai. It is an interesting juxtaposition of Moses and Elijah at Sinai and may be seen as the tradition behind the transfiguration scene in the gospels. Justin, D. 8:4; 49:1; Wiener, *Elijah*, pp. 62-77. The *gezerah shavah* indicated in the text consists of the word "spirit" at Gen. 1:2 and Is. 11:2, the latter referring to the Messiah; and of "waters" at Gen. 1:2 and at Lam. 2:19; the latter reference to pouring out one's heart like water being taken to signify repentance.

78. B.B.B. 123b; B. Suk. 52a; P. Suk. 55b. The "son of Joseph" does not occur with "Messiah" in the latter reference, but otherwise it follows B. Suk. This material is elaborated in later midrashim known as Sefer Zerubavel, Perek Eliyahu, and others. The descent of a heavenly Jerusalem is cited by Wiener, p. 67, from midrashim called Maase Daniel and Sefer Eliyahu. Gen. R. 5:6 tells of the great primeval light stored up for the righteous for the messianic era; Is. 30:26 is cited there, to support the idea that the primeval light was greater than the light of the sun, and that in messianic times the light of the moon will become like that of the sun and the sun will become as bright as the primeval light. Healing and light are mentioned in tandem at Mal. 3:20, where the *shemesh zedakah,* "the sun of righteousness" signifies the great light of the messianic times with "healing on its wings." Cf. Hul. 60b. See Wiener, pp. 67-77. See B. Suk. 52b; Ned. 32b.; Ps. 110. The four messianic figures are "the four craftsmen" of Zekh. 2:3. See Tanna de Be Eliyahu Rabbah 18. The lore concerning Melchizedek is also of interest, but cannot be indulged here. B. Suk. 52b, Munich Ms., identifies Melchizedek with the "righteous priest," one of the "four craftsmen" of the vision at Zekh. 2:3. The fact that this pagan priest-king appears with Elijah and two Messiahs indicates the belief that at the eschaton the pagan world will be joined to Israel in a universal faith. See Heb. 7 and passim. Gen. R. 43:6 records two interpretations to Gen. 14:18, "Malki Zedek, king of Shalem, brought forth bread and wine, he being the priest of El Elyon. . ." R. Samuel b. Nahman says that he taught priestly procedures to Abraham; other sages say he revealed Torah to him, bread and wine taken as the teaching of personified Wisdom at Prov. 9:5. See above, Pt. 1, Ch. 6, n. 72 and Ch. 7.

79. See Moore, II, 362-376; Mekh. II, 120; B. San. 98b; Shab. 118a; cf. Is. 26:17-19; Mi. 4:9f.; Jer. 22:23. The term refers to the suffering of the age or of Zion which is in labor to give birth to the Messiah, not to the suffering of the Messiah.

80. II Bar. 29:5ff.; Sif. Deut. 317; B. Shab. 30b; Ket. 111b. The biblical references to the ingathering are so explicit and numerous they need not be listed here. The hope for a return of Israel to its land is also found in the intertestamental literature, e.g. Bar. 2:30-35; 4:36-5:9; Ben Sira 33:13-23; Ps. Sol. 8:33f. and frequently in the Testaments of the Twelve Patriarchs. Cf. Jer. 23:7f.; B. Ber. 12b. On the ten northern tribes: Sifra 112b; M. San 10:3; B. San. 110b; T. San. 13:12. The copious blessings to ensue at the coming of the Messiah are also described at Sib. Or. 3:702ff.; 741ff. 785ff.

81. See Zeph. 3:9; Is. 2:2-4; etc. The Sib. Or. 3, 767ff. clearly includes all humans in the new era: "Then He will raise up a kingdom to all eternity over men. . ."

82. B. San. 99a; Sif. Deut. 310; P.R. 1:7. The latter source describes how the righteous dead will come in underground channels to the holy land, there to be resurrected and enjoy the messianic era.

83. The following main works may be pursued for details: Enoch, Testaments of the Twelve Patriarchs, Sibylline Oracles, (especially Bk III), II Baruch (Apocalypse of Baruch), II Esdras (Apocalypse of Ezra). These are contemporary with proto-rabbinic teachers and the early post-70 rabbis. Bk III of the Sib. Or. is dated to about 96 B.C. (Charles, *Apocrypha* and *Pseudepigrapha,* II, 371).

84. The Hebrew *bene hayizhar* is translated literally as "sons of oil." The word *yizhar,* however, may also be related to *zahar,* to shine, and might signify the two splendid ones, "the sons of splendor." It is difficult to know what was in the mind of the Greek translator of our LXX who used *piotētos,* "sons of richness," or "fatness," aside from the indirect relationship of this term of oil. My supposition is that the LXX once read differently. The P. Targ. translates *rebrebayà,* "the great princes." In its context it did not originally refer to two Messiahs but rather to the kingship and priesthood at the time of the post-exilic restoration.

85. Ps. Sol. 17. See Jn. 7:41-42 in tandem with Mt. 21:9. The crowds take it for granted that he is the "son of David."

Cf. Mt. 22:41-46 where Jesus tries to dispel the notion; Mk. 12:35-37; Lk. 20:41-44. Only Mark supplies the puzzling ending to the episode, that the people heard Jesus' denial of a Davidic Messiah "with delight." This indicates Mark wrote last, for by the second century Christians no longer believed in the Davidic political messianic hero, and Mk. retrojects.

86. The Hebrew reads, *ulshabai,* "to those who turn." The LXX renders *apostrepsei* "he will turn away"; apparently the translator had before him a Hebrew source which read *veyashib,* "he will turn away." Cf. Rom. 11:26. Urbach, I, 671 says Paul "changed" the first part of the verse of LXX in order to say "out of Zion will come a redeemer," and Urbach adds that Paul signifies, to the gentiles, and not to Zion. This is problematic. Paul might have had that reading before him, or because he rendered from memory he erred. In any case, the context refutes Urbach, for Paul is indicating there that "Israel will be saved." As a matter of fact, he points out the whole relationship of gentiles and Jews and their respective salvation, is a *mysterion* (mystery), and he does not change the sequence of the verse but emphasizes that a redeemer will come out of Zion and turn away the sins of Jacob, not "to the gentiles."

87. On the month of redemption: B.R.H. 11a; Mekh. I, 115f. At M. Ed. 2:10 Akiba relegates the end-time war of Gog and Magog (Ez. 38:2ff.) to "the future to come," thus implying that the tumultuous end-time events are separate from a this-worldly, historical messiah. Such a view continues in the opinion of the Babylonian Samuel, who says there is no difference between the days of the Messiah and the present historical time other than the liberation of Israel (B. San. 99a and many times). See Urbach, I, 676-683 for further references to the reaction that set in to the Bar Kokhba failure leading to a renewed emphasis upon the apocalyptic-spiritual messianism.

88. Based upon S of S R. 2:7, 1, some rabbis argued that Israel must not prematurely bring the eschaton, and said that God adjures the nations not to so mistreat Israel that she will prematurely force the end. The European holocaust of 1942-1945 was the proverbial straw that broke the camel's back. The verse reads, "I adjure, daughters of Jerusalem. . . lest you disturb, lest you interrupt our love, until it is desired." Twice occurs the term *im,* here represented by "lest," signifying two oaths. The term *kez* as the eschatological hour, and the adjuration to wait for it with faith was derived from Hab. 2:3, and became a significant theological concept, especially in mystical and later popular hasidic circles. See Urbach, II, 1002, n. 11 for references to contemporary views

related to the reestablishment of Israel. The last words of the verse, "until it is desired" or is "pleasing," is taken by the midrash to refer to the eschaton.

89. B. San. 106a. The Talmud is taken to have a word missing. Translators read "Woe to the nation that may be found (attempting to hinder). . ." The Aramaic *shetimẓa,* taken as "found" may be a misprint or misreading for another word signifying a "quarreller," from *neẓa,* "to wrangle." See Jastrow *maẓáya,* p. 826.

90. Urbach, I, 184-213; Moore, I, 380-384. God is the creator: Is. 42:5; 40:28; Jer. 32:17.

91. Gen. R. 1:9; Creation passages are found at Job 26: 7-14; 38f; Ps. 19:1-7; 104. Ps. 104 certainly breathes the air of creation *ex nihilo.*

92. M. Ḥag. 2:1; T. Ḥag. 2:1; Ben Sira 3:21f.; cf. B. Ḥag. 13a; P. Ḥag. 77c. The creation is a frequent theme in pre-rabbinic literature, e.g. Bar. 3:32ff.; Ben Sira 16:26-17:9; En. 69:16-24; Jub. 2:1-33.

93. Gen. R. 3:2; 10:9; 12:1; Sif. Deut. 307.

94. Urbach, I, 198.

95. Prov. 8; Ben Sira 29:8-9; at Gen R. 1:1 to Prov. 8: 30, the midrash says that the Torah calls itself the "working tool" of God. Gen. R. 1:10; P. Ḥag. 77c; Sif. Deut. 307; Gen. R. 10:6-7; Ben Sira. 38:4, 7, 8.

96. Gen. R. 8:4, 7-9; 17:4; B. San. 38b. See Pt. 1, Ch. 6.

97. B. Hag. 12a; Gen. R. 3:6; 42:3; PRK 21; that this notion of God's having wrapped Himself in a white robe which then radiated light throughout the universe was taught "in a whisper" points to the recognition that despite its presence in scripture (Ps. 104:2), the application of the scriptural verse was esoteric. Some rabbis believed there was a succession of worlds which were destroyed. See Gen. R. 3:7; Mid. Ps. 4:13; Philo, *On Creation* 7(20); see also *The Eternity of the World,* (39-44), where Philo rejects the concept of Democritus and others, who postulated that many worlds were created and destroyed. At B. Ḥag. 12a we have a rabbinic view that Time ("the nature of day and the nature of night") was created on the first day, and was not pre-existent, in accordance with Philo.

98. Urbach, I, 286-342; Schechter, *Aspects*, 116-169; Heschel, *God in Search*, pp. 167-280.

99. See the remarks by Rene Latourelle, *Theology of Revelation* (Staten Island, N. Y.: 1967), pp. 29f.

100. Sif. Num. 112; B. San. 90b; 64b; B. Kid. 17b; etc.

101. Reference to theophanies in the Pentateuch as having occurred in a cloud are so numerous it is needless to list them. But see e.g. Ex. 24:16; Lev. 16:2; Num. 12:5; Deut. 1: 33; Ps. 97:1-2 attests to the general understanding that "cloud" is a way of describing deity in its mystical unknowableness. See Heschel's remarks, *op. cit.* pp. 198f. "To sum up, revelation is a moment in which God succeeded in reaching man. . ."

102. See Sigal, *New Dimensions,* Chap. 2, for a discussion of how the rabbis dealt with the tension of Divine Revelation and Human Authority.

103. See also Sifra 112b.

104. See Heschel's remarks, pp. 273ff. The quotation is from p. 275.

105. Urbach, I, 286-290. I have taken this up in a hitherto unpublished paper addressed to the Eastern Great Lakes Biblical Society in 1977, entitled, "A Brief Inquiry Into the Use of the Term *Nomos*." See W. D. Davies, "Torah and Dogma: A Comment." *HTR*, 61 (1968), 87-105.

106. B. Git. 60b; Sheb. 39a; Hul. 60b; P. Peah 17a; Hag. 76d; B.B.B. 12a; M. Kid. 4:14; Apoc. Ab. 8:1-7; Gen. R. 64:4; Num. R. 14:2; in Jub. both views are found: Abraham discovers true religion on his own, 11:7; 12:8-20; he receives revelation 12:25-27. Philo sees Abraham as striking out on his own and then God reveals Himself to help and perfect the process. *Abr.* 15 (68)-17 (80).

107. R. Hanina ben Hama of our text died around 250 after a long and influential career. See B. Ber. 33b; Nid. 16b; Meg. 25a. A variant is cited at B. Hul. 7b: "a person does not stub his little finger here below unless it has already been decreed from above." On astrology and the effect of planetary movements see Gen. R. 44:10, 12. Those who opposed astrological efficacy in human life drew upon Jer. 10:2. Others held that the reason God changed Abram's and Sarai's name to Abraham and Sarah was to change their planetary fate.

On free will see G. F. Moore, "Fate and Free Will in the Jewish Philosophies According to Josephus," *HTR*, 22 (1929), 371-389. (Incidently, Moore here incorrectly has Ḥanina as Ḥanina b. Papa, p. 381).

108. Josephus, *War*, II, 8.14 (162f.); *Ant*. XIII, 5.1 (172f.); XVII, 1.3 (13); 1.5 (18). See Wolfson, *Philo*, I, 424-462 for a detailed treatment of Philo's view.

109. Akiba: M. Ab. 3:19; R. Judah: *ibid*. 2:1. Urbach, I, 257 calls attention to early commentators who long ago interpreted Ab. 3:19 in the light of 2:1; but cf. Mekh. I, 134f. R. Yanai at M. Ab. 4:19 is probably the little-known first-second century tanna, father of R. Dosthai (*ibid*. 3:10). See Herford's note to the text of Ab. Ben Sira 15:11-17; Ps. Sol. 9:7-9. At Tan. Pekude 3, to Ex. 38:22 there is a very long passage on what occurs with the drop of semen about to fertilize an egg at the time of the creation of a fetus. When the angel in charge asks God what the destiny of this drop is God decrees immediately the events, conditions and character of its life on earth. But "whether he will be righteous or wicked is placed in the hands of the person alone," citing Deut. 30:15-20.

110. P. Taan. 65b; B. Shab. 32a; see especially B.R.H. 16a-18a; in general the whole question of determinism and providence must be modified by the implications of human freedom inherent in the theology of repentance related to Rosh haShanah and Yom Kippur.

111. M. Ab. 1:3; Gen. R. 62:2; B. Hul. 142a. On Elisha and his grandson see P. Ḥag. 77a; cf. T. Hul. 10:16.

112. T. Suk. 2:6; B. Suk. 29a; Mekh., I, 19. At T. Suk. 2:5, however, eclipses are ascribed to Providence as retribution for specific human evils, and are not seen as autonomous predetermined laws of nature. See also B. Shab. 156a-b; Tan. Shofetim 10. See Lieberman, *Greek*, 97-114. Lieberman points out, with references, that pagans conceded that astrological signs have no effect on Jews. He also discusses how the rabbis handled the similar problem of "charms" which the then-civilized world believed in and the rabbis condemned as superstition (B. Shab. 67a). When the rabbis saw that certain charms contained some natural remedial benefit they allowed it (P. Shab. 8c). So too magic and superstition were "judaized" by giving ancient popular practices such as placing ashes on the head of the bridegroom, originally to divert the demons into thinking this is a place of mourning rather than joy, new interpretations such as the ashes being symbolic of

mourning for the destruction of the Temple. See also J. Z. Lauterbach, *Studies in Jewish Law*, on various rituals preserved in Judaism with new interpretations that circumvent the older magical and folkloristic explanations. This was the case with the ritual of breaking a glass at weddings; and in details related to the naming of children.

113. Selected bibliography: Heinemann, *Prayer in the Talmud*; Abudraham, *Sefer Abudraham*; tractate *Soferim* of the Minor Tractates of the Talmud; *Contributions to the Scientific Study of Jewish Liturgy*, ed. J. Petuchowski; David de Sola Pool, *The Kaddish* (New York: 1964); A. Z. Idelsohn, *Jewish Liturgy* (New York: 1967); Leopold Zunz, *Die gottesdienstlichen Vortrege der Juden Historisch Entwickelt* (In Hebrew: *Haderashot be Yisrael*, ed. H. Albeck, (Jerusalem: 1954); a variety of articles in *HUCA* and *JQR* can be consulted with profit; W. S. Towner,"'Blessed be Yhwh' and 'Blessed Art Thou, Yhwh': The Modulation of a Biblical Formula." *CBQ*, 30 (1968), 386-399.

114. Vicarious atonement is at Gen. R. 44:5, but has not been included in liturgy.

115. Sigal, *Emergence II*, Chap. 3; Abudraham, *Sefer*, pp. 34ff.; B.R.H. 17b.

116. On the language of prayer: M. Sot. 7:1; B. Sot. 33a; Ber. 40b; Sheb. 39a.

117. The Psalms give extensive evidence for verbal prayer, and in the prayer of David at II Sam. 8:18-29 we find the term *tefilah* for prayer for the first time (v. 27). See Idelsohn's brief survey of worship in ancient Israel and Judah up to the rabbinic period, pp. 3-25; see in general on the use of psalms and hymns in the sacrificial cult, Kraus, *Worship in Israel*. The origin of the synagogue will be discussed below in Chap. 4.

118. The rabbis after 70 emphasized that God is present wherever there is a congregation in worship: P. Ber. 8d; B. Ber. 6a; Deut. R. 7:2; B. Meg. 29a.

119. On the antiquity of the liturgy as referred to by the rabbis, see B. Meg. 18a; Ber. 26b-33a; Sif. Deut. 343; P. Ber. 11c, all ascribing their liturgy to the legendary Great Assembly, the prophets and even Moses. Ben Sira 36:1-17 is a prayer for Israel; at 35:12-20 Ben Sira speaks of God hearing the prayers of the distressed. The Hebrew Ben Sira has a psalm set between 51:12 and 13 consisting of sixteen verses of prayer of two lines each. The first line resembles paragraphs

of the ámidah and the second line which is a refrain, "For
His mercy endures forever" resembles Ps. 136. Box and Oesterly, Charles' *Apocrypha*, I, 514, are reluctant in their note to
this section, to accept the idea that it was omitted from the
Greek version of Ben Sira because of stanza ix which lauds the
Zadokite priesthood which has been overthrown by the Hasmonean
at the time Ben Sira's grandson translated the work. But it
appears logical that Ben Sira's grandson would omit the whole
prayer rather than mutilate or falsify it. Stanza viii looking forward to a Davidic restoration would also fall under
such scrutiny, and so in order not to offend the Establishment
he omitted the entire prayer. See *The Hebrew Text of the Book
of Ecclesiasticus*, ed. Israel Levi, 3rd ed. (Leiden: 1969). M
Yom. 7:1 also points to the passages reminiscent of the ámidah
just as M. Tam. 5:1 indicates that the priests followed an
order of worship similar to the present structure of the daily
worship. See Louis Ginzberg, "The Mishnah Tamid," *Journal of
Jewish Lore and Philosophy*, I (1919), on the early dating of
the material.

120. See Heinemann, "Introduction." I do not agree with
Heinemann, however on his use of "legal norms" and "statutory
prayers" which is susceptible to the usual misguided attack on
rabbinic halakhah as "legalism." A convenient comparative
liturgical table is found at Idelsohn, pp. 21f.

121. *Emergence* II, 40ff. Abudraham; p. 24; for a cursory
exposition of the elements in the traditional prayerbook see
Israel Abrahams, *A Companion to the Daily Prayerbook* (New York
1966). The berakhah form is at Ps. 119:12, I Chron. 29:10.
That people should not indiscriminately devise berakhot: P.
Ber. 12d. The berakhah formula without *atah, barukh adonay*,
"praised is the Lord" is used numerous times by persons thanking God for some kindness: Gen. 14:20; 24:27; Ex. 18:10; I
Sam. 25:39; I Ki. 8:15; Ps. 66:20; Ezra 7:27, and many more.

122. B. Ber. 28b; on *piyutim* see Idelsohn's brief survey,
pp. 34-46 and on the influence of kabalah, pp. 47-55; see
Sigal, *Emergence* II, 297-302, and index entry *piyut*.

123. Heinemann, pp. 18, 23. Finkelstein, "Development of
the Amidah," *Contributions*.

124. M. Ber. 7:3; Meg. 4:3f.; *pesuke dezimra* are psalms
and passages from I Chron. 29:10-13; Neh. 9:6-11; Ex. 14:30-15
18; they are flanked by *barukh shèamar* and *yishtabah*, two
berakhot-paragraphs that are modelled after the way Hallel is
to be said, at B. Pes. 117a-118a. The hallel is referred to
in the synoptic gospels in the accounts of the last supper,

and the *haftarah* at Lk. 4:18f. There are many different problems concerning the cycle of Torah and *haftarah* readings compounded by puzzles related to the annual and triennial cycles, which are too technical to enter into here. See Jacob Mann and Isaiah Sonne, *The Bible as Read and Preached in the Old Synagogue*, 2 vols. "Prolegomenon" by Ben Zion Wachholder (Cincinnati and New York: 1966, 1971); Joseph Heinemann, "The Triennial Lectionary Cycle," *JJS*, 19 (1968), 41-48. The format of the worship order outlined here can be followed in any standard traditional prayerbook. See, for example, Hertz, *Authorized Daily Prayerbook*; Rabbinic Assembly *Sabbath and Festival Prayer Book* (New York: 1967). Abbreviated prayers: T. Ber. 5:24; variants: T. Ber. 1:9; 3:25; 3:11; M. Ber. 5:2; B. Ber. 48b.

125. *A-e*, relate to the first berakhah, called *yozer; f,* to the second, *ahabah; g-n,* to the shemà; *m-o,* to the berakhah after the shemà, *geulah*.

126. The pre-Christian venue of the prayer for the Davidic monarchy in terms of the "shoot" and "horn" is borne out by its use at Lk. 1:68-69.

127. Another example of a mini-theology embedded in one small prayer is found in the *kiddush*. The kiddush is the formal proclamation of the sanctity of the Sabbath or holy day and is recited at the opening dinner. It contains within two paragraphs the affirmation of God as creator and the source of Sabbath sanctity, the doctrine of election, the notion that the Sabbath is the token of the covenant recalling both creation and the redemptive exodus from Egypt. Implicit in the line "who has sanctified us with His mizvot" is the doctrine of revelation. And thus in kiddush alone may be found creation, election, revelation, redemption and the quality of the Sabbath as token of the covenant. There is thus, too, conjured up the two sets of the Decalogue, the one in Exodus attributing the Sabbath to creation and the one in Deuteronomy asserting that the Sabbath recalls the exodus. In sum, the Sabbath, a sign of the covenant, the legacy of revelation, and the bond of election also affirms creation and redemption. It is therefore little wonder that theologically the Sabbath is a central *sine qua non* of Judaism and helps explain the great reluctance of early Christian Jews, and those pagans who learned from them, to allow its observance to lapse. Of the prayers mentioned in the text, the *kaddish* is one of the least understood though best known. Like the term kiddush which relates to holiness, and expresses the sanctification of time, the kaddish prayer also embodies the holiness idea but relates directly to the sanctity of God, enunciating the hope that the

great Name will be sanctified in the advent of His Kingdom.
It is named kaddish for the first time at Sof. 10:7; 16:12;
19:1, 12; 21:6. Otherwise it is referred to generally by its
central line, "Let the great Name be praised forever and ages
eternal." It was first used as a doxology after a study session (P. Sot. 16d) when messianic ágadah was often used as a
closing homily, climaxed by this eschatological doxology looking toward the time of divine sovereignty. (See de Sola Pool,
The Kaddish, 6ff.). By the end of the talmudic period it had
a regular position in the synagogue worship order, serving as
a divider between sections of worship, and later on by a
puzzling and still undeciphered process it became a mourner's
prayer although it is by no means a prayer for the dead. It
appears from Sof. *ibid.* that the kaddish was a regular part
of the call to worship with *barkhoo* and also concluded the
Torah reading and the worship order as a whole. The mystical
belief was present from earliest times that when congregations
recite the central line referred to above ("Let the Great
Name" etc.) with fervor they can annul evil decrees (B. Shab.
119b; de Sola Pool, *ibid.* pp. 101ff.). A midrash concerning
Ákiba is cited in medieval literature in which Ákiba teaches
the son of a man suffering in *gehinnom* to say kaddish and allow his father relief (de Sola Pool, p. 102, and references,
n. 3). There was a concept that a son can vindicate a father
(B. San. 104a) and that he should study torah in his father's
name for the first twelve months after death and consider himself as expiating for him (Sif. Deut. 210; P. San. 29c).
These various traditions coalesced into the medieval custom
of a son reciting kaddish for both the father and mother for
twelve months to free them from the torment of *gehinnom.*
Later it was reduced to eleven months in order not to imply
that the parent was actually in *gehinnom* for the maximum time.
But nevertheless, the real lines of development of the kaddish
custom remain obscure. There is an expanded kaddish reserved
for the hour of burial. Obviously the eschatological nature
of the prayer accounted for its importance from the beginning.
Talmudic tractates end with eschatological hopes (B. Tam. 33b;
M.K. 29a; Hul. 142a, M. Sot. 9:15; M.K. 3:9; Taan. 4:8; Ed.
8:7). It is this eschatological quality that made it popular
as a mourner's prayer, for the messianic era implies resurrection of the dead and the triumph of humans over death, a
natural and consoling thought at the time of bereavement.

Much has been written concerning the relationship between
the kaddish and the Lord's Prayer (see de Sola Pool. pp. 111f.
but cf. C. Taylor, *Sayings of the Jewish Fathers,* pp. 124-130,
who finds many affinities between it and prayer passages in
Judaism as well as Old Testament sayings, but correctly does
not relate it to kaddish). Some see in Mt. 6:9b, c, 10a, b,

c, affinities with some of the words of kaddish: "may the great name be hallowed," "may His kingship be sovereign," "according to His will in the world." But it is conceded that the second half of the Lord's Prayer which is petitional for personal need is not related to the kaddish. Others connect the Lord's Prayer with Ez. 36:23-31 just as kaddish relates to Ez. 38:23. There is, however, a great distance between seeking the Lord's Prayer in the kaddish, an idea I reject, and finding "Jewish origin" in it as so many scholars do (de Sola Pool, p. 112, n. 4), an obvious reality. See also W. D. Davies, *The Setting*, pp. 309ff. In my view the Lord's Prayer is not a counterpart to the ȧmidah because it has no berakhah formula; the Lord's Prayer is designed as a public devotion just as the ȧmidah was intended as a central item of public liturgy (Did. 8:3 requires it thrice-daily), but both are also private and recited in the traditional plural style of Judaic prayers. It is not an abbreviated ȧmidah because it lacks the Name and Malkhut required for every berakhah formula, a requirement maintained in the abbreviated ȧmidah (B. Ber. 29a-b). Rather, the Lord's Prayer is a brief private prayer said in the plural to accommodate it to public worship, but serves as a private addendum to the ȧmidah (B. Ber. 16b-17a). See also Heinemann, pp. 192f. He regards the Lord's Prayer correctly as a private prayer, but argues that it shows that Jesus prefers private prayer over prayer of the synagogue. This view is wide of the mark.

128. Deut. R. 2:1; Abudraham, p. 9.

129. See Heinemann, Chapters 3 and 9.

130. T. Ber. 3:24. By combining the berakhot, the ȧmidah was to be held to eighteen paragraphs. But it evolved into nineteen anyhow because the prayers for Jerusalem and the Davidic throne once together were separated. The ȧmidah texts I have seen do not contain the term *perushim* in the twelfth paragraph against *minim* and other sinners, but the language of Tosefta is pregnant with meaning: "one includes that of *minim* with that of *perushim*." The explanation for its removal from the text at a time after that referred to by Tosefta, might be that the *perushim* become of little consequence in the second century and were never of importance in Babylonia.

131. See Pt. 1, Ch. 2. See also T. H. Gaster, *Festivals of the Jewish Year* (New York: 1955); Haim Leshem, *The Sabbath and Festivals of Israel* (Hebrew) 2 vols. (Tel Aviv: 1965); Solomon Zevin, *Hamoadim Behalakhah* (Tel Aviv: 1955); Hayyim Schauss, *The Jewish Festivals*, trans. Samuel Jaffe (New York: 1938).

132. The volumes are in Seder (The Order) MOED. There is no tractate for Pentecost, but it is equalized in all halakhah with the other festivals, while Hanukah is not. M.B.K. 1:3 and Hal. 4:10 stabilizes first-fruits at Shabuot. See n. 176.

133. For the modern problem of the Second Diaspora Day see Sigal, *New Dimensions*, "Rejoice on Your Festivals."

134. Even Sukot was connected with the exodus from Egypt at Lev. 23:42. Shabuot was first historicized in the post-exilic period as this is first evident at Jub. 6:17-22.

135. It is clear that in our source, II Ki. 25, the dates do not match the calendar dates for *c* and *d*. The date for *a* is not specified. Cf. Jer. 52:4, 6 which give the same dates for *b* and *c*, but v. 12 gives the 10th day of the fifth month for *d*. Cf. Jer. 39 where no dates are given for *b, c, or d*, and no date is given for the murder of Gedalyah at Jer. 41:1-3. Nevertheless, at 41:1 it appears the murder took place at a meal of the seventh month. Since special note is taken of this it is possible it happened at the feast of the first day of the seventh month. When the rabbis decided to commemorate this occasion as a warning against duplicity and as a caution that Jews should rather accept Roman arrangements after 70 A. D., they probably instituted it on the third day to bypass Rosh haShanah. Zekh. 7:3 indicates the fast of the fifth month marking the destruction of the temple was more meticulously kept and 7:5 indicates that it and the fast of the seventh month were generally observed. Josephus, *War VI*, 2.1 (93f.) informs us that the daily *òlah* offering came to an end on the seventeenth of Panemus, Tamuz, and the temple was burned on the tenth of Lous, Ab (*ibid.* 4:3ff, 236-250). Josephus (*ibid.* 250) tells us that the tenth was the day it had been burned by the Babylonians (Jer. 52:12). Nevertheless, the tradition (B. Taan. 29a) accepted the ninth probably because on that day the conflagration began. For anthropological views see T. H. Gaster, *Festivals*, pp. 193f. n. 2, and in general, pp. 191-195.

136. See Mishnah R. H., passim, N. H. Snaith, *The Jewish New Year*; Philo, *Spec. Laws II*, 31 (188f.).

137. M.R.H. 1:2; B.R.H. 8a; These ideas are certainly first-century as they come to us from circles in which R. Meir was active, B.R.H. 16a-b. The New Year Day was a Babylonian day of judgment since time immemorial but it was celebrated in spring. It appears, therefore, that although details vary we have here too the judaization of a pagan day. Precisely what were the steps by which the nature of this Baby-

lonian day was ascribed to the Pentateuchal "trumpet festival" is not presently known. But it is clear that by the end of the first century this was the case. R. Akiba and his colleagues are credited with arranging a Rosh haShanah liturgy (M.R.H. 4:5-7), but it is clear that even if this came at Yavneh at the end of the first century the prayers to be used are spoken of in a manner that indicates they were well-known and used in times past. It is also apparent that the Hallel (Ps. 113-118) was recited at that time and points to the antiquity of the liturgy. Later on, probably owing to the length of the Rosh haShanah liturgy as it evolved, Hallel was removed. The idea of a heavenly book is a very old motif in Israelite religion (Ex. 32:32). It recurs frequently in biblical and intertestamental writings and has been referred to in earlier chapters. B.R.H. 16a-18b is an exceptionally interesting homiletical section and one of the most significant theologically in all of the Talmud. The student can easily pursue details of custom in any number of popular books on Jewish customs. Post-talmudic rituals arose sometimes as part of the process of the judaization of ancient folkloristic motifs. See Gaster and Schauss. Some customs, e.g. eating an apple dipped in honey, are an outgrowth of views in the Talmud which had not yet become ritual. See B. Hor. 12a, and on this Abudraham, p. 143.

138. A perusal of the entire liturgy and most especially a careful study of the ámidah will yield the various motifs of Rosh haShanah, and reveal the central emphasis upon creation, judgment, kingship of God, and God's forgiving compassion. The creation theme is found at *Bib. Ant.* 13:4 where God is quoted as saying He oversaw His creation on the Feast of Trumpets.

139. It should be borne in mind that this *malkhuyot, zikhronot, shoferot,* liturgy is very old. It is discussed at M.R.H. 4:5f. as a well-known liturgy, references to the sections being made without explanation. There is no reason to doubt that it is pre-70 proto-rabbinic.

140. Lev. 16 is the basic Yom Kippur passage. But details are provided at Lev. 23:26-32.

141. The goat sent to Azalzel is popularly known as a "scapegoat." Sir James Frazer's *Golden Bough* has much information on the worldwide practice of using a scapegoat to bear the sin of a community. But, as Gaster, p. 142, properly points out, the original meaning of a scapegoat was not someone "blamed" for our sins, but a medium used to carry off the sin which we first confess. The act of confession is

present in other scapegoat rituals. In modern times the
scapegoat ritual of confession and carrying-off of the sin is
a psychological purgation of society. The person or community
is relieved of encumbrance and can make a fresh beginning. In
a very real sense Jonah is the goat thrown to the Azalzel of
the sea. He carries off the sin that encumbers the boat, for
it is indeed his own sin of flight from God. The reading of
Jonah on Yom Kippur afternoon, therefore, is appropriate for
more than one reason. Gaster, pp. 176f. refers to other
folklore stories of persons swallowed by great fishes and then
disgorged like Jonah. See Elias Bickermann, *Four Strange
Books of the Bible* (New York: 1967).

142. "Dew" is a code-word in references to salvation and
resurrection, and the last line alludes to Isaac at Gen. 24:
63. For dew, see Is. 26:19; B. Hag. 12b; etc.

143. The *geshem* prayer is by Eliezer Kalir, 6th-7th
century. Sifra 102b; Lev. R. 30:5-15. An interesting ethical
principle is stressed in the halakhah of the *lulab*: that a
stolen one is unfit. The exegesis is from the words "to you"
at Lev. 23:40, that one is to take the branch that is his own,
Lev. R. 30:5f.; B. Suk. 29b. The altar circuits are described
at B. Suk. 45a. The *lulab* is waved to all points of the com-
pass to symbolize the omnipresence of God; M. Suk. 3:9; B.
Suk. 37b.

144. I Ki. 8:60, "that all the nations of the world will
know that the Lord is God and no other" is reminiscent of
Zekh. 14:9. For Shemini Azeret, see T. Suk. 4:17; B. Shab.
48a.

145. See Rankin, *Origins of the Festival of Hanukah* for an
indepth discussion of the pre-Hasmonean Hanukah antecedents.
See also Goldstein, *I Macc.*, pp. 276-284; Gaster, *Festivals*,
pp. 233-253; Zevin, pp. 156-181. On dedication of altar in
eight days: Moses, Ex. 40:2, 17 in tandem with Lev. 9:1;
Hezekiah, II Chron. 29:17; Zerubbabel does it at Sukot, I Esd.
5:50-52. It is of interest that no miracle is said to have
occurred at this dedication as in the case of the dedications
by Moses and Solomon (Ex. 40:22-27; Lev. 9:11; II Chron. 4:
19-20; 5:1-7:1). This may have something to do with the
rabbinic tradition that the Shekhinah and divine fire were
absent in the second temple, which was generally defective of
sacred elements in their view. The defective state of the
temple, however, must be taken back to 518 B.C. and not
blamed upon the Hasmoneans. See P. Taan. 65a; Mak. 32a; Hor.
47c; B. Yom. 21; Ab. de R.N. A. 41 and elsewhere. In addition
to the absence of divine fire and the Shekhinah these sources

list the absence of the Holy Spirit, ark, anointing oil, Urim and Tumim, the vessel of manna set aside by Moses, Moses' rod and Aaron's rod.

146. Goldstein, p. 18, n. 33.

147. See Carey A. Moore, *Esther*. The *Anchor Bible* (New York: 1971); Jacob Hoschander, *The Book of Esther in the Light of History* (Philadelphia: 1923); N. S. Doniach, *Purim, or The Feast of Esther* (Philadelphia: 1933); Gaster, *Festivals*, 215-232; Schauss, 237-271.

148. *Ant.* XI, 6, 13 (292-296); the rabbinic work devoted to Purim is tractate Megilah of Mishnah, Tosefta and Talmud; see de Vaux II, 516f. The earliest independent reference to Purim is at II Macc. 15:36 which refers to a "Day of Mordecai" on the fourteenth of Adar after the "Day of Nicanor." The latter is established at I Macc. 7:49. According to the postscript to the apocryphal Greek edition of the Book of Esther, the "Purim letter" of Mordecai and Esther (Est. 9:29-32) was brought to promote Purim in Egypt "in the fourth year of the reign of Ptolemy and Cleopatra," which is taken by some scholars to be Ptolemy XII and Cleopatra V, around 78 B.C., by others Ptolemy VII or Soter II, ca. 114 B.C. See Moore, p. 112. But almost a century later Philo does not refer to it. For a discussion of arguments for and against the historicity of the events recorded in the Book of Esther see Hoschander, *Book of Esther;* Moore, *Esther,* pp. xxxiv-xlvi; Doniach, *Purim.* As far as the name is concerned, many scholars doubt whether the common etymology of *purim* as "lots" is correct (Est. 3:7). Josephus does not refer to lots being cast as a means to determine the day on which Jews were to be destroyed (*Ant.* XI, 6, 7 (219)). Josephus, *ibid.* (6, 13, 295) refers to the Purim days as *phruraios* as LXX to Est. 9:26 reads *phrurai.* It is possible that the name derives from an old Persian word meaning "first" and relates to the New Year. In Arabic *phur* is still used colloquially to denote the New Year although there is no satisfactory etymology to explain the term. See Gaster, 217, 221; Moore, XLVIf. Nevertheless, the benefit of the doubt should be given biblical tradition which interprets *pur* to refer to *goral,* casting a lot, or determining destiny. This is an interpretation and not a translation. The term *puru* in Assyrian means "lot" from its primary meaning of "stone" upon which the destiny was written, and in Babylonian *puru* means "lot" in the sense of destiny, which is precisely what Est. 3:7 states, *pur* is *goral,* "destiny."

149. Moore, *ibid.* XLVI-LIII.

150. The religious elements in the apocryphal Greek additions to Esther: the mention of God, prayer, the references to election, redemption, kashrut, are all deemed later additions and not evidence of an earlier fuller, more theological Hebrew original, and in any event, were not incorporated into the rabbinic version. See Moore, XXXIIf.

151. See, however, the argument offered by Robert Gordis, *Studies in the Esther Narrative, JBL,* 95 (1976), 43-58. He construes 8:11 to mean the Jews may defend themselves against anyone attacking "them, their children and their wives. . .," that is, taking these words not as indicating that the Jews are to attack women and children but as a citation from Haman's edict at 3:13, and allowing them to defend themselves. Gordis provides grammatical and philological force, but is unconvincing and appears apologetic. The verse is an ironic paraphrase of Haman's edict: what he planned to do to the Jews will now be done to his supporters, a typical outcome of retributive justice.

152. See Zevin, pp. 194-203; B. Meg. 3a; this is all in accordance with the idea that what is received in tradition is as legitimate as what is in the Torah, B.R.H. 19a. Cf. B. Meg. 7b for the blurring of Mordecai and Haman. See also Sandra B. Berg, *The Book of Esther* (Missoula, Mont.: 1979), who sees "the hiddenness of Yhwh's presence in the world" (p. 178) requiring human activity, as a theological statement in the book.

153. The sculpture is mentioned at M. Mid. 1:3; Kel. 17:9; B. Men. 98a; Bekh. 40a; Pes. 86a. See Bickermann, *Four Strange Books,* pp. 171-240 for an interesting approach to the composition of the Book of Esther and the establishment of Purim. At p. 201, he suggests that Purim was originated at Susa, and while I do not adopt all of his particulars, Iranian-Zoroastrian elements are found in the book. Aramaic was used by Zoroastrians during the hellenistic period and some believe the book was originally written in Aramaic which was the language of the eastern Jews. Possibly an unsuccessful effort to establish Purim in Alexandria is reflected by a parallel story referring to a peril ca. 144 B.C.

154. See especially J. B. Segal, *The Hebrew Passover.* The Passover liturgical and calendrical texts in the Pentateuch are at Ex. 12; 23:15; 34:18, 25; Lev. 23:5-8; Num. 9:1-14; 28:16-25; Deut. 16:1-8. See Pt. 1, Ch.2 above for a discussion of the Israelite festival calendars.

155. See de Vaux, II, 484-493, and Segal, *op. cit.* There is no certainty about the derivation of the name of the festi-

val, Pesah. The word is connected with *pasah*, "to limp, to jump" thus giving the English name "Passover," indicating God passed or jumped over the houses of Israelites during the tenth plague. DeVaux, II, 488 hastily rejects derivation of *pesah* from the Akkadian *pashahu*, "to appease," on the grounds that the paschal offering did not have an expiatory purpose. Conceivably it did have an expiatory soteriological purpose. This tradition is preserved in the Isaac lore discussed above and in Christology. See Segal, pp. 95-106 for a review of different hypotheses concerning the meaning of the word. The P. Targ. is of interest, however, as a major source for considering the paschal lamb in an expiatory sense. At Ex. 12:13 the targum refers to the paschal lamb as *mearev*, serving as surety or bail for Israel, and to God's sparing Israel by virtue of the merit of the lamb. So too, at v. 23 it translates the term *pasah* as "protect" and at v. 27 refers to the sacrifice as one of "mercy." As far as the term *mazot* is concerned, it means "unleavened bread" and marks the beginning of the barley harvest, the first crop. A gift had to be offered on the pilgrimage (Ex. 23:15; 34:20) and the first sheaf offering was a special rite (Lev. 23:9-14). See Segal, pp. 107-113 for his rejection of various hypotheses concerning the meaning and origin of the mazot festival, including the view that it was a harvest festival. Segal hypothesizes that Pesah originated as a New Year festival, pp. 114-154.

156. Segal, p. 157ff. touches upon the ideas I present here and led me to my view, but he does not reach the same conclusion. References to the "blood" of Isaac in the Isaac-typology lore I have discussed earlier may be a reminiscence of this tradition that an expiatory offering was made by blood and not only by annihilation. See Mekh. I, 57 to Ex. 12:13; at n. 7, Lauterbach cites Mekh. de R. Simon, ed. Hoffman, p. 4, to the effect that one-fourth of a log of Isaac's blood was offered on the altar. So too in Christology the body of Jesus is not annihilated and the expiation is by the shedding of blood. Both he and Isaac are, therefore, paschal lambs and not whole burnt-offerings. Segal argues that the blood ceremonies resemble those of New Year commemorations of other near eastern religions. He makes the point that the Akkadian word *kuppuru* describes the ceremony of smearing the shrine with blood, and that the Arabic *fidyah*, redemption, describes the motive for the Islamic ritual, and both are used at New Year celebrations. By juxtaposing the ancient ritualistic term with that of Islam he concludes that the Passover blood ritual is a *kippurim*, a smearing and cleansing at the New Year, and that this supports the idea that Passover was a New Year festival. The paschal lamb was therefore a *pidyon*, a redemption, by which humans could avert distress in the coming year. Segal's view, pp.

162ff., is suggestive, and I think the notion of the paschal
lamb being "redemptive" is only a stone's-throw from the idea
that it is expiatory, if not fully identical. To "expiate"
is "to avert by religious ceremonies; to purify with religious
rites" as well as "to extinguish by suffering to the full"
(*The Oxford Universal Dictionary* 3rd rev. ed. 1955). "Redeem"
has many meanings, among them "to buy off by payment"; "ransom, rescue, save, deliver, deliver from sin and its consequences, to make amends or atonement" (*ibid.*). It is unnecessarily pedantic to see any distinction between expiation
and redemption. If the paschal lamb is redemptive (Segal, p.
164; 183: "We have seen that the Pesah ceremony was a sacrifice of redemption") it is expiatory. Yet Segal denies this
at pp. 105f. See Segal's useful review of the details to be
observed in the preparation and eating of the paschal communion
meal, pp. 166-174. Note also that Ex. 12:10 accommodates the
paschal lamb to a whole burnt-offering by ordaining its total
annihilation by human consumption and burning of the remainder.
Ex. 12:13 makes it clear that it is redemptive and the purpose
of this expiation is the exodus (v. 17). I think the paschal
lamb is the prototype *ʿolah*.

157. The Torah prohibits *seor, maḥmeẓet* and *ḥameẓ,* three
forms of basic terms which denote leaven or fermentation (Ex.
12:19f., 15). The punishment for eating leaven is *karet,* being
"cut off" from Israel (Ex. 12:15, 19). In all likelihood unleavened bread was to be eaten with the paschal lamb because
the celebrant was the priest and his altar represented the
sanctuary altar, and no leaven was to be eaten by priests in
the sanctuary (Lev. 6:7ff). The bread is considered part of
God's sacred sacrifice (v. 10) and for this purpose leaven is
improper. The traditions must be deep-rooted in the most primitive origins of the cult. In later times, Mt. 16:6; Mk. 8:15;
Lk. 12:1; I Cor. 5:6, etc., B. Ber. 17a; R.H. 3b-4a, indicate
that this notion of leaven as an agent of corruption was still
prevalent. It also played a role in kabalism.

158. *Spec. Laws* II, 27 (145)-28 (161). See Colson's note
a at p. 394.

159. *Ibid.*, 27 (148); M. Pes. 9:5; T. Pes. 8:11-22 catalogues the distinctive halakhot applicable to each category,
and at 8:15 specifies that blood is not smeared on the door-
posts and lintels. Even at II Chron. 35:11 the priests merely
"sprinkle" blood as is usual in all sacrifices.

160. Segal, pp. 9, 221. Cf. Cowley, *Aramaic Papyri,* No. 21.
Segal, pp. 222f. argues that this papyrus only indicates that
the week of Passover was observed. He rejects the notion that
the paschal sacrifice was offered at Elephantine. The papyrus

is too mutilated to determine which view is correct. Segal
offers an imaginative interpretation of Philo (p. 240) and he
argues that there is no evidence for the paschal lamb offered
outside of Jerusalem in post-exilic times except for what he
terms "the heretical Samaritans and possibly by the Falashas
in Ethiopia." See Segal, pp. 251ff; 255f. He believes Philo
refers to Jerusalem and to the proto-rabbinic permission to
eat the paschal meal anywhere in Jerusalem. Instead of seeing
alternative practices in the diaspora in Philo, Segal adjudges
Philo to be in error, p. 29. For post-exilic paschal: Ezra
6:19-22; II Chron. 35. Wine: Jub. 49:6; paschal limited to
the sanctuary: Jub. 49:16-21. Segal, p. 231f. rejects the
notion that the wine is a substitute for the blood. But the
rabbis did require red wine for Pesah, P. Pes. 37c; and wine
and blood were compared, e.g. at Gen. 49:11, Deut. 32:14; Is.
63:3; Ben Sira 39:26; 50:15; B. San. 70a, all of which Segal
is aware. He offers no arguments or evidence for his conclusion that it is "improbable" that an analogy was drawn between
wine and blood. The term *afikomen*, M. Pes. 10:8 is obscure.
At B. Pes. 119b, P. Pes. 37d it has received various explanations. It probably means that one ought not to leave the
paschal gathering to join in the *epikomios*. The Greek term
means a "festival procession" and probably signifies that the
celebrant should not join any other banqueting group of which
there were many in Graeco-Roman society, which often ended
with drinking bouts. It became customary to put aside a
piece of mazah to be eaten at the end of the Seder. In
Sefardic and Oriental liturgy the last piece of mazah is taken
with the formula: "In memory of the Passover sacrifice. . ."
Cited in *The Passover Hagadah*, ed. Nahum Glatzer (New York:
1953), p. 57, note. See also Louis Finkelstein, "Pre-
Maccabean Documents in the Passover Hagadah," *Pharisaism*,
Additional note C, pp. 111ff.

161. Segal, pp. 29ff; 35.

162. Lk. 2:41; 23:49, 55; Mt. 27:55; Mk. 15:40f. The Last
Supper is at Mt. 26:17-30; Mk. 14:12-26; Lk. 22:7-38; Jn. 13.
One comment is needed here on the absence of a paschal lamb
connected with the Last Supper. It is my contention that A.
Jaubert is correct that the sectarian Pesah occurred on Tuesday night at which time the Last Supper took place. See her
Date de la Cine, and J. A. Walther, "Chronology of Passover
Week," *JBL*, 77 (1958), p. 116. A lamb would not be offered
in the Temple because the priests would not accommodate any
dissenter. On the one hand it is possible the evidence that
lambs were offered outside Jerusalem has been suppressed except for the inference we can make from Philo and an assumption we can make for Qumran. On the other hand Jesus had to

be in Jerusalem for the climax of his career, and either he
could not offer a lamb for the reason stated, or he would not
want to offer a lamb in a dramatic demonstration that he is
the lamb. He eats the Last Supper on Tuesday knowing that he
will not then be the lamb. First, because he wishes to observe
the festival according to the non-Establishment calendar as a
gesture of loyalty to its authority, or perhaps because he
always followed the Qumran calendar. And secondly, if he is
the paschal lamb the gesture of dying on the cross will have
its major impact on the masses if it is done on the day and at
the hour when the paschal lamb is offered. John reports the
Last Supper as having taken place on Thursday night either because of lapse of memory or because a later redactor thought
that to be correct. And again, as in the synoptics, Jesus
dies at the hour of the Jerusalem paschal offering. Moreover,
neither the Synoptic Gospels nor John endeavor to give a fac-
tual and careful portrayal of the Pesah Seder. They merely
provide the natural setting, their major motive being to
teach how Jesus transformed the traditional paschal communion
meal into the eucharist.

163. See Segal, pp. 259f. for details of Pesah observance
before 70 A.D., and notes for the references to rabbinic literature. Wine: M. Pes. 10:1-4, customs abandoned: 9:5; T. Pes.
8:11ff. See Segal, 261. For removal of leaven and other
practices: M. Pes. 1:1ff; Pes. 3:1; 2:7-8; Tem. 7:5; Pes.
2:1; 7:9.12; Meg. 1:11; Pes. 7:13; 10:9; T. Pes. 5:13. Modify-
ing the Torah's requirement to burn the left-overs that same
night: M. Pes. 7:10; B. Shab. 24b.

164. The Seder ritual is at M. Pes. 10:1-3; the statement
"in the sanctuary they brought before him the body of the paschal lamb" intimates that M. Pes. 10:1-3 referred to a post-
70 ambiance when the lamb was no longer used. The four
questions: *ibid.* 4. See Louis Finkelstein, "Pre-Maccabean
Documents," p. 93, n. 114. It is apparent in the Palestinian
Mishnah that there are only three questions, as at P. Pes. 37b.
See *The Babylonian and Jerusalem Mishnah,* ed. Melech Schachter,
p. 76. The three questions cover dipping twice, eating only
mazah, and eating roast. Another text, The Berlin Edition,
cited by Blackman at 10:4, records the three questions as:
why mazah, dipping twice, *maror?* Obviously these three constitute the relevant questions today when these rituals are
still performed. Actually there was flexibility in the ritual
and children could ask other questions: B. Pes. 115f; 116b.
Children are obligated to participate in the rite because they
too were involved in the redemption. See B. Pes. 108b-109a.

165. The anecdote is traced to no other source and is found

only in the Passover Hagadah. A parallel is at T. Pes. 10:10.

166. For a discussion of the dating of Dayyenu and the affinities it has with earlier literature, see Finkelstein, "Pre-Maccabean Documents," pp. 83-90, 117f.

167. The great Hallel is to be recited with the fourth cup, B. Pes. 118a; this is Ps. 136 (B. Ber. 4b; M. Taan. 3:9).

168. See Zevin on the halakhah of Pesah, pp. 231-262; on the problem of utensils, and *kashering,* B. Pes. 30a-31a; A.Z. 75b; search for leaven, B. Pes. 2a; 7b; 12b; left-over leaven prohibited, B. Pes. 28a, 29a; selling the leaven, T. Pes. 1 (2):24-26, (ed. Zuckermandel, p. 157). It should be noted that the circumstances of selling *ḥameẓ* in the Tosefta are very limited and not designed to become an annual ritual. This developed in the middle ages and is increasingly falling into disuse in modern times. See also Ex. 12:19; 13:7, etc. Options in the halakhah are evident at B. Pes. 5b-6a; 27b-28a; M. Pes. 2:1.

169. Some questions were touched upon in my *New Dimensions,* but a full monograph toward the radical revision of the halakhah of leaven is a current desideratum.

170. See deVaux, *Ancient Israel,* 493ff; Shemaryahu Talmon, "The Calendar Reckoning of the Sect from the Judaean Desert," *Scripta Hierosolymitana IV,* (Jerusalem: 1958), pp. 162-199; Segal, *Passover,* 247-269; see also Pt. 1, Chaps. 2; 5, IV, C and notes, above.

171. At Jub. 1:1 God speaks to Moses on the sixteenth day of the third month (Sivan in later reckoning), Moses ascends Sinai to be enveloped in the divine cloud for six days (16-21 Sivan), and God calls to Moses on the seventh day, or Sivan 22. From that date, for forty days and nights, Moses experiences the revelation. At Jub. 6:1-4 God is said to have made a covenant with Noah on Sivan 1, and with Abram on the same date (14:20). This date is regarded as the date of the covenant with Israel (6:11). Thus at 6:17 when the Feast of Weeks is ordained "in this month" as a covenant renewal festival it is impossible to determine its date. At v. 21 Weeks is identified with the feast of first fruits as in the Pentateuch and it is declared to be a dual feast: celebrating both the harvest and the Sinai covenant. At 15:1 Abram celebrates the harvest festival on the fifteenth day of the third month, as does Jacob at 44:4. But here the covenant with Abram is not made on the first of Sivan but "in the middle of" Sivan (vv. 1, 4ff.). At 16:13-14 it is clear that the author of

Jubilees believed that Isaac was born on the same date as God spoke to Abraham, and that this date was the date of the harvest of the first fruits and occurred "in the middle of the month." From all of these verses it emerges that there is no coherent statement on the date of the revelation to Moses and the making of the covenant, and the date of the festival of first fruits which is twice placed "in the middle of the month." We have at least three variant dates, Sivan 1, 15, and 22 for a revelation-harvest-covenant renewal festival called Weeks and Pentecost (II Macc. 12:31-32). See Pt. 1, Chap. 5, IV, c, for the calendar.

One of the main problems is how to interpret "from the morrow of the Sabbath," (Lev. 23:15). If Sabbath (hashabat) here signifies a day of cessation from work other than the Sabbath, it can apply to either a) the first, or b) seventh day of Passover (Lev. 23:7f.) and still leaves the day of the sheaf offering undetermined. According to a) the ȯmer would be offered on Nisan 16 and Pentecost would occur on the fiftieth day or Sivan 5 if each month would have thirty days by the solar calendar, or Nisan 6 if we follow the lunar calendar and Iyar (the second month) has twenty-nine days. This latter computation ultimately became the proto-rabbinic and rabbinic way to determine the date of Shaḇuot. See Charles, "Jubilees," *The Apocrypha II*, pp. 34f., note to 15:1. Onk., P. Targ. Lev. 23:11, 15, LXX, Philo and Josephus all clearly adopt this approach. Philo, *Spec. Laws II*, 29 (162), writes ". . .within the feast there is another feast following directly after the first day. This is called the 'Sheaf'. . ." (trans. F. H. Colson). See Josephus, *Ant*. III, 10.5 (250). M. Ḥag. 2:4 speaks of an aẓeret (Pentecost) that could fall on a Friday or a Saturday which indicates it too assumes the ȯmer occurs on any day of the week. But contrary to Charles, *ibid*., while this affirms that it need not occur necessarily on Sunday it does not tell us whether the ȯmer is brought after the first festival day or the last festival day, when work is also forbidden, giving it equally the air of a *shabbat*. M. Men. 10:1-3 indicates the ȯmer could be cut on the Sabbath, again reflecting that it could be offered on any day of the week and not only on Sunday, but not clearly telling us whether it was brought after the first or the last day of the festival. The mishnaic evidence, therefore, is not ironclad, but that the ȯmer was brought during Passover is supported at T. Men. 10:23. Since the rabbinic Pentecost is observed on Sivan 6, furthermore, it is reasonable to conjecture that the proto-rabbis followed the interpretation offered by the sages who are responsible for the LXX, and that this view was adopted by the targumists and Philo, and Josephus already reflects the similar post-70 rabbinic halakhah.

There are various alternative datings which we cannot go into here. For example, the Qumran calendar cited by Segal, pp. 39-41, reflects the waving of the sheaf on a Sunday. But contrary to Segal, p. 247, it is not clear whether this would be a Sunday during Pesah or after Pesah. Similarly at P.R.H. 57c, when the rabbis discuss whether cutting the ȯmer grain supersedes the Sabbath it is not clear whether Passover I or Passover VII is meant as having occurred on the Sabbath. But at Sifra 100b, where "the Sabbath" is taken as it is by Onk., to refer to the festival, it is also specified that it refers to the first festival day. It is argued that Deut. 16:8 "six days shall you eat unleavened" does not contradict 16:3 and other verses elsewhere that require one to eat unleavened for seven days, because the six refers to the remaining days when unleavened bread is made of new grain after the ȯmer was brought on the second day of Passover. Thus out of all of the confusion one point emerges: the rabbinic celebration of Pentecost on the fiftieth day from the second day of Passover is based upon a tradition that belongs to at least the first century B.C. or early first century A.D. (Philo), but possibly even to the third century B.C. (LXX), providing the LXX at v. 11, "the morrow of the first day" and v. 15 "the day after the Sabbath" refers to identical days, the day following the first day of Passover.

172. IQS 1:14-15; cited by Vermes, *The Dead Sea Scrolls in English*, p. 72; Burrows, *The Dead Sea Scrolls*, p. 371. In rabbinic literature we have reflected debates over precise calendar intercalations and consequently when certain festivals occur. But the difference is that all schools of proto-rabbis and their successors, the rabbis, argued for rabbinic authority in calendar regulation even if they divided over precise particulars. See M.R.H. 2:9; B.R.H. 25a; P.R.H. 57a-58b, where Gamaliel II asserts his patriarchal authority over R. Joshua. See Solomon Zeitlin, *Studies*, I, 183-211 on the question of the calendar. He points to the complex problem of tracing the history of Israel's calendrical changes from lunar to solar and back to a lunar calendar; see especially J. Morgenstern, "The Three Calendars of Ancient Israel" *HUCA*, 1924. The post-exilic lunar-solar compromise (a lunar calendar of 354 days in a twelve-month year with one month intercalated seven times in nineteen years to accommodate the 365-day solar year) led to a year in which Nisan always had thirty days and Iyar twenty-nine. This resulted in Pentecost always occurring on Sivan 6 (Zeitlin, p. 196). The Jubilees circles dissented from these calendar reforms even before some of them turned against the Hasmoneans to emerge as Qumranites and Essenes.

173. T. Men. 10:23; M. Men. 10:9; 10:2-3; see Talmon, "Calendar Reckoning," pp. 185-187. At pp. 187-198 Talmon attempts to support the notion that the pietists began the day at sunrise by examining the order of prayer discovered at Qumran. But to maintain this point of view he is compelled to declare (pp. 192f.) CDC 10:14-15, not to work late Friday afternoon, "the extension of Sabbath," to be an interpolation by a later copyist. This is not very convincing. And as far as Jubilees is concerned, at 50:7, "six days shall you work. . ." and other references to preparation on the sixth day, prove nothing about Friday night anymore than the similar biblical verses. The question is when the seventh day begins, at sunset on Friday, at sunrise on Saturday, or perhaps at midnight between Friday and Saturday. We simply have no way of knowing at the present time. It is possible that all the groups began the Sabbath on Friday evening, or that Qumran and Jerusalem did and that the Jubilees circle did not. The latter maintained the death penalty (50:13) and Qumran did not (CDC 12:4), so one need not expect complete unanimity among the various denominations as if there are two only: "the orthodox" and "the sectarians." Talmon, p. 194, seems to be subject to this overgeneralization when he juxtaposes "sectarians" and "normative Judaism." As a matter of textual precision, when we follow the rabbinic texts we can conclude that Sadducees and Boethusians were two separate groups and not necessarily synonymous as Zeitlin and other scholars take them to be, as is apparent from Ab. de R.N. A, 5; B, 10. T.R. H. 1:15; P.R.H. 57a; Zeitlin, *Studies II*, 267f.

174. B. Yom. 4b; Shab. 86b; Taan. 28b. The attribution of revelation to Pentecost is in *beraita* literature of a period before Akiba. But the view can be dated even earlier because of Jub. 1:1, and an anonymous tradition recorded at Mekh. II, 99; P. Targ. Ex. 19:16. At B.R.H. 6b we find that there was fluidity on when Pentecost occurred, depending upon the lunar calendar prior to its stabilization.

175. For the Pentecost first-fruits ritual see tractate Bikkurim. From M. Bik. 1:3 and Hal. 4:10 we infer that the first-fruits ritual was stabilized at Pentecost. Although Lev. 23 does not imply the kind of first-fruits ceremonial we find developed in later times, its colorful nature is implied at Deut. 16:10f. and its formalistic ritual at Deut. 26:1-11.

176. See above Section A. The discrepancies involved in the dates of the fasts have been brought to the reader's attention previously. Some held that the Tebet fast should be on the fifth of the month when the diaspora heard that Jerusalem was attacked. See B.R.H. 18b; M. Taan. 4:6; B. Taan. 26b.

A special feature of the Fast of the Ninth of Aḅ, Tisha B'Aḅ, is the reading of Lamentations at synagogue worship: B. Taan. 30a; see also Gaster, *Festivals*, pp. 192-211; Schauss, *Jewish Festivals*, 96-105. See Zevin, pp. 342-349.

177. See Gaster, pp. 57-58; New Year for trees is the fifteenth of Shebat, at M.R.H. 1:1. For the geonim see *Emergence* II, Chapters 2-3. Modern Judaism, except for those who style themselves "orthodox" has eschewed the *sefirah* halakhah.

178. Moore, II, 21-39; for a popular level discussion of the subject, see Abraham E. Millgram, *Sabbath The Day of Delight* (Philadelphia: 1952); for a romantic view, A. J. Heschel, *The Sabbath* (New York: 1951); Schauss, *Festivals*, pp. 3-37; Lauterbach, "The Origin and Development of Two Sabbath Ceremonies" in *Studies in Jewish Law*. See also the discussions of the Sabbath in Pt. 1, Chaps. 2, 3, 5-7, and bibliography.

179. Moore, II, 24, following Augustine's usage.

180. Judith 8:6; I Macc. 1:39; 2:29-41; 10:34; II Macc. 5:25ff.; 6:6ff; 8:25-28; 12:38; 15:1-5; Jub. 1:10; 2:23, 27, 29-30; 50:6-13; Philo, *Dec.* 20 (96-101); *Spec. Laws* II, 15 (56-64), 16 (65-70); 45 (249-251); *Moses* II, 4 (21-22); 39 (209-216); 40 (217-220) and elsewhere; Josephus, *War* I, 7.3 (146); II, 17.10 (456); *Ant.* III, 10.1 (237); XII, 6.2 (274f., 276ff.) and elsewhere. For the Sabbath at Qumran, Pt. 1, Chap. 6.

181. Baron, *History*, I, p. 9. Baron cites Cranmer and Luther for the usage in English and German.

182. Sifra 83a; Philo, *Mig. Aḅ.* 16 (91); see also Boaz Cohen, "Sabbath Prohibitions Known as Shebut" in *Law and Tradition in Judaism* (New York: 1959), 127-166; a variety of such secondary rabbinic prohibitions are listed throughout talmudic literature, e.g. M. Bez. 5:2; R.H. 4:8; Shab. 10:6; B. Shab. 95a; 114b; Bez. 33b. These and dozens of other references are of the pietistic quality which have as their major thrust the imposition of a quiescent day, utter abstention from the mundane being regarded as the only way to proper sanctification of the day. Such rules as governed carrying (not serious "transportation") became trivialized and beset by many complex details. See M. Er. 10:3; B. Shab. 97a.

183. These rabbinic principles are: *pikuah nefesh*, saving life (Mekh. III, 197f.), *safek nefashot*, even if there is only a doubt concerning danger to life (M. Yom. 8:6; T. Shab. 15:11, 15, 16; B. Shab. 57a) the items that are *doheh shabbat*, supersede the Sabbath, such as circumcision, sacred worship, a mes-

senger for a mizvah; and the many ramifications of these.
See T. Shab. 15:16; M. Shab. 19; Pes. 6:1-2; Er. 10:13, etc.
Some items are no longer relevant such as the permission to
violate the Sabbath in the interest of the cult, but when we
understand the cult in its extensive sense of sacred worship
it becomes apparent that such halakhah can be applied to the
synagogue as other cultic elements were after 70. The thirty-
nine primary prohibitions are called *aḇot* (principal) and the
numerous derivative prohibitions are called *toledot* (subdivisions or derivatives). The *toledot* were not formulated before the period of the ámoraim.

184. This is the theme underlying my *New Dimensions*. This
is also recognized by G. F. Moore, *Judaism*, II, 31.

185. The explanations for the use of spices and a light
along with wine at *haḇdalah* vary. See Lauterbach, "Two Sabbath Ceremonies." Although originally the blessing for light
was in thankfulness for Adam's discovery at the onset of the
new week (Gen. R. 12:6) it is understood today that light
and spices are taken as symbolic of the radiance and fragrance
that the family prays will be its blessing in the coming week.
The wine represents fertility and hence prosperity, and perhaps is also in some way reminiscent of the blood element in
the sacrificial cult. In this way the drinking of wine in
both the *haḇdalah* and kiddush is participating in a sacramental act in affirming the sanctity of the Sabbath. There is
much kabalistic mysticism related to the *haḇdalah* which does
not belong to our period, but whose roots are in this early
rabbinic period. Various rabbis linked the drinking of *haḇdalah* wine with future salvation (B. Pes. 113a) and other
blessings (PRE 21). See also B. Pes. 53b, 54a. It is recorded
in some sources that Elijah appears at the beginning of the new
week to sustain those waiting for redemption. The wine, therefore, has some relationship to the cups of redemption connected
with Passover. See B. Er. 43b. Along with the various humanitarian principals that the rabbis invoked to circumlocute some
of the restrictiveness of Sabbath halakhah they also utilized
exegetical and halakhic arguments such as: a) when a *melakhah*
is not intended it is not a sin; b) when one does not require
the actual forbidden act but seeks a permitted objective the
forbidden act is not a sin (B. Shab. 73b; Bez. 8a; Ḥag. 10a-b).
A simple example is offered: when a person carries a dead
person from a building on the Sabbath he is not guilty of
violating restrictions of transporting from one domain to
another, for his intent is not "to transport" but to do honor
to the dead. Cf. B. Shab. 93b.

186. Moore, II, 39.

187. See Sidney B. Hoenig, "The Designated Number of Kinds of Labor Prohibited on the Sabbath," *JQR*, 68 (1978), 193-208. The attempt by Hoenig to explain the connection between the thirty-nine prohibited activities and the construction of the sanctuary is not persuasive. For an exposition of the Sabbath by one who considers himself "orthodox," see I. Grunfeld, *The Sabbath* (London: 1954). It is my intention to write a monograph on the Sabbath in the not-too-distant future in order to explicate the meaning of *melakhah* for contemporary society and provide the historico-halakhic underpinnings for a contemporary form of Sabbath observance.

CHAPTER 4

The Media of Judaism: Synagogue and Sources

I. PREFATORY COMMENTS

That a coalition of movements, which is really what
Judaism constitutes, should have had the resiliency and stam-
ina to withstand the tumultuous centuries of persecution, the
rise and separation of Christianity in both its gentile and
Judaic forms, a variety of burgeoning and debilitating messianic movements, the challenge of Mazdeism, Mithraism, gnosticism, Islam, Karaism, internal denominational struggles, and
not only survive but continue a flourishing spiritual evolution, is nothing short of miraculous. It had to have some
special power to achieve this. In this chapter we will briefly survey the instrumentalities of the faith. These include
the synagogue, the scriptural canon, the Greek and Aramaic
targums which opened the canon to the entire diaspora and
limited the element of mystery in the texts which would otherwise have to be authoritatively interpreted by the Jerusalem
priests, and finally, the great literary corpus which evolved
out of the interpretive activity of the hakhamim, sofrim, and
rabbis, the Midrash, Mishnah, Tosefta, and Talmud. Much of
this took place in Palestine, but increasingly after the first
century the center of Judaic religious creativity was Babylonia.

II. THE SYNAGOGUE[1]

A. *Origin*

The origin of the synagogue is lost in a mist of obscurity.
Various theories have been propounded but none can be sustained
with documentable certainty. I tend to accept the view that
the ultimate origin of the synagogue is in the early monarchical period.[2] In every society there are people who search for
ways to express their religion outside of established institutions. This may be either because they wish to supplement the
formalistic rites with more personal forms, or because they
come to disdain the formalistic rites. In ancient Israel people

sought alternative forms of worship either because they desired
to surmount what appeared to them the impersonality of the
priestly-sacrificial cult, or because too frequently the established priesthood and the sanctuaries and high places were
given over to idolatrous rites. In the circumstance it would
appear to the devout that seeking out a holy man and searching
for torah from him, and perhaps reciting psalms and prayers
under his inspiration and guidance would be a solution to a
religious crisis.

That some such process was at work is at least suggested,
if not proven by II Ki. 4:23 which informs us that it was customary to visit the home or religious center of an *ish elohim*,
a man of God, on Sabbaths and New Moons. Even after Josiah's
reform the Temple did not remain pure of religious taint, and
people would continue to find an alternative worship system
attractive. Moreover, the emphasis upon a centralized sacrificial system in Jerusalem which was accelerated by Hezekiah
and Josiah with the destruction of *bamot* (rural high places),
would make local prayer-gatherings in towns and villages distant from Jerusalem important. Furthermore, the Judaic diaspora which existed as early as the ninth century B.C. in
Damascus required a solution to the problem of worship distant
from the sanctuaries of Israel and Judah. The argument that
synagogues did not exist because there is no epigraphic or
archaeological evidence for the existence of such centers of
worship cannot be accepted. The statement by a leading scholar,
"The utter absence of testimony forbids our thinking of a pre-
exilian origin," must be rejected.[3] People have to have a way
of satisfying religious yearning when the established way is
unacceptable, inadequate or inaccessible. It is conceivable
that the term *bet hamidrash* as a place of study and exposition
grew out of this early prayer center, for one went originally
to a presiding prophet at a shrine *lidrosh*, to inquire of the
Lord, to receive an oracle.[4]

As far as the term "synagogue" is concerned (Greek *synagōgē*), again we are in the dark as to when the term arose as
the almost-exclusive way to refer to the Judaic house of worship. Similarly we are in the dark concerning the Hebrew term
bet hakeneset. Both the Greek and the Hebrew signify "place
(or house) of assembly." The Israelites are a *kahal* or an
edah in the Bible, and these words for "congregation" or "assembly" are usually rendered as *synagōgē* in the Greek (LXX
Num. 14:5; 13:27). But a place of worship is also rendered
proseuchē in the Greek as for example when the anonymous preacher refers to God's *bet tefilah*, "house of prayer" (Is. 56:7).
The term *proseuchē* is used by Philo and Josephus, and is ascribed to Paul. Philo usually uses the term *proseuchē* but he
also uses *synagōgē* as do the New Testament and Josephus.[5] To

distinguish themselves Christians began to use the term *ekklēsia* which means the same thing (Acts 16:5).

The *maǎmadot* were rotations of lay-people corresponding to the twenty-four rotations of priests at the Temple.[6] These lay people assembled in their towns while priests and levites went to Jerusalem to participate in their *mishmar*, the priestly watch or rotation which changed every two weeks. While some scholars see these *maǎmadot* as the origin of the synagogue I think it is more plausible that the alternative worship centers going back to early monarchical times helped stimulate the rise of *maǎmadot*, and these were conducted in the worship centers that came to be called *proseuchē* and *synagōgē* under Greek influence, and *kenishta* among the Aramaic-speaking Jews of the eastern diaspora.[7] The dual meaning of the term "church" in modern times as the building or place of worship and the congregation or the polity can be applied in various contexts to the Greek, Hebrew or Aramaic terms that refer to a Judaic center of study and worship. Rabbinic sources frequently use another term, *zibur* (an association) to speak of the community of believers or worshippers.[8]

As has already been pointed out by others, a first-century inscription summarizes the function of the synagogue in ancient Judaism. This tells that the synagogue was built ". . .for the reading of the Torah and inquiry into the commandments; furthermore, the Hospice and the Chambers and the water installation for lodging of needy strangers."[9] Josephus and Philo emphasize the Sabbath gatherings at which Torah and teaching was a major feature of the synagogue.[10] This is also clear from the New Testament (Lk. 4:15f.). It is natural that travellers would need a place to stay and synagogues provided this service well down into the middle ages. By the same logic the woman of Shunem who was a disciple of Elisha's is paradigmatic for the pre-exilic period. When people travelled to the center of worship where an *ish ělohim* presided they too must have availed themselves of facilities for eating and sleeping. Although it is precarious to infer that what we find in the first century A.D. had its pristine origins in the eighth century B.C., it is equally precarious to allow the argument from the silence of our sources to mute such an inference.

The tradition that the Sabbath synagogue activity had high antiquity, even that it was established by Moses, pervades the hellenistic and rabbinic tradition. To argue that this is an utter fiction with no roots in historical reality is without warrant.[11] Just as we have *bet tefilah* in post-exilic writings and *proseuchē* which is derived from *proseu-*

chomai, to pray, we also have in the Dead Sea Scrolls the term *bet hishtaḥavut*, a place of prayer, or prostration before God (CDC 11:22).

It is of course true that there is no explicit mention anywhere in canonical scripture or in Ben Sira of an established institution housed in a building as we would imagine a place of worship to be. In its earliest period it could face the same kind of devastation as rural high-places and would naturally not find an elevated or definitive position in the opposition literature which we have inherited. But this alternative worship center is alluded to in II Kings, Ezekiel and in Psalms. Only after the rise to prominence of the proto-rabbis is freer reference to this alternative worship made, and in due course this popular alternative institution is stabilized in permanent physical structures and becomes predominant.[12] It was for the very reason that it was an *alternative*, frequently dissenting center of worship and teaching before the late Hasmonean period that Antiochus IV has no need to include it along with his proscription of the cult of the Jerusalem temple. On the other hand, since Antiochus sought to uproot the Torah he made a special campaign against it (I Macc. 1:56f.).

It is not known with certainty when the *maàmadot* originated. But it may be presumed that the diaspora experience had a strong impact upon Judeans who returned with Ezra and Nehemiah, and that in the post-Nehemian age this was one of the reforms instituted in Temple procedure. The rabbinic tradition[13] ascribed the institution to the pre-exilic prophets. This tradition also refers to the fact that the men of the *maàmad* gathered in their local synagogue. This implies that it was believed on the basis of traditions and evidence known then that such an institution, even if not in a permanent physical structure, existed in the earliest times of the *maàmadot*, namely in the pre-exilic era (B. Meg. 27b). In time this would tend to influence the establishment of a permanent physical structure. Possibly this structure, as distinguished from the Temple in Jerusalem, was called the *bet àm*, "the people's house," a term the rabbis later opposed. The reason for this opposition is not clear, but since it comes from the second century A.D. it constitutes part of the generally vehement opposition of the rabbis to the *àmmei haàrez* whose synagogues are placed off-limits (B. Shab. 32a; M. Ab. 3:14). Possibly the *àmmei haàrez* used their synagogues as secular social centers, and partly in reaction to this the rabbinic halakhah developed in a way to give increasing sanctity to this worship center which replaced the Temple after 70 A.D.[14]

The rabbinic tradition established that one is not to conduct oneself in a disrespectful manner in a synagogue, one is not to eat, drink, or sleep therein, but confine oneself to studying sacred literature, and preaching and lecturing aside from praying there (B. Meg. 27b, 28a-b). And indeed this is what the synagogue was designed to be from the earliest times, a place of instruction and devotion. The New Testament is an independent witness to the antiquity of "reading Moses" in the synagogue "from earliest generations." (Acts 15:21).

B. *The Synagogue: Its Officers, Functions and Impact*

The synagogue generally belonged to the corporate community, at least in tannaitic times. It was administered by appointed elders. It is not clear who made the appointments. The scriptural reading, preaching and prayer-leading was done by any member of the congregation who volunteered or who was invited to lead. The official who assured the functioning of the synagogue is known in literature reflecting the entire Graeco-Roman society as *archisynagōgos*, ruler or elder of the synagogue, or *Rosh hakeneset* in the Hebrew. This was the official who appointed the scripture-reader and invited the preacher.[15] He was assisted by a superintendent, the *hazan hakeneset*, an official probably comparable to the contemporary sexton, who helped in the public worship activity by bringing forth the scroll, helping direct worshippers and sounding trumpets; he sometimes taught reading to children and administered floggings.[16] There were also those who collected and distributed alms, the *gabaei zedakah*, and the *shaliah zibur*, the leader of worship, the delegate, agent or apostle of the congregation. The congregation was not headed by a rabbi, but it can be presumed that the rabbis served as halakhic consultants.[17]

The synagogue contained a closet or *tebah*, for the scrolls which were wrapped in linen and held in cases. In some instances the scriptures were read from a *bimah* or elevated platform, a feature that goes back to the time of Ezra and Nehemiah. The synagogues and study houses were equipped with lamps, and the synagogues possessed horns and trumpets.[18]

The congregation may have been seated according to socio-economic status or age, possibly varying among groups and from town to town. There is no evidence that women were segregated. When Philo tells of women segregated at the sacred banquet of the Therapeutae he is not implying this is done in synagogues. Mindful of the sexual promiscuity at Greek symposia Philo is careful to preclude any suggestion of this happening among the Therapeutae. But in his description of the Essene synagogue seating arrangement, on the other hand, he does not indicate women sat apart. There is no mention of separate seating for women in the talmudic literature, nor even when Paul suggests women be silent in the churches does he recommend segregated seating. Segregated seating in the synagogue, like the covering of the head, which became deeply entrenched and was the prevailing mode until the nineteenth century, is a post-talmudic development.[19]

It appears that by the first century there was a regular pattern of public worship, and that this public worship required a minimum prayer quorum of ten, or a *minyan*. The prayers included the shemá, ámidah, the priestly blessing, the torah reading, and a *haftarah* or prophetic reading. The scriptural readings were translated. Other liturgical occasions required a *minyan* of ten as well. The shemá in this context includes the liturgical paragraphs that precede it and follow it which express the doctrines of creation, revelation and redemption. This liturgy is to be fulfilled in community. A community of believers, a synagogue in its essential sense, is seen to be the agency of redemption for the individual. Thus public worship is a *sine qua non* in Judaism.[20]

Basing themselves upon Ps. 69:14 the rabbis called "the favorable hour" for worship the hour when the congregation is united in prayer. All the above enumerated passages and all others considered *kedushah*, expressive of holiness, such as *kaddish* and *kedushah* among others, were to be recited only if a quorum of ten is present (B. Ber. 6a, 8a, 21b). The *kaddish*, originally an eschatological prayer, was not introduced as a reaffirmation of faith by a mourner during his first year of bereavement until the middle ages. Because of its "holiness-passage" status it is proper that a mourner observe this obligation at synagogue worship and not as a matter of private devotion.

The explanations for why the number ten was selected as a minimum prayer quorum are various. It might be the adaptation of the *perushite* practice of dividing their communities into units of ten. Some scholars believe the reverse, that the Qumran community established congregations of ten because they followed general Judaic practice.[21] Whenever a quorum was present the leader could begin worship with the invocation *Barkhoo et adonai*, "give praise to the Lord," thus summoning the congregation to worship, and it in turn responded *barookh adonai hamevorakh leòlam vaèd*, "praised is the Lord the source of blessing, forever." This procedure remains the practice in Judaic worship to this date, except that preliminary psalms are recited, for which a quorum is not required, and then the formal worship begins with *barkhoo* (M. Ber. 7:3).

The New Testament, Philo, Josephus, and rabbinic literature all reflect that preaching and teaching was normal custom in the synagogue. The rabbinic literature arranges formal scriptural readings and translations for all festivals, indicating they were treated like Sabbaths. The literature also speaks of the *meturgeman*, a translator who functioned along with teachers who taught halakhah.[22]

The basic prayer, ámidah, as noted in Pt. 2, Chap. 3, was quite old. But apparently the form in which it appears today was given to it at Yavneh. Simon Ḥapakoli arranged the traditional order of eighteen paragraphs for Gamaliel II, but when the latter decided to expel the Christians from the synagogues he asked Samuel the Small to institute a special new paragraph against the *minim*, Christian Jews. At a later date this paragraph was amended, and the term *noẓrim* (Christians) as well as the term *minim*, were both removed, although the latter is still found in a thirteenth century English prayerbook.[23]

The foregoing indicates that from the earliest times the synagogue offered study, prayer, charity and hospitality. This is the model that remained historically functional. In this way the synagogue is one of the major instrumentalities in the continuity of Judaism. After the destruction of the Temple and the virtual cessation of the sacrificial cult it took primacy in Judaism.[24] The synagogue became the substitute for a political organization and the survival of the Jew was seen to be dependent upon the continuity of study. The terms "house of worship" and "house of learning" became almost synonymous and are frequently used together in the literature. Attending synagogue became a major *miẓvah* and was equated in the diaspora with living in the holy land. Moreover, some texts read emphatically that prayer is not heard except in the synagogue. The synagogue was a democratizing institution. Individuals could lead the worship and be called to the Torah and read it before the entire congregation. But in time the office of Torah reader evolved and individuals merely recited berakhot before and after the reading, thanking God for the revelation, election, and eternal life. As Torah-readers evolved so did prayer-leaders, later called cantors, as the knowledge and competency of individuals decreased and more and longer prayers were added to the worship order.[25]

The synagogue and Torah were portable sanctuaries. Even if the building was destroyed and the scroll burned,

Judaism had so many buildings and so many scrolls and books
that no enemy could undo it. Ten Jews were a congregation.
No clergy and no cultic trappings were actually required. Eve.
in a gathering of two or three talking words of Torah, there
was the Shekhinah believed to be and the participants were as
partaking of a sacrificial meal (M. Ab. 3:3f.). If this
spiritualization of the religious process influenced a lack
of interest in synagogue architecture, it should not lead to
an exaggeration of the antipathy to art believed to be endemic
among the rabbis. They refrained from emulating the Temple,
including the seven-branched *menorah*, and opposed sculptured
figures, but they did not oppose all art.[26]

III. THE CANON[27]

     The Greek term *kanōn* appears to be used for the first
time by Athanasius around 367 A.D. From the usage of this
term in various contexts the meaning to be attributed to it is
that the books listed as "canonical" conform to a certain
standard. According to some views, what marks certain books
as "canonical" is the fact that they are deemed appropriate
to be read at cultic assemblies. But this does not tell us
why they became canonical in the first place. Furthermore, it
is especially questionable whether we can actually define what
makes for canonicity in Judaism. Books that are not canonical
not considered sacred, for example, Ben Sira, are quoted in
the talmudic literature.[28] Even in ancient times there were
differences of opinion over canonicity, and the criteria that
were used to settle the disputes are not clear to us. Thus,
during the first century Bet Shammai and Bet Hillel differed
over whether Ecclesiastes (Kohelet) should be considered part
of the sacred scriptures. It was disputed again at Yavneh and
only after Gamaliel II was temporarily deposed from leadership
was it voted to declare Ecclesiastes sacred. We do not have a
record of the arguments for and against the book. That it
should be considered sacred was the earlier view of Bet Hillel
and that scholars at Yavneh decided to include it in the collection of official sacred writings is an example of how they
often followed Hillelite halakhah (M. Ed. 5:3; Yad. 3:5).

     But even the use of books at religious worship or for
private devotionals only attests to their canonicity and does
not explain why they were canonized in the first place (M. Yom.
1:6). Thus, there were many books used for study, or perhaps
cultically, in ancient times, that are referred to in the
Bible, and which we no longer possess. Evidently those who
had charge of literary developments in Judaism chose not to
preserve them. We have no precise idea how, why, where or

when the canon was formed to include the books that we possess
except that this was in all probability a reflection of the
theology and halakhah of different leaders. Such men as Ezra
and Nehemiah and others at different stages of the development
of Judaism, such as those at Yavneh and Usha were responsible
for selecting and omitting books. The two divisions of scripture as we have it, the Pentateuch and Prophets, were known
and accorded special status by 200 B.C. for they are listed
by Ben Sira (45:1-5; 46:1-49:13). Furthermore in the view
of some scholars Job was known to Ben Sira and used by him,
while his grandson attests to other writings of the third
division of our scripture, Hagiographa or Sacred Writings.
It goes without saying that all or most of the Psalms were
already gathered. And so it may be fairly asserted that by
200 B.C. most of the "canon" was known, perhaps all of it except Daniel, even if it was not yet all regarded as sacred
scripture.[29]

Rabbinic literature refers to twenty-four books and this
without consistency. Josephus refers to twenty-two. The
lists vary in different contexts. The evidence from Alexandria
and Qumran indicates that books later excluded by the rabbis,
such as Jubilees, were once freely used along with other
scriptural works. The Septuagint, and the lists of Church
Fathers vary. But the books present at Qumran do not prove
there was a larger canon at one time anymore than rabbinic use
of Ben Sira indicates that the book was in their canon. There
was no settled canon before the second century A.D. and it was
then settled because of the rise of Christianity. This was
not done at the Synod at Yavneh and we have no knowledge of
how it came to be. The scholarly consensus which dates the
fixing of the canon to Yavneh and specifically to around 90
A.D. when Gamaliel was deposed, is not accurate. The questions
raised about Ecclesiastes and Song of Songs, and doubts about
Esther are still in dispute during the second and third centuries.[30]

It is difficult to ascertain why the rabbis decided to
exclude certain books. It is plausible that books were excluded by the following criteria: a) they were not pre-
Maccabean; b) they were used by Christians or had affinities
with the Christian emphasis upon the Son of Man-Messiah concept; c) they were halakhically wholly unacceptable such as
Jubilees; d) they were composed in Greek. These criteria resulted in the exclusion of all those works we have come to
call Apocrypha and Pseudepigrapha, the New Testament (and its
Apocrypha) and the writings that originated at Qumran. For
reasons given in my discussion of Philo earlier, his writings
were not given the same status as rabbinic writings. The

great puzzler which fits none of these criteria is the exclusion of Ben Sira. The exclusion of the Maccabee books despite the continuation of Hanukah basically relates to the
continued rejection of the Hasmoneans for the usurpation of
priesthood and kingship. Despite the pietistic rigor that
was taken over by the rabbis from the *perushim* they did not
adopt the Qumran books because of the controversial nature
of elements of their halakhah, their eschatology, the Teacher
of Righteousness material, and basic opposition of rabbinism
to monastic separatism. To make official all the exclusions,
we have the attempt on the part of the Mishnah to threaten
loss of salvation to those who read "extraneous books," that
is, the books excluded from sacred literature. But it is not
yet clear to which books this referred. This threat had some
force over large groups of Jews over the centuries but has
lost all import in modern times except among some fundamental-
ist circles.

The collection of sacred writings is vastly enlarged by
the rabbinic literature which took on near-canonical status
itself. Like the synagogue, the literature is portable and
both together make possible continuity and affinity of thought
among widely scattered congregations. The term "torah" was
extended to all discussions of Judaic religion and to all
writings interpreting it. Thus synagogue and canon became
two vital media of post-70 Judaism that enabled it to survive
two-thousand years of often trying vicissitudes.

IV. THE TARGUMS

An important element in enabling the canonical literature
to serve its educational and edifying purpose was the early
recognition for the need and legitimacy of translations. We
have already noted the impact of the Greek translation. Here
we will briefly sketch the role of the *targums*. These are the
Aramaic translations which often are not literal translations
but take on the nature of interpretation and virtually border
on being *midrash*. There are several *targums* that come under
our purview, although we cannot do more than identify them and
briefly indicate their significance.[31]

There is a group of Palestinian targums which are desig-
nated in books by the names of Targum Yerushalmi, Fragment
Targum or Targum Yerushalmi II, one version of which is gen-
erally found in a well-equipped standard traditional Hebrew
Bible. There also exists a parallel to this called Targum
Pseudo-Jonathan. In addition there is the more famous and

popular Targum Onkelos. The authorship of the literary corpus in our possession is entirely obscure, and is regarded as
a "hopeless question" by a targum specialist. All in all
there is what one scholar has called a "synoptic problem"
with the Palestinian targums for there was never a fixed text
and no two manuscripts are the same. This fact had much to
do with diversity in rabbinic Judaism as well as in early
Christianity.[32]

A recent manuscript discovery of Palestinian targum is
published and discussed under the name of Targum Neofiti I.
It is believed that Neofiti I contains old halakhah, including
pre-Christian halakhah, and that it is therefore a valid
source for the background of rabbinic halakhah. Sometimes
the Pseudo-Jonathan differs from Neofiti I and we can see
therein part of that perennial Judaic halakhic diversity expressed in the translations. On the other hand the targums
have later interpolations such as the name of the city of
Constantinople (at Num. 24:24), and possibly some versions
have undergone rabbinic recensions to bring them into line
with at least one view in rabbinic halakhah.[33]

The translation was offered in the synagogue at the time
of the scriptural reading by a *meturgeman* (M. Meg. 4:4), a
tradition ascribed to Ezra (B. Ned. 37b). There might have
been two schools of translation: the one rendering the verse
almost literally, the other midrashically. The latter incorporated supplementary traditions that were not found in
scripture, or offered exposition of the verse rather than mere
translation.[34]

The messianic doctrine is an example of how targum expounded upon the Pentateuch to bring it into line with the
thinking of various schools.[35] Some rabbis were opposed to
speculation concerning the end of days, probably continuing
an older tradition that wanted to avoid the frustrations
occasioned by unfulfilled calculations made in Daniel and intertestamental writings.[36] It is of interest to find in the
Palestinian Targum, therefore, that when Jacob called his sons
together to relate to them the events of the end of days (Gen.
49:1), it is said that he meant to tell them when the eschaton
(*kez*) will occur but at the very instant that the revelation
was granted him it was withdrawn. In this way the targumist
reflects the point of view which opposed speculation about the
end-time.

The same process can be traced in halakhah. We can see
an example of how the sages sought to revise halakhah through
new exegesis expressed in the vernacular to the congregation

gathered in worship. The verse forbidding cooking a kid in
its mother's milk yields diverse results in targum Neofiti I,
the various Palestinian targums found in traditional texts,
and in Onkelos. Onkelos forbids only the eating of flesh and
milk, curiously ignoring the Hebrew "boil." The Palestinian
targums expand this to prohibit both the boiling and the eating of the two together. The rabbinic literature reflects a
triple prohibition against cooking, eating, and deriving benefit from the mixture in any way, such as selling it. The
Palestinian targums do not mention a prohibition against benefit, and Onkelos mentions neither benefit nor cooking. The
latter remains an enigma since it was the popular targum recited weekly along with the Pentateuchal text. The absence
of a prohibition of benefit in the Palestinian targums is to
be explained by the fact that they reflect the views of those
among the rabbis who only maintained a prohibition against
cooking and eating. In any event, we see here an example of
two developments. First, the targum reflects halakhic diversity; secondly, the P. Targ. coincides with one view of later
rabbinic halakhah, there having been no "normative" Judaism;
thirdly, we see the sages in the process of teaching the public that the prohibition to cook a kid in its mother's milk
is not to be taken literally but to be understood as forbidding the cooking and eating of any meat and dairy products.
The targum reveals for us the transformation of a cultic prohibition into a dietary prohibition. Scholars are therefore
not accurate when they say, for example, that Targum Pseudo-
Jonathan contains "deviations from established halakhah."
There was no established halakhah when these targums were in
the process of formation. Even later, as we see in the Talmud, there was no absolute agreement on the halakhah, and
consequently the targum never was altered to include the prohibition on benefit. Onkelos, strangely, was allowed to retain only the prohibition against eating.[37]

The targums provided the worshipper with information and
understanding and provided the average synagogue-goer with at
least a modest "adult education" program down through the
centuries.[38] From the targums the worshipper sometimes im-
bibed the oldest traditions. The antiquity of targumic traditions, as those of midrash and halakhah in general, is difficult to ascertain. But when they are paralleled in hellenistic literature we have the assurance of their pre-Christian
venue.

V. THE RABBINIC LITERATURE[39]

A. *General Observations*

The rabbinic literature includes àgadah and halakhah, and these genres are embodied in the literature referred to as midrash, Mishnah, Tosefta, and Talmud. Àgadah is expository material encompassing folk-lore, biographical data, science, history, and whatever else needed to illuminate a text. It seeks at times to inspire and edify and to influence one's conduct, but it does not relate to how one should conduct himself. The expository or interpretive torah that seeks to form and regulate one's conduct is halakhah. The àgadah is contained in midrashim which are termed halakhic as well as in those that are considered àgadic. The halakhah is similarly contained in both types of midrashim. There is even a small amount of àgadah in the Mishnah and Tosefta, although otherwise these two collections embody the halakhah. There are two Talmuds, one that was formed and collected in Palestine, mainly at Caesarea and Tiberius, the other in Babylonia, mainly at Nehardea, Sura and Pumbedita. Mishnah and Tosefta generally provide a succinct statement of halakhah without citing scriptural sources, although occasionally they provide a proof-text. Midrash, on the other hand, reveals the process of exegesis and the application of hermeneutical rules to scripture in the course of developing the theological point of view or the halakhah. One might say that midrash represents the discussion in process, the Mishnah and Tosefta represent the conclusion extracted as the implication for behavior. The Talmud in essence repeats the midrashic process upon the Mishnah, Tosefta and midrashic texts. In a real sense the Talmud is to the Mishnah and Tosefta what midrash is to scripture. The Talmud then reproduces both àgadah and halakhah. And just as it was at some point necessary to extract a simple reference-form of halakhah for public and school use from the mass of midrashic material found in Mekhilta, Sifra and Sifre to form Mishnah and Tosefta, so after the close of the talmudic corpus it became necessary to extract a simple reference-form of halakhah from the Talmud. This led to the medieval collections of halakhah which are often incorrectly termed "codes of Jewish law." They are not codes. They are digests or manuals of reference collected for convenience and not for the exercise of authority.[40]

Midrash and its result, halakhah, was not the only way the proto-rabbis and rabbis dealt with changing circumstances. They also issued *gezerot*, decrees to prohibit that which was previously permitted, and *takanot*, positive enactments to innovate a new practice. All of this emerging interpretive material, the halakhic conclusions and the positive and negative enactments came to be called oral torah. This oral torah of the sofrim-hakhamim-proto-rabbis and rabbis was regarded as of divinely revealed status.[41]

B. *The Literature*

1. *The Mishnah*

From the beginning it was necessary to transmit the literature as carefully as possible since it was regarded as sacred, and as of the very essence of revelation. The process was that of oral transmission in which the material was recited by the instructor and memorized by the students, but much literature was also gathered in written form. There is almost a fetish about being negative in modern critical studies concerning the question of oral transmission. This misleads scholars into adjudging even the earliest of the written rabbinic literature as post-70 A.D. and even later. There is little reason to doubt that the tannaitic midrashim contain much pre-70 and pre-Christian material and that many traditions recorded in the Talmud in the name of later scholars are earlier traditions. Thus the view that insists "a person is obligated to use the language (*leshon*) of his teacher (*rabbo*)," does not necessarily say he is to give the name of his teacher or his source like a modern footnote. It insists upon accuracy of transmission not fealty to sources.[42] But what we see here, as in all else, is a diversity of views. Some insisted on speaking in the name of the teacher, others only on using the accurate words. But even if one spoke in the name of his teacher he is not obligated to give the name of the teacher's teacher ad infinitum. Logic, therefore, dictates that the traditions reported by later teachers may indeed be very old.

The basic text of rabbinic Judaism is the digest of halakhah which came into existence around 200 A.D., is ascribed to Rabbi Judah haNasi, and is called the Mishnah. Rabbi Judah is frequently referred to simply as "Rabbi." Rabbi Judah adopted earlier collections and put them together to form the Mishnah. Different schools of thought and diverse opinions are recorded in the Mishnah, indicating that R. Judah did not design his work as a "law code" but as a digest for easy reference. As has been pointed out by scholars of the subject, the fact that editorial work is attributed to Akiba makes clear that the sages of Yavneh were engaged in putting together material that predated their era. Perhaps at a minimum they were classifying

Temple cultic halakhah in the wake of the disaster of 70 in
order to preserve the Jerusalem traditions and to consolidate
their own views on this and other matters against any attempted revival of the Sadducees. The question concerning the
"anonymous mishnah" with which term we refer to an anonymous
pericope, is whether indeed R. Judah "carefully selected" it
as some scholars maintain and intended it to be the "canonical"
halakhah. There is no warrant for this.[43]

The rabbinic literature evinces much confusion and uncertainty about all matters related to the so-called "anonymous mishnah." All we can say definitely is that an anonymous
pericope is one for which the editor of the Mishnah knew neither the originator nor the transmitter of the statement.
Many references can be adduced to indicate that talmudic
teachers, the amoraim of later generations, believed that the
anonymous pericopes were "consensus" views of rabbis and
therefore had the status of the official halakhah, but there
are also examples where the anonymous pericope, although
identified as a view of *rabbanan* or *ḥakhamim* is not selected
as the preferred halakhah. Similarly, little can be said
with certainty about the formation of the Mishnah. The Bet
Shammai and Bet Hillel scholars probably were the first to
collect ḥalakhot, and these were studied and expanded at
Yavneh. Akiba arranged a proto-Mishnah which was used by R.
Judah in his compilation. An intermediate stage attributed
to R. Meir is not warranted by the sources. Finally, since
the Mishnah includes statements by men who lived after R.
Judah it is evident that our form of it is a late recension.
The Mishnah should therefore be seen as a collection of a number of documents and even small units of halakhah derived
from varying schools of thought and individuals who had the
strongest role in shaping Judaism between the time of Ben
Sira and R. Judah the Nasi, 200 B.C. to 200 A.D. Its nature
as a repository rather than serving as a code supports the
thesis that there was no centralized authority or normative
halakhah in rabbinic Judaism.[44]

2. *The Tosefta*[45]

The Tosefta is similar to the Mishnah in arrangement.
Its name "supplement," derives from the fact that it provides
supplementary halakhah to that of the Mishnah, in the sense
of *alternative* halakhah. The two works are frequently in conflict. The Tosefta lacks certain tractates that are in the
Mishnah, and its halakhot are often styled *beraita*, "extraneous" material in the Talmud. Theories concerning the compilation of the Tosefta range from claiming it is the original

Mishnah of Rabbi which was supplanted by the present version
in Babylonia, to the idea that it was edited in Babylonia after
the Talmud. I tend to favor the view that much in Tosefta is
older halakhah regardless of when Tosefta was edited, which may
very well have been in the third century by R. Hiyya as tradition has it. My view, which there is no space here to explicate, is based partly upon my own studies of Tosefta halakhah
in the light of Philo.[46]

3. *The Midrashim*[47]

The term *midrash* applies to a process and a product, to
the exposition of scripture and to the collected results of
that exposition in a large number of books. The midrashim
are tannaitic when the scholars mentioned therein are those
who lived and functioned between 200 B.C. and 200 A.D. These
tannaitic midrashim report exposition of scripture from two
basic schools of thought that flourished during the second
century, that of R. Akiba and that of R. Ishmael. Basically
a midrash "contemporizes" scripture, as one scholar has astutely phrased it.[48] The tannaitic midrashim became the
reservoir of later halakhic compilation.

Other midrashim are basically homiletical in character
and consist of collections of material gathered for what must
have been lectures for the purpose of creating sermons, or
the sermons themselves. The Torah had been divided into
sedarim, sections for Sabbath and festival readings as well as
readings for special days and special Sabbaths. The Torah
seder was followed by a *haftarah* from the prophets. As noted
earlier, the targum aided in the explication of these readings,
and in a sense also "midrashized." But the sermons expanded
both the homiletical or àgadic and halakhic teaching of the
lection. It is thought that the earliest collections of
homilies are in Pesikta de R. Kahana, Pesikta Rabbati and
Tanhuma. The Midrash Rabbah is a comprehensive commentary on
all of the Pentateuch and the five Megilot (scrolls) read in
the Synagogue.[49] Another group of midrashim are called narrative or historical midrashim, such as Pirke de R. Eliezer,
which includes many aspects of rabbinic mysticism related to
such subjects as creation and the chariot-throne. Another
example of this type of midrash is the Chronicle of Jerahmeel.[50] There are probably forty different works of the genre
midrash, some of them multi-volumed.

4. *The Talmud*[51]

Talmud is a term which means "teaching," and is a midrash on Mishnah and Tosefta, serving the combined function of the tannaitic and homiletical midrashim. The Palestinian Talmud is the product of the schools of Caesarea, Sepphoris and Tiberias; the Babylonian of Sura, Nehardea, Pumbedita, Nisibis and other lesser centers. This "midrash" or exposition follows the Mishnah, almost paragraph by paragraph.

The teachers of the Talmud are called amoraim, the word *amorà* signifying "expositor." Both Talmuds omit some tractates, but not the same ones. Genizah fragments indicate that at one time the Palestinian Talmud included some of the missing tractates. In time, owing to the activity of the Geonim, the Babylonian Talmud gained hegemony in Judaism.[52] The Babylonian Talmud was further expanded and glossed by post-amoraic rabbis, the saboraim, who were the editors of the Talmud.[53] They flourished during the sixth century and bring us to the chronological limits of this volume.

The two talmuds are a massive testimony to the continued effort of Judaic spiritual leaders to continue the work theoretically begun at Sinai. The Talmuds were seen as a form of revelation and took their places as "canonical" works in Judaism. Over the intervening centuries since the compilation of the Babylonian Talmud, this Talmud in particular has perhaps had as much or more influence upon Judaism as scripture. The Talmuds constitute a literature that requires a lifetime of energy in order that one comprehend the idiom and the technical nuances of the terminology. It is in fact a giant stumbling block to the unequipped who seek to use it in modern comparative religious studies.

It is highly questionable whether the Talmuds were edited in our modern sense of the term. Rather, it appears that a mass of inchoate written material was brought together as one might collect minutes of a meeting or records of any academic discussion. Since the discussions were of mishnaic pericopes they were gathered in accordance with the sequence of the mishnaic texts. But the material is not at all thematic. Discussions flow from one subject to another often unrelated, and halakhic discussions are punctuated by agadic and mystical discussions and even table-talk.

Both Talmuds are written in Aramaic except for the Hebraic material of the tannaitic literature, the Palestinian Talmud in a western dialect and the Babylonian in eastern Aramaic. The Talmuds are records of discussions taking place in a variety of schools in both Palestine and Babylonia. This means there must have been more than one version of Talmud in circulation in their respective countries. It is hypothesized that the Palestinian version that is presently known took its final form at Tiberias toward the end of the fourth century and the Babylonian at Sura.[54]

The scholars of the two centers were in constant communication and the texts refer to scholars traveling to and fro, and to opinions held "here" or "there" or in "the west" (Palestine). The Palestinian Talmud contains views of Babylonian scholars and the Babylonian Talmud records the views of Palestinians, providing much space for the prominent Palestinian scholars, R. Yohanan, R. Simon b. Lakesh and Abbahu. The same Yohanan was one of the major movers of the Palestinian Talmud.[55]

The Babylonian Talmud was largely the product of the activity of several major sets of scholars such as Rab and Samuel during the third century, Abaye and Raba in the fourth century, and R. Ashi and Rabina in the fifth century. The study of the Babylonian Talmud was then undertaken throughout the diaspora as the Mishnah before it had been. Copies ultimately reached Egypt, North Africa, Italy, Spain and France. For the most part the Palestinian Talmud was neglected although here and there its study was emphasized. With the spread of the Babylonian Talmud and the hegemony of the Geonim, the rites and theology of Judaism were shaped in accordance with it.[56] Thus, like the Synagogue, the canon, the targums, the midrash and Mishnah, it became a vital medium for the preservation of Judaism. While Judaism continued its metamorphosis, all change was now measured against talmudic literature. All in all, the Talmuds mark the close of an era of remarkable literary achievement which followed the debacles of 70 and 135. This fascinating evolution says something for the power and efficacy of rabbinic Judaism.

VI. THE BABYLONIAN DIASPORA: CHRYSALIS[57]

Babylonia emerged as a great new center of Judaism to surpass Syria (Antioch), Alexandria, and Asia Minor as a major center of Judaic population and to witness a great effulgence of Judaism. That the Judaic diaspora was widespread is seen from the fact that a synagogue is mentioned as far away as Crimea in modern Russia. But in places like Damascus or Salamis, Cyprus, closer to Palestine and Babylonia, there were several and even many (Acts 9:20; 13:15). From frequent references in Philo we learn of many synagogues in Rome. From remaining inscriptions even on tombstones it is apparent that the people were Greek-speaking. This does not mean they did not use Hebrew at worship any more than modern English tombstones attest to the disappearance of Hebrew in North America.[58] But undoubtedly at worship they used both languages, and read scripture in both. In Babylonia, also, Judaism availed itself of both Hebrew and Aramaic, and the monumental Babylonian Talmud attests to the fact that the everyday language of study was Aramaic, as it was in Palestine. Hebrew was now generally only the language of worship and used in study. Even when new Hebrew poetry was written in Palestine as late as the seventh century, it was preserved in Hebrew by virtue of its use in the synagogue.

At first the Jews of Babylonia lived in the hellenistic area of Seleucia and other hellenistic centers such as Dura. By the time the Parthians conquered the country under Mithridates I around 140 B.C. the Jews had already lived in Babylonia for half of a millenium. Yet very little is known of their life and religious development throughout that time, in Babylonia, in Mesopotamia to the north, or Iran to the east. There is no evidence to link Babylonian Jews in any way to the tumultuous Hasmonean events. Quietly and inexorably a widespread and populous Jewish community developed from the northern end of the Tigris-Euphrates plain to the southern tip of the Persian Gulf. Historically this is the community which has been termed broadly, the "Babylonian" diaspora.[59]

It is not possible to determine whether Herod's appointment of a Babylonian Jew as high priest was for astute political reasons, or signals the fact that the Babylonian community was already a highly developed one. Perhaps it maintained intact its priestly families as "pretenders" to the high priesthood in Jerusalem. It was also during Herod's time that Hillel, said to have been of Babylonian origin, appeared in the constellation of ancient proto-rabbinic leaders in Palestine. Hillel's story is a confused rags-to-riches drama. He is sometimes said to have been an Alexandrian. He is said to have been poor. But in an instant he bests the proto-rabbinic leaders of the day, the enigmatic Bene Bathyra and is elevated to the position of Nasi (President) of the Sanhedrin. That he lived for awhile in Alexandria is quite plausible on the basis of a tradition of Tosefta (Ket. 4:9), even if he was not born there. That he arose to leadership in Jerusalem is clear. But what his Babylonian roots and background were is entirely obscure. Yet, it is apparent that the tradition was willing to ascribe to a Babylonian a high degree of sophisticated academic competence and an extensive knowledge of the preceding traditions of such teachers as Shemayah and Abtalion. This implies that as early as the

first century B.C. there already were major schools in Babylonia where a higher proto-rabbinic-type of training in the
oral interpretive torah could be attained. Moreover, the
sources reveal that upon his being elevated Hillel taunted the
Palestinians for their indolence in scholarship, thus having
to turn to "this Babylonian," a taunt which possibly reveals
the rivalry that already existed between the two communities
for hegemony in Judaism.[60]

Communication, travel and immigration between the eastern
diaspora and Palestine was frequent and there is no reason to
doubt that each community knew what was happening in the
other. They interchanged religious ideas and halakhah. This
partly explains the parallels in traditions in the two Talmuds. Letters from Palestinian leaders such as Gamaliel I,
went to the diaspora communities. Either the Palestinians
endeavored to assert their authority in Babylonia or the Babylonians sought it. In the person of R. Judah ben Bathyra,
whose importance is independent of any solution to the problem
of who the Bene Bathyra were, we have a major pre-70 tannaitic
scholar at Nisibis. Similarly, at the end of the first century the Babylonian Nehemiah at Nehardea, who was a Galilean
of Bet Deli, had an important influence on the rabbis in the
halakhah of testimony which normally requires two witnesses.
He brought them to allow a woman to remarry on the evidence
of one witness alone that her husband is dead. Here we have
a clear example of Babylonian influence upon tannaitic halakhah albeit by one born in Palestine. This implies not merely
that Palestinian scholars migrated to Babylonia but allows
the conjecture that these scholars founded schools. Moreover, during the second century we find that R. Nathan of
Babylonia was in a conspiracy to depose R. Simon b. Gamaliel
II (B. Hor. 13b). This may mark an effort on the part of the
Babylonians to unseat the Gamaliel dynasty.[61]

As was the case in Palestine and in the Graeco-Roman
diaspora Jews of the eastern diaspora also acculturated. But
this did not prevent Judaism from continuing its growth. R.
Hiyya, late second century, is already a Babylonian figure of
much influence in the evolution of rabbinic Judaism. He was
the uncle of Rab (Abba Arekha) who became the cornerstone of
Babylonian rabbinic-talmudic Judaism which placed its stamp
upon the entire future evolution of Judaism. He is much
quoted in Sifra; many halakhot that remained outside of the
Mishnah (beraitot), and the accuracy of form are ascribed to
him. These men mark the shift of gravity to Babylonia, and
ultimately of authority. The Bar Kokhba war caused a flight
of Akiban scholars to Nisibis and R. Ishmael's disciples to
Huzal, near Nehardea in the south. Some of these scholars

remained in Babylonia and conducted schools in which the Palestinian tannaitic traditions were taught. There is no way to determine to what extent the Mishnah incorporates Babylonian tannaitic traditions. Some scholars returned to Palestine. There must have been a mingling of traditions not only as a result of the refugees returning, but in general as a result of Babylonian scholars' input at Palestinian schools, and especially at Sepphoris as we have seen in the case of R. Hiyya. In the fourth century it was said that in Babylonia one can find the Shekhinah at Huzal![62]

The rabbinic tradition in Babylonia therefore, does not begin as it is traditionally described, with the opening of schools at Sura and Pumbedita with Rab and Samuel respectively. The influence of R. Ishmael of Palestine, through Huzal, is very strong in the Babylonian Talmud through the medium of Rab. But rabbinic learning originated even earlier and the Babylonians are known to have had their independent *hilkhata* or halakhot of which we read in a midrash in a second-century context (Gen. R. 33:3), as well as an independent mishnah-tradition. One might conceivably see the combined Palestinian-Babylonian product in the Mishnah in the light of the combined Karo-Isserles Shulḥan Arukh of the sixteenth century, which is discussed in the next volume. As has been noted by others, along with schools and scholars goes a style of exegesis, and along with the rational study of halakhah and ethics goes the esoteric and mystical midrash. Even if they did not hold the title by virtue of Palestinian ordination, the early Babylonian sages were rabbis. This is certainly evident in the case of Abba bar Abba the father of the famous rabbi Mar Samuel of Nehardea.[63]

Judaic literature has rather sparse allusions on developments within Sassanian Iran or on relations between Iran and the Byzantine Empire, and the Christian and Mazdean religions. From the middle of the third century through the sixth, which is the period of our literature, the Judaic community seems to have concentrated upon its inner life, and this appears to have been dominated by the rabbis and their academies. Although we cannot be certain of our information, especially of the chronological sequence concerning which there are many discrepancies in different sources, it is clear that a rich academic and spiritual life flourished, especially in the two major centers of which we know the most, Sura and Pumbedita, among others. The academies functioned to create an ideal Judaic community and became one of the most remarkable phenomena of religious history. Moses was held to be the prototype rabbi. But the academies were never monasteries where rabbis lived out their lives in seclusion. Rabbinical rite and ethics did not call for encratism or any form of ascetic behavior. The rabbis lived at home, in families, and functioned in society as judges, teachers, preachers and pastors. The main distinction between the rabbi and the lay person when the latter lived the ideal Judaic life proposed by rabbinism, was that the rabbi was a scholar, an expert in Judaica, and engaged in study for an inordinate proportion of his time. Rabbis had a great influence upon the public by their control of synagogue teaching and preaching.[64]

Abba Arekha (Rab), who died in 247, was the founder of the academy at Sura in 219 where the Talmud was ultimately compiled. There already was a college at Nehardea (P.B.B. 15a; B. Yom. 20b) and for awhile Rab taught there. Samuel became head of Nehardea, and the two great scholars and their schools engaged in constant mutual intellectual challenge. Rab specialized in liturgical and ritual matters and Samuel specialized in civil law. Rab was also a foremost agadist and numerous homilies are ascribed to him. A major portion of the Babylonian Talmud is occupied with the material of Rab and Samuel. Rab also engaged in esoteric studies and is a prime example of the rabbinic interest in mysticism that was not stilled by their intensive rationalistic halakhic activity (B. Ber. 17a; Ḥag. 12a; Kid. 71a).

Mar Samuel (165-254) was born at Nehardea, studied at Nisibis and in Palestine, and ultimately headed the academy at Nehardea. Along with Rab he made the independence of Babylonian Judaism from the authority of Palestine inevitable. He taught that it is forbidden to migrate from Babylonia (B. B.K. 111a). thereby encouraging students to study in Babylonia. Indeed, the leading Palestinian scholar, R. Yoḥanan, recognized in Samuel a superior authority (B. Hul. 95b). He collected halakhot which are referred to often as *beraitot* of the school of Samuel (B. Shab. 54a, etc.).[65] It is to him that the rule *dinà demalkhutà dinà* (sovereign law, or the law of the land is binding) is ascribed. But undoubtedly he was merely reformulating an old tradition which was exegeted from the famous letter of Jeremiah to the exilic community in Babylon.[66]

After Samuel's death a disciple of both Rab and Samuel opened what became another major center, the school of Pumbedita. This remained a leading center of scholarship and authority through the geonic era. Space constraints demand that we not discuss the great galaxy of rabbis who predominated from the third to the sixth centuries. Mention has already been made of R. Ashi. In sum it may be said that from the time the work of Rab and Samuel became effective, Babylonian Judaism moved to supremacy. Samuel insisted, for example, that some mishnaic halakhah is relevant only to Palestine and that Babylonia may pursue its own course (B.B.B. 26a). His disciple, R. Judah b. Ezekiel taught that "whoever emigrates from Babylonia to Palestine" violates God's command at Jer. 27:22, "they shall be carried to Babylon and remain there until the day I remember them." To this Judah is attributed great expansion of learning in Babylonia (B. San. 106b). Ultimately (probably 358-359) the Palestinians gave up their last major symbol of authority, the promulgation of the calendar, and issued a permanent computation which is still in use as the Judaic liturgical calendar. The Babylonian community was now prepared, with media and expositors, to become what the geonim made of it: spiritual father to the diaspora for fifteen hundred years.

VII. THE ETHICS OF RABBINIC JUDAISM[67]

We have already noted in previous chapters the Judaic norms related to the conduct of members of the family toward one another and the rights of women, and in passing have lightly touched upon various elements that are subsumed under our term "ethics." For Judaism there were two branches of miẓvot, those that obtain between the human and God, and those that obtain between the human and the fellow person, and it is the latter which moderns categorize under ethics. There is no tractate in the Mishnah on ethical or moral behavior. All of the ethical and moral precepts are interlaced in other themes of halakhah, in the civil, criminal and cultic halakhah, and in this section I can offer only a summary sampling.

There are no definitive limits in benevolent behavior, for it is left to human conscience to translate Lev. 19:18, to love one's fellow human, into concrete terms (Sifra 109b). Thus in the obligation to save one's fellow from peril (B. San. 73a) one need not surrender his own life. Here we have the famous conundrum of the two travellers in the desert where one had a little water sufficient to save one life, and the other had none. Ben Paturi argued that they should divide it and that both should die, while R. Akiba maintained that the one to whom the water belongs may save himself (Sifra 109b; B.B.M. 62a). On the other hand, human mutual responsibility was also stressed. A parable suggests this by pointing out that when a person drills a hole under his own seat on a ship, the water will enter and sink the ship with all of its passengers (Lev. R. 4:6).

The employer is to recognize rights of his employees and

to treat them in no way less than in accordance with the
standards of the region, compelling no overtime, and providing meals if this is customary (M.B.M. 7:1). In regard to
labor-management relations rabbis invoke the principle of
lifnim meshurat hadin, to go beyond what the law requires and
to act with special compassion in accordance with Prov. 2:20
(B.B.M. 83a).

One is not to threaten violence or humiliate someone in
public (B. San. 58b; B.M. 58b). Although the giving of charity is deemed a major miẓvah rabbinic ethics emphasized that
it is more virtuous to help one become economically independent (B.B.K. 112a). One should not acquire personal advantage
through the giving of charity (Ex. R. 31:18). An interesting
catalogue of ethical concerns is provided at M. Peah 1:1,
where we read that there is no fixed measure for the virtue of
leaving the corners of the field during harvest for the poor
(Lev. 19:9) or for the doing of benevolent deeds in general;
one receives reward in this world and in the next for honoring
parents and promoting peace along with the miẓvah which has
primacy, the study of Torah.

The ideal rabbinic Judaist is one who exercises great
self-control in order to exorcise envy, greed and pursuit of
self-exaltation or honor, for these are self-destructive (M.
Aḅ. 4:28). Anger, too, is regarded as a self-destroying vice
(B. Ned. 22b), and in a quarrel between two people the one who
desists first is commended (B. Kid. 71b). Among the many sayings concerning upon what the survival of the world depends is
the one in which God is personified as the supreme Righteous
One (B. Ḥag. 12b), and righteousness is declared to be more
significant than the cult (Deut. R. 5:3). Basically the ethical and moral life is predicated, as we have seen earlier,
upon the principle of imitating God (B. Sot. 14a).[68] There
are times when God is not to be imitated, for example in His
vengeful anger. The rabbis then become apologetic. But what
stands out perhaps, is that the rabbis reached for an even
higher level of saintliness than is evident in the Bible, in
full recognition that the Bible dates to an earlier time and
to a time when the earthy pagan gods of nature who roared and
stormed in eternal caprice were first eschewed for a spiritual
and ethical monotheism.

Sufficient has already been said earlier about the love
command as the basis of all halakhah and need not be repeated.
The corollary of love is not to hate, and the great first-
century disciple of Yoḥanan b. Zakkai, R. Joshua admonished
that *sinàt haberiyot*, hatred of people, is one of those qualities that are self-destructive (M. Aḅ. 2:16). In sayings such

as these the rabbis reach their crest. In sayings of less nobility we must recall they speak from the midst of a community turning into itself after tumultuous and traumatic debacles (the catastrophes of 70 and 135) and a severe rift (the separation of Christianity), in a largely pagan world between 70-600, for in Babylonia they still lived in a non-Christian Iranian society. But on the whole, as one author has indicated, as relates to whether the rabbis advanced or retrogressed from the Bible, "The advance is more conspicuous than the retrogression. . ."69

NOTES

1. See the essays gathered in *The Synagogue: Studies in Origins, Archaeology and Architecture,* ed. Joseph Gutmann (New York: 1975); Salo Baron, *The Jewish Community,* I, Chap. Three, III, 10-13; Emil Schürer, *A History of the Jewish People* (New York: n.d.), II, 44-89; Baron, *History,* II, 280-292.

2. Louis Finkelstein, "The Origin of the Synagogue," *The Synagogue,* ed. Gutmann, pp. 3-13; also found in *Pharisaism,* pp. 1-11. It appears that while Finkelstein sees II Ki. 4:23 as evidence of prayer gatherings earlier (ed. Gutmann, p. 4) he ascribes the rise of the "established institution" of the time of Jeremiah to the reign of Menasseh when the temple was polluted for half-a-century (pp. 6f.).

3. Schürer, II, 55. See below, n. 10. The Damascus diaspora: I Ki. 20:34.

4. See Finkelstein's discussion of this as linguistic evidence for the pre-exilic synagogue, pp. 8ff., which I do not accept entirely, but agree with in the particular I have noted in the text. See Ben Sira 51:23ff. It should not be forgotten that worship and holy days were a feature in Greek schools: Hengel, *Judaism and Hellenism,* I, 67b.

5. Philo's use of *synagōgē* is at *Every Good Man* 12 (81); at Moses II, 39 (216) he uses *proseuchē*. See Zeitlin, "The Origin of the Synagogue," in Gutmann, pp. 14-26. I reject his view that the synagogue had its origin in social and economic conditions (p. 17). From Philo's remark, *ibid.,* concerning the gathering of Essenes at "sacred spots which *they* call synagogues" (*kalountai synagōgai*) it should not be inferred

that in Palestine they were called synagogues and in the Greek-speaking diaspora a place of worship was called *proseuchē*. See John Bowker, *The Targums and Rabbinic Literature*, pp. 11f., where he follows Zeitlin's view that the synagogue became a center of worship as a result of the *maàmadot*, the lay-rotations in cities and towns which corresponded to the priestly divisions (*mishmarot*) that served two-week rotations in the Jerusalem Temple. See below. Another view of the origin of the synagogue is expressed, for example, by G. F. Moore, *Judaism*, I, 283, following others, that it had its origin in post-587 B.C. Babylonia where Jews had to make-do without the Temple. But this need existed earlier. See Josephus, *Life*, 54 (277, 280), 56 (293); *Ag. Ap.* II, 2 (10); *War* II, 14.4 (285).

6. Sif. Num. 142; M. Taan. 4:2; T. Taan. 4 (3):2. The Mishnah bases the *maàmadot* upon Num. 28:2 which is taken to require each individual to make his own offering. This is taken to imply his presence at the altar. Consequently "the first prophets," we are told, (the "prophets of Jerusalem" according to T.) established the twenty-four priestly divisions, and with each one there was a *maàmad*.

7. Acts 16:13, 16 uses *proseuchē* while Acts 9:2 and in other places uses *synagōgē* as does Lk. 4:15; 7:5, and James 2:2. At P. Meg. 74d we find *kenishta* without *bet*.

8. M. Ber. 5:5; R.H. 4:9; Shek. 4:1,6; Suk. 5:7; Pes. 7:4; Taan. 1:5; etc. and in the Talmud, passim.

9. I have slightly revised the translation cited by Bowker, p. 11, n. 2., from E. L. Sukenik, *The Ancient Synagogue of El-Hammeh*.

10. Philo, *Creation*, 43 (128) emphasizes the role of Sabbath in the search for wisdom, improvement of character and scrutiny of conscience. Cf. references, n. 5 above. Josephus, *Ag. Ap.* II, 17 (175); *Ant.* XVI, 2. 4 (43).

11. See Philo, *Hyp.* 7:11-7:14 and previously cited Philo and Josephus references; P. Meg. 75a. I therefore reject the views of Sidney Hoenig, "The Supposititious Temple-Synagogue," Gutmann, *ibid.* 55-71, and the views of Ellis Rivkin, "Ben Sira and the Non-Existence of the Synagogue," *In The Time of Harvest*, ed. Daniel Jeremy Silver (New York: Macmillan, 1963), 320-354. So too, the Babylonian rabbis at B. Meg. 29a accepted a tradition that the exilic "temporary sanctuary" of Ez. 11:16 refers to synagogues.

12. Ez. 8:1; 14:1; 20:1; 33:30f. See Baron, *Community*, III, 10, n. 5. Ps. 40:4 which speaks of a new mode of worship taken in tandem with the psalmist's rejection of the sacrificial cult at v. 17 may point to the tension that existed between the proponents of the exclusive validity of the Temple cult and those who championed the alternative system. So too, Ps. 51:17-19. It is of interest that v. 17 was selected as the opening line of the amidah. Ps. 51:20-21 praying for the future restoration of the cult, was added by an editor who was disturbed by the antecedent verses, and wanted them to mean that only while the Temple is not available is an alternative worship system valid. At Ps. 74:8 the words *moadei el* are puzzling. They can mean "the festivals of the Lord," but the enemy hardly "burns" festivals. The words therefore signify "gathering places" and refer to alternative worship centers which were destroyed along with the Temple (v. 7).

13. Finkelstein, *New Light*, p. 49, and Chapter IX as a whole. See n. 6 above.

14. M. Meg. 3:2f.; B. Meg. 28a-b; T. Meg. 3 (2) 7. Old traditions cited by Rashi took the phrase "and every great house" at Jer. 52:13 to refer to the synagogues. The parallel account at Jer. 39:8 reads *bet haam*, also taken by Rashi there as synagogues.

15. M. Ned. 5:5; Meg. 3:1f.; see Schürer, *History*, II, 59ff. and his notes; see also M. Sot. 7:7-8; Yom. 7:1; Acts 13:15.

16. M. Sot. 7:7-8; Yom. 7:1; Mak. 3:12f.; Shab. 1:3; T. Suk. 4:6, 11f. The office of *hazan* is also known in the Temple, as at M. Suk. 4:4; Tam. 5:3. At Lk. 4:20 the scroll is given to Jesus and received again from him by a *hypēretēs*, an attendant or assistant, probably the *hazan*. This should not be confused with the modern term, *hazan* which refers to the cantor.

17. For alms-collectors, M. Dem. 3:1; Kid. 4:5; Peah 8:7. For the "apostle" or prayer-delegate, M. Ber. 5:5; R.H. 4:9.

18. M. Meg. 3:1; Ned. 5:5; Taan 2:1-2; Ber. 5:4; Shab. 9:6; Kil. 9:3; Kel. 28:4; Shab. 16:1, and see also pertinent talmudic discussions. Neh. 8:4; P. Meg. 73d; it is also clear from M. Pes. 4:4 that there were lamps in synagogues; R.H.3-4, Taan. 3-4 passim. See Schürer, pp. 74f. For general synagogue halakhah see Sof. 10-21 which summarizes talmudic liturgy.

19. Philo, *Cont. Life* 8 (68)-9 (69); *Quod Omnis* 12 (81); I Cor. 14:34ff. Segregated seating ceased first with the reform movement during the nineteenth century and later with the conservative movement, but ḥasidic and other groups who refer to themselves as "orthodox" continue to practice it. On covering the head see Vol. IV of this series.

20. M. Meg. 4:3f.; B. Meg. 23b. The fact that the items enumerated required ten indicates they were the indispensible portions of the liturgy. Priests, or rather those who claimed descent from *kohanim* continued to have a role in public worship, reciting the priestly benediction and being called first to the Torah. They were no longer functioning priests since all of their functions as teachers and cultic figures passed to the rabbis. Since the nineteenth century the priestly benediction performed by *kohanim* is increasingly replaced by its recital by the rabbi. Many synagogues no longer recognize the priority of a *kohen*-descendent to be called to the Torah first. For an explanation of the phrase *pores et shemà* which is used in the sources that require a quorum of ten for the shemà section of the liturgy, see Finkelstein, Chap. 13, *Pharisaism*, 385-398. It is of interest that some Palestinian scholars recognized seven as a proper quorum (Sof. 10:7).

21. See Phillip Sigal, "Women in a Prayer Quorum," *Judaism*, 23 (1974), 174-182. This is also now reprinted in *Conservative Judaism and Jewish Law*, ed. Seymour Siegal (New York: 1978). The most cogent explanation for the *minyan* is at P. Meg. 75c; Ber. 11c, where an analogy is drawn through the common use of the Hebrew word *betokh* [the hermeneutical rule of *gezerah shavah* is here employed]. At Gen. 42:5 Jacob's sons are said to come *betokh*, in the midst of other purchasers of Egyptian grain. At Lev. 22:23 God is to be sanctified *betokh* Israel. Who is the minimum Israel among whom God is to be sanctified, is set by the Israel of Gen. 42:5, the *ten* sons of Jacob. See Vermes, *Dead Sea Scrolls*, p. 18; CDC 13:1-2. IQS 6 contains a longer discussion of the role of ten as the basic unit.

22. Mt. 4:23; Mk. 1:21; Lk. 4:15; Jn. 6:59; Acts 13:14ff. etc. M. Sot. 9:15; B. Ber. 24a; T.B.K. 7:3; B. Sot. 15a; San. 38b, etc.

23. M. Ber. 4:3; 5:2; R.H. 4:5; Taan. 1:1-2. We are told that Simon Hapakoli *hisdir*, arranged the 18 paragraphs, while Samuel the Small *tiken*, enacted the *birkhat haminim*. The careful distinction in terminology teaches an essential difference between what the two men did. The text of the thirteenth century English ritual is found in *Contributions*, ed. Petuchowski,

pp. 459-502, the text of *minim* at p. 481.

24. There are some who argue that sacrifices were still brought to Jerusalem after 70 A.D. See Chap. 1, n. 26; K. W. Clark, "Worship in the Jerusalem Temple After 70 A.D.," *NTS*, 6 (1959-60), 269-280. The thrust of the argument is just as some sacrifices were brought to the ruins between the destruction of 587 B.C. and the rebuilding of 516 B.C., so too between 70 A.D. and the final Hadrianic ban in 135 A.D. The evidence is not persuasive but the possibility has to be considered. M. Ed. 8:6 argues for sacrifices without a Temple. Possibly Justin, D. 46:2 supports Clark's view. Cf. also B. Meg. 10a; Zeb. 62a.

25. B. Ber. 8a. The evolution of synagogue liturgical leaders to replace spontaneous leadership from among the assembled is described in *Sefer Hamaasim*. See Baron, *History*, II, 423, n. 57. Cf. B. Ber. 11b where the berakhah still recited for the Torah is an already fixed formula. *Sefer Hamaasim* is a halakhic work from the seventh century which embodies many older traditions. See Baron, III, 111f.; 283, n. 46; IV, 64f.; 355, n. 71.

26. See above, Pt. 2, Chap. 2, V. Cf. Baron, II, 284f.; see the essays by Gideon Foerster, Michael Avi-Yonah, Martin Hengel and others in *The Synagogue,* ed. Gutmann.

27. See Gunnar Ostborn, *Cult and Canon* (Uppsala and Leipzig: 1950); Sid Z. Leiman, *The Canonization of Hebrew Scripture: The Talmudic and Midrashic Evidence* (Hamden, Conn.: 1976).

28 Ostborn, pp. 12ff.; 96f. See above Pt. I, Chap. V, II. C, 2, for Ben Sira.

29. Leiman, pp. 17f.; 141, n. 36. Examples of lost books: "Books of the Wars of the Lord" at Num. 21:14; "Book of Yasher," Josh. 10:13; II Chron. 24:27 indicates as early midrash on Kings and I Chron. 27:24 that prophets wrote chronicles that apparently have not survived. See Solomon Schecter, *Studies in Judaism*, Second Series, pp. 46f.; 58f.

30. B.B.B. 14b-15a; *Ag. Ap.* I, 8 (38-43); Leiman, pp. 37ff; p. 157, n. 207; other rabbinic sources that refer to twenty-four books: B. Taan. 8a; Num. R. 13:16; 14:4; 18:21; S of S R. 4:11; Ecc. R. 12:11f. and elsewhere. Deposition of Gamaliel II, B. Ber. 27b-28a; for continued dispute, B. Shab. 30b; M. Yad. 3:5; B. Meg. 7a; T. Yad. 2:13f; B. San. 100a; Yom. 29a; See Leiman, pp. 37-40 on the LXX, and pp. 120-124 on Jamnia.

31. For targum see also Pt. 1, Chap. 2 above, and bibliography at n. 6. The reader is directed to the following works: John Bowker, *The Targum and Rabbinic Literature,* and bibliography, pp. 329-348; P. Churgin, *Targum Jonathan to the Prophets* (New Haven: 1927); Paul Kahle, *The Cairo Genizah,* pp. 191-208; A. Diez Macho, *Neophyti I Targum Palestinense,* 2 vols. (Madrid: 1966, 1970); M. McNamara, *The New Testament and the Palestinian Targum; Targum and Testament* (Shannon: 1972); Alexander Sperber, *The Bible in Aramaic* (Leiden: 1973); P. Wernberg-Moller, "An Inquiry into the Validity of the Text-Critical Argument for an Early Dating of the Recently Discovered Palestinian Targum," *VT*, 12 (1962), 312-31; A. P. Wikgren, "The Targums and the New Testament," *Journ. Rel.,* 24 (1944), 89-95. In addition the reader should consult the writings of Geza Vermes, R. Bloch (French) and Roger Le Deaut (French).

32. Sperber, p. 3; McNamara, *Targum,* pp. 167f.

33. See A. Diez Macho (n. 31). McNamara provides a survey of targum scholarship, pp. 15-33; see p. 63.

34. Bowker, *Targum,* p. 6, conveniently lists methods of explanation as seen in the Dead Sea Scrolls: verse by verse commentary or *pesher,* the extension of scripture by inclusion of other traditions, anthologies on specific themes (such as the Messianic Anthology), among others.

35. See Levey, *The Messiah.*

36. Rabbinic opposition to calculation: B. San. 97b; B. Meg. 3a; Gen. R. 98:2.

37. Ex. 23:19; 34:26; Deut. 14:21. The P. Targ. to Deut. uses the hermeneutical rule, *kal vehomer,* deducting the major from the minor, to prohibit eating as derived from boiling. It thus sees the eating as the greater sin. This prohibition is expressed by Neofiti I and P. Targ. to Ex. accompanied by a warning that if Israelites violate this they will find themselves eating wheat and chaff inextricably mixed together. See M. Hul. 8:1, 4 where cooking and deriving benefit are forbidden but eating is not specified. Eating is specified at T. Hul. 8:9. There is no hint of the new interpretation of the text in LXX. It is therefore a product of the second century B.C. or later, perhaps originating among the *hasidim-perushim.* The triple prohibition against cooking, eating and deriving benefit from a dairy-meat mixture, appears in rabbinic literature attributed to the School of Ishmael. See B. Hul. 115b. But actually at Mekh. III, 187ff. where R. Ishmael

himself (1st-2nd century) is cited, his reason given for the verses occurring three times is that they emphasize the triple covenant between God and Israel (Ex. 24:7-8; Deut. 29:11; 28: 69). R. Ishmael here reveals his awareness that the prohibition not to cook a kid in its mother's milk had no relationship to the dietary practices and is not to be expanded exegetically to eating and deriving benefit. He correctly sees the cooking of a kid in its mother's milk as a cultic, anti-covenantal rite. See Pt. 1, Chap. 2 above for its Canaanite connection. Others of his school went off into different exegetical paths and expounded each word beyond its literal meaning to include all dairy products, all meat products, and more than cooking. Out of their exegesis grew the standardized Judaic practice not to cook or eat the mixture of dairy and meat products with mixed ingredients, and even to separate utensils. Some rabbis never agreed on the prohibition of deriving benefit. See B. Kid. 57b; Pes. 24b; Bekh. 10a; Men. 101b; Hul. 116a. The *kal vehomer* offered by P. Targ. is also found in rabbinic literature, as is also a *gezerah shavah* to prohibit eating. For recital of targum see B. Ber. 8a-b. Onkelos is not specified, however. It is possible that no specific version was used until the middle ages. See Bamberger, "Halakhic Elements," p. 28.

38. The contemporary synagogue-goer has the same opportunity when his or her synagogue is accustomed to using English targum. It is to be deplored, however, that this is not done adequately and the contemporary Jew does not become as literate in classical texts as his forbears were. The European vernaculars were discouraged during the middle ages. See Tosafot, top of page, B. Ber. 8b, and the commentary of R. Asher b. Yehiel, Berakhot 1:8.

39. The reader may draw on numerous works already cited above and in previous chapters. It is useful to read all the "Introductions" to the Soncino translations of Midrash Rabbah and the Babylonian Talmud. See the following: H. L. Strack, *Introduction to the Talmud;* Bowker, *op. cit.*, Chapter Four, "Classical Rabbinic Literature"; Julius Kaplan, *The Redaction of the Babylonian Talmud;* L. Ginzberg, "Introductory Essay" to his *Commentary on the Palestinian Talmud.* Among other works in Hebrew see Zekhariah Frankel, *Mavo Hayerushalmi* (Breslau: 1870); *Darkei Hamishnah* (Lipsia: 1859); J. H. Weiss, *Dor Dor Vedorshav.* There are also English translations of a number of individual midrashim, including the following: *The Midrash on Psalms,* trans. W. G. Braude (New Haven: 1959); *Pesikta Rabbati,* trans. W. G. Braude (New Haven: 1968); *Pirke de R. Eliezer,* trans. G. Friedlander, (New York: 1965); *Pesikta De-Rab Kahana,* trans. W. G. Braude and J. Kapstein (Philadelphia: 1975); *The Fathers According to Rabbi Nathan*

(Abot de R. Nathan), trans. Judah Goldin (New York: 1974).
Various translations of the Mishnah are in circulation, the
best still being Herbert Danby's; a translation of the Tosefta
under Jacob Neusner is now in process. All references in this
volume, however, are the author's own translations from the
original Hebrew and Aramaic sources unless otherwise noted.

40. The material presented in this section is a composite
drawn from the various introductions cited above, filtered
through my own understanding of the sources. For the view
expressed on halakhic collections see Sigal, *New Dimensions,*
pp. 60-65, Chap. 11; *Emergence II,* 18f., p. 414, n. 12; p.
322.

41. See Z. H. Chajes, *The Student's Guide* where a useful
summary of *gezerot* and *takanot* is provided. Although as an
orthodox scholar Chajes' judgment on historical matters must
be questioned, his discussion of the data is useful. For
example, throughout Chap. 7 he accepts as historical the talmudic attribution of *gezerot* to biblical figures, instead of
seeing this as a way to express the antiquity of a given
halakhah. For use of term torah for oral material see for
example, Ex. R. 47:7 and Sif. Deut. 351. For a catalogue of
most of the oral torah see Strack, pp. 26-28, Appendices I and
II, pp. 29-76, 206-232.

42. See Gerhardsson, *Memory and Manuscript* for a comprehensive discussion of the theme of oral transmission and the
nature and function of the schools. See also Bowker's brief
sketch, *op. cit.* pp. 48-53, and the discussion above in Pt. 2,
Chap. 2. Attestation of written literature is found at P.
Maas. 49d; Kil. 27a; B. Shab. 6b; 89a; 96b; 156a; B.M. 92a;
Men. 70a; Hul. 60b. On citing teachers M. Ed. 1:3; B. Ber.
47a; at M. Ab. 6:6, the habit of teaching a tradition in the
name of its teacher is extolled as a virtue; B. Meg. 15a;
Hul. 104b; Nid. 19b.

43. There are references to an earlier Mishnah or earlier
Mishnayot at T. Maas. Shen. 2:1; M. Ket. 5:3; Naz. 6:1;
Git. 5:6; Ed. 7:2. R. Akiba is described as arranging collections of halakhot at T. Zab. 1:5, and midrash, halakhot and
agadot at P. Shek. 48c. See David Hoffmann, *The First Mishnah*
trans. Paul Forchheimer (New York: 1977). One must, however,
read Hoffmann with caution and not accept all his conclusions.
R. Yosi, early second century, already knew M. Kel. and so
too at B. Hor. 13b we have reference to the tractate Ukzin as
existing before R. Judah. The same may be said for all or
parts of other tractates going back to pre-70 days: B. Yom.
14b, 16a; Zeb. 67b, 68a. M. Pes. 10:4, where the child asks
the questions about the roasted lamb at the Passover Seder,

points to the chapter on the Seder as pre-70. All the arguments cited by Bowker, *The Targums*, pp. 59-60, made by
scholars to argue that R. Judah designed a "canonical code"
could be used to argue that he designed a digest. To satisfy
variegated viewpoints a compiler would anthologize material
in a simple style and with some effort at thematicization.
At B. Shab. 46a; Bez. 37b and at over twenty other places the
dictum, "the halakhah is according to the anonymous mishnah"
is given in the name of a third-century scholar, R. Yoḥanan.
Yet in certain cases he followed another view of the Mishnah
on a given subject (B. Men. 52b). R. Judah, no more than R.
Yoḥanan intended the anonymous mishnah to be "canonical." At
P. Yeb. 6b we find differences of opinion on the status of
the "anonymous mishnah," and whether the anonymous mishnah
should be attributed to R. Meir. R. Yoḥanan who attributes
anonymous mishnah to R. Meir at B. San. 86a attributes it to
"the rabbis" at P. Yeb 6b! See on this question Alexander
Guttmann, "The Problem of the Anonymous Mishnah," *HUCA*, 16
(1941), 137-155. See also Saul Lieberman, "The Publication of
the Mishnah," in *Hellenism*, pp. 83-99. See Guttmann, pp. 148-
154. The matter requires much further study. Thus when the
twelfth-century Maimonides is cited as the decider in favor of
the anonymous pericope it tells us nothing about its status in
the first or second century. Yet Guttmann includes these
examples in his catalogue. On the other hand we find that at
M. Ed. 6:1; B. Git. 52b; Er. 62b, and elsewhere the Talmud
itself records a decision against the anonymous pericope.
See B. Yeb. 10a for evidence of various Mishnah versions in
circulation: R. Levi is said to have his own version.

44. See *The Modern Study of the Mishnah*, ed. Jacob
Neusner (Leiden: 1973), another work, like that of Hoffmann's,
which must be taken with much critical reserve, albeit for
reverse reasons. While Hoffmann is not sufficiently "untra-
ditional" Neusner and his students who authored the essays in
this volume, are super-critical of nineteenth century scholarship on the Mishnah, even terming it "primitive and puerile."
I am in sympathy with some of Neusner's views but not with the
disdain with which he has expressed them. But I totally reject his facile view that one should not begin to trace the
oral torah with the post-exilic period simply because our
literature is post-70 A.D. Here he moves in the kind of cir-
cular argument of which he accuses the nineteenth century
scholars. He assumes that because the written corpus is post-
70, the content is post-70 in origin, and cannot embody
material carefully, orally transmitted for generations. He is
ignoring all that modern anthropology teaches about oral transmission. My view on the Mishnah as repository of halakhah is
contra Strack, *Introduction*, p. 21. There are no sources that
refer to R. Meir as a systematizer or redactor. B. San. 86a

does not, although it is often cited.

45. The most advanced commentary on the Tosefta is Saul Lieberman, *The Tosefta and Tosefta Kifshuta*. An accessible complete text is *Tosefta*, ed. Moses Zuckermandel (Jerusalem: 1963).

46. B. San. 86a only hints at Nehemiah, a pupil of Akiba, as the source of anonymous Tosefta; R. Hiyya is named as compiler by the Gaon Sherira in his famous Epistle. See Baron, *History*, VI, 204f.; Boaz Cohen, *Mishnah and Tosefta* (New York: 1935) studies tractate Shabbat and reaches the conclusion that Tosefta halakhah is often earlier, even if the work was compiled later. This view is supported by the examination of more tractates by B. de Vries, "The Problem of the Relationship of the Two Talmuds to the Tosefta" *Tarbiz*, 28 (1959), 158-170.

47. For a brief sketch see Bowker, *The Targums*, 69-92, and Strack, 206-232; Roger Le Deaut, "Apropos a Definition of Midrash," *Interpretation*, 25 (1971), 259-282; Geza Vermes, *Scripture and Tradition*.

48. Le Deaut, p. 259.

49. See Jacob Mann, *The Bible as Read and Preached in the Old Synagogue*.

50. Bowker, p. 85. See also the "Introduction" in Friedlander's edition where he expands upon the affinities between PRE and Jubilees and I Enoch, as well as other apocryphal writings. Jerahmeel and PRE are excellent examples of how the old mysticism and esoteric theosophy of the excluded apocalyptic writings re-entered rabbinic literature through the later collections of midrash. See *The Chronicles of Jerahmeel*, trans. Moses Gaster, "Prolegomenon" by Haim Schwarzbaum (New York: 1971).

51. See n. 39 above; Schechter, "On The Study of the Talmud," and "The Talmud," *Studies*, I, 143-237; *Understanding Rabbinic Judaism*, ed. Jacob Neusner (New York: 1974); *The Talmud of Jerusalem*, vol. I. Berakhoth, trans. Moses Schwab rpt. (New York: 1969); Baron, *History* II, 215-321; the bibliography in Kaplan, *Redaction*.

52. Maimonides in his Introduction to his Commentary on the Mishnah indicates he did not have the fifth order, Kadashim, which is missing in all extant texts of the Palestinian Talmud. See Sigal, *Emergence* II, Chapters Two and Three on geonim.

53. Kaplan, *The Redaction*, Chapters 15, 21-22. The term *gemara* is usually used as a synonym for talmud, and is applied to the discussions of the Mishnah. But it should be noted that Kaplan's technical distinction between *gemara* and *talmud* is interesting. He sees the term *gemara* as derived from *gamar* "to conclude" therefore, having the significance of a conclusive statement summing up a discussion. In this sense it comes close to halakhah. Kaplan also seeks to revise the conventional view of the saboraim as mere links between the two great bodies of rabbis, the amoraim and geonim. But he might err on the side of granting them too great a role in the completion of the Talmud. The term *saboraai* signifies to reflect or to examine, and the saboraim were those who went over the talmudic corpus, revised, expanded and completed it.

54. The Palestinian Talmud is sometimes called "the Talmud of Erez Yisrael" which is a correct appellation. "The Yerushalmi" or "The Jerusalem Talmud" shown in reference by "J.", "Jer.", or "Yer." are incorrect since the Talmud was neither compiled nor promulgated in Jerusalem. The Babylonians called it *Talmud demaaraba*, "the Talmud of the West." See Strack, pp. 65f. The extant P. Talmud covers thirty-nine tractates of the Mishnah while the B. covers thirty-six and a half. The latter is much larger, however, because of its verbosity compared to the laconic manner of the former. For the redaction of the Baylonian Talmud see Kaplan. See also *The Formation of the Babylonian Talmud*, ed. Jacob Neusner (Leiden: 1970). Kaplan's data are useful even if some of his conclusions are sometimes questionable. This is not the place for a specialized critique of his work, or of the Neusner critique of 19th century scholars, or a technical treatment of the subject. One thing is clear from the B. Talmud, and that is that R. Ashi (d. 427) is alluded to as editor, but not expressly so named. Perhaps the most significant references to R. Ashi as a compiler, editor and author are at B.B.B. 157b, where his first and second "edition" is referred to, and at B.B.M. 86a where he is compared to R. Judah the Nasi as marking the close of an era in a particular academic genre. In this case it is *horaah* or teaching definitive expository conclusions. That R. Ashi is prominent is also clear (Kaplan, Chap. 4, catalogues much data), for he is mentioned probably more than any other single *amora*. Kaplan, pp. 71ff. calculates 1700 instances, and draws attention to the high status of the school of R. Ashi in many talmudic references, and to the implication in many passages that R. Ashi solved long-standing uncertainties. But none of this documents that he was the editor. Furthermore there is much in the Babylonian Talmud that is datable to a time after the death of R. Ashi. See Kaplan, Chap. 8. There is also no direct evi-

dence in the Talmud of Rabina I having been a co-editor or associate of R. Ashi in the redaction of the Talmud. He died around 420, so that there is much in the Talmud that originated following his death. This along with other considerations leads Kaplan, Chap. 10, to reject the tradition of his associate editorship. One of the unsolved problems is the confusion that can arise between Rabina I and his nephew Rabina b. Huna who died ·ca. 500, who is also credited with associate editorship of the Babylonian Talmud. What R. Ashi was probably responsible for during his long period of activity (352-427) was the collection of *gemara* or halakhic decisions in a manner similar to pre-mishnaic collections which became the Mishnah. In the case of the Talmud, R. Ashi's collection possibly revised by him (B.B.B. 157b) and Rabina (B.B. M. 86a) became the backbone of the Talmud put together by saboraim during the sixth century, and was embedded in it.

55. At times Babylonian scholars recognized superior Palestinian competence in some subjects as is reflected at B. Hul. 110b. Second century rivalry for authority between Babylonians and Palestinians is reflected at an important passage at B. Ber. 63a-b.

56. The geonim rarely use the Palestinian Talmud and it barely plays any role in the earliest halakhic compilations of the geonic period such as Sheiltot and Halakhot Gedolot. Evidence seems to point to its more frequent use in Southern Italy. But it was the other compilations that played the larger role in the future unfolding of Judaic religious practice especially in Spain and Northern Europe which became the sources of eastern European Judaism and therefore, of American Judaism. See Vol. II.

57. For socio-economic, cultural and historical material on the Jews of Babylonia see Neusner's volumes, *A History of the Jews of Babylonia;* for general history, A. T. Olmstead, *History of the Persian Empire* (Chicago: 1948). On Zoroastrianism: R. C. Zaehner, *The Dawn and Twilight of Zoroastrianism,* (London: 1961); and the useful extensive bibliographies in Neusner I, 191-213; II, 291-301; III, 359-365; IV, 437-442; V, 376-387. On the diaspora in general, Emil Schürer, *A History,* II, 220-327 is still useful for the early Christian period, although one must be cautious with Schürer's handling of the rabbinic material. See also Appendix B, below.

58. See Schürer, *ibid.* pp. 283f. and notes. The modern analogy makes scholarly debate on the Hebrew question futile.

59. Neusner, I, 10ff. In the Mesopotamian region of Nisibis where a Jewish community thrived were the remnants of

northern Israelite exiles from the Assyrian conquest. Cf. M. San. 10:3.

60. *Ant.* XV, 2.4 (22) for Herod's appointment of a Babylonian; Neusner, I 37f. For Hillel see the summary, N. Glatzer, *Hillel the Elder, The Emergence of Classical Judaism* (New York: 1956). T. Ket. 4:9 indicates clearly that Hillel made a halakhic decision in Alexandria, for the nature of the statement does not imply that a stray question came before the sages and Hillel on one occasion on the part of an Alexandrian who happened to be in Jerusalem; B.B.M. 104a. See for Hillel's rise to leadership, P. Pes. 33a; B. Pes. 66a. The Bene Bathyra are among the most obscure persons in rabbinic literature and there is much technical, scholastic debate. See Sidney Hoenig, *Great Sanhedrin*, p. 179; Neusner, *Life of R. Yohanan*, pp. 156-57; *JE* I, 598; Mantel, *Studies in the History of the Sanhedrin*, p. 19. nn. 113-125.

61. For letters see T. San. 2:2; B. San. 11b; see also for other early connections, M. Hal. 4:11; Shek. 3:4; Yom. 6:4; Men. 11:7; B. Shab. 26a. See Mantel, pp. 175-254. For Nehemiah's influence and a visit by Akiba see P. Yeb. 12c; B. Yeb. 102a; Pes. 3b; Neusner, *History* I, 46-53; for Nehemiah's halakhah see M. Ed. 8:5; M. Yeb. 16:7; B. Yeb. 115a; P. Yeb. 16a. For a different view of the conspiracy of R. Nathan see Neusner, *ibid.*, 79-85.

62. On acculturation see Neusner, I, 100-103; the origin and relationships of R. Hiyya and Rab, and their connection with R. Judah the Nasi are at B. San. 5a; Hiyya's academic activity is referred to at B. Hul. 141a-b. See also Baron, *History*, II, 204-209. On the tannaitic period in Babylonia see Neusner, I, 122-177. The Shekhinah at Huzal; B. Meg. 29a.

63. Ishmael's influence on the Babylonians: B. Shab. 151b; Hul. 36a; Ker. 21a; Git. 45a; Lev. R. 34:9. Babylonian halakhot are also referred to at B. Ket. 93a; Tem. 16a; B.M. 86a. At the last source it is clear that R. Nathan the Babylonian is placed on a par with R. Judah as having brought the Mishnah era to an end. If so, there must have been some recognition of Babylonian input into the final product. For Karo and Isserles see *Emergence* II, 319-324. For Babylonian exegesis see Neusner I, 164ff., and a mystical tradition based on Ezekiel, pp. 166ff. The latter indicates it is no accident that the Dura Synagogue highlights Ezekiel's vision. We have already examined some of these aspects of Babylonian Judaism in Pt. 2, Chap. 3 on rabbinic theology. For Samuel's father: B. Bez. 9a, 16b; Ket. 51a; B.B. 36a; San. 63b; P. Shab. 8c.

64. Neusner, V, 133ff; for the problems of chronology: pp. 135-146. On the life-style of the rabbi it is necessary to read the Talmud, for references are so prolific and widespread that it is impossible to offer them in a footnote. A monograph on the rabbi is still a desideratum for Judaic scholarship. Similarly there are a large number of references to indicate rabbinic control of synagogues.

65. B. Er. 70b; Pes. 39a; R.H. 29b, and often.

66. See Pt. 1, Chap. 2. B.B.K. 113b; B.M. 108a; B.B. 55a.

67. See Moore, *Judaism,* II, Part V; Cohen, *Everyman's Talmud,* Chapters VI, VII; Chap. VIII on the person's obligation toward himself is of interest; Montefiore and Loewe, *Rabbinic Anthology,* Chapters XV-XXI. M. Ab, although sometimes translated "Ethics of the Fathers," is not an ethical treatise as such, but like all ancient wisdom literature, a genre it resembles, has much of ethical importance in it.

68. See also Sif. Deut. 49. At B. Sot. 14a the virtues listed are: to clothe the naked, visit the sick, comfort mourners, bury the dead; at Sif. the virtues are: to act with compassion and graciousness, offer gifts to the needy, to act righteously and lovingly. Cf. B. Sot. 5a, and many other references. How did the rabbis get around qualities attributed to God which humans could not emulate, such as anger (Nah. 1:2)? They appealed to the notion that God is master of His anger and can control it while in humans it will flow uncontrollably (Gen. R. 49:8).

69. Some of the inadequacies of rabbinism are discussed by Montefiore, *op. cit.*, xxiii ff.

CHAPTER 5

A Backward Glance

Our survey of the first millenium and a half of the life of the Religion of Israel and Judaism has concentrated upon Palestine. But it has taken excursions into the hellenistic Graeco-Roman and Iranian diasporas. In a sense the birth of the faith took place in the diaspora. It is not possible to describe this birth of the Religion of Israel because its origins are wrapped in historical mists too deep to penetrate. The haze is sufficiently lifted, however, to reveal that a figure of immense grandeur and heroic proportions, known as Moses to tradition and history, placed his imprint upon a coalition of hebraic tribes in Egypt some time during the late second millenium. The tradition of these tribes, known to history as Israel, recalled a bondage endured in Egypt and celebrated Moses as the divinely-appointed redeemer figure. But they believed that more than a mere uprising and a flight of slaves to freedom had occurred. The tradition of Israel told of miraculous events, the very breakthrough of God into history, even of the unnatural drying up of waters so that Israel may pass in safety to freedom. It told a saga of salvation-history.

But more than this is recalled. The traditions of Israel commemorate a supernatural event which it associates with a Mount Sinai somewhere in the Sinai wilderness. There, it is believed, God and Moses were, so to speak, closeted in a cloud and Moses received the word of God. This revelation is believed to be embodied in the Pentateuch. But tradition has it that not all of the revelation was written down by Moses, but rather that he taught textual meaning and provided supplementary information in oral lectures. This oral torah which interpreted and supplemented the written torah was transmitted from the time of Sinai to the time of the rabbis, over one thousand years later, and they, for historical and cultural reasons began to put it into writing. Ultimately, it is said, this dual torah was finalized in what we call the Talmud.

The foregoing is a brief sketch of faith-history, how tradition explained the evolution of sixth-century rabbinic-talmudic Judaism out of the event at Sinai. But what we real-

255

ize is that so much of that which we call history is conjecture. We know that the name of the man who brought God's word down from Sinai is an Egyptian nominal suffix, and we really do not know the true name of the redeemer and mediator of revelation. We do not know how Israel originiated, and we do not know where Sinai stands. We do not truly know the beginnings or the process of the evolution of the oral torah before the post-exilic period, and even after Ezra and Nehemiah perhaps not until the third century B.C. Then, with the Septuagint we begin to glimpse how Judaic faithful would seek to understand their traditional Hebrew scripture by means of translation which included here and there supplementary information from parallel traditions.

The people called Israel was a loose federation of twelve tribes that worshipped the same God called Yahweh, and professed a stern monotheism which was more commonly breached than upheld. From the beginning the people were torn by a great tension between being a religious federation, the people of God, and playing the role of a national state on the scene of history. The tension is perhaps best described at I Sam. 8. Disasters occurred in their early history until many in Israel clamored for a central monarchy. This reliance upon the astuteness and bravery of a heroic human king may have been the ultimate idolatry, for it signalled the shift of the character of Israel from a holy assembly, a religious federation, an association rooted in faith, to a national-state with all the trappings and the traps of near eastern monarchy and national and international aspirations. Out of the initial wreckage came David who built a great empire for its day and expanded the national frontiers of Israel into what has since become the ideal borders of the promised land as his reign became the symbol of an ideal future.

There arose in Israel a phenomenal group of men who are called "prophets" but whom I prefer to name the canonical "preachers" who were opposed to the official prophets of their day. They made claim to speak in the name of Yhwh and they came bearing tidings of the Day of the Lord, the end of days, as a time of judgment. They made severe demands for repentance for sins of idolatry or adultery against God and inhumanity against fellow humans. And they preached visions of a better time to follow the day of judgment, an era of peace and order in the world of nature and in human society. History has come to call this the "messianic era," but for Israel's preachers it was the *eschaton, aharit hayamim,* the end of days, when a new world will take the place of the old, and the human heart will be attuned to God's word. The vision at times included the return of a Davidic king to the throne of a restored repentant Israel which will have suffered cataclysm in judgment. Indeed, the foretold disasters of judgment occurred to the northern kingdom of Israel in 722 B.C. and to the southern kingdom of Judah in 587 B.C. But never again did a Davidide sit on the throne at Jerusalem. The theme of the return of this anointed king, the *mashiaḥ*, which gives us our transliterated term "messiah," lent its name to the eschatological hope. Henceforth people yearned for the appearance of the messianic-figure, the Lord's anointed one of the house of David, to inaugurate or to accomplish the miraculous events of the eschaton as Moses once executed the great historic redemption of old. The messiah-figure became a complex one embodying the figure of a divine spokesman like Moses, the figure of Elijah promised as herald, the servant of Yhwh who would suffer on behalf of many, and the Davidic kingship.

For a fleeting instant there were those who thought that the moment was arriving near the end of the sixth century B. C. when the Temple was restored. But it was not to be. The schism in Israel which took place in the tenth century B.C. after Solomon died and the north seceded from David's union, was now exacerbated. The post-exilic community rejected the Samaritans and the north-south dichotomy became even more profound. This was a historical thread that wound its way through antiquity. It was later reflected again in rabbinic Judaism when Galilee and Judah had many differences. But in those far-off post-exilic days the very persistence of the schism, the absence of the messianic reunification of north and south implied that the time had not come. The promise was not yet fulfilled.

And then hellenism invaded the biblical lands. Selucid kings ruled Palestine and Syria. As Israel had once acculturated to pagan Canaan, Judah and Jerusalem now absorbed hellenistic culture. Ben Sira and Ecclesiastes stand as monuments to acculturation in Jerusalem. And in the far-flung diaspora Judaism was hellenized in even greater measure. But its monotheism and its basic theology was less affected than it was wont to be when its believers followed Baal and the Ashera in pre-exilic days as we can see in the devout writings of Philo. Nonetheless, there were those who were determined to resist even a small degree of hellenization, and out of the rivalries of Jerusalem's parties in which traditionalist pietism was poised against modernist revisionism there grew a revolutionary movement for control of the priesthood. This led to a Seleucid-Syrian suppression of Judaism and an effort to re-establish the old pagan idolatry that once distorted the temple's monotheism in pre-exilic days. This, in turn, brought forth the famous Maccabee rebellion and transformed the ḥasidim, the pietistic circles who had basked in the Ezraic-Nehemian retrenchment as religious liberationists. The success of the movement signalled by the rededication of the Jerusalem Temple to the pure monotheistic worship was not sufficient, however, to those now in power. The Hasmonean family continued a national-political war of imperial aspiration, and Judaism succumbed once again to the old tension of relgious association versus national state of Samuel's day. Those who opposed worldly power withdrew and are known to history as Pharisees, Essenes, Qumranites, Therapeutae, and others, all a medley of *perushim*, separatistic pietists. In varying degrees these groups opposed Jerusalem and the Hasmoneans for their usurpation of the priesthood from the true hereditary line, as Samaritans argued that Judah's priesthood is a usurpation of the true priesthood of Mount Gerizim. They also opposed the Hasmoneans for their usurpation of the kingship from the House of David. That a great rift had developed in Judaism is evident from the halakhah and theology of the Book of Jubilees and the literature of Qumran.

Meanwhile a great new institution was in the making, the synagogue. From the earliest times when there were rural altars along with central regional shrines as well as the major shrine where rested the Ark of the Covenant, there were alternative worship opportunities in Israel. One of these took the form of a gathering at the home or the center presided over by a man of God. Stimulated by the compulsory centralization of the cult in Jerusalem and by the growth of the post-exilic diaspora the alternative form in which prayer and teaching were combined, grew in significance, and it became a major religious presence in every Judaic community. This gathering place, the synagogue, looked at first to prophets and later to proto-rabbis for leadership. In this way the proto-rabbis became popular interpreters of torah and inevitably became spiritual advisors to the people. They prayed on their behalf and became surrogate priests. When the recurrent religion-state tension led to disastrous civil wars and war with Rome, the Temple cult and its priesthood was swept away in the year 70. Now the synagogue and its spiritual leaders, the rabbis, were in a position to supersede Temple and priesthood. Prayer and study replaced the cult, and benevolent and loving deeds became the surrogate for the cult's expiatory rites. Another chapter in the saga of salvation-history was written. Rabbinic Judaism was born, and this form of Judaism, albeit radically modified, continues to appeal to the loyalty of Jews at the present time.

Four major characteristics of twentieth-century Judaism which we will see unfold during the middle ages in Volume Two, were already present in pre-exilic Religion of Israel and in post-exilic Judaism. Each trait is closely intertwined with the others. These distinctive marks were strengthened by the emergent rabbinic Judaism and became its hallmark. I speak of: 1) acceptance of diversity in observance and belief; 2) the supremacy of localism over centralization; 3) a theoretical obeisance to tradition with a practical legitimization of change; 4) the primacy of contemporary authority. Within the Bible itself are embedded several layers of halakhah and cultic procedures from different periods and different schools. Judaists developed their independent styles of faith and practice in their *perushite* cells and communities, or as Samaritans, Babylonians, Alexandrians, and even closer to home they differed as Galileans and Judeans, and within Judah as followers of one school or another among the rabbis. Like the Bible, the Mishnah, Tosefta and Talmud attest to this notion that options are available in halakhah, change is possible and that contemporary authority takes precedence.

At times, under the impact of some great challenge like that of Christianity there were efforts on the part of some to standardize at least a mini-orthodoxy on a few specific questions. But this had limited efficacy. Even when it had some effect for awhile, the old freedom to choose would soon reassert itself and the limited dogmatic demands would be ignored without peril to the one who ignores them. The truth is that salvific dogma never took hold in Judaism and one's salvation was not inextricably tied to a particular dogma or a miẓvah index. Yet there exists a roster of people who, for various halakhic and doctrinal reasons are not to enjoy salvation (M. San. 10:1), or are to be condemned to eternal damnation. Perhaps these views originated in the effort to quash Jubilees, the halakhic Temple Scroll of Qumran, and Paul, but they are only views, wishful thinking, and although recorded as dogma in the Mishnah were never urged for some kind of catechetical or creedal recital. They remain like all else in Judaism, a question of conscience between the individual and God. The person's salvational risks in opting one belief over another and eschewing certain doctrines, or in selecting his own options for observance from the reservoir of halakhah, are risks he takes with God alone. In different periods of history as we will see in Volumes Two and Four, various groups endeavored to establish an "orthodoxy" but were unsuccessful.

Obeisance to tradition coupled with the recognition of the legitimacy of revisionism made for a consistent continuity in Judaism. At times this continuity obscured radical change. The Religion of Israel shades delicately into post-exilic Judaism. The synagogue is certainly radically different from the

Temple but it must be realized that by 70 A.D. Jews were quite familiar with the synagogue as already being an ancient institution, and aware that the core of the liturgy had also been present in the Temple. At a later time a rabbi (Num. R. 16: 22) expressed the idea that though God fills all the universe (Jer. 23:24), He compressed himself to meet Israel between the cherubim on the Ark (Num. 7:89). This ancient notion of God's contraction shows up later as the doctrine of *zimzum* in medieval kabalah. We could go on at great length to illustrate this continuity. It indicates that perhaps one of the wisest critical remarks ever penned or preached was that of the famous Kohelet-Ecclesiastes when he said that there was nothing new under the sun. For in fact that is what both Jewish and Christian ideas of typology are all about. The ancestors are types for the descendants, and history consists of endless thematic repetition.

The Bible itself came out of a matrix. Debate in coming years will center on whether it was at Ebla that things Jewish originated or whether Ebla was after all merely a center of Mesopotamian culture. Either way, we have seen that Canaanite, Egyptian and Mesopotamian influences are "Israelized" in the Bible. This is wedded to hellenism and some Zoroastrian influence to become the matrix of rabbinic Judaism. Judaic art symbols were borrowed out of their Graeco-Roman environment. Jews rejected the mythology behind them and Judaized these symbols. But they represent the wide influence upon the faith, for iconographical representations of bread or cakes and wine are found in synagogues and in cemeteries throughout the Graeco-Roman world. In all probability this art attests to the great importance of the mystical notions attributed to these symbols when they were used in ritual. Wine enters into every single Judaic Sabbath, festival, and life cycle ritual. Although we cannot ascertain when wine first became a significant ingredient of Judaic ritual it goes back to the Pentateuchal description of cultic offerings (Num. 15) and is regarded as indigenous to religion and as indispensable to the proper achievement of communion with God. The sacred meal of bread and wine is depicted as the way in which Melchizedek, the High Priest of Jerusalem in a dim pre-Israelite past, greets Abraham. With bread, staple of life, symbol of creation and wine, the mystic symbol of blood, the life or very *nefesh* of the person, as well as the messianic cup of eternal life, Melchizedek refers to God as creator and redeemer. One can almost see this as the prototype *kiddush*.[1]

Scholarship has a tendency to be myopic about halakhah, and frequently faults the ancient rabbis for cold legalism. This overlooks their theology I have sketched in Pt. 2, Chap.

3, albeit all too briefly. It also ignores the extensive
material that reveals the rabbis as mystics. Their gathering
up of ritual and placing a heavy proportion of it in the home
as a constant source of religious expression and communion
with the divine, points not to vapid legalism but to esoteric
mysticism. Every Judaist was to become finally the priest who
tends the altar and links himself with God on behalf of his
own congregation, the family. Rabbinic Judaism did not want
all Jews to be rabbis; it wanted at last to bring the kingship of God into visible reality when all who profess Judaism
constitute the kingdom of priests and a holy people (Ex. 19:6).
If they have been no more successful in their program than the
great canonical preachers were in their program to win Israel
to high morality and stern monotheism, it is not halakhah
which is at fault, but the human condition. Rabbinic Judaism,
however, did enjoy limited achievement. The effort to turn
each household into a miniature sanctuary, the dining table
into an altar and the presiding officiant into a local priest
at a local high place, not only restored to Judaism its
quintessential nature of a religious association, it made
possible the survival of Judaism into the twentieth century.
Rabbinic Judaism spawned the geonic era which was to follow,
and the intrepid men who served in that exalted office placed
the stamp of rabbinic Judaism upon those who professed Judaism
in every country of the civilized world. It survived the
challenge of Zoroastrianism, Christianity and Islam and sur-
mounted a new great schism, Karaism, which for awhile seemed
to threaten as profound an earthquake as the separation of
Christianity. Karaism and the relationship to Islam are
pursued in Volume Two.

Judaism, as it emerged from the rabbinic schools of
Palestine and Babylonia to enter into medieval times, was a
great complex of different influences. Rabbis sought to establish their hegemony but developed a homogeneity instead.
Judaic belief and observance in Babylonia, Palestine, Asia
Minor, and throughout the Roman provinces of North Africa and
Europe, were similar but lacked monism. There was a degree
of conformity on a local level or with the views of a highly
respected scholar, but no uniformity. Authority was in the
hands of individual scholars, not in any synod or institution.
There was respect for the past and affirmation of continuity,
but commitment to the present and to the freedom of reinterpretation took precedence.

In this survey of early Judaism I have devoted a lengthy
chapter to Christianity. The reason for this is my conviction
that early Christianity was not only the product of its Judaic
matrix, but that it was a version of Judaic halakhah and the-

ology into the second century. It is also my conviction that
if the Christian world is serious about ecumenicism it must
include Judaism and its own Judaic content in such explora-
tions. Moreover, that chapter is designed to stress to Jews
as well that they must be aware of this historic reality and
rethink their attitude toward Christian origins and the sentence of apostasy pronounced upon Christianity by a legion of
modern Jewish scholars. We must recognize a distinction between first-century Christianity which was expelled from the
synagogue and second-century Christianity which became pre-
dominantly gentile and divested itself of its Judaism. And
yet, as I have endeavored to show, even gentile Christianity
struggled with its Judaic tension into the fifth century and
later. There is mystery in this, a mystery which deserves
fresh academic initiatives.[2]

What the rabbis had achieved by 650 when the geonic
period is in germination and the seeds of Karaism are also
being sown was a massive revision of biblical Judaism, a
revision which had continuity and flux as its watchword. This
massive revision made possible first the survival of Judaism
in the face of Mazdeism and the triumph of rabbinism in the
persons and institutions of the geonim over Karaism, and its
subsequent survival in the face of Islam. The rabbis maintained intact biblical theology. They wedded biblical ethics
and morality to new socio-economic and political realities.
These three elements constituted the Judaism of 650 which was
launched into the medieval world to metamorphose into the
Judaism of 1650.

NOTES

1. The student should pursue Erwin Goodenough, *Jewish
Symbols in the Graeco-Roman Period,* without necessarily adopting all his suppositions and conclusions.

2. See Appendix C as a preliminary statement.

APPENDIX A

Samaritanism

I. *Schism or Movement?*

It is a moot question whether the separation of the Samaritans from other adherents of Judaism is simply the product of a development of an independent tendency, of their secession, or of their being expelled. The biblical view is that Zerrubbabel and his high priest Joshua rejected the participation of Samaritans in the rebuilding of the Temple around 518 B.C. (Ezra 4). The presumption is that they were rejected on the grounds that they were not true Israelites, but an admixture of people who were highly syncretistic in their religion (II Ki. 17). According to this view the effective separation took place immediately after the Assyrian deportation of Israelites following their futile revolt in 720 B.C. which they staged after the conquest of Samaria in 721 B.C. On the other hand, the Samaritans themselves date their secession to the eleventh century B.C. claiming that Eli the priest perverted the true priesthood and abandoned the true shrine on Mt. Gerizim. It also appears that although kings of Judah espoused an irredentism toward the north and Hezekiah invited the northerners to join in a repentant Passover in Jerusalem, many of the latter rejected Judean overtures.[1] Yet, it is also significant that some accepted (II Chron. 30:11). Again, later on we hear that some retained their loyalty to Jerusalem even after 587 B.C. (Jer. 41:4ff.).

The fact of the matter is that the preaching prophets are equally critical of both Israel and Judah as guilty of apostasy-adultery-idolatry as the sin is variously regarded. Ezekiel's allegory of the two sisters emphasizes that both will suffer the same fate for the same reason, and that both will one day experience a unified restoration.[2] It appears that Nehemiah crystallizes the break when he brings to an end participation of the northern priesthood (Neh. 13:28f.). Not even Ezra's policy against mixed marriage (Ezra 9-10) included Samaritans among the forbidden. It is puzzling, therefore, why the Samaritans blame Ezra along with Eli for the separation and for falsifying the text of scripture in order to demote Mt. Gerizim unless they blame him for Nehemiah's action.[3]

264

The best one can say of Old Testament sources is that the
Samaritan-Judean schism known to us in the hellenistic and
Roman-rabbinic period is in the historical tradition. There
was always a north-south tension. The southern traditions
indicate that Judah upheld the Davidic monarchy, the Aaronite-
Zadokite priesthood (in a line through Eli) and the exclusive
sacral legitimacy of Jerusalem (II Chron. 13), while the north
rejected the Davidic house, accepted non-Aaronides as priests
(I Ki. 13:33f.), and legitimized rural sanctuaries. As late
as the time when IV Macc. 6:1-2 was written, certainly no
later than the first century B.C. the northerners and south-
erners were both considered "Jews" and their two sanctuaries
at Jerusalem and Mt. Gerizim as belonging to the same religious fraternity.[4]

Scholars who think John Hyrcanus destroyed the temple on
Mr. Gerizim in 128 B.C. because the north was opposed to the
Hasmonean wars are in error. Many Judeans were also opposed
for opposite reasons: hasidim-*perushim* opposed the national-
istic-expansionist venture, and extreme hellenists opposed the
separation from the Seleucid Empire. But John Hyrcanus was,
in reality, attempting to undo the secession of Jeroboam I
after the death of Solomon and suppress the historic individu-
ality of the north. Perhaps he hoped that he might appease
those who oppose the Hasmonean usurpation of the Davidic
kingship by binding up the severed nation into the old Davidic
unity. In this way and by also restoring the Davidic kingdom
he can present himself as a new David and acquire the mystique
of the original David.[5] This action of John Hyrcanus led to
irrevocable hostility on the part of the north which ended in
mutual hostility. By the first century A.D. the Samaritan is
held in contempt as is reflected at Lk. 9:51-56, Jn. 4:9, and
in some rabbinic references.[6] This contempt is reflected in
Josephus' record which claims that during the time of Antiochus
IV the Samaritans denied their Israelite origins and asked
that their temple be dedicated to Zeus Hellenios.[7]

The Samaritans have their own self-perception which can
be gleaned from their *Sefer hayamim*, a chronicle which covers
from the entry of Joshua into Canaan and corresponds to the
biblical material in Joshua, Judges, Samuel and Kings.[8] They
charge Eli, descended from Itamar, son of Aaron, and not from
the high priest Eleazar, with leaving Shechem to form a new
and illegitimate priesthood at Shiloh, building a copy of the
sanctuary and its holy objects and taking along torah books
which were Itamar's version.[9] From this perspective the true
Israel and the true Aaronide-Zadokite priesthood is in the
north and Judah owes its separate existence to a schismatic
usurper, Eli. Indeed, the priestly conservatism prevailed so
pervasively that all of the prophets, including the northerners

Elijah and Elisha are either ignored or are rejected.[10]

It seems logical nevertheless, that if the Samaritans use the biblical historical books, including Chronicles, that they were not irrevocably separated from the rest of Judaism before 400 B.C. Furthermore, since they do not recognize, for example, non-biblical aspects of Sabbath observance they must have separated before the hegemony of the emergent rabbinate and the proto-rabbinic halakhah after 70 A.D. On the other hand the presence of synagogues in Samaritanism attests to the fact that it did not separate before the expansion of that institution in the third or second century B.C. In general it exhibits common characteristics with Judaism which lead to a conclusion that the separation took place sometime between 300 B.C. and the rise of rabbinism in 70 A.D. Moreover, both the New Testament and Josephus attest to a serious separation during the first century. And rabbinic literature indicates Samaritans had not adopted proto-rabbinic standards of purity or the doctrine of resurrection. There is some ambiguity about the latter, however.[11]

The foregoing indicates that the issues between Samaritanism and Judaism led to a separate development during the crucial centuries when other Judaic groups were differentiating themselves, including but not limited to, Qumran, Essenes, the ubiquitous *perushim*, Sadducees, and others. Thus, a study of the script, orthography and textual tradition of the Samaritan Pentateuch leads one scholar to conclude that the sectarian redaction took place during the Hasmonean period precisely when all this other individuation proceeded apace.[12] It appears the rabbinic view of Samaritans is a balanced one: they are a non-rabbinic denomination of Judaism. This could only have come about if their own testmony is to be accepted. Thus when Solomon died in 922 B.C. the two kingdoms went their own way, but after 721 B.C. when Assyria moved pagan settlers into the north, the loyal Israelites remained attached to Yhwh and to their holy place at Mt. Gerizim. They remained even more conservative in their norms than the people of Judah, and were sundered from Samaria as they were from Jerusalem. They might have seen an opportunity to regain control of the priesthood by functioning in Jerusalem which had a hiatus of the priestly cult for some fifty years from 587 B.C. to 538 B.C. But when they were finally rejected by Nehemiah there appeared to be no possibility of reunion. As they were rejected so they rejected the post-exilic authority of Jerusalem and the split in the fellowship of Israel continued.[13] John Hyrcanus' action in 128 B.C. undoubtedly was undertaken for the additional reason that the Hasmoneans claimed descent from Phineas and therefore to be of the true priestly line. In this claim the Samaritans were competitors and John Hyrcanus saw cause to eliminate the Samaritan sanctuary and its priesthood.[14]

Samaritanism was not allied with Sadduceeism for the latter recognized the centrality of Jerusalem. Samaritanism was not allied with Qumran for the latter shows no interest in Mt. Gerizim. But all three did have affinities in their individuation from proto-rabbinic Judaism and greater conservatism in biblical interpretation.[15] In sum, as some scholars have recognized, Samaritanism is another of the many variations of Judaism that arose during the proto-rabbinic period, the hellenistic and Graeco-Roman era, more particularly from 200 B.C. - 70 A.D. Samaritanism received a new lease on life when Pompey restored northern separatism in 64 B.C. Since there is no orthodox or orthopraxic Judaism from which it would separate it is a moot point whether to consider Samaritanism a "schismatic" movement.[16] As the ambivalence toward Samaritans prevailed in proto-rabbinic circles it was natural for New Testament writers to prefer them to their main Judaic opposition. Rabbinic Judaism struggled for hegemony over all the factions of first century Judaism and these factions may have sought their common ground. Qumranite and Samaritans may well have appreciated their common hostility to the Hasmoneans. But Samaritans, no more than other Jews, developed a monolithic religion. They too spawned many sects, among them the best known being the Dositheans.[17]

II. *Aspects of Samaritan Theology and Halakhah*[18]

The people we call Samaritans called themselves "Israel," and *Shamrin*, guardians of the Torah. It is quite conceivable that the people identified by the Septuagint as Samaritai are not the Shomronim (I Ki. 17:29), and that while the former is a term that refers to the syncretistic northern admixture, the latter is the term that refers to Israelites who remained true to Torah and the sanctuary at Mt. Gerizim. The Church Father, Epiphanius explains their name as meaning "guardians" and refers the term to the "entire people." Historically perhaps the terms Samaritans and Shomronim were confused in general usage, and in time they tended to fuse together so that the Samaritans known since the middle ages into the present period are descendants of the fusion. It is clear from Assyrian annals that less than 30,000 Israelites were deported and that an Israelite population never ceased to exist in the north.[19] These northern Israelites preserved a version of the pre-exilic Religion of Israel which has some very basic affinities with Judaism. The Samaritan creed includes the doctrine of monotheism, an emphasis upon Moses, and loyalty to Torah and to Mt. Gerizim. In the worship of the Sabbath eve, there is also asserted a doctrine of vengeance and retribution at the end of days, in some versions also containing the belief in a *taheb*, an eschatological redeemer.[20]

As is the case with Judaism, Samaritanism acquired much new material and developed new literature, liturgy, theology, and *hillukh*, the Samaritan halakhah. The Samaritans went to Mt. Gerizim three times a year in accordance with their belief that Moses had deposited the holy ark there.[21] The Samaritans have seven festivals: a) Passover; b) ḥag hamaẓot, the feast of unleavened bread; c) Shaḅuot (Pentecost); d) Trumpets, based on biblical first day of the seventh month; e) Yom Kippur; f) Sukot; g) *ha'asif*, another harvest festival; *b* and *f* last seven days and pilgrimages are made to Mt. Gerizim, as they also are at Shaḅuot, and there too the paschal lamb is still offered. (Only five are listed at Bowman, *Samaritan Documents,* pp. 223-232).

Much of what we learn about Samaritan theology and halakhah is derived from *Memar Marqah*, upon which is based the work of later Samaritan theologians. This is adjudged to be a fourth century "thesaurus," in part a midrashic commentary on the Pentateuch, in part a compilation of philosophical and scientific discourses as well as prayers, hymns and kabalistic passages.[22] It may be fair to presume that Marqah reflects all of the basic doctrinal teachings of antiquity and that what is not found here may be later. Perhaps Book Five is the most interesting for the christological flavor applied to Moses in dealing with the ancient notion of the death, ascension and glorification of Moses. The recurring phrase *let alah elah ahad* "there is no God but One" might signify Samaritan influence upon Islam.[23] In acclaiming heroes of the past only Joseph is named of the twelve sons of Jacob and he is hailed as "the most honored of his father's house," an obvious allusion to the supremacy of the north.[24]

Marqah records Samaritan tradition as teaching that repentance is vital for the great Day of Vengeance, that there will be a resurrection of all and that the *taheb* will restore the chosen place of God just as Joseph (=Samaritans) was recompensed with a kingdom after his servitude. This passage is climaxed with the dual paean, "there is none like Joseph the King" and "there is none like Moses the prophet." Thus Moses *redivivus,* the *taheb,* will restore the sovereignty of the north.[25]

Among other clearly Judaic theological principles taught by Samaritanism are the divine election of Israel; the revelation of the Torah as a means of grace; circumcision as a sign of the election; their possession of the covenant with God, which entitles them to the blessings promised by God to the patriarchs; the centrality of Sabbath observance as a further special sign of the elect status of Israel and its special blessing of grace. Samaritanism espouses the doctrines of creation, revelation, and resurrection. They emphasized the primacy of the Aaronide priesthood through Phineas and Zadok, and possessed a messianic idea in the form of the *taheb* . The *taheb* will reunite Ephraim and Judah. The period of the *taheb* will follow an apocalyptic war. It will be one of peace and justice, the restoration of true faith and the renewal of worship on a purified Mt. Gerizim in the rediscovered ancient sanctuary which is hidden away in a cave. The period of the *taheb*, however, will end with his death, and at an undetermined time after this the world will experience a great cataclysm as a prelude to the resurrection. The resurrection is followed by judgment. It is difficult to tell whether the notion is pre-Christian, but there is a belief that Moses will stand in the midst of the resurrected and be their intercessor.[26]

The *hillukh* referred to above describes Samaritan practice in such matters as the Sabbath, circumcision, Passover and other festivals, the observances related to male and female purity, the description of permitted animals and birds and how to slaughter them for food, marriage practices and the marriage ceremony, divorce, death and burial. Along with halakhic material the *hillukh* provides theological interpretation and polemic against Judaism. A striking difference between Samaritanism and Judaism is that the former denies the status of Israel to an uncircumcised person which Judaism does not, and rejects any postponement of the circumcision to after the eighth day for illness of any other reason, which Judaism allows. The *hillukh* notably fills Pentateuchal gaps for Samaritans as halakhic literature does for rabbinic Judaism. Thus, for example, the Torah contains no *ketubah* (marriage certificate) or the divorce document, both of which are supplied by the Samaritan *hillukh*. In this and other ways Samaritans, no less than other Jews in all periods, were compelled to supplement the Torah in order to maintain a viable religion.[27]

A notable difference between Samaritanism and Judaism is found in the Decalogue. The first nine commandments are divided differently so that they constitute eight. The tenth commandment, not to covet, is the ninth, and a tenth commandment is added from Deut. 27:3-8 in various versions, but clearly ordaining Mt. Gerizim as the chosen place of God.[28]

Another significant halkhic item is the rabbinic interdiction of marriage with Samaritans (B. Kid. 75a; Kuthim 1:2). On the whole it can be assumed that the differentiation of Samaritanism and rabbinic Judaism was completed by the fifth century A.D. Later on, interaction and mutual influences between Samaritanism and Karaism, as well as the literary influence of Islam would somewhat distort the process of the original separation.[29]

It is logical to surmise that the affinities between Samaritan halakhah and pre-rabbinic halakhah is the result of both having recourse to a common tradition. Pre-70 Samaritans would not derive their halakhah from the priests of Jerusalem, nor would post-70 Samaritans seek their halakhah from the rabbis at Yavneh. The Samaritan calendar is an outstanding source of division between Judaism and Samaritanism. The Samaritans claim that their calendar goes back to Adam, passing through all generations to Moses who taught it to Phineas who in turn provided its mysteries to the priesthood of Gerizim. No festivals occur on the same day in the two traditions, and the ȯmer counting among Samaritans begins on the Sunday following the Sabbath of Passover, resulting in Shabuot always falling on a Sunday. The method of slaughtering meat among Samaritans is another example of high antiquity. Since nothing in the Pentateuch describes the method, both rabbinic Judaism and Samaritanism adopted interpretive tradition, the rabbis dating it to Moses at Sinai, the Samaritans calling it a tradition of the elders. Similarly, the injunction against cooking or eating any mingled meat and dairy based upon the verse not to seethe a kid in its mother's milk, is also followed by the Samaritans. Both traditions, therefore, go back to an earlier time albeit when the real meaning of the precept was forgotten, but not to a later time when Samaritans would have been reluctant to adopt a rabbinic halakhah. On the other hand, the Samaritans do not use the *tefilin*, indicating that this is a later proto-rabbinic tradition dating to a time after the separation during the Hasmonean era.[30]

III. *The Samaritan Moses*

The Moses lore in both Samaritanism and rabbinic Judaism is fascinating. It is difficult to determine whether christological theory is derived from an antecedent Mosesology or whether the reverse is the case. Certainly much Moses-lore is post-Jesus, but much is earlier, and much of the post-Jesus liturgy tradition might in actuality contain pre-Christian material. In any event the Samaritan Moses reflected in the writings of Marqah is a virtual christological figure.[31]

It is at the burning bush (Ex. 3:2) that Moses receives full mystical knowledge of the past and the future. It is believed that God established the name of Moses on the seventh day of creation, that is, the Sabbath, when God's Name and Moses' name (Aramaic *Sheme* and *Moshe*, each having the same consonants, *mem*, *shin* and *hay*), were made one. On a number of occasions midrash and narrative interrupt to sing paeans to Moses. He is the one who reveals truth and destroys the lie, exalts the good and crushes the guilty, and thus takes on the typology of the *taheb*. Here we receive a hint that the *taheb* will be Moses *redivivus* and Moses is given messianic qualities. Moses is glorified and is the recipient of mysteries. All creation exults with him and he sustains the living and exalts the dead. It is said that Moses stood at the very foundations of creation and knew its mystery, and thus his origin is projected back from the seventh day of creation to pre-existence as that of Wisdom, the Torah and the Johannine Jesus. Often the author calls upon the reader to believe in Moses in order to be saved from the wrath of the Day of Vengeance when Moses will be the intercessor.[32]

The death of Moses is taken up in Book V, and is a midrash on Deut. 34:5. There is an acrostical play on the word Elohim, with each letter pleading for Moses not to die because he is related to each of the letters. It concludes with the statement that Moses ascended into a cloud, crowned with light, and disappeared from view. Since then "the sun of Divine Favor" has been concealed. Moses was the one who "supplied the world with the light of life."[33]

IV. *Samaritanism and Qumran*

The Samaritans and Qumranites agreed on the absolute and exclusive legitimacy of the Zadokite priesthood and had certain halakhic affinities in which they differed from rabbinic Judaism. Among these was the prohibition of marriage between a man and his neice. But it is not until after the thirteenth century that the Qumran teachings about "sons of light" and "sons of darkness" emerge in Samaritan literature. In this regard the catechism *Malef*, teaches that the light of Gen. 1:3 is the Holy Spirit, pre-existent Moses, and that this light passed through Adam through all generations until it was reincarnated in the human Moses who brought the Torah to the Samaritans. They believed this to be an instrument of grace to recapture the light of Adam as it was before the fall, a goal that was shared at Qumran. In addition to some particulars of this sort the Samaritans and Qumran shared a very strict approach to the Pentateuch, a special status for Moses and antipathy for the Jerusalem Establishment. While some of these affinities suggest themselves to be reasons for Qumranite absorption into Samaritanism after 70 A.D., the opposition of Qumran to Jerusalem must be distinguished from that of the Samaritans. The former opposed the priests there but hoped one day to liberate and purify it.[34] Other affinities include the use of a solar calendar, the absence of Purim and Hanukah in the roster of festivals, and observance of Pentecost on a Sunday. When one considers the nature of their affinities it can be hypothesized that after 70 A.D. some Qumranites may have felt more comfortable entering Samaritanism than rabbinic Judaism. Others felt a stronger pull to Christianity.

V. *Samaritanism and Christianity*

According to some scholars the Gospel of John is directed at Samaritans, and Luke sees Samaritans as the first arena for evangelism. Acts reflects the fact that Judea, Galilee and Samaria were all "Judaic" and not "pagan." Motifs in Samaritan ágadah and John have many points of contact and which could attract Samaritans to the christology. There is not only the question of the pre-existent Moses and Jesus, but also the emphasis upon such motifs as the word and light, and the attributes ascribed by the Samaritans to Moses which were now taught of Jesus, and the previously noted midrash on Moses which is found in Merqah. It is conceivable that many Samaritans saw in Jesus the *taheb* or Moses *redivivus*.[35] Jesus does not even deny that he may be Samaritan (Jn. 7:41; 8:48f.) Ezekiel and John are both represented as juxtaposing water and spirit in the rebirth of the believer (Ez. 36:25f.; Jn. 3:5). Luke presents a pro-Samaritan picture when he has Stephen refer to Jacob's burial at Shechem in the tomb purchased by Abraham contrary to the tradition that it was at Hebron.[36] This Samaritan emphasis may also help explain why Luke is harsher toward the Sadducees, for although they and the Samaritans had much in common, the Samaritans would tend to oppose them most vigorously since they were the party that supported the discredited priesthood in Jerusalem.

NOTES

1. R. J. Coggins, *Samaritans and Jews* (Atlanta, Georgia: 1975), p. 7; 20f.; J. MacDonald, *Samaritan Chronicle II* (Berlin: 1969) II, 178; II Chron. 31:1; 30:1-20. It is apparent from II Chron. 30:6-9 that the northerners were regarded as Israelites and that they had but to repent the apostasy into which their ancestors fell in order that Yhwh restore Israel and deliver the deportees from Assyria. II Ki. 18:34 points to the syncretism in Samaria even before 721 B.C. But that is no different from the Judaite lapses which included the ásherah in the Temple. These and other passages only evince the idolatry that went on in both Israel and Judah all through the pre-exilic period and prove nothing about specific Samaritan syncretism for which they should be expelled from "theological Israel." See also John Bowman, *Samaritan Documents*.

2. Hos. 2:1f.; Zekh. 10:6; Ez. 23. Ez. 48 indicates there is no consciousness of a schism. Cf. Ez. 36-37; Jer. 30-31; 50:19 20; Ez. 16:3.

3. Cf. Ben Sira 50:26 for an anti-Samaritan attitude ca. 200 B.C.

4. Cf. Macc. 5:22f. North and South, Jerusalem and Mt. Gerizim constitute the same "people." See Coggins, p. 86.

5. See Coggins, p. 88ff. See Josephus, *Ant.* XIII, 9.1 (254-258) for the forced conversion of the Idumaeans, suppression of the Samaritans, and the destruction of their temple on Mt. Gerizim. John Hyrcanus destroyed Samaria in 107 B.C. in a further effort to annul the old northern secession. Pompey restored northern separatism in 64 B.C. See F. M. Cross, *The Ancient Li brary of Qumran*, p. 211.

6. M. Shebi. 8:10, "one who eats the bread of Cuthim (Samaritans) is as if he eats swine's flesh," reflects contempt.

7. *Ant.* XIII, 5.5 (257-264).

8. *Samaritan Chronicle II* (n. 1 above). Coggins, pp. 117ff. provides a brief survey of these writings as well as

other Samaritan writings edited by MacDonald. By using Samaritan chronology MacDonald (App. V, pp. 220-223) arrives at an Exodus date of 1478-1451 B.C.

9. *Samaritan Chronicle* II ed. MacDonald, pp. 111ff. They claim Eli copied all the objects of Moses' tabernacle (mercy seat [*kaporet*],·cherubs, the table for shewbread, etc.), the Mosaic original remaining at Mt. Gerizim which is called Bethel (ibid. p. 113).

10. See Coggins, pp. 123-131, for a discussion of the interpretation of the historical events from 1000 B.C. to 587 B.C. The rejection of Elijah and Elisha is at Chronicle II, p. 168.

11. J. A. Montgomery, *The Samaritans,* pp. 27-33. See the talmudic tractate Kuthim for a succinct testimony to Samaritan practices. Cf. M. Ned. 3:10 for rabbinic testimony to Samaritan emphasis upon the Sabbath equally with the Jews. See also M. Nid. 4:1; Coggins, pp. 138ff.; David Daube, "Jesus and the Samaritan Woman," *JBL,* 69 (1950), pp. 137ff. for the translation of Jn. 4:9. The woman there has reference to the halakhah that Samaritan women are considered constant menstruants because they do not practice the purity norms, and therefore, their vessels are impure, M. Kel. 1:1ff; and cf. T. Shab. 1:14, not to eat with a menstrual woman.

12. James D. Purvis, *The Samaritan Pentateuch* (Cambridge, Mass.: 1968), p. 86f., 96. The rabbinic attitude indicates the Samaritan individuation was no more radical than that of Qumran, for the literature concedes that although some practices of Samaritans are like those of the gentiles, in part they are "like those of Israel, mostly like Israel." See Kuthim 1; B. Kid. 76a; Ber. 47b; Git. 10a; Hul. 4a; where rabbis regard Samaritans as more trustworthy than the *ʿam haʾareẓ* in some religious matters.

13. See F. M. Cross, "The Discovery of the Samaria Papyri," *B.A.,* 26 (1963); "Papyri of the Fourth Century B.C. from Daliyeh" in *New Directions in Biblical Archaeology,* 41-62. See also Tcherikover, *Hellenistic Civilization and the Jews* for the historical setting, pp. 81-89; 127-142; 153-174.

14. I Macc. 2:54 Mattathias also invoked Elijah in his farewell address whom the Samaritans rejected as a false prophet.

15. But see also the views of Montgomery, *Samaritans,* p. 187; John Bowman, *The Samaritan Problem* (Pittsburgh: 1975).

16. The ambivalence of rabbinic literature is due to the long span of time and numerous views it represents. At M. Dem. 3:4 the Samaritan is classed with the *àm haàrez* (a class of Jew), distinct from the *nakhri* (a gentile), but 5:9 distinguishes a Jew and a Samaritan. Yet at M. Ber. 7:1; B. Ber. 47b the Samaritan is included in a quorum for Grace After Meals.

17. Bowman, *Samaritan Problem*, pp. 26f.; at pp. 40f. Bowman cites a Samaritan annalist to the effect that hasidim were Samaritans. Qumranites and Samaritans both emphasized Deut. 18:18 in their eschatology. On Samaritan sects, p. 57 and Chapter Two. See also below on Samaritanism and Qumran and Christianity.

18. See Montgomery, *op. cit.*; John MacDonald, *The Theology of the Samaritans* (London: 1964), Bowman, *Samaritan Documents*.

19. Coggins, pp. 9ff.; p. 17, n. 7; de Vaux, *Ancient Israel*, p. 66, for population estimates. Epiphanius, *Panarion* 9-14.

20. The creed is cited by John Bowman, "Samaritan Studies," *BJRL*, 40 (1957-58), p. 310. Christian and Islamic creedal recitals could just as well have been influenced by Samaritanism. The idea of the *taheb* must be an old one since it is mentioned indirectly by Josephus, XVIII, 4.1 (85-87), who refers to a messianic pretender who tried to convince the Samaritans that he will reveal to them the hidden sacred objects in Mt. Gerizim where Moses deposited them. This revelation is still part of the *taheb* lore. See Bowman, *Samaritan Documents*, pp. 267-270. The Samaritan Book of Joshua includes the statement that Moses was taken up alive to God and is destined to return as the *taheb* (Bowman, *The Samaritan Problem*, p. 19).

21. The Samaritan Pentateuch at Ex. 23:17 reads that all males should be seen three times a year before the *àron* (the holy ark holding the tablets of commandments) rather than *adon* "the Lord," as it is in the masoretic text.

22. *Memar Marqah*, 2 vols., ed. John MacDonald (Berlin: 1963), p. xviii. On dating the work, our text of which is fourteenth century, see pp. xx ff.

23. *Ibid.* II, 43 (translation), and the original at I, 27, and passim.

24. *Ibid.* II, 40f.; Joseph is exalted at p. 94f. See

below the section on Moses.

25. *Ibid.* II, 181-189; I, 110f.

26. See MacDonald, *The Theology of the Samaritans*, 276-313; 359-390; Jn. 4:25f. shows that Samaritans had a pre-Christian messianic idea despite not having the prophetic books in their canon and our sources being very late. Their source was Deut. 18:18. The belief in resurrection the Samaritans exegeted from their own version of Gen. 3:19 which reads, "You are dust and to your dust you will return," reading the second *àfar* (dust) as *àfrekha* (your dust), signifying that the human will return to the same composition as he is in his lifetime. See MacDonald, p. 374f. The intercession of Moses is believed to be a function typified by his previous intercession at Ex. 32:31f. Some scholars question whether the doctrine of resurrection in Samaritanism is ancient or a medieval interpolation. See Stanley Jerome Isser, *The Dositheans* (Leiden: 1976), pp. 143-150. One of the difficult problems attached to the question is the statement in both Judaic and Christian sources that Samaritans did not believe in resurrection. See Kuthim 2 which requires Samaritans to accept resurrection as a pre-condition to being received as Jews, and Epiphanius, *Panarion* 9-14, where he speaks of the Samaritans and indicates that because they did not have more scripture than the Pentateuch, and because resurrection is not clearly announced in it, Samaritans did not believe in the resurrection of the dead. But Epiphanius claims that a Samaritan faction called Dositheans, founded by a Jew Dositheus, did believe in resurrection. It is possible, therefore, that as in the case of the Jews, some Samaritans did believe in resurrection while others did not. Furthermore, the reference in Kuthim is not found in earlier rabbinic literature and may not reflect what some believed at an earlier time. See Isser, *op. cit.* pp. 38-48. It is important that the doctrine of resurrection is already fully developed in Memar Marqah's fourth century exposition and it is unlikely that it was interpolated later. See Montgomery, "Eschatology," pp. 239-251.

27. See Bowman, *Documents,* "The Hilluk," pp. 298-330. The circumcision *hilluk* is translated by Bowman, *ibid.* pp. 305ff. See B. Hul. 4b; A.Z. 27a; the Samaritan stringency is found in Jub. 15:26f. and is one of the pointers to affinity between Jubilees, Qumran and Samaritanism. The *hilluk* is wrong, however, in saying that Jews postpone the circumcision from the Sabbath or Day of Atonement to the next day. Circumcision supersedes the Sabbath: T. Shab. 15:16; M. Shab. 19:2f.

28. Bowman, *Documents,* 9-16.

29. See, in addition to MacDonald (note 26, above), Montgomery, *The Samaritans*, pp. 165-195.

30. See Moses Gaster, *The Samaritans*, pp. 40-95; ȯmer: pp. 68, 168, 178. Bowman, *Documents*, p. 227, cites a medieval Samaritan commentator who specifies Sunday as the day of ȯmer. On slaughtering: Gaster, pp. 68f.; cf. B. Hul. 28a; 42a. On seething a kid: Gaster, p. 70. See both P. Targ. and Onk. to Ex. 23:19. The former forbids cooking and eating, the latter only eating.

31. See *Memar Marqah* I for texts and II for translations. What follows in the text is gleaned from the original. See also MacDonald, *Theology*, 147-222.

32. An example of this type of often-reiterated paean to Moses is at I, Bk. V, Sec. 9, p. 45; II, 71; cf. I, 50-52; II, 80-83; I, 88; II, 142f.

33. I, 117-128; II, 193-209; I, 144.

34. Bowman, *Samaritan Problem*, p. 94-101; CDC 5:8; B.B.B. 115b.

35. See John Bowman, "Samaritan Studies," *BJRL*, 40 (1958), pp. 299f.; *The Fourth Gospel and the Jews* (Pittsburgh: 1975). See Acts 1:8; 8:1, 5, 9, 14, 25; 9:31; 15:3; Lk. 10:33-37; 17:11f. See Jn. 1; 8:12; 9:5; cf. Bowman, "Samaritan Studies," p. 306; *Samaritan Problem*, pp. 63-69. See also Jn. 4:39; 41f.; at 6:14; 7:40 they see Jesus in the light of Deut. 18:18.

36. Lk. 7:15f.; Acts 7:15-16. Actually Gen. 23:17-20; 49:30; 50:13, do not specify Hebron. Gen. 23:2 only indirectly implies it. Sarah might have died at Hebron but the burial could have been at Shechem. Not even Gen. 35:27-29 clearly indicates where the burial cave was.

Additional Note:

MOSES

I. *Moses in Judaic Tradition*

The Samaritan Moses, like the Philonic Moses, is not the product of imaginative exegesis by Samaritans and hellenistic Jews, but is derived from within the historic tradition itself. From earliest times Pentateuchal verses must have been understood in both mystical and metaphorical manner and impressed different people in a variety of ways. Thus, the designation of Moses as *elohim* (Ex. 4:16; 7:1), the statements that Israel believed in or trusted God and Moses equally (Ex. 14:31), that Moses was transfigured by radiant divine light so that he is feared as if he were a celestial being (Ex. 34:28-35), and the account of his death (Deut. 34:5-7), must all have made a deep impression upon people. One can take these verses literally or metaphorically, and we can see that they were indeed taken both ways. When they were taken literally a very mystical concept of Moses emerged.

The rabbinic tradition on Moses is quite prolific in mystical lore. B. Sot. 11a to 14a, and Ex. R. 1:9f., 16, 18, 20, 22, 24; Lev. R. 1:3, contain extensive midrashic or àgadic exegesis on Moses birth, and one could easily fashion from this material a birth narrative in the style of that of Matthew or Luke for Jesus. Ex. 2:4 is given powerful meaning. "His sister stood afar off to know what will be done to him" is given a word for word exegesis that results in the idea that the Shekhinah (Wisdom, the Lord) was nearby and divine knowledge was active in Moses' protection. The entire verse was interpreted to refer to the Holy Spirit (Ex. R. 1:22). There is even a hint of the application of divinity to Moses.

It is said that Egyptian seers warned Pharaoh that a child is to be born who will be the redeemer of Israel. Variant traditions have Miriam prophesy the birth, or God appear in a dream to Amram, Moses' father, to tell him of the forthcoming birth, (Josephus, *Ant.* II, 9, 2-4 (205-223); Ex. R. 1:22). When Moses is born divine radiance filled the room according to the Moses àgadah. This exegesis is made possible by use of *gezerah shavah,* the analogy of *toḇ*, in which Moses is recognized as "good" (Ex. 2:10), just as the light of Gen. 1:4 is declared *tob*. The Eyptian seers are said to foresee that the Israelite savior is to be punished through the medium of water and therefore Pharaoh ordered the drowning of all male children (Ex. 1:22). But they do not understand that Moses' punishment is to be for striking the stone at Meribah to get water for Israel instead of speaking to the stone (Num. 20:8-13). Moses is placed in the water instead of being exposed in the field in order to make Pharaoh think he will perish. Moses is called "good" because of the radiance of his birth, but it is said that he is called "good" also because the Torah is called "good" at Prov. 4:2, and the Torah is therefore called by the name of Moses (Mal. 3:22) for both are named *tob* and both are "light." When the daughter of Pharaoh opens the basket (Ex. 2:6) she sees *et hayeled* "the child." According to the Nahum Gimzo type of hermeneutics, every *et* in the Torah is linguistically superfluous, but in order that no word in the Torah be considered superfluous it is exegeted. In this case the extra *et* signifies something in addition to the child, and it is said that Pharaoh's daughter saw the Shekhinah in the basket with the child (Ex. R. 1:24), and the Shekhinah in turn is identified as God (*ibid.* 1:25).

Moses is accorded ten or eleven names (Lev. R. 1:3), depending upon how one reckons the midrashic terms. All of the names signify major theological notions and in some cases a near-divine status for Moses: he brought the Torah and the Shekhinah down from heaven and united the children (Israel) with their Father in heaven. It must be recalled that nobody was present at Moses' death and therefore it is not difficult to see the emergence of the tradition that he did not die. He is even considered pre-existent and declared to immortally function as a mediator and intercessor before God (Ass. Moses 1:14; 3:12; 12:6; B. Sot. 13b; Sif. Deut. 357). At Deut. 33:1 Moses is called "man of God" and this is taken to mean that he was both divine and human; he was a man compared to angels, divine compared to humans, divine when he worked miracles or when he ascended to God and had no need of material sustenance (Deut. R. 11:4).

There developed a generally mystical approach to Moses' death (Philo, *Moses* II, 51 (288-291); *On the Virtues* 12 (76ff.) and Part I, Chapter 6 above, as well as Erwin Goodenough, *By Light, Light*, p. 199). It even appears that the "lamb" as an image of the savior was used for Moses. This is found in P. Targ. Ex. 1:15 when Pharaoh is reported to dream of Egypt on one side of a scale and a lamb on the other which outweighs Egypt. The Egyptian seers explain that the lamb is the child to be born in Israel who is to be the redeemer and will destroy

Egypt. The Aramaic *talya* (lamb) is explained as *bar*, a child, just as the term "kid" is used in English for a human and an animal offspring. (See G. Vermes, *Scripture and Tradition*, pp. 93f., n. 5; cf. Jn. 1:29).

Two other interesting points may be added here. First, a midrash to Deut. 26:5-8 recited at the Passover Seder avers that "God saw the affliction of Israel in Egypt means he pondered their sexual abstention (Ex. R. 1:15; 2:25; B. Yom. 74b; B.B. 60b). This is connected with Ex. 2:25 which reports that "God knew," suggesting the use of the term "know" in its sexual nuance, that is, God caused a divine birth in Egypt. Secondly, one may note that in *gematria*, the numerical value of the letters of Moses' name (Mem=40; Shin=300; Hay=5;) provides a total of 345. When these three separate numbers are added together they total 12. Moses then becomes the twelve tribes of Israel personified. (Much Moses material is gathered by Louis Ginzberg, *Legends*, II, 245-375; III; V, 391-439; VI, 1-168).

II. *Moses in Pagan Tradition*

There is also a pagan tradition concerning Moses which is discussed and documented by John G. Gager, *Moses in Graeco-Roman Paganism*. He had a reputation as a wise man and a great lawgiver. But there were also negative attitudes towards him and some considered him a deficient lawgiver. Some hostile views saw him as a renegade Egyptian priest who was expelled along with defiled Egyptians in a religious revolution against the extant faiths. One other aspect of Moses-lore bases itself upon the biblical verses that pit Moses against Egyptian wise men and see him as a magician and alchemist (See Gager, Chapter Four). He is mentioned in papyri as one of special divine wisdom who wrote books and magical recipes, and his name is found on amulets. But all accounts, whether erroneous in details or not, include his role as leader of the Israelite exodus and as the Jewish lawgiver. The literature surveyed by Gager covers a six-hundred year span from Hecataeus of Abdera to Julian the Apostate. Some of the literature is of the anti-Jewish Alexandrian genre which pictures Moses as having little theological wisdom, and as the founder of a system that inculcated in its followers a hatred for everything not Judaic. But as Gager points out (p. 132) these accounts generally are the consequence of the great hostility that arose as a result of the political and religious conflicts between the Hasmoneans and the Seleucids, and the subsequent animosity that arose

between pagans and Jews from the middle of the second century
B.C. This was exacerbated during the anti-Roman conflicts
from 63 B.C. to 70 A.D. and beyond, to the end of the Bar
Kokhba revolt in 135. The interested reader might find the
following brief additional bibliography of value in pursuing
various aspects of Moses-lore: H. Teeple, *The Mosaic Eschatological Prophet*; J. Danielou, *From Shadows to Reality*, pp.
153-226 on typological use of Moses and the exodus; W. A.
Meeks, *The Prophet-King: Moses Traditions and the Johannine
Christology*.

APPENDIX B

Zoroastrianism[1]

Rabbis of differing standpoints on many halakhic questions were united in their opposition to Christianity. For
example, both Rab and Samuel are said not to have entered a
niẓrefi, the gathering place of Christian Jews. But while
Rab would also not enter a house of a Zoroastrian Magus
Samuel was willing to enter one (B. Shab. 116a). This reflects
the view that Christians who are apostates from Judaism are
worse than pagans who never knew the truth (T. Shab. 14:5).
But Rab was equally antagonistic to Mazdeans (worshippers of
Ahura Mazda, the "Wise Lord," that is, Zoroastrianism), because he saw in them a repressive threat to Judaism.[2] There
were periods in Sassanian Persia (third to seventh century
A.D.) when Magi had the government prohibit the ritual preparation of meat and purification baptisms, exhume the dead
for exposure of the bodies (B. Yeb. 63b), and regulate the use
of fire, for them the power that overcomes darkness, the symbol of truth, important for Jews in Sabbath and Hanukah observance (B. Shab. 45a; Git. 17a). The Talmud, again in the name
of Rab, refers to Mazdeans destroying synagogues (B. Yom. 10a).

Nevertheless, just as Christian repression of Judaism in
medieval times did not preclude mutual influences, so too
Judaism and Zoroastrianism experienced mutual influences. One
does not look only at third century Sassanian Iran for this,
but rather to the earliest connections between Zoroastrianism
and Judaism, in the first years of the Babylonian exile, before the time of Ezra and Nehemiah. Scholars debate whether
Zarathustra (the correct Avestan form for Zoroaster) was born
in the seventh century B.C., a contemporary of Jeremiah and
Ezekiel, or in the tenth century B.C. In either case his
teachings would have been encountered by the Jerusalem exiles.[3]
Affinities between religions do not necessarily imply that one
influenced the other, but it is interesting that when Zarathustra was purified while drawing water for a ritual he had a
vision at the bank of the river where he was purified. He saw
a being wearing a garment of light and when he was brought into
the presence of Ahura Mazda he saw only great light. Ezekiel
too has his mystic vision at a bank of a river where the heavens open and great flashing light is a medium of his vision

(Ez. 1:1-4). And Jesus, at baptism, also sees the heavens open (Mt. 3:16) and the Holy Spirit descends upon him. We have already previously referred to God's wearing the light as a garment (Ps. 104:2), which is precisely the imagery in Zarathustra's vision.

The foregoing merely points to a similarity in the style of religious language which can come from a common source, develop by coincidence, or be the result of mutual influences. Similarly it is taught that a son born to Zarathustra post-humously by a virgin who will be impregnated by sperm miraculously preserved in a lake, will be the cosmic *saosyant*, or savior who will destroy all evil and bring about the full realization of goodness in the universe. Part of the savior's achievement will be to bestow immortality.[4] The miraculous virgin birth of the savior is a theme repeated with variations in Christianity. The precise mode of birth, from sperm absorbed in water is attributed to Ben Sira's conception by the daughter of Jeremiah in a public bath where she received the sperm of her own father. (We cannot deal here with the obvious chronological impossibility for the daughter of Jeremiah (sixth century B.C.) to be the mother of Ben Sira (200 B.C.) regardless of mode of conception.)[5] The differences in the legends indicate a common reservoir of folk-lore.

The complex halakhah of purities in Judaism antedate Zoroastrianism, but so too did Indo-Iranian practices antedate it. All primitive religions practiced various washings and bathings for cultic purification. Like the Bible, Zoroastrianism regards a woman after childbirth as polluted for forty days.[6] On the other hand, Zoroastrianism and Judaism differ in the manner of disposing of the dead. The former exposes the body naked under the sun to be devoured by vultures, and apparently as noted earlier, at one time even exhumed Jewish bodies for exposure. Judaism insists upon burial of the dead in the ground. Both religions, however, have a belief that the soul lingers on earth for three days after leaving the body, and both provide liturgies relevant to the soul (Yasna 28-34).[7] The term *frasegird* (or as given by Zaehner, *frash-kart*) which is translated as "rehabilitation," the condition at the end-time when the *saosyant* destroys evil, signifies the condition of the world in which there will be no further natural affliction or human-imposed suffering. It is akin to the "messianic age" in its utopian sense in Judaism.[8]

A major difference between the two faiths is in the God-idea. Judaism's monotheism was not compromised by Zoroastrianism's dualism in which Ohrmazd (Ahura Mazda) is constantly beset by the challenge of Angra Mainyu or Ahriman, the spirit of

evil. The Qumran idea of "two spirits" was a dualistic notion
with much affinity with Zoroastrianism, but like the *yezer*
harà (evil inclination) and *yezer hatoḫ* (good inclination) in
rabbinic literature, was less damaging to pure monotheism.[9]
In Judaism it is the human alone who is beset by an inner
struggle. God is not threatened by another power. Yasna 43
and its idea of judgment at the end of days, as well as Yasna
44 with its great resemblance to Job 38 on creation, are examples of religious affinity. On the other hand there is no
doctrine of forgiveness in Zoroastrianism.

Among the ideas that have points of contact between
Judaism and Iranian religion are the chronological division
of history into millenia, the last judgment, a book in heaven
in which human deeds are inscribed, the transformation of the
earth into excellence at the end, and others.[10] There is also
the thrice-daily prayer custom in the two religions, at dawn,
noon and dusk.[11] But perhaps a matter of special interest is
the doctrine of resurrection.

In the relevant chapters above I have discussed the ambiv-
alent approach to the doctrine of resurrection. From earliest
times there was what one scholar has called a "nascent faith,"
and it became stronger during the Hasmonean period.[12] Jews
came into contact with Zoroastrians in Syria as well as Persia during this era. The question here is whether this doctrine was imported from Zoroastrianism. Yasna 43:4-5 give
Zarathustra's teaching that God weighs the deeds of the righteous and the wicked and metes out reward and punishment (see
also Yasna 51:6f; 12-13). Although Zarathustra speaks of the
"last turning-point of existence," that is, the end of days,
he never refers to resurrection. At Yasna 53 which is believed not to be by Zarathustra, but by a close disciple, who
wrote it soon after Zoroaster's death and ought to have had
intimate knowledge of his teaching, we have a lucid statement
of the doctrine of immortality and eternal bliss, but not of
resurrection. Yasna 48:2-3, 5 evinces the kind of ambiguity
present in the Zoroastrian literature in which there is a
degree of confusion between this-worldly renewal and post-
death bliss and suffering, but no specific statement of a
meta-historical resurrection-existence. The conclusion one
must reach after reading these and other Yasnas is that there
is no clear statement of a doctrine of resurrection of the
dead in Zoroaster's Gathas. Probably the doctrine of resurrection in Zoroastrianism is later than that of Judaism.[13]
Early Zoroastrianism, the religion that Judaism first encountered during the sixth century B.C., did not have this doctrine whereas it was already "nascent" in Judaism. Whether
Zoroastrianism took it from Judaism is immaterial. During a

period of severe persecution during the fourth century many
Jewish children were seized and brought up as Zoroastrians.
We have no way of knowing their influence. Zoroastrians could
have taken it from ancient Vedic religion just as Judaism
might have acquired it from its remote Canaanite past, not
making it into a dogma until the first century. In Zoroastrianism this doctrine is found in the later Pahlavi texts of
the Parsi religion when the trauma of Islamic conquest had
upon the Zoroastrians the same effect of stimulating the acceptance of an extant doctrine of resurrection as the trauma
of 587 B.C. had in Judaism.[14]

An interesting influence upon Judaism could have been the
quality of the Magus as astrologer, physician, magician and
the like, which induces rabbis to undertake a mixture of these
sciences, including the occult with theology. It was believed
that rabbis, no less than Persian Magi could associate with
the dead, interpret dreams, omens and signs, and had the
power to utter both an effective blessing and curse. In general the Magus functioned like a rabbi, and in these ways the
rabbi adopted qualities of the Magus. Nevertheless, since
Palestinian rabbis also functioned this way the question must
be posed whether the development was indigenous and coinciden-
tal, or whether the Mazdean Magus influenced the Babylonian
rabbis who in turn influenced the Palestinians.[15]

When we consider all the other affinities between the two
faiths, in the doctrine of hell and heaven, reward and punishment, an emphasis upon ritualism, we can recognize the challenge Mazdeism was to Judaism when it was all-powerful and in-
tolerant in Sassanian times. Yet we can also see signs of
Judaic acculturation in Persia from a reference at B. Yeb.
63b that Palestinians believed that Babylonian Jews were
"punished" by God through the agency of the Magi for sins they
committed, that there was an element of relaxation from strict
observance and that Jews even in some way celebrated the
Mazdean holidays.

NOTES

1. Suggested bibliography: Mary Boyce, *A History of Zoroastrianism* (Leiden: 1975); R. C. Zaehner, *The Dawn and Twilight of Zoroastrianism* (New York: 1961); George W. Carter, *Zoroastrianism and Judaism* (Boston: 1918); Carter's work must be taken with great caution. His thesis of an inordinate influence of Persian religion upon Judaism is achieved by sleight of hand. He dates late Zoroastrian literature early and early Judaic literature late! See also Miles M. Dawson, *The Ethical Religion of Zoroaster* (New York: 1969); *The Hymns of Zarathustra,* trans. Jacques Duchesne-Guillemin, trans. from French, Mrs. M. Henning (London: 1952).

2. For a discussion of the meaning of Ahura Mazda see Boyce, pp. 37-40. The primary profession of faith by a Zoroastrian or a Mazdean is cited by Boyce (p. 253f.), from Yasna 12:1, "I profess myself a Mazda-worshipper, a Zoroastrian, rejecting the *daevas* (demons), accepting the Ahuric doctrine. . ."

3. On his date see Boyce, pp. 3, n. 4; 184-191. See also Zaehner, *The Dawn and Twilight,* p. 33.

4. Boyce, pp. 282f., from Yasna 19:88-89.

5. The Talmud also reflects this mode of impregnation as a possibility at B. Ḥag. 14b-15a.

6. Boyce, Chap. 12; childbirth: p. 308.

7. *Ibid.* "Excursus on Funerary Rites," pp. 325ff. Cf. P.M.K. 82b.

8. *Ibid.* p. 233; Zaehner, pp. 296, 308f.

9. For the idea of deity see Carter, pp. 41-54; Zaehner, 43-55. For Zoroastrian affinities at Qumran see George Widengren "Iran and Israel in Parthian Times," *Temenos,* 2 (1966), 139-177.

10. See J. Duchesne-Guillemin, *The Western Response to*

Zoroaster (Westport, Conn.: 1958), pp. 95f.

11. The Zoroastrian custom is cited by Franz Cumont, *The Mysteries of Mithra*, trans. Thomas J. McCormack (New York: 1956).

12. Gordis, *The Book of God and Man*, p. 84.

13. The ambiguity is sustained by careful reading of a wide variety of Yasnas in the Henning translation. See 33:1; 34:12-15; 44:16-20; 48:1, 4; 46:10-11; and Yasna 30. See also also translations in James H. Moulton, *Early Zoroastrianism* (Amsterdam: 1972).

14. Dawson, p. 250. Zaehner, p. 57, recognizes that the idea of resurrection is not found in the earlier literature of the Avesta, but nevertheless goes on to hypothesize that the doctrine of resurrection was "probably original to Zoroastrianism."

15. See Jacob Neusner, "The Rabbi and the Magus," in *Talmudic Judaism in Sassanian Babylonia* (Leiden: 1976), 78-86.

APPENDIX C

Dual Covenant Theology

Part I, Chapter Seven of this volume stressed the Judaic matrix of early Christianity. In effect this is saying that regardless of the direction Christianity took after the Council of Nicea, 325, which led it to a historic hostility against Judaism, the origin of Christianity is as a version or denomination of Judaism. The problem of the contemporary era is to re-examine these roots with a view toward establishing the possibility and feasibility of Judaism and Christianity once more seeing themselves as twin expressions of biblical religion, each allowing appropriate theological space for the other and each conceding covenantal legitimacy to the other. In further research I would endeavor to broaden this concept to include Islam.

It is my view that the very first requirement in this process is to eschew the endless debate over anti-Judaism in the New Testament and the drawing of a straight line to Auschwitz from Christian theology based upon the Epistle of Barnabas (13:2-6) which declares Judaism subordinate to Christianity. Antagonism to its sister religion is not a monopoly of Christendom (see Ernst Bammel, "Christian Origins in Jewish Tradition," *NTS*, 13 (1966), 317-335). The anti-Christian literature written and circulated among Jews stretches over a millenium in various languages, and is crowned by an extremely pejorative version of the gospels, *Toledot Yeshu*. Ernst Bammel has termed the mutual denigration of Judaism and Christianity as "a war in the trenches which is fought out with considerable ammunition and with tactical skill" (p. 319).

In the shadow of Auschwitz both Christian and Jewish dialogists presently engage in defensive apologetics. This detours us from the serious level of theological discourse. What is needed is less discussion of the tragic centuries between the fourth and the twentieth, between, shall we say, Nicea and Vatican Two, and less emphasis upon where the two religions are distinctive and irreconcilable, and more candid intellectual pursuit of how to come to formulations that will bridge the gap. Christian ecumenicism without the participation of Judaism is inadequate, as others have noted.[1]

Subjects that must be placed on a serious interreligious theological dialogue, among others, are: conversion, the doctrine of election, the perennial problem of faith and works or the nature of grace and merit, the Christology, and the meaning of a "dual covenant." Christianity is not alone in its desire for conversionism. Jews must realize that the álenu prayer that closes each occasion of Judaic public worship is an expression of Judaic conversionism. It looks to the time, not simply when all humans will have their religion recognized as valid by Judaism, but when all humans will accept Judaic monotheism. The text looks to the day when all humans will accept *òl malkhut*, the yoke of God's sovereignty, which means *òl mizvot*, the yoke of the halakhah. Indeed, it is true that Judaism declares "the pious of the gentiles" enjoy salvation (T. San. 13:2), but it must be conceded that this means only those who are pious by Judaic norms. In essence the álenu looks forward to the eschatological attainment of the hope that all will confess and comply with Deut. 6:4-9.

Both Alan Davies and Rosemary Ruether see Rom. 9-11 as Paul's requirement for Jews to accept Jesus.[2] What Paul is really saying is not all that clear in those two chapters which are probably the two most enigmatic chapters in the whole Bible. Clearly what emerges is that Paul refers to all believers in Christ as the "remnant" of Israel, whether these believers are originally Judaic or pagan (10:9-13).[3] The Christian Church is the remnant of Israel because it originated with Israel, and gentiles in the remnant are foreign branches that have been grafted on to the tree (11:16-24). Paul is here as exclusivist as Judaism in general: one can be part of Israel if one believes in a particular dogma. No more than the author of the álenu nor Zekh. 14:9 is Paul able to universalize the hope. The Christian invitation to all to baptism and faith, and the Judaic invitation to all to accept the *òl malkhut* leads us with resignation to the prescient remark of Ezekiel, "like mother, like daughter" (16:44).

Judaism and Christianity are rival claimants to the status of elect, covenanted people of God through whose theology salvation is possible. The problem before us, therefore, is to search for formulations that allow for theological space under the monotheistic, biblical umbrella. Much has already been said in Part I, Chapter Seven on faith and works, and some comments were made earlier in this volume on the Judaic idea of the possibility of divine incarnation. There is nothing unJewish in John's approach to the essence of his theology At Jn. 14:21 we are given a ladder to salvation:

> Jesus will manifest himself to one whom he loves--
> Jesus will love the one whom God loves,
> God will love the one who loves Jesus,
> The one who loves Jesus is the one "who
> has my commandments and *observes* them."

(See also Jn. 15:10). Rudolph Bultmann, in his *Theology of the New Testament,* apparently finds it too painful to comment on this or on its original formulation at Mt. 28:20 which informs the disciples that after baptism which symbolizes faith stands the command to *observe* all the teachings, and that only then "I am with you always."

Establishing the basic Judaic quality of John is always a rather surprising matter to those who believe John is outside of Judaism. The fact is that not even with his reiteration of incarnation is he outside of one version of pre-70 Judaism, which is the Judaism he believes and teaches. The messianic idea requires much discussion. I have already made reference to the notion of a divinely begotten messiah in pre-Christian Judaism.[4] The messianic concept as a whole is one of the most complex theological problems in the biblical-rabbinic continuum. Even Christian theologians sometimes wonder whether Jesus was the Messiah in terms of the simplistic view of a Messiah bringing a utopian age. And if he does not fit this conception of a Messiah, which does he fit? Or is it at all proper to refer to him as the Messiah? Is it perhaps better to begin dialogue by examining the function of Jesus for the post-30 disciples as the embodiment of the Servant of Yhwh-ákedah principle, even if before 30 they thought he was the Messiah in Davidic-political terms? And this can be turned around for Jews. Is there any way to concede theological space to a Jesus who took upon himself the ákedah destiny and was seen by his post-30 disciples to be the Servant, while other Jews struggled with whether Moses was the Servant or collective Israel was the Servant? Can a Christian notion of a Jesus personifying Israel and a Judaic notion that Israel continues to be the Servant find a theological bridge? If the crucifixion goes on as a process of ever-recurring history what is the meaning of the resurrection? Are Christians prepared to discuss this question? Hans Küng is apparently prepared to say at least this much,

> "Surely the history of this people and its
> God, this people of tears and life, of lamen-
> tation and trust culminates in the one figure
> of Jesus and his history as a spectacular sign
> of the crucified and resurrected Israel?"[5]

Perhaps we can amend Küng's text to read "illustrates" in place of "culminates" and then inquire whether Judaic thinkers can participate in dialogue which declares Jesus to be an illustration of the historic role of Israel. Can Jews and Christians enter into theological negotiation from the posture of Jesus as a symbol of the resurrection of God's Elect at the Eschaton, a latter-day re-enactment of the bondage and exodus?

After all, is it really possible, or rather *necessary*, to say that the world is redeemed in the messianic-redemption sense? Küng has indicated that "the present with its poverty and its sin is and remains too sad and too discordant to be already the Kingdom of God. . ."[6] Similarly Jakob Petuchowski sees the failure of the "Messianic Era" philosophy that arose in the Jewish self-redemption notions of both Reform Judaism and Zionism.[7] He, therefore, concludes that we continue to live in a pre-messianic and unredeemed world. The expectation of both Christianity and Judaism is centered in Hab. 2:3, "though it tarry, expect it; it will surely come. . .

In this sense the doctrine of the resurrection of Jesus becomes the proleptic paradigm for the resurrection or restoration of non-Jewish mankind to the perfect state of original creation. This is what the command to make disciples of *panta ta ethnē*, "all the gentiles," (Mt. 28:19) is all about. For indeed this final pericope (Mt. 28:18-20) is perhaps more significant in some ways than has been noticed. At v. 18 Jesus tells the disciples that all authority is given to him in heaven and on earth, an idea allusive to the creation in the notion of universal authority that belongs to a creator. Thus the three-fold name of v. 19 is here alluded to as well: the identification of the Son and the Father along with the Holy Spirit, and the beginning of the notion of Jesus as the medium of creation, the equivalent of the Logos-Wisdom-Torah-Sophia as the source-book of creation. At v. 19 Jesus tells the disciples to transmit his revelation, and at v. 20 to live in obedience so that he will be with them. Thus v. 18 alludes to creation, v. 19 to revelation and v. 20 to his redemptive presence. This is the structure of worship familiar to any first-century Jew as we have noted in our comments on liturgy. Thus where the end of the Shema, Num. 15:37-41, precedes the berakhah of redemption, it speaks of remembering to do the mizvot, an idea alluded to by Mt. 28:20.

A re-study of the New Testament and rabbinic literature from a new perspective on theological discourse may result in temporary mystification, but lead to permanent clarity. After all, Mt. 28:20 and LXX Mal. 1:11 have much in common in idea and in terminology. The one speaks for Christianity, the

other for Judaism.   Is this not proleptic of dual covenant
theology?

NOTES

1.   Alan Davies, *Anti-Semitism and the Christian Mind*
(New York: 1969) p. 96; Hans Küng, *On Being a Christian* (New
York: 1976), p. 170.

2.   Rosemary Ruether, *Faith and Fratricide* (New York:
1974), pp. 105ff.; Davies, *op. cit.* 94-107.

3.   The reader should not be confused by the term "Israel"
in this context.   It does not refer to the modern Republic of
Israel, but rather to the theological entity composed of followers of Judaism.

4.   R. Gordis, "The 'Begotten Messiah' in the Qumran
Scrolls" *VT*, 7 (1957), 191-194.

5.   "Introduction," pp. 14f., *Christians and Jews*, ed.
H. Küng and Kasper (New York: 1974).

6.   Küng, *On Being a Christian*, p. 222.

7.   In Küng and Kasper, *op. cit.* pp. 58f.

Additional Note:

THE PROBLEM OF "ANTI-SEMITISM"

I. *Pagan Negativism Toward Jews and Judaism*

It is believed that the term "anti-Semitism" was first
used around 1878 or 1880 (Sandmel, p. xx; Sevenster, p. 1),
for the complex of feelings, sayings and actions of a negative and physically harmful nature against Jews and/or Judaism. Since the term "semitic" is that of a language group
(Syriac and Arabic among others, in addition to Hebrew) and
there are many Semites who are not Jews, and many Jews who
are basically no longer "semitic" in their language, the
term ought to be replaced. One should really refer to
"anti-Jewish" and "anti-Judaism" as two separate phenomena
cf. Sandmel, p. xxi). One may hate Jews but appreciate
Judaism, or one may disdain Judaism while having no quarrel
with Jews as persons. Furthermore, one should not refer to
intellectual polemic or critique as "anti-Judaism" even if
that polemic or critique is negative. A position should not
be termed "anti-Judaism" until its adherent actually urges
the suppression of forms of Judaic expression, whether of
academic or spiritual nature, such as its publications and
its synagogues and schools.

In the pagan world no writer of note attacked Jews on
racial grounds. The typical terms in Greek were *phylon,
genos, ethnos,* or the Latin *gens,* frequently translated as
"race" in English. Technically, the translations might be
correct, but when the term "race" is thought of in its disastrous 19th-20th century pseudo-scientific connotations it
carries with it a total misconstrual of what the ancient
author meant. He had none of the modern pejorative racial
ideas in mind. He was simply referring to a political, social,
or religious "aggregate of people." Writers like Juvenal
attack the Greeks even more viciously than the Jews. Poliakov, I, 6 has correctly drawn attention to an idea which is
one of the theses of my work: the Jews regularly acculturated,
and only their religion differentiated them. They were attacked for their "superstition," as were others. A study of
pagan writers leads to the conclusion that "anti-Jewism" in
the ancient world was the product of Judaic loyalty to Judaism
although during one period this was exacerbated by Hasmonean

conquest. The exclusivity and isolation of Judaism and its practices which were contrary to the entire pagan world around them, gave rise to animosity. The covenant-claims to possession of the truth, the taunting of paganism as a no-religion, the refusal to participate in civic religion in Graeco-Roman society, all coupled with the special legal position accorded to Jews to practice their religion undoubtedly had the greatest impact upon "anti-Jewism" in the pagan world. Haman's argument at Est. 3:8 probably sums up the mixture of truth and falsehood that prevailed in the classical world. The pagan hostility was aimed at the *amixia* (the isolation, the refusal to amalgamate) of the Jews. Thus, Sevenster, p. 144, is correct in concluding that Judaic "strangeness, emanating from the way of life and thought prescribed by the Torah (read: torah, including the interpretive torah) lies the profoundest cause for the anti-Semitism of the ancient world." Poliakov (I. 12), correctly points out that the ancient world had no "state anti-semitism" in which government laws were employed to suppress Jews, although on two occasions there occurred the aborted efforts of Antiochus IV (167 B.C.) and Hadrian (135 A.D.) to suppress Judaism.

II. *The Christian Factor*

Samuel Sandmel, p. 5, emphatically negates the notion that there is any relationship between pagan anti-Semitism and what he refers to equally as "Christian anti-Semitism." Basically I would argue that in the case of Christianity, New Testament negativism is a theological critique. By my own criteria stated earlier I see this critique neither as anti-Semitism nor anti-Jewism nor anti-Judaism. What emerges in Christian circles after Nicea (325) is another problem. But at the inception of the new movement in Judaism later to be called: "Christianity," the most articulate critic of Judaism was Paul. I have already sketched my view of Paul's teaching in Part I, Chapter Seven which is at some variance with Sandmel's. The problem at hand simply is: can Paul's attitude toward the Torah, when he uses phrases like "the *nomos* kills" or "the *nomos* is a curse," be considered the father of a form of Christian anti-Semitism? Is I Thess. 2:14-16, which is the only passage in which Paul accuses "the Jews" of killing Jesus, to be seen as Pauline anti-Semitism? It hardly appears that way to me. In the light of my understanding of Paul, his critique of the salvific efficacy of the *nomos* is his way of looking, rightly or wrongly, at inherited Judaic traditions. If he had meant to hurt Jews with the charge of killing Jesus it would have been far more pervasive in his writings.

The gospels are interlaced with a critique of Jews and Judaism. It is at Mt. 5:12 and 23:31 in which the evangelist accuses prior generations of persecuting prophets. Although this is a charge which is not wholly unfounded (Neh. 9:2-6) here we have one of the seeds of future anti-Judaic arguments by Christians which prepares the ground for the historic accusation of deicide. Mt. 23, a lengthy denigration of scribes and Pharisees can be seen as an early Christian attack on Judaism. But it can also be seen as an internal diatribe against extremist pietists. What has been made of Mt. 23 by enemies of Jews and Judaism is not what Mt. or Jesus might have wanted it to convey. This is a crux for inter-religious dialogue: the Christian obligation to place harsh statements into their first-century context, something it would appear to me honest teachers and clergy persons do in their classes and pulpits. The Passion Narrative is capable of arousing much anti-Judaic sentiment, but was not necessarily designed to do that. In this regard Mt. 27:25, "'His blood be upon us and on our children'" is the most dangerous verse in all the gospels and has reinforced the popular taunt even against Jewish youngsters in modern times as "Christ-killers." But it is very important to note, as Sandmel (p. 68f) does, that Mt. is vindictive against "scribes and Pharisees" and not "the Jews." This suggests that Mt. and his church are still in Judaism and are still Jews and that Mt. tries to represent the struggle in the context of the time of Jesus. If we were not so accustomed to defending Pharisees incorrectly as synonymous with rabbinic Judaism we would not be as disturbed about this internal quarrel between Judaic Christians and their pietist opposition. For moderns to disassociate Mt. 27:25 from later generations is not a giant step. Lk. 23:34 informs us that Jesus had already provided for that on the cross, not only exhonorating future generations, but the very ones that were active in his death. No Christian dare do less. The fact that New Testament textual critics indicate that there is a high degree of doubt as to whether this Lucan text is authentic, indicates not that it does not give the words of Jesus, but that many people tried to eliminate them and hence varying manuscripts came down with and without them. We find far less anti-Judaic sentiment in Mk. because when he wrote the quarrels with rabbinic Judaism were not as severe and he could place the matter in the context of Jesus' time. He portrayed the opposition to Jesus as being centered in the establishment at Jerusalem except for the "crowds" in the Passion Narrative. But "crowds" are fickle, and after following a hero (Mk. 12:18) in his hour of glory they do not shrink from abandoning him in his hour of distress (Ecc. 4:15-16). Moreover, Sandmel, pp. 46f., is correct in indicating that Mk. treats the Jewish disciples critically too, and it is possible

that Mk. is promoting gentile Christianity against the continuing Judaization that went on apace at the turn of the
century.

The author of Luke-Acts furthers the Pauline position
that Christianity is Judaism and Christians are heir to the
promises of the Old Testament. Here, along with Paul's theology, are the seeds of the position ripened in Barnabas and
reaped in patristic literature, that Judaism is subordinate
to Christianity and that Christianity possesses the covenant.
Sandmel (p. 73), ascribes to Luke "a frequent subtle, genteel
anti-semitism" which becomes more overt in Acts. But again,
it is a moot point whether critical polemic can be considered
anti-Semitism. It is evident from the letters of Paul that
Paul had a great series of controversies with "Judaizers."
His references to these conflicts imply that they were severe.
There is no surprise, therefore, in Luke's effort to establish Christianity as authentic and to claim that it is the
Jews who refuse to believe that they are deviating from a
proper understanding of the faith. The charge that Jews
crucified Jesus (Acts 2:36; 3:15, and elsewhere) is mitigated
by the concession that it was God's will and that Jews acted
unwittingly (3:17). It appears to be an exercise in futile
apologetics for Jews to deny the complicity of Jews in the
crucifixion, or to try to compute how few could have been responsible (Sandmel, p. 136). Similarly it is an exercise in
Christian myopia to give it any further thought. It is entirely within the realm of the possible that a cryptic remark
attributed to Abigail in a conversation with King David points
to the possibility that Sanhedrin procedures were allowed to
be altered for the trial of a traitor (B. Meg. 14a-b), which
is what Jesus was being tried for, and not in any sense for
sins of theology of halakhah.

It is the Gospel of John which is considered the most
anti-Semitic gospel. Here the opponents of Jesus are "the
Jews." But while it is important to note that the term "Jews"
has a variety of meanings in John (Sandmel, p. 101), more
significant is that Jn. 9:22 and 16:2 indicate the author
writes from the posture of one expelled from the synagogue.
His vituperation is understandable from his side of the fence.
Perhaps over half of a century of controversy has gone on and
the Christians, still oblivious of the eventual triumph they
will enjoy, are being thrown out of Judaism. Has anyone
tried to compare the polemical literature of the controversies
between followers of Sabbatai Zvi and anti-Sabbateans of the
eighteenth century, or that of the orthodox-reform polemic of
the nineteenth? This would make a fine monograph and help in
the establishment of new guidelines in the inter-religious

dialogue of our time as it affects the question of "anti-Semitism."

The real problem is the turn that occurred with the
Church Fathers. Their anti-Judaic posture is no longer internal polemic. It is a sinful vindictiveness that is unbe-
coming spiritual giants such as Origen who turned Mt. 27:25
into an excuse for diatribes against contemporary Jews, calling them three centuries later, "Murderers of the Lord,
assassins of the prophets, rebels and detesters of God. . .
Companions of the devil, race of vipers, informers, calum-
niators. . ." (Gregory of Nyssa), or with St. John Chrysostom
seeing the synagogue as a "Brothel and theatre. . .a cave of
pirates and the lair of wild beasts. . ." and that Jews "can
do one thing only: gorge themselves with food and drink"
(quotations cited by Poliakov, I, 25).

The foregoing is an effort to place an angonizing problem
into some form of unemotional perspective in order to facili-
tate dialogue. I do not see a straight line from the Church
Fathers through Innocent III (see *Emergence* II) and on to
Auschwitz. In Volume IV I will devote more space to the distinction between Christian theological presuppositions that
resulted in the subordination of Judaism, and the rise of a
new kind of anti-Jewism in the nineteenth century which led
to the Holocaust.

Suggested Bibliography:

Leon Poliakov, *The History of Anti-Semitism,* 4 vols.
trans. Richard Howard (New York: 1965); J. N. Sevenster, *The
Roots of Pagan Anti-Semitism in the Ancient World* (Leiden:
1975); Samuel Sandmel, *Anti-Semitism in the New Testament*
(Philadelphia: 1978); Fred Gladstone Bratton, *The Crime of
Christendom* (Boston: 1969); see also relevant bibliography
in Part I, Chapter Seven above, such as A. Davies, Ruether,
Wilken, and the various writings of James Parkes. See also
Part I, Chapter Seven, and Part II, Chapter Three, above.
The reader should consult D. R. A. Hare, *The Theme of Jewish
Persecution of Christians in the Gospel According to St.
Matthew* (Cambridge: 1967).

APPENDIX D

The Impact of Christianity at Yavneh*

During the last three decades of the first century CE the rabbinic academy at Jabneh issued a significant number of decisions, whose intention was to bring unity to Jewish worship and practice. If the assumption is correct that Jewish Christians were actively seeking converts to their messianic faith within the synagogue communities of Palestine and the Diaspora, it appears probable that some of the actions taken at Jabneh were directed against the Christians, whose sectarian activity threatened the unity of the Jewish community.

W. D. Davies is one of the few contemporary scholars who has made a serious attempt to assess the Christian influence at Jabneh. His section entitled "Jamnia" in *The Setting of the Sermon on the Mount* (1964) remains unsurpassed. At various points, however, Davies' presentation can be modified or supplemented.[1] We will examine the evidence in the order in which it is treated by Davies.

1. *The Canon*

Among those who have no part in the world to come according to Sanh. 10:1 is "he who reads the outside books." Davies accepts Ginzberg's opinion that the outside books are not heretical books but merely non-canonical, and that the stricture concerns not private reading but public reading in the synagogue service.[2] He likewise accepts the results of K. G. Kuhn's research on "the books of the *minim*" (Tos. Shabb. 13:5) and the *gilyonim* (Tos. Yad. 2:13); neither of these terms is employed in the early period to refer to Jewish Christian writings.[3] Davies concludes:

> The outcome of Kuhn's work is to make us more
> cautious in connecting the fixation of the

* Presented to the CBA Task Force on Matthew; Duquesne University, August 24, 1976, by Douglas R. A. Hare and Phillip Sigal. (Note: This material is presented in its original form without change.)

canon at Jamnia directly with the Christian
gospels and writings, despite the impressive
list of scholars who have urged this. Nevertheless, Kuhn's understanding of the *'minim'*
as including Jewish Christians leaves the
door open for the view that the fixation of
the canon at Jamnia was not unrelated to the
awareness of a growing Christianity, as was
the later codification of the Mishnah with
the growing authority of the New Testament.[4]

It is important to remember that the *conjecture* of Christian
influence is here based upon the insecure foundation of the
hypothesis that the sages at Jabneh made definitive decisions
concerning the canon, for which there is no clear evidence.
For a careful assessment of the alleged evidence the reader
is referred to an article by Jack P. Lewis.[5] It would seem
to be safer to abandon the conjecture of Christian influence
at Jabneh in this connection.

2. *The Birkath ha-Minim*

The most important element in Davies' argument concerning
Christian influence at Jabneh is the *Birkath ha-Minim*. Davies
accepts Kuhn's finding that in the first and second centuries
minim was a broad term referring to various kinds of heterodox
Jews, including Jewish Christians. He also accepts the majority view that the Cairo Genizah fragment represents an early
Palestinian form of the Twelfth Benediction, and that *noṣrim*
specifically refers to the followers of Jesus of Nazareth
(pp. 275f.) He concludes: "The *Birkath ha-Minim* makes it
unmistakably clear that the Sages at Jamnia regarded Jewish
Christians as a menace sufficiently serious to warrant a
liturgical innovation" (p. 276).

If a good case could be made for the view that *noṣrim*
did not occur in the original form of the benediction prepared
by Samuel the Small but was added later and/or elsewhere than
at Jabneh, *or* that *noṣrim* refers not to Jewish Christians but
to some other Jewish sect, then it could be argued that the
central element in Davies' argument has been demolished.[6]
The consensus, however, still favors the view that *noṣrim* was
part of the original text, and that it did designate Jewish
Christians.

3. *The Use of the Ban at Jabneh*

Davies makes only passing reference to the hypothesis
that the authorities at Jabneh employed the ban as a weapon

against Christians: "Largely similar in its intent to isolate Jewish Christians was the use of the ban at Jamnia" (p. 2
276). "And it is also clear that the reason for the frequent
use of the ban by Rabban Gamaliel was his fear of dissentients,
among whom were Jewish Christians, against whom he instigated
the *Birkath ha-Minim*" (p. 277). More recent study has found
no evidence that either the *niddui* or the *ḥerem* was employed
against Jewish Christians as such at this early period; not
minuth but halakic nonconformity provoked such discipline,
and it was used primarily, perhaps exclusively, against fellow rabbis.[7] The alleged evidence in the N.T. (Lk. 6:22, Jn.
9:22, 12:42, 16:2) is better explained on other grounds.[8]

4. *Anti-Christian Propaganda Spread by Apostles from Jerusa-
   lem/Jabneh*

Justin's *Dialogue With Trypho* charges that ". . .you
[the Jews] selected and sent out from Jerusalem chosen men
through all the land to tell that the godless heresy of the
Christians had sprung up, and to publish those things which
all they who know us not speak against us" (ch. 17; ch. 108
repeats the charge).

The allusion to Jerusalem indicates that Justin believed
that Jewish *shaliḥim* were sent out to counter the Christian
mission even before the war. In any event, it seems to be a
safe conjecture that when the Tefillah was standardized at
Jabneh--including the addition of the *Birkath ha-Minim*--these
liturgical decisions were communicated to the synagogues of
the Diaspora by means of *shaliḥim/apostoloi*, and that Diaspora
Jewish Christians perceived these messengers as guilty of dis-
seminating anti-Christian propaganda. There is, of course, no
evidence extant to demonstrate that this was a correct perception.

5. *Social Exclusion*

In Justin's *Dialogue* 138, Trypho reports, "Sir, it would
be good for us if we obeyed our teachers, who laid down a law
that we should have no intercourse with any of you, and that
we should not have even any communication with you on these
questions." Davies does not cite any Rabbinic material in
support of Trypho's report, but the following passage from the
Tosefta is clearly pertinent: "One does not sell to them [the
minim] or receive from them or take from them or give to them.
One does not teach their sons a trade, and does not obtain
healing from them. . ." (Tos. Hullin 2:20f.).

6. *The Shema', Tefillin and Mezuzah*

"There can be little doubt that not only the prominence
given to the Shema but to the Tefillin (phylacteries) and the
Mezuzah (doorpost text) at Jamnia had a polemic intent. These
last items were standardized in the interests of orthodoxy and
unity" (Davies, p. 280). An earlier statement on the same
page is more cautious: ". . .all that can be claimed is that
the menace of Christianity increased a credal significance
which the Shema alrady possessed."

Perhaps even more caution is advisable on these matters.
There is little evidence of thorough standardization. As
late as the twelfth century the grandson of Rashi still differed from the accepted view concerning the contents of the
Tefillin, and today there are orthodox Jews who use two sets
of Tefillin, representing these divergent traditions. Kuhn's
arguments in support of the view that uniformity was imposed
by the authorities at Jabneh to counter Qumran heteropraxy
are therefore not wholly convicing.[9]

Perhaps support for Davies' hypothesis of a polemical use
of the Shema' after 70 can be drawn from a liturgical innovation in the Shema'. The response *Baruk shem,* "Praised is his
sovereignty forever" (more literally, "Blessed is the name of
his glorious kingdom forever") was inserted between the affirmation of the creed ("Hear, O Israel," Dt. 6:4, and the paragraph beginning, "You shall love, etc.," vv. 5-9). The exposition of this formula provided in the Palestinian Talmud
(Berak. 9:1) is that it signifies that the "One" in the creed
is unquestionably One. This was in response to the argument
that the creed itself supports the notion of three aspects to
the deity in the words, "The Lord, our God, the Lord." The
counter-argument was: the liturgical addition speaks of *his*
sovereignty (using the third singular possessive suffix).

It was at this same period, sometime after 70, that the
"sovereignty verses" (*malkuyot*) were introduced into the High
Holy Day liturgy. They are absent from the pre-70 liturgy reflected in Taan. 2:3, where the *shoferot* and *zikronot* verses
are listed as part of a special Amidah for drought. In Rosh
ha Shanah 4:5, however, the series includes *malkuyot,* ten
verses selected from all three divisions of the Hebrew scriptures to reinforce the emphasis upon the sovereignty of God.
New prominence may have been given to the *Tefillah* worn on the
head by broadening the leather straps which held it in place;
this is the most probable interpretation of the denunciation
of Matthew 23:5.[10] The tradition from R. Meir suggests that
he emphasized those very things which, according to Mt. 23:5,

Christian Jews were de-emphasizing, in the expectation that such practices would render Jews "inaccessible," i.e. protect them from *minuth* and apostasy by accentuating symbols of Jewish identity. Berakoth 15a contains a tradition which asserts that saying the Shema' and wearing Tefillin is accepting completely the *Malkuth ha-Shamayim,* the sovereignty of heaven. Although of later date, this may point back to that earlier time when such practices as the recitation of the Shema' and the wearing of Tefillin became more important among Jews loyal to Jabneh simply because Christian Jews were discounting their importance. [Note also T. Ber. 7:24f. where R. Meir emphasizes the recital of berakhot, the ámidah, tefillin, mezuzah, fringes, as protective for the Jew].

7. *The Decalogue*

Davies points to evidence suggesting that at one time both the Mezuzah and the Tefillin included the decalogue, and that it was recited regularly in the temple and in the synagogue services, just prior to the Shema' (p. 281). Berakoth 12a reports that the recitation in the synagogues was not permitted "on account of the insinuations of the *minim.*" Because R. Nathan (who flourished at the same time as R. Gamaliel II) is mentioned in support of this tradition, it is possible that the discontinuance of the recitation of the decalogue also dates from the Jabnean period. A number of scholars have proposed that it was Christian emphasis upon the decalogue which provoked the rabbis to institute this liturgical change. Davies concedes that the evidence for Christian emphasis on the decalogue is not strong, but nonetheless maintains that it is a "real possibility" (p. 282).

Recently this understanding of Berak. 12a has been challenged by G. Vermes.[11] The clue to the underlying controversy is to be found, according to Vermes, in the Palestinian Targum to Dt. 5:22 (19). The Hebrew text *we lo yasaph* "states plainly that God limited himself to the Ten Commandments in his direct communication with the whole congregation of Israel on Sinai" (Vermes, pp. 173f.). The LXX translates literally: *kai ou prosetheken.* The targums, however, agree in a paraphrase which contradicts this: "These words the Lord spoke to all your assembly at the mount. . .with a loud voice which/and he/ ceased not" (Vermes, p. 174). The "orthodox" forces in Judaism are here to be seen opposing a heretical group whose position is alluded to in the Palestinian Talmud in a statement attributed to Korah, the prototype of all heretics: "God has given us only the Ten Commandments. Of dough-offering, heave-offering, tithes and fringes we have not heard except from yourself [Moses]. You have spoken in order to establish rulership for yourself and glory for Aaron your brother" (P. San.

10:27d-28a). On *a priori* grounds Vermes finds it unlikely
that Jewish Christians made so great an impact on Judaism at
this early date (p. 175). More important, "none of the parties within the early Church taught an 'antinomianism' as
radical as the complete denial of the divine origin of the
Torah" (*ibid.*). Even the "Hellenist" Stephen, who declares
that the Torah was not delivered to Israel by God but rather
by the angels, does not, in Vermes' opinion, represent the
radical rejection of the Torah by the *minim* who claim that
only the Ten Commandments are of divine origin (p. 177). He
concludes that these *minim* constituted an important faction
of hellenistic Judaism as found at Alexandria; the intellectual elite of their day, they were "the ancient forebears of
what is known today as 'progressive Judaism'" (p. 177).

Although Vermes gathers together in this article many
fascinating pieces of evidence, we must not lose sight of the
fact that conjecture plays a role in his reconstruction. For
example, the precise meaning of *tar'umoth* in Berak. 12a, rendered "insinuations" by Davies (p. 281), is not entirely
clear. On the other hand, it must be admitted--as is done by
Davies (*ibid.*)--that there is no evidence that early Jewish
Christians gave exaggerated prominence to the decalogue.
What we know of the Jewish Christians suggests rather that
circumcision and the dietary laws, i.e. prescriptions of the
Torah which lay outside the decalogue, were of special importance to them. We could conjecture that it was *gentile* Christians who gave prominence to the decalogue, but there is no
evidence that the *entire* decalogue was ever taken seriously
by gentile Christians. Supposed echoes of the decalogue in
the Didache and Pliny's Letter to Trajan contain knowledge of
gentile sabbatarians in the first two centuries.

In the absence of certain evidence to the contrary, we
must conclude that Vermes provides the best hypothesis for
the controversy underlying Berak. 12a. Further support in
its favor is perhaps provided by Philo's attack on the "al-
legorists" who ". . .regarding the laws in their literal sense
in the light of symbols of matters belonging to the intellect,
are overpunctilious about the latter, while treating the former with easy-going neglect" (De migr. Ab. 16:89f.).

If Vermes is correct in his identification of the *minim*
who made exaggerated claims for the decalogue, he is clearly
mistaken in his assumption that *minim* was not used at all of
Jewish Christians in the Tannaitic period.[12] The passage from
the Tosefta cited above is especially illuminating. Among
those forms of contact with the *minim* which are forbidden is
seeking healing from them. The description of *minim* as espe-

cially sought out for healing hardly fits the intellectual elite of Alexandria regarded by Vermes as constituting the *minim*! In case any doubt should remain, however, the Tosefta passage continues immediately with a report of an incident in which Jacob of Kephar-Soma sought to heal R. Eleazar ben Dama (ca 130 CE), nephew of R. Ishmael ben Elisha, of a snake bite in the name of Jeshua' ben Pantera ('Pantera' is probably a corruption from *parthenos*). The next anecdote concerns R. Eliezer ben Hyrcanus, who was arrested by the Roman authorities on account of *minuth*. After his acquittal he was questioned by R. Akiba concerning the possible reasons for this false charge. He then remembered that once in Sepphoris Jacob from Kephar Sekanya told him a word of heresy in the name of Yeshua' ben Pantera, and it pleased him. When the great age of the Tosefta is taken into account, this whole section of Hullin 2 provides clear evidence of the antipathy of the Rabbis toward the Jewish Christians, the followers of Yeshua' ben Pantera, who were known for their healing power and were still considered Jews but were called *minim* because they were perceived as a severe danger to the peace and stability of the synagogue community.13

8. *Evidence not considered by Davies: The Proselyte Blessing*

Immediately following the *Birkath ha-Minim* in the Amidah is the Thirteenth Benediction, which invokes God's blessings upon the righteous and the proselytes. It presently reads: "Towards the righteous and pious. . .elders. . .scribes. . . towards true proselytes. . .may thy tender mercies be stirred . . ." Originally, however, it was a briefer paragraph and began with the words "Upon the righteous proselytes may your compassion be stirred." Dr. Louis Finkelstein is of the opinion that this paragraph was inserted in order to elevate only those proselytes who became fully Jewish, thus relegating the "other" proselytes then being admitted into Christianity to a lesser status. Should this suggestion be correct, the Thirteenth Benediction becomes a companion to the Twelfth in ordering the liturgy in a way that will make Christian Jews uncomfortable in the synagogue.14

Conclusions

Respecting the proposal of W. D. Davies that the Jewish authorities at Jabneh were in part reacting to Jewish Christianity when decisions concerning the canon were made, in their use of the ban, and in the removal of the decalogue from the liturgy (items 1, 2, and 7), we have found the evidence inadequate. With respect to the *Birkath ha-Minim*, the Jabnean *shalihim* the imposition of social ostracism, and the new prominence given to the Shema', Tefillin and Mezuzah (items 2, 4, 5 and 6) we have proposed additional evidence in support of Davies' view that the academy at Jabneh did in fact regard Jewish Christianity as a menace. Hopefully, further research into the *halakoth* and liturgy of this period will provide still more evidence of the interaction between the rabbinic authorities and the followers of Jesus.

NOTES

1. We acknowledge our indebtedness to the "Annotated Bibliography on Yavneh and Yohanan ben Zakkai" prepared by Daniel J. Harrington for the Task Force on Matthew.

2. L. Ginzberg, "Some Observations on the Attitude of the Synagogue to the Apocalyptic-Eschatological Writings," *JBL*, 41 (1922), p. 115, cited by Davies, p. 274.

3. "Giljonim and sifre minim," *Judentum--Urchristentum--Kirche*, ed. W. Eltester (Berlin, 1960).

4. *Setting*, p. 274.

5. "What Do We Mean By Jabneh?" *Journal of Bible and Religion*, 32 (1964), pp. 125-32.

6. M. Simon, *Jewish Sects at the Time of Jesus*, (Philadelphia: Fortress, 1967) pp. 103ff., proposes that *Nazōraioi/nosrim* were originally a pre-Christian Jewish sect which became allied with one brance of Jewish Christianity at a later date. This opinion is reiterated by Simon in a more recent study, "Reflexions sur le judeo-christianisme," *Christianity, Judaism and Other Greco-Roman Cults*, ed. J. Neusner (Leiden: Brill, 1975), Part II, pp. 69ff.

7. D. R. A. Hare, *The Theme of Jewish Persecution of Christians in the Gospel According to St. Matthew*, (London: Cambridge, 1967) pp. 48-53.

8. *Ibid.* pp. 53-56.

9. K. G. Kuhn, *Phylakterien aus Höhle 4 von Qumran*, (Heidelberg, 1957).

10. I. Abrahams, *Studies in Pharisaim and the Gospels,* Second Series (London: Cambridge, 1924) pp. 203-5.

11. "The Decalogue and the Minim," *In Memoriam Paul Kahle,* ed. M. Black and G. Fohrer (Berlin: 1968), pp. 232-40; reprinted in his collected essays, *Post-Biblical Jewish Studies* (Leiden: 1975) pp. 169-77.

12. *Post-Biblical Jewish Studies,* p. 175 (Kahle *Festschrift* pp. 237f.): "But although M. Simon has recently shown *Verus Israel,* p. 218 that Christians were referred to as Minim in the fourth century, the title scarcely fits the Judeo-Christians of the apostolic and sub-apostolic age." Here Vermes ignores that fact that Simon has also argued, even more recently, that *minim* includes Jewish Christians; *Jewish Sects,* p. 93.

13. This association of healing with *minuth* is evidenced also by Sanh. 10:1. Among those who have no part in the age to come is ". . .he who reads the outside books, or that utters charms over a wound and says, 'I will put none of the diseases upon thee which I have put on the Egyptians; for I am the Lord that healeth thee." Even if the outside books are not specifically Christian writings but non-canonical books in general (cf. *Setting,* p. 273 and literature there cited), and the objection is primarily concerned with the *public* reading o of such writings in the synagogue services, the fact remains that the paragraph is dealing with different manifestations of *minuth* (without using the term), and included among these Jews who have fallen into heresy are those who are known for their healings.

14. Louis Finkelstein, "The Development of the Amidah," *Contributions to the Scientific Study of the Liturgy,* ed. Jakob Petuchowski, (New York, KTAV: 1970), pp. 91-177.

GLOSSARY

ABELUT - Mourning; the halakhah of grief and bereavement.

ABODAH - a technical term for the temple cult; also used of
    secular "labor."

ABOT - "patriarchs, fathers;" the first blessing in the
    amidah which refers to the God of Abraham, the God of
    Isaac, and the God of Jacob; the term also refers to
    early rabbis during 300 B.C.-200 C.E., and to a volume of
    the Mishnah.

AGADA (AGADIC) - all non-halakhic (non-legal) matter in Talmud
    and Midrash; folklore, legend, homily, theosophy, biogra-
    phy, etc. Also spelled *hagadah*, not to be confused,
    however, with the Passover Manual called "The Hagadah."

AKEDAH - "binding"; biblical account of God's command to offer
    his son Isaac as a sacrifice.

AM HAAREZ - "people of the land"; term used in Bible for
    citizens, or some particular class of citizens; in rab-
    binic literature, for a group that dissented from rabbin-
    ic halakhah and rigorous purity and tithing norms. It
    sometimes signifies the unlearned.

AMIDAH - "standing"; the main section of prayers said in a
    standing posture; also known as *tefilah* or *shemoneh esreh*.

AMPHICTYONY - "religious federation," or "faith community";
    an association of neighboring states or tribes in ancient
    Greece who banded together for their common interest and
    protection.

ANTHROPOMORPHISM - attributing human characteristics to what
    is not human, e.g. the deity; such as God sees, hears,
    knows, and loves.

APOCALYPSE (APOCALYPTIC) - a Greek word meaning "revelation"
    and a body of literature based upon revelations claimed
    by the authors; usually mystical and containing doctrines
    of the end-time.

306

APOCRYPHA – from the Greek meaning "to hide"; refers to books "set apart," to the intertestamental books found in the Septuagint and included in the Catholic canon but not in the Jewish or Protestant canons.

BAT KOL – a heavenly divine voice.

BERAITA – "outside"; statement of a *tanna* not found in Mishnah; term covers tannaitic halakhah, halakhic or agadic midrash not included in the Mishnah. See Tosefta.

BERAKHA(OT) – "blessings"; thank-you offerings that praise God for a benefit conferred or a great event experienced.

BET MIDRASH – place of study, discussion and prayer; in ancient times a school of higher learning.

BET SEFER – elementary school.

BET TALMUD – advanced school.

BIRKHAT HAMINIM – "benediction concerning heretics"; prayer that invoked divine wrath upon Christian Jews.

DINA D'MALKHUTA DINA – the sovereign law of the land is binding upon the Jew.

EBIONITES(ISM) – Judaeo-Christian sect 2nd-4th century; accepted much of Mosaic Torah (circumcision, Sabbath, etc.) but rejected sacrifices; accepted Jesus as Messiah but not his divinity; opposed Pauline doctrine.

EKKLESIA – an assembly; synonym for Synagogue.

ESCHATON (ESCHATOLOGY) – a study or science dealing with the ultimate destiny or purpose of mankind and the world.

GEMARA – "completion"; word popularly applied to the Talmud as a whole, to discussions by rabbinic teachers on Mishnah, and to decisions reached in these discussions.

GER – proselyte who formally joined the Judaic faith.

GEZERAH (ot) – a prohibitive enactment.

HABDALAH – "separation"; the ceremony using wine, spices and candle at the conclusion of the Sabbath. Smelling the spices signifies the hope for a fragrant week; the light signifies the hope for a week of brightness and joy.

HAGADAH - "narration"; a liturgical manual used in the Passover Seder.

HAKHAMIM - title given to pre-70 A.D. proto-rabbinic scholars
and post-70 rabbinic scholars.

HALAKHAH (HALAKHIC) (OT) - a pattern of conduct; includes
ethics, man's relationship with his fellowman, and
ritual, man's relationship with God; guidance; religious
practice.

HASIDIM (HASIDISM) - "the pious"; a movement which flourished
during the second century.B.C. in response to the religious persecution of Antiochus Epiphanes; (not to be confused with 13th century and modern hasidim).

HABURAH (OT) - associations or fellowships of pietists who had
rigorous purity and tithing norms, later they constituted
voluntary organizations which particpated in rituals such
as marriage, circumcision, gathering the remains of the
dead, and comforting mourners.

HEILSGESCHICHTE - "salvation history"; refers to the revelator
and saving acts of God whereby he was thought to save the
world and to which the Old Testament primarily bears
witness.

HELLENISM - period from 323 B.C. to 30 B.C. in which there was
penetration into the Near East of elements of Greek Civilization (Greek names, language, institutions) which
fused with Oriental religion.

HEMEROBAPTISTS - "morning bathers"; Jewish sect for which a
daily baptismal rite was crucial.

HYKSOS - dynasty of Asiatics who exercised control over Egypt
1635-1570 B.C. It is thought by some that during their
rule Israel entered Egypt.

JUDAIC - adjective for the faith of Judaism and a person professing the faith.

JUDAIST - a believer in Judaism.

JUDAITE - a person from Judah.

KABALAH (KABALISM) - "receiving, tradition"; a system of Jewish theosophy and mysticism.

KADDISH - a doxology recited at the conclusion of each major
section of each service and also used as a prayer by
mourners during the first year of bereavement and on the
anniversary of the death of next-of-kin.

KASHRUT - dietary practices.

KERYGMA - the preaching or proclaiming of the Christian gospel.

KIDDUSH - "sanctification"; a ritual of Sabbath and other
holy days; it proclaims the holiness of the day, derived
from "kadosh" (holy), and is usually done accompanied by
a cup of wine.

LEVIRATE - a biblical system of marriage in which the levir
(brother-in-law) marries his brother's widow; no longer
practiced.

LOGOS - a Greek term for "word," "reason"; refers to the chief
emanation of God.

MAGI - Zoroastrian priests.

MEZUZAH - "doorpost"; parchment scroll with selected Torah
verses (Deut. 6:4-9; 11:13-21) placed in container af-
fixed to doorpost of rooms occupied by Jews, or to outside door of a home.

MIDRASH - from *darash*, "to inquire"; the literature which attempts to interpret Scripture to its fullest meanings.
May be either agada dealing with theological ideas,
ethical teachings, popular philosophy, imaginative exposition, legend, allegory, animal fables, etc. or on
the halakhic material directing man to specific patterns
of practice.

MIN (IM) - a term loosely meaning "sectarian" or "schismatic"
and applied in earlier centuries to Christians; heretic.

MINYAN - a quorum of ten Jews (male or female), above age
thirteen necessary for public services and certain other
religious ceremonies. Females are not acceptable among
the orthodox.

MISHNAH - "teaching"; digest of the recommended halakhah as it
existed at the end of the second century.

MIZVAH - "commandment, obligation"; a duty or act of obedience
to God's will which is an act of religion, whether of
ritual or ethics.

MUMAR - a Jew who leaves the faith; apostate.

NABÎ (NEBIIM) - a term designating the "prophet" of ancient Israel.

NOMOS (NOMOI) - a Greek term meaning "law" and referring to the Pentateuch, all of scripture and even proto-rabbinic halakhah; an expert in *nomos* is termed a *nomikos*.

NOZRIM - Christians.

OMER - "sheaf"; first sheaf of grain offering brought to the Temple on Nisan 16; also the name of the seven-week period between Passover and Shabuot.

PERUSHIM - a catchword in Hebrew for a broad spectrum of inherently conflicting or differing groups; it can denote separatists, dissenters, pietists. See Pharisees.

PESHER - interpretation; term used in Dead Sea Scrolls for application of biblical prophecies to circumstances of end of days.

PHARISEES - the *perushim*; although their origin is uncertain and the nature of the movement unclear, this is the name given to an ancient group in Judaism.

PIKUAH NEFESH - an elliptical phrase meaning "to remove debris in order to save a person," from which it came to mean "saving an endangered life"; supersedes Sabbath observances.

PROSELYTE - a Greek term meaning a newcomer, a convert to the Jewish religion.

PROTO-RABBIS - pre-70 sages who set the foundations of post-70 rabbinic Judaism.

PSEUDEPIGRAPHA - from *to pseudos,* "a deceit, untruth," and *hē epigraphē,* "an inscription," a writer inscribed his work with a pen name purporting to be an ancient worthy; the name given to a number of Intertestamental apocryphal writings.

REDIVIVUS - brought back to life, alive again, reborn.

ROSH HASHANAH - "beginning of the year"; Jewish New Year celebration.

ROSH HODESH - beginning of a lunar month.

SADDUCEES - a priestly party; they rejected traditions not directly grounded in the Pentateuch such as the concept of life after death; although their origin and all their ideas are uncertain, they are considered the major opponents of the Pharisees.

SEDER - evening meal and service opening the celebration of Passover.

SHABUOT - "weeks"; observed 50 days from the day the first sheaf of grain is offered to the priests; Pentecost.

SHEKHINAH - the Divine Presence. In kabalism it sometimes took on the aspect of the feminine element in deity. The Holy Spirit.

SHEMA - "hear"; Deut. 6:4-9; 11:13-21; Num. 15:37-41, required to be read every morning and evening. Deut. 6:4 is the Jewish affirmation of the monotheistic creed.

SHOFAR - ram's horn sounded at Rosh Hashanah morning worship and at the conclusion of Yom Kippur.

SICARII - a dagger; an anti-Roman Jewish terrorist fringe of Zealots in first-century Palestine who concealed daggers beneath their cloaks.

SOFER (SOFERIM) - "scribes"; used as a general designation for scholars and copyists in both talmudic and later literature.

SUKOT - "booths," or "tabernacles"; seven-day festival beginning on Tishri 15 commemorating the *sukot* where Israel lived in the wilderness after Exodus.

SYNCRETISM - synthesis of variegated religious beliefs.

TALIT - a four cornered cloth with fringes used by males as a prayer shawl.

TALMUD - "study" or "learning"; the collection of rabbinic writings which comprise the commentary and discussion of the amoraim on the Mishnah.

TAMID - daily morning and evening burnt offering in the Temple; is also used for tractate in Mishnah.

TANNA - sage from period of Hillel to compilation of Mishnah (20-200 C.E.) distinguished from later amoraim. Primarily scholars and teachers; the Mishnah, Tosefta and Midreshei Halakhah were among the great literary achievements of this group. Later: schoolmen who recited texts.

TARGUM - "translation"; Aramaic translation of Bible; also used for Aramaic portions of Bible.

TEFILIN - box-like appurtenances that accompany prayer; worn by Jewish adult males at the weekday morning services, one each is placed on the head and left arm and held by a strap; they contain shemá passages; usually translated as "phylacteries."

THEODICY - from *theos* "God, deity," and *díkē* "justice," signifies "the justification" or "vindication" of God's government of the world; (refers to the attempt to reconcile the goodness of God with the manifold evil present in the world).

THERAPEUTAE - "healers"; sect of Jewish ascetics, possibly a radical off-shoot of pre-Christian Judaism, perhaps Essenism, severe in its discipline and mode of life.

TOSEFTA - supplements, collection of tannaitic beraitot, arranged according to the order of the Mishnah.

YEHUDI (IM) - a Judaist, believer in Judaism or a resident of Judah.

YOM KIPPUR - "Day of Atonement"; annual day of fasting and atonement, occuring on Tishri 10, the most important occasion of the Jewish religious year.

ZIZIT - "fringes"; (see talit).

Note:

This glossary does not pretend to be exhaustive. Some terms not listed here have been defined in the text or notes of the book. This listing should also be used in conjunction with the listing in Volume II on the medieval period.

ABBREVIATIONS

(Note: All the works of the Old and New Testaments and the
Talmud are listed. Otherwise only the books cited in abbre-
viation are listed.)

THE OLD TESTAMENT
(The Order According to Masoretic Text)

O.T.	–	Old Testament	Mic.	–	Micah
Gen.	–	Genesis	Nah.	–	Nahum
Ex.	–	Exodus	Hab.	–	Habakkuk
Lev.	–	Leviticus	Zeph.	–	Zephaniah
Num.	–	Numbers	Hag.	–	Haggai
Deut.	–	Deuteronomy	Zekh.	–	Zekhariah
Josh.	–	Joshua	Mal.	–	Malakhi
Judg.	–	Judges	Ps.	–	Psalms
I Sam.	–	I Samuel	Prov.	–	Proverbs
II Sam.	–	II Samuel	Job	–	Job
I Ki.	–	I Kings	S of S	–	Song of Songs
II Ki.	–	II Kings	Ruth	–	Ruth
Is.	–	Isaiah	Lam.	–	Lamentations
Jer.	–	Jeremiah	Ecc.	–	Ecclesiastes
Ez.	–	Ezekiel	Est.	–	Esther
Hos.	–	Hosea	Dan.	–	Daniel
Joel	–	Joel	Ezra	–	Ezra
Am.	–	Amos	Neh.	–	Nehemiah
Ob.	–	Obadiah	I Chron.	–	I Chronicles
Jon.	–	Jonah	II Chron.	–	II Chronicles

THE TRANSLATIONS

LXX	–	Septuagint	P. Targ.	–	Palestinian Targum
Onk.	–	Targum Onkelos			

APOCRYPHA AND PSEUDEPIGRAPHA

Apoc. Ab.	–	Apocalypse of Abraham
Apoc. Est.	–	Apocryphal Esther
Bar.	–	Barukh
II Bar.	–	Syriac Apocalypse of Barukh
Ben Sira	–	The Wisdom of Sirach
I, II En.	–	I, II Enoch
I Esd.	–	I Esdras
II Esd.	–	II Esdras = IV Ezra
Jub.	–	Jubilees
Jud.	–	Judith
I, II, III, IV Macc.	–	I, II, III, IV Maccabees
Ps. Sol.	–	Psalms of Solomon
Test. Asher	–	Testament of Asher
Test. Benj.	–	Testament of Benjamin
Test. Dan	–	Testament of Dan
Test. Gad	–	Testament of Gad
Test. Iss.	–	Testament of Issachar
Test. Jos.	–	Testament of Joseph
Test. Jud.	–	Testament of Judah
Test. Levi	–	Testament of Levi
Test. Reub.	–	Testament of Reuben
Test. Zeb.	–	Testament of Zebulon
Tob.	–	Tobit
Sib. Or.	–	Sibylline Oracles
Wisd.	–	The Book of Wisdom

THE DEAD SEA SCROLLS

C D C	–	Zadokite Document
I Q S	–	Manual of Discipline
I Q M	–	Scroll of the War
I Q H	–	Thanksgiving Scroll, *Hodayot*
I Q pHab.	–	Habakkuk Commentary
Gen. Apoc.	–	Genesis Apocryphon

THE NEW TESTAMENT

N. T.	–	New Testament	I Tim.	–	I Timothy
Mt.	–	Matthew	II Tim.	–	II Timothy
Mk.	–	Mark	Tit.	–	Titus
Lk.	–	Luke	Phm.	–	Philemon
Jn.	–	John	Heb.	–	Hebrews
Acts	–	Acts	James.	–	James
Rom.	–	Romans	I Pet.	–	I Peter
I Cor.	–	I Corinthians	II Pet.	–	II Peter
II Cor.	–	II Corinthians	I Jn.	–	I John
Gal.	–	Galatians	II Jn.	–	II John
Eph.	–	Ephesians	III Jn.	–	III John
Phil.	–	Philippians	Jude	–	Jude
Col.	–	Colossians	Rev.	–	Revelation
I Thess.	–	I Thessalonians			
II Thess.	–	II Thessalonians			

PHILO

Abr.	–	On Abraham
Alleg. Int.	–	Allegorical Interpretation
Cher.	–	On the Cherubim
Cont. Life	–	On the Contemplative Life
Dec.	–	On the Decalogue
Hyp.	–	Hypothetica
Mig. Ab.	–	On the Migration of Abraham
Q G	–	Questions and Answers, Genesis
Q E	–	Questions and Answers, Exodus
Quod Omnis	–	Every Good Man is Free

JOSEPHUS

Ag. Ap.	–	Against Apion
Ant.	–	Jewish Antiquities
Vita	–	The Life
War	–	The Jewish War

EXTRA-CANONICAL CHRISTIAN WRITINGS

Ap.	–	Justin's Apology
Apost. Const.	–	Apostolic Constitutions
Barn.	–	Epistle of Barnabas
Did.	–	Didaché
D.	–	Justin, Dialogue with Trypho
Rec.	–	Clementine Recognitions
Pan.	–	Epiphanius, Panarion
Hom.	–	Clementine Homilies
Vis.	–	Shepherd of Hermas, Visions

THE TALMUD

(M or T before the name of a tractate in the text signifies
Mishnah and Toseftà, respectively; B or P before the name of
a tractate signifies Babylonian and Palestinian Talmud, respectively; R preceding a name signifies Rabbi.)

Ab.	—	Aḅot	Men.	—	Menaḥot
Aḅ.de.R.N.	—	Aḅot de Rabbi	Mid.	—	Middọt
		̦Nathan	Mik.	—	Mikvaọt
Ahal.	—	Ăhalot	M.K.	—	Moĕd Katan
Ar.	—	Ặrakhin	Naz.	—	Nazir
A.Z.	—	Aḅodah Zarah	Ned.	—	Nedarim
B.B.	—	Baḅa Batra	Neg.	—	Negăim
Bekh.	—	Bekhorot	Nid.	—	Niddah
Ber.	—	Berakhot	Or.	—	Ŏrlah
Bez.	—	Bezah	Par.	—	Parah
Bik.	—	Bikkurim	Peah	—	Peah
B.K.	—	Baba Kama	Pes.	—	Pesaḥim
B.M.	—	Baba Mezi^c a	R.H.	—	Rosh Hashanah
Dem.	—	Demai	San.	—	Sanhedrin
Ed.	—	Ĕduyot	Sem.	—	Semaḥot
Er.	—	Ĕrubin	Shab.	—	Shabbat
Git.	—	Gittin	Shebi.	—	Sheḅiit
Ḥag.	—	Ḥagigah	Sheb.	—	Sheḅûot
Ḥal.	—	Ḥalah	Shek.	—	Shekalim
Hor.	—	Ḧorayot	Sot.	—	Sotah
Ḥul.	—	Ḥulin	Suk.	—	Sukkah
Ǩel.	—	Ǩelim	Taan.	—	Taănit
Ker.	—	Keritot	Tam.	—	Tamid
Ket.	—	Ketubot	Tem.	—	Temurah
Kid.	—	Kiddushin	Ter.	—	Terumot
Kil.	—	Kilayim	Tah.	—	Taharot
Kin.	—	Kinnim	Teḅ Y.	—	Teḅul Yom
Maas.	—	Maăsrot	Uk.	—	Ukẓin
Maas. Sh.	—	Maăser Sheni	Yad.	—	Yadayim
Mak.	—	Makkot	Yeb.	—	Yebamot
Makh.	—	Makhshirin	Yom.	—	Yoma
Meg.	—	Megilah	Zab.	—	Zabim
Meil.	—	Meilah	Zeb.	—	Zebaḥim

MIDRASHIM

Gen. R.	–	Genesis Rabbah (Note: Each volume of Midrash Rabbah is cited in this manner: The biblical book followed by R.)
Mekh.	–	Mekhilta de R. Ishmael to Exodus
PRK.	–	Pesikta de R. Kahana
PRE.	–	Pirke de Rabbi Eliezer
Sifra	–	Sifra to Leviticus
Sif.	–	Sifre to Numbers and Deuteronomy
Tan.	–	Tanhuma
Mid.	–	Midrash
P. R.	–	Pesikta Rabbati.

PERIODICALS

ATR	–	*Anglican Theological Review*
AUSS	–	*Andrews U. Seminary Studies*
BA	–	*Biblical Archaeologist*
BAR	–	*Biblical Archaeology Review*
BASOR	–	*Bulletin of the American Schools of Oriental Research*
BJRL	–	*Bulletin of John Rylands Library*
BSOAS	–	*Bulletin, School of Oriental and African Studies*
BTB	–	*Biblical Theology Bulletin*
CBQ	–	*Catholic Biblical Quarterly*
ET	–	*Expository Times*
ETR	–	*Études Theologiques et Religieuses*
HTR	–	*Harvard Theological Review*
Heyth J.	–	*Heythrop Journal*
HUCA	–	*Hebrew Union College Annual*
JBL	–	*Journal of Biblical Literature*
JBR	–	*Journal of Bible and Religion*
JEH	–	*Journal of Ecclesiastical History*
JES	–	*Journal of Ecumenical Studies*
JJS	–	*Journal of Jewish Studies*
JMEOS	–	*Journal of the Manchester University Egyptian and Oriental Society*
JQR	–	*Jewish Quarterly Review*
JSS	–	*Journal of Semitic Studies*
JTC	–	*Journal of Theology and Church*
MTZ	–	*Münchener Theologische Zeitschrift*

PERIODICALS
(Continued)

NKZ	–	*Neue kirchliche Zeitschrift*
NTS	–	*New Testament Studies*
PIJSL	–	*Papers of the Institute of Jewish Studies, London*
REJ	–	*Revue des études juives*
RQ	–	*Revue de Qumran*
SJT	–	*Scottish Journal of Theology*
SVT	–	*Supplements to Vetus Testamentum*
Theol. St.	–	*Theological Studies*
VG	–	*Vigiliae Christianae*
VT	–	*Vetus Testamentum*
ZAW	–	*Zeitschrift für die alttestamentliche Wissenschaft*
ZNW	–	*Zeitschrift für die neutestamentliche Wissenschaft*
ZRG		*Zeitschrift für Religions und Geistesgeschichte*
ZTK		*Zeitschrift für Theologie und Kirche*

OTHER

ANET	–	Pritchard's *Ancient Near Eastern Texts*
Bib. Ant.	–	*The Biblical Antiquities of Philo*
ddd	–	dinā demalkhutā dinā
EJ	–	*Encyclopedia Judaica*
JE	–	*The Jewish Encyclopedia*
JPS	–	*Jewish Publication Society*
ICC	–	*International Critical Commentary*
TDNT	–	*Theological Dictionary of the New Testament*
TWNT	–	*Theologisches Wörterbuch zum Neuen Testament*
UAHC	–	*Union of American Hebrew Congregations*

Note on Transliterations:

a) Certain Hebrew terms have been regarded as anglicized and have not been rendered in translation nor italicized as foreign words.

BIBLIOGRAPHY

The following is neither an exhaustive reading list nor comprehensive guide to research materials. Space prohibits listing numerous worthwhile volumes and periodicals, or more than a fraction of the works consulted in the preparation of this volume. The notes after each chapter include dozens of such titles with full bibliographical data in addition to those listed here and may be consulted by the reader. Many of the volumes referred to in the notes and of those listed here have extensive bibliographies which may be consulted with profit. The reader is advised to consult standard Dictionaries, Atlases, Encyclopedias, and Commentaries referred to in the notes. The translations of Scriptural, Qumran and rabbinic materials are by the author, unless otherwise noted. The reader should also refer to the Note on Indices in both Parts 1 and 2.

Aḅot de Rabbi Nathan, Ed. Solomon Schechter, N.Y.: Philip Feldheim, 1945.

Abrahams, I., *Studies in Pharisaism and the Gospels*. rpt. New York: Ktav, 1967.

Ackroyd, Peter R. *Exile and Restoration*. Phil.: Westminster, 1968.

Albright, W. F. *Archeology and the Religion of Israel*. Baltimore, Md.: Johns Hopkins Press, 1953.

Albright, W. F. *From the Stone Age to Christianity*. Baltimore, Md.: Johns Hopkins Press, 1940.

Albright, W. F. *Yahweh and the Gods of Canaan*. Garden City, N.Y.: Doubleday, 1968.

Alon, Gedalyahu, *Jews, Judaism and the Classical World*. Trans. Israel Abrahams, Jerusalem: The Magnes Press, 1977.

Ancient Christian Writers. Ed. Johannes Quasten, Joseph C. Plumpe. Westminster, Md.: The Newman Press, 1948.

Ancient Near Eastern Texts, 2nd Ed. Ed. James B. Pritchard. Princeton, N.J.: Princeton University Press, 1955.

Ante-Nicene Christian Library. Ed. Alexander Roberts and James Donaldson. Edinburgh: T. and T. Clark, 1870.

The Apocrypha and Pseudepigrapha of the Old Testament. Ed. R. H. Charles, 2 vols. Oxford: Clarendon Press, 1913.

Aramaic Papyri of the Fifth Century B.C. Ed. A. Cowley. Oxford: Clarendon Press, 1923.

Auerbach, Elias. *Moses.* Trans. Robert A. Barclay and Israel O. Lehman. Detroit: Wayne State University Press, 1975.

Bagatti, Bellarmino. *The Church From The Circumcision.* Trans. Eugene Hoade. Jerusalem: Franciscan Press, 1971.

Bamberger, B. J. *Proselytism in the Talmudic Period.* New York: Ktav, 1966.

Banks, Robert. *Jesus and the Law in the Synoptic Tradition.* Cambridge: Cambridge University Press, 1975.

Baron, Salo, W. *A Social and Religious History of the Jews.* Phil.: JPS, 1952-1973.

Baumgarten, M. *Studies in Qumran Law.* Leiden: E. J. Brill, 1977.

Belkin, Samuel. *Philo and the Oral Law.* Cambridge: Harvard University Press, 1940.

Bentzen, Aage. *Introduction to the Old Testament.* Copenhagen: Gad, 1957.

The Biblical Antiquities of Philo. Trans. M. R. James. "Prolegomenon," Louis H. Feldman. New York: Ktav, 1971.

Bickerman, Elias. *From Ezra to the Last of the Maccabees.* N.Y.: Schocken, 1962.

Black, Matthew, *The Scrolls and Christian Origins.* London: Nelson, 1961.

The Book of the Dead. Trans. E. A. Wallis Budge. N.Y.: Bell, 1968.

Bornkamm, Gunther. *Jesus of Nazareth.* Trans. Irene and Fraser McLuskey, N.Y.: Harper and Row, 1975.

Bornkamm, Gunther. *Paul*. Trans. D. M. G. Stalker. New York: Harper and Row, 1971.

Bowker, John. *The Targums and Rabbinic Literature*. New York: Cambridge University Press, 1969.

Bowman, John. *The Fourth Gospel and the Jews*. Pittsburgh: Pickwick Press, 1975.

Bowman, John. *The Samaritan Problem*. Pittsburgh: Pickwick Press, 1975.

Boyce, Mary. *A History of Zoroastrianism*. Leiden: E. J. Brill, 1975.

Braude, William G. *Jewish Proselyting in the First Five Centuries of the Common Era*. Providence, R.I.: Brown University Dissertation, 1940.

Brown, Raymond E. *The Birth of the Messiah*. New York: Doubleday and Co., 1977.

Buchler, A. *Types of Jewish Palestinian Piety From 70 B.C. to 70 C.E.* London: Jews College, 1922.

Cambridge Ancient History, Vols. 1-6. Ed. J. B. Bury, et al. 7-12. Ed. S. A. Cook, et al. Cambridge: The University Press, 1923-1939.

Charles, R. H. *Eschatology*. N.Y. Schocken Books, 1963.

Chajes, Z. H. *The Student's Guide Through the Talmud*. Trans. Jacob Shachter. New York: Philip Feldheim, Inc., 1960.

Coggins, R. J. *Samaritans and Jews*. Atlanta, Georgia: John Knox Press, 1975.

Cohen, A. *Everyman's Talmud*. London: J. M. Dent, 1932.

Cohen, Boaz. *Jewish and Roman Law*. 2 vols. New York: The Jewish Theological Seminary, 1966.

Contributions to the Scientific Study of Jewish Liturgy. Ed. Jakob J. Petuchowski. New York: Ktav, 1970.

Corpus Papyrorum Judaicarum. Ed. Victor A. Tcherikover, Alexander Fuks, Menahem Stern, 3 vols. Cambridge, Mass.: Harvard University Press, 1957-1964.

Cross, Frank M. *The Ancient Library of Qumran*. Garden City, N.Y.: Doubleday, 1958.

Cullman, Oscar. *Early Christian Worship*. Trans. A, Steward Todd, James B. Torrence. Chicago: Henry Regnery Co., 1953.

Danielou, Jean. *The Theology of Jewish Christianity*. Trans. J. A. Baker. Chicago: Regnery, 1964.

Daube, David. "Rabbinic Methods of Interpretation and Hellenistic Rhetoric." *HUCA* 22 (1949) 239-264.

Daube, David. *The New Testament and Rabbinic Judaism*. London: Athlone Press, 1956.

Davenport, Gene L. *The Eschatology of the Book of Jubilees*. Leiden: E. J. Brill, 1971.

Davies, Alan. *Anti-Semitism and the Christian Mind*. New York: Herder and Herder, 1969.

Davies, W. D. *Paul and Rabbinic Judaism*. New York: Harper and Row, 1958.

Davies, W. D. *The Setting of the Sermon on the Mount*. Cambridge: Cambridge University Press, 1977.

Discoveries in the Judean Desert of Jordan. 6 vols. Ed. Barthelemy, J. T. Milik, et al. Oxford: Clarendon Press, 1955-1977.

Documents From Old Testament Times. Ed. D. Winton Thomas. London: Thomas Nelson & Sons, 1958.

Driver, G. R. *Aramaic Documents of the Fifth Century B.C.* Oxford: Clarendon Press, 1954.

Dunn, J. D. G. *Unity and Diversity in the New Testament*. Philadelphia: Westminster Press, 1977.

Dupont-Sommer, A. *The Essene Writings From Qumran*. Trans. G. Vermes. Oxford: Blackwell, 1961.

Eissfeldt, Otto. *The Old Testament*. Trans. Peter R. Ackroyd. New York: Harper and Row, 1974.

Epstein, Louis M. *Marriage Laws in the Bible and the Talmud*. Cambridge: Harvard University Press, 1942.

Eusebius, *The Ecclesiastical History*. Trans. Kirsopp Lake. 2 vols. Cambridge, Mass.: Harvard University Press, 1953.

Farmer, W. R. *Maccabees, Zealots and Josephus*. New York: Columbia University Press, 1956.

Farmer, W. R. *The Synoptic Problem*. New York: Macmillan, 1964.

The Fathers According to Rabbi Nathan. Trans. Judah Goldin. New York: Schocken Books, 1974.

Finkelstein, Louis. *New Light From the Prophets*. New York: Basic Books, 1969.

Finkelstein, Louis. *Pharisaism in the Making*. New York: Ktav, 1972.

Finkelstein, Louis. *The Pharisees*, 2 vols. Philadelphia: JPS, 1946.

Fitzmyer, Joseph. *The Dead Sea Scrolls, Major Publications and Tools for Study*. Missoula, Mont.: Scholars Press, 1977.

Frankel, Zekhariah. *Darkei Hamishnah*. Lipsiae: H. Hunger, 1859.

Frankel, Zekhariah. *Mavo Hayerushalmi*. Breslau: Schletter, 1870.

Gaster, T. H. *Festivals of the Jewish Year*. New York: William Sloane, 1955.

Gaster, T. H. *The Holy and the Profane*. New York: William Sloane, 1955.

Gerhardsson, B. *Memory and Manuscript*. Uppsala: C. W. K. Gleerup, 1961.

Ginzberg, Louis. *A Commentary on the Palestinian Talmud*. New York: Ktav, 1971.

Ginzberg, Louis. *An Unknown Jewish Sect*. New York: Ktav, 1976.

Ginzberg, Louis. *Legends of the Jews*. 7 vols. Philadelphia: JPS, 1947.

Goodenough, Erwin R. *By Light, Light.* Amsterdam: Philo Press, 1969.

Goodenough, Erwin R. *Jewish Symbols in the Graeco-Roman Period.* 13 vols. New York: Pantheon Books and Princeton University Press, 1953-1968.

Gordis, Robert. *The Book of God and Man.* Chicago: University of Chicago Press, 1965.

Gordis, Robert. *Kohelet-The Man and His World.* New York: Schocken, 1968.

Gowan, Donald E. *Bridge Between the Testaments.* Pittsburgh: Pickwick Press, 1976.

Grant, Michael. *The Jews in the Roman World.* London: Weldenfeld and Nicolson, 1973.

Gray, G. B. *Sacrifice in the Old Testament.* Oxford: Clarendon Press, 1925.

Guilding, Aileen. *The Fourth Gospel and Jewish Worship.* Oxford: Clarendon Press, 1960.

Guttmann, Alexander. *Rabbinic Judaism in the Making.* Detroit: Wayne State University Press, 1976.

Hadas, Moses. *Hellenistic Culture.* New York: Columbia University Press, 1959.

Heichelheim, Fritz M. "Ezra's Palestine and Periclean Athens," *Zeitschrift fur Religions und Geistesgeschichte.* 3 (1951) 251-253.

Heinemann, Joseph. *Prayer in the Talmud.* Berlin and New York: Walter De Gruyter, 1977.

The Hellenistic Age. Ed. Abraham Schalit. New Brunswick, N.J.: Rutgers University Press, 1972.

Hengel, Martin. *Hellenism and Judaism.* Trans. John Bowden, 2 vols. Philadelphia: Fortress Press, 1974.

Herford, R. Travers. *Christianity in Talmud and Midrash.* Clifton, N.J.: Reference Book Publishers, 1966.

Herzog, Isaac. *The Main Institutions of Jewish Law.* 2 vols. 2nd ed. London and New York: The Soncino Press, 1965.

Heschel, A. J. *God in Search of Man*. Philadelphia: JPS, 1956.

Heschel, A. J. *The Prophets*. Philadelphia: Jewish Publication Society, 1962.

Hoenig, Sidney B. *The Great Sanhedrin*. Philadelphia: Jewish Publication Society. 1953.

Hoffman, David. *The First Mishna*. Trans. Paul Forchheimer. New York: Maurosho Publications, 1977.

The Hymns of Zarathustra. Trans. Jacques Duchesne-Guillemin, Trans. from the French, Mrs. M. Henning. London: John Murray, 1952.

Jews and Christians in Egypt. Ed. Idris Bell. Westport, Conn.: Greenwood Press, 1976.

Jongeling, Bastiaan. *A Classified Bibliography of the Finds in the Desert of Judah 1958-1969*. Leiden: E. J. Brill, 1971.

Josephus. With an English translation by H. St. J. Thackeray, R. Marcus, A. Wikgren⁻ and L. H, Feldman. 9 vols. Loeb Classical Library. London, New York and Cambridge, Mass.: William Heinemann and Harvard University Press, 1926-1965.

Judaism and Christianity. Ed. W. O. E. Oesterly, rpt. 3 vols. in one. New York: Ktav, 1969.

Justin Martyr. *The Dialogue with Trypho*. Trans. A. Lukyn Williams, London; New York: Macmillan Co., 1930.

Kahle, Paul E. *The Cairo Geniza*. London: Oxford University Press, 1947.

Kaufmann, Yehezkel. *The Religion of Israel*. Abridged and trans. by Moshe Greenberg. Chicago: University of Chicago Press, 1960.

Kaufmann, Yehezkel. *Toldot Ha'Emunah Hayisra'elit*. (Hebrew), 4 vols. Tel Aviv: Devir, 1952-1956.

Kittel, G. *Theological Dictionary of the New Testament*. Trans. Geoffrey W. Bromeley. 10 vols. Grand Rapids, Mich.: Wm. B. Eerdmans, 1964-1976.

Klausner, Joseph, *From Jesus to Paul*. Trans. William Stine-spring. London: George Allen and Unwin Ltd., 1946.

Klausner, Joseph. *Jesus of Nazareth*. Trans. Herbert Danby. New York: Macmillan Co., 1946.

Klausner, Joseph. *The Messianic Idea in Israel*. Trans. W. F. Stinespring. London: George Allen and Unwin Ltd., 1956.

Kraus, H. J. *Worship in Israel*. Trans. Geoffrey Buswell, Richmond; Va.: John Knox Press, 1966.

Kümmel, W. G. *Introduction to the New Testament*. Trans. H. C. Kee. New York: Abingdon Press, 1975.

Lambert, W. G. *Babylonian Wisdom Literature*. Oxford: Clarendon Press, 1960.

Lauterbach, Jacob Z. *Rabbinic Essays*. Cincinnati: Hebrew Union College Press, 1951.

Lauterbach, Jacob Z. *Studies in Jewish Law, Custom and Folklore*. New York: Ktav, 1970.

Leaney, A. R. C. *The Rule of Qumran and its Meaning*. Philadelphia: Westminster Press, 1966.

Leiman, Sid Z. *The Canonization of Hebrew Scripture, The Talmudic and Midrashic Evidence*. Hamden, Conn.: Archon Books, 1976.

Lieberman, Saul. *Greek in Jewish Palestine*. New York: The Jewish Theological Seminary, 1942.

Lieberman, Saul. *Hellenism in Jewish Palestine*. New York: Jewish Tehological Seminary, 1950.

Lieberman, Saul. *Texts and Studies*. New York: Ktav, 1974.

Lieberman, Saul. *The Tosefta and Tosefta Kifshuta*. 10 vols. New York: Jewish Theological Seminary, 1955-1973.

The Lord's Prayer and Jewish Liturgy. Ed. Jakob J. Petuchowski and Michael Brocke. New York: Seabury Press, 1978.

I Maccabees. The Anchor Bible. Trans. Jonathan A. Goldstein. New York: Doubleday, 1976.

Mann, Jacob and Isaiah Sonne. *The Bible as Read and Preached in the Old Synagogue.* 2 vols. Prolegomenon by Ben Zion Wachholder. Cincinnati: Hebrew Union College, 1966 and New York: Ktav, 1971.

Mantel, Hugo. *Studies in the History of the Sanhedrin.* Cambridge, Mass.: Harvard University Press, 1965.

The Manual of Discipline. Trans. P. Weinberg Moller. Leiden: E. J. Brill, 1957.

Marmorstein, A. *The Doctrine of Merits in Old Rabbinical Literature* and *The Old Rabbinic Doctrine of God,* three volumes in one, rpt. New York: Ktav, 1968.

McNamara, M. *The New Testament and the Palestinian Targum to the Pentateuch.* Rome: Pontifical Biblical Institute, 1966.

McNamara, M. *Targum and Testament.* Shannon, Ireland: Irish University Press, 1972.

Megilot Midbar Yehuda. Ed. A. M. Habermann. Tel-Aviv: Devir, 1959.

Mekhilta de Rabbi Ishmael. 3 vols. Ed. J. Z. Lauterbach. Philadelphia: JPS, 1949.

Memar Marqah. 2 vols. Ed. John MacDonald. Berlin: A. Topelmann, 1963.

The Midrash on Psalms. Trans. W. G. Braude. Yale Judaica Series. New Haven: Yale University Press, 1959.

Midrash Rabbah. New York: Grossman, 1951.

Midrash Tanhuma. Warsaw: 1910.

Mielziner, Moses. *Introduction to the Talmud.* New York: Block, 1968.

The Mishnah. Trans. Herbert Danby. London: Oxford University Press, 1954.

Mishnayoth. Trans. Philip Blackman. 6 vols. Gateshead, England: Judaica Press, 1973.

Montefiore, C. G. and Loewe H. *A Rabbinic Anthology.* London: Macmillan and Co., 1938.

Montefiore, Claude G, *The Synoptic Gospels*. 3 vols. London: Macmillan, 1909.

Montgomery, James A. *The Samaritans*. rpt. New York: Ktav, 1968.

Moore, G. F. *Judaism in the First Centuries of the Christian Era*. 3 vols. Cambridge: Harvard University Press, 1950.

Morgenstern, Julian. "The Three Calendars of Ancient Israel." *HUCA*, 1924

Neufeld, E. *Ancient Hebrew Marriage Laws*. London: Longman's Green and Co., 1944.

Neusner, Jacob. *From Politics to Piety*. Englewood Cliffs, New Jersey: Prentice-Hall, 1973.

Neusner, Jacob. *A History of the Jews in Babylonia*. 5 vols. Leiden: E. J. Brill, 1965-1970.

Neusner, Jacob. *The Rabbinic Traditions About the Pharisees Before 70*. 3 vols. Leiden: E. J. Brill, 1971.

Newman, J. *Halachic Sources From the Beginning to the Ninth Century*. Leiden: E. J. Brill, 1969.

Nicene and Post-Nicene Fathers. Ed. Philip Schaff. rpt. Grand Rapids, Michigan: Wm. B. Eerdmans, 1971-1975. Vols. I, IV, V.

Nickelsburg, Jr. George W. E. *Resurrection, Immortality, and Eternal Life in Intertestamental Judaism*. Cambridge: Harvard University Press, 1972.

No Graven Images. *Studies in Art and the Hebrew Bible*. Ed. Joseph Gutmann. New York: Ktav, 1971.

Noth, Martin. *The History of Israel*. 2nd Ed. Trans. P. R. Ackroyd. London: A and C Black, 1960.

The Old Testament and Modern Study. Ed. H. H. Rowley. Oxford: Clarendon Press, 1952.

Orlinsky, H. M. "The Tribal System of Israel and the Related Groups in the Period of the Judges." *Oriens Antiques*, 5 (1965), 11-20.

Parkes, James. *The Conflict of the Church and the Synagogue.* Cleveland and New York: Meridian, 1961.

Patai, Raphael. *The Hebrew Goddess.* New York: Ktav, 1967.

Patte, Daniel. *Early Jewish Hermeneutic in Palestine.* Missoula, Mont.: Scholars Press, 1975.

Pesikta de Rab Kahana. Trans. W. G. Braude and J. Kapstein. Philadelphia: Jewish Publication Society, 1975.

Pesikta Rabbati. Trans. W. G. Braude, Yale Judaica Series XVIII. 2 vols. New Haven: Yale University Press, 1968.

Pfeiffer, Robert H. *History of New Testament Times.* New York: Harper and Row, 1949.

Philo. Trans. F. H. Colson, G. H. Whitaker, Ralph Marcus. 11 vols. Loeb Classical Library. Cambridge and London: Harvard University Press and William Heinemann, 1950-1953.

Pines, Shlomo. "The Jewish Christians of the Early Centuries of Christianity According to a New Source." *Proceedings of the Israel Academy of the Sciences and Humanities.* Jerusalem: 1966.

Pirke Aboth. Trans. Travers Herford. New York: Jewish Institute of Religion, 1945.

Pirke de R. Eliezer. Trans. G. Friedlander. rpt. New York: Hermon Press, 1965.

Pool, David de Sola. *The Kaddish.* New York: Union of Sephardic Congregations, 1964.

Porten, Bezalel. *Archives From Elephantine.* Los Angeles: University of California Press, 1958.

Purvis, James D. *The Samaritan Pentateuch and the Origin of the Samaritan Sect.* Cambridge, Mass.: Harvard University Press, 1968.

Rabin, Chaim. *Qumran Studies.* New York: Schocken, 1975.

von Rad, Gerhard. *Old Testament Theology,* trans. D. M. G. Stalker. 2 vols. New York: Harper and Row, 1962-1965.

Rankin, O. S. *Israel's Wisdom Literature.* New York: Schocken, 1969.

Rankin, O. S. *The Origins of the Festival of Hanukah.* Edinburgh: J and J Clarke, 1930.

Reitzenstein, Richard. *Hellenistic Mystery Religions.* Trans. John E. Steely. Pittsburgh: Pickwick Press, 1978.

Ringgren, Helmer. *Israelite Religion.* Trans. David E. Green. Philadelphia: Fortress Press, 1966.

Rivkin, Ellis. *The Hidden Revolution.* Nashville, Tenn: Abingdon, 1978.

Rowley, H. H. "Moses and the Decalogue." *BJRL,* 34 (1951-1952) 81-118.

Russell, D. S. *The Method and Message of Jewish Apocalyptic.* Philadelphia: Westminster Press, 1964.

Samaritan Documents. Trans. and Ed. John Bowman. Pittsburgh: Pickwick Press, 1977.

Sanders, E. P. *Paul and Palestinian Judaism.* Philadelphia: Fortress Press, 1977.

Sandmel, Samuel. *Judaism and Christian Beginings.* New York: Oxford University Press, 1978.

Sayings of the Jewish Fathers. Ed. Charles Taylor. Prolegomenon by Judah Goldin. New York: Ktav, 1969.

Schachter, Melech. *The Babylonian and Jerusalem Mishnah.* Jerusalem: Mosad Harav Kook, 1959.

Schechter, Solomon. *Some Aspects of Rabbinic Theology.* New York: Behrman House, 1936.

Schiffman, Lawrence H. *The Halakha at Qumran.* Leiden: E. J. Brill, 1975.

Schoeps, H. J. *Jewish Christianity.* Trans. D. R. A. Hare. Philadelphia: Fortress Press, 1969.

Schoeps, H. J. *Paul: The Theology of the Apostle in the Light of Jewish Religious History.* Trans. H. Knight. Philadelphia: Westminster Press, 1961.

Scholem, Gershom. *Jewish Gnosticism, Merkabah Mysticism and Talmudic Tradition.* New York: Jewish Theological Seminary, 1960.

332

Schürer, Emil. *The History of the Jewish People in the Age of Jesus Christ,* rev. ed. Trans. Geza Vermes and Fergus Millar. Edinburgh: T and T Clark, 1973.

Schürer, Emil. *The Literature of the Jewish People in the Time of Jesus.* Ed. Nahum N. Glatzer. New York: Schocken, 1972.

Segal, Alan F. *Two Powers in Heaven.* Leiden: E. J. Brill, 1977.

Segal, J. B. *The Hebrew Passover.* London Oriental Series, vol. 12. London: Oxford University Press, 1963.

Sifra. Ed. I. H. Weiss. Vienna: Schlossberg, 1861. rpt. New York: Om, 1946.

Sifre debe Rab. Ed. Meir Friedman. Vienna: n.p. 1863. rpt. Jerusalem, 1967.

Sifre on Deuteronomy. Ed. Louis Finkelstein. 2nd ed. New York: Jewish Theological Seminary, 1969.

Sigal, Phillip. *The Emergence of Contemporary Judaism, II.* Pittsburgh Theological Monograph Series, 12. Pittsburgh: Pickwick Press, 1977.

Sigal, Phillip. *The Halakhah of Jesus of Nazareth According to the Gospel of Matthew.* Dissertation, University of Pittsburgh, 1979. (Available, University Microfilm International, Ann Arbor, Mich.).

Sigal, Phillip. "Unfinished Business (The Role of Halakhah in the Future of the Conservative Movement)" *Judaism* (Summer, 1977).

Sigal, Phillip. *New Dimensions in Judaism.* Jericho, New York: Exposition Press, 1972.

Sigal, Phillip. "Women in a Prayer Quorum," *Judaism,* 23 (1974) 174-182.

Simon, Marcel. *Jewish Sects at the Time of Jesus.* Trans. James H. Farley. Philadelphia: Fortress Press, 1967.

Smith, Morton. *Palestinian Parties and Politics That Shaped The Old Testament.* New York: Columbia University Press, 1971.

Smith, Morton. *Tannaitic Parallels to the Gospels*. Philadelphia: Society of Biblical Literature, 1951.

Snaith, Norman H. *The Distinctive Ideas of the Old Testament*. New York: Schocken, 1975.

Sowers, S. G. *The Hermeneutics of Philo and Hebrews*. Richmond: John Knox Press, 1965.

Sperber, A. *The Bible in Aramaic*. Leiden: E. J. Brill, 1973.

Spiegel. S. *The Last Trial*. Philadelphia: Jewish Publication Society, 1967.

Stamm, J. J. and Andrew, M. E. *The Ten Commandments in Recent Research*. Studies in Biblical Theology, Second Series. 2. Naperville, Ill.: Allenson, 1967.

Strack, Hermann L. *Introduction to the Talmud and Midrash*. New York and Philadelphia: Meridian Books and Jewish Publication Society, 1959.

Strack, Hermann, and Billerbeck, P. *Kommentar Zum Neuen Testament, Talmud und Midrash*. 5 vols. Munich: C. H. Becksche, 1965.

Studies and Essays in Honor of Abraham A. Neuman. Ed. Meir ben Horin et al. Leiden: E. J. Brill, 1962.

The Synagogue: Studies in Origins, Archaeology and Architecture. Ed. Joseph Gutmann. New York: Ktav, 1975.

Talmud Babli (The Babylonian Talmud). New York: Shulsinger Bros., 1947.

Talmud Yerushalmi (The Palestinian Talmud). New York: Shulsinger Bros., 1948.

Tarn, W. W. *Hellenistic Civilization,* rev. ed. New York: World Publishing Co., 1969.

Tcherikover, Victor. *Hellenistic Civilization and the Jews*. Trans. S. Applebaum. Philadelphia: Jewish Publication Society, 1959.

The Temple Scroll. 4 vols. Ed. Yigal Yadin. Jerusalem: Israel Exploration Society, 1977.

Toldot Am Yisrael. Ed. H. H. Ben Sassoon, 3 vols. Tel Aviv: Devir, 1969 (Hebrew).

Tosephta. Ed. M. S. Zuckermandel. Jerusalem: Wahrmann, 1963.

Urback, Ephraim. *The Sages. Their Concepts and Beliefs.* Trans. Israel Abrahams. 2 vols. Jerusalem: Magnes Press, 1975.

VanderKam, James C. *Textual and Historical Studies in the Book of Jubilees.* Missoula, Mont.: Scholars Press, 1977.

De Vaux, Roland. *Ancient Israel.* 2 vols. New York: McGraw Hill, 1965.

Vermes, Geza. *Post-Biblical Jewish Studies.* Leiden: E. J. Brill, 1975.

Vermes, Geza. *Scripture and Tradition in Judaism.* Leiden: E. J. Brill, 1961.

Vitae Prophetarum (Lives of the Prophets). Trans. C. C. Torrey. Philadelphia: Society of Biblical Literature, 1946.

Weiss, I. H. *Dor Dor Vedorshov.* 5 vols. Wilna: Joseph Zawadski, 1911.

Werner, Eric. *The Sacred Bridge.* New York: Columbia University Press, 1959.

Wiener, Aharon. *The Prophet Elijah in the Development of Judaism.* London: Routledge and Kegan Paul, 1978.

Wilken, Robert L. *Judaism and the Early Christian Mind.* New Haven: Yale University Press, 1971.

Winter, Paul. *On The Trial of Jesus.* Berlin: de Gruyter, 1961.

Wolfson, Harry Austryn. *Philo.* The Foundation of Religious Philosophy in Judaism, Christianity and Islam. 2 vols. Cambridge, Mass.: Harvard University Press, 1962.

Yadin, Yigal. *The Scroll of the War.* Trans. Batya and Chaim Rabin. Oxford: University Press, 1962.

The Zadokite Document. Ed. Chaim Rabin. Oxford: Clarendon Press, 1954.

Zaehner, R. C. *The Dawn and Twilight of Zoroastrianism.* New York: G. P. Putnam, 1961.

Zeitlin, Solomon. *The Rise and Fall of the Judaean State.* 3 vols. Philadelphia: Jewish Publication Society, 1968.

Zeitlin, Solomon. *Studies in the Early History of Judaism.* 4 vols. New York: Ktav, 1973.

Zevin, Solomon J. *Hamoàdot Behalakhah.* Tel Aviv: Zioni, 1955.

INDICES

NOTE ON INDICES

a) All Old Testament citations are from Biblia Hebraica, ed. R. Kittle, P. Kahle.

b) LXX and Targum citations are from standard printed editions of the Bagster Septuagint and Mikraot Gedolot respectively.

c) Apocrypha and Pseudepigrapha citations are either from R. H. Charles' monumental work or from texts and translations listed in bibliographical information in the notes in context.

d) In the case of the Dead Sea Scrolls both the Schechter and Rabin editions of CDC are cited. Other scrolls are cited from Haberman, *Megilot Midbar Yehudah,* or from texts and translations referred to in the notes.

e) The New Testament text used is the 2nd edition of the *Greek New Testament,* ed. Aland et al. The latest Aland-Nestle edition was not yet available at the time of preparation of this Ms. For the extra-canonical Christian and patristic writings, texts and translations cited are given in the notes in context.

f) Standard traditional printed texts of the rabbinic literature are used except when otherwise noted. The Mishnah, except for Abot, is cited according to the tractate, chapter and paragraph order given in the edition of P. Blackman. Abot is cited according to the Herford edition. Although Saul Lieberman's Tosefta text and commentary was consulted throughout, citations are from the edition of Zukermandel because it is still the more accessible. The references to the Mekhilta are given according to volume and page of the Lauterbach edition. References to Sifra are by the pagination in the Weiss edition.

g) The Author Index includes only modern authors, who are cited when the reference is of special significance, or contains important bibliographical information. Some ancient and medieval authors are included in the Subject and Name Index. Otherwise, the notes to each chapter include comprehensive bibliographical selections.

h) In the Subject and Name Index I have included entries with no more than one or two references only when they are of special significance. The indices of Part 1 and Part 2 may be used in tandem.

i) Finally, in the interest of space economy, as the source indices grew in length it appeared pragmatic to omit some ancient sources, among them Philo and Josephus, as much as this was to my regret. Some remedy is attempted by listing them in the Subject and Name Index.

For the same reason of economy of space the Appendices have not been indexed.

SOURCE INDEX

A. *Old Testament*

344

B. *Old Testament Transla-tions*

1. *Septuagint*

2. *Targum Onkelos*

348

7. *Palestinian Talmud*
    (Krotoschin ed., 1865,
    based on Venice, 1521).

9. *The Minor Tractates*

AB. De R. NATHAN (Solomon Schechter ed., NY 1945)

AUTHOR INDEX

SUBJECT AND NAME INDEX

370

DR. PHILLIP SIGAL was born in Toronto, Canada. He has studied at the University of Toronto and Yeshiva University. He earned his M.A. at Columbia University and was ordained and received an MHL at the Jewish Theological Seminary, New York City. Dr. Sigal received his Ph.D. in New Testament Studies at the University of Pittsburgh for his dissertation entitled "The Halakhah of Jesus of Nazareth According to the Gospel of Matthew." Author of many articles and halakhic responsa, Dr. Sigal has written *New Dimensions in Judaism* and is engaged in the writing of this four-volume series, *The Emergence of Contemporary Judaism*. He is lecturer in Judaic Studies at Duquesne University, adjunct faculty at the Pittsburgh Theological Seminary and at Chatham College.

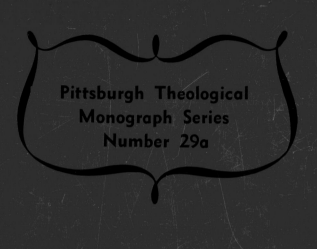

Pittsburgh Theological
Monograph Series
Number 29a

THE WRITING OF BOOKS ON JEWISH HISTORY has
attracted many a scholar during the last century and a half.
The multifaceted background of today's Jews and Judaism
is itself an invitation to see relationships and to propound
historiosophical theories and constructions. Yet it is only
the rare Jewish historian who has actually mastered the
intricacies of Rabbinic literature, and who can thus speak
with real authority about a system of beliefs and practices,
of legal decisions and theological opinions, which both regulated and reflected the actual life of the Jews in various
parts of the world during a time-span of almost two thousand years. Rabbi Phillip Sigal has mastered that literature, and he therefore does speak with authority—and not
only about that literature itself, but also about the challenges to which Rabbinic Judaism had been subjected ever
since it had come into existence.

DR. JAKOB J. PETUCHOWSKI   ·
Hebrew Union College—Jewish Institute of Religion
Cincinnati, Ohio